The Golden Age of Data Visualization

We are living in the Golden Age of Data Visualization. The COVID-19 pandemic has demonstrated how we increasingly use data visualizations to make sense of the world. Business analysts fill their presentations with charts, journalists use infographics to engage their readers, we rely on the dials and gauges on our household appliances, and we use mapping apps on our smartphones to find our way.

This book explains how and why this has happened. It details the evolution of information graphics, the kinds of graphics at the core of data visualization—maps, diagrams, charts, scientific and medical images—from prehistory to the present day. It explains how the cultural context, production and presentation technologies, and data availability have shaped the history of data visualization. It considers the perceptual and cognitive reasons why data visualization is so effective and explores the little-known world of tactile graphics—raised-line drawings used by people who are blind. The book also investigates the way visualization has shaped our modern world. The European Renaissance and the Scientific Revolution relied on maps and technical and scientific drawings, and graphics influence how we think about abstract concepts like time and social connection.

This book is written for data visualization researchers and professionals and anyone interested in data visualization and the way we use graphics to understand and think about the world.

Kim Marriott is a Professor in Computer Science at Monash University, where he leads the Monash Assistive Technology and Society (MATS) Centre. His research interests include data visualization and assistive technologies for people who are blind or have low vision.

AK Peters Visualization Series

Visualization plays an ever-more prominent role in the world, as we communicate about and analyze data. This series aims to capture what visualization is today in all its variety and diversity, giving voice to researchers, practitioners, designers, and enthusiasts. It encompasses books from all subfields of visualization, including visual analytics, information visualization, scientific visualization, data journalism, infographics, and their connection to adjacent areas such as text analysis, digital humanities, data art, or augmented and virtual reality.

Series Editors: Tamara Munzner, University of British Columbia, Vancouver, Canada
Alberto Cairo, University of Miami, USA

The Golden Age of Data Visualization: How Did We Get Here?
Kim Marriott

Data Visualization for People of All Ages
Nancy Organ

Data Visualization in Excel
Jonathan Schwabish

Building Science Graphics
Jen Christiansen

Joyful Infographics
Nigel Holmes

Making with Data
Edited by Samuel Huron, Till Nagel, Lora Oehlberg, Wesley Willett

Questions in Dataviz
Neil Richards

Mobile Data Visualization
Edited by Bongshin Lee, Raimund Dachselt, Petra Isenberg,
Eun Kyoung Choe

Data Sketches
Nadieh Bremer, Shirley Wu

For more information about this series please visit: https://www.routledge.com/
AK-Peters-Visualization-Series/book-series/CRCVIS

The Golden Age of Data Visualization

Visualization

How Did We Get Here?

Kim Marriott

CRC Press
Taylor & Francis Group
Boca Raton London New York

CRC Press is an imprint of the
Taylor & Francis Group, an **informa** business

AN A K PETERS BOOK

Designed cover image: Map of the world (as it was then known) after the work of Claudius Ptolemy (second-century Egyptian Roman, mathematician, astronomer, astrologer, geographer), by Johannes Schnitzer (Ulm), 1492

First edition published 2025
by CRC Press
2385 NW Executive Center Drive, Suite 320, Boca Raton FL 33431

and by CRC Press
4 Park Square, Milton Park, Abingdon, Oxon, OX14 4RN

CRC Press is an imprint of Taylor & Francis Group, LLC

© 2025 Kim Marriott

ISBN: 978-1-032-83079-7 (hbk)
ISBN: 978-1-032-83077-3 (pbk)
ISBN: 978-1-003-50764-2 (ebk)

DOI: 10.1201/9781003507642

Typeset in Minion
by Newgen Publishing UK

Contents

Series Editors Foreword

KIM MARRIOTT TELLS US a story of sweeping scope across time and space, pulling together many threads about how visualization has been used to weave a tapestry of unprecedented breadth and depth. The examples of visual representations discussed in this book span thousands of years of history and a multitude of thoughtfully chosen cultural contexts. Marriott's analysis of how and why they were constructed, and even more importantly their impact on the world, is a tour de force. This book will entice people who are new to visualization to connect with it deeply yet will provide new information to even the most avid aficionado. A great adventure awaits you. Dive on in!

Alberto Cairo and Tamara Munzner
Series Editors
AK Peters Visualization Series

Preface

EVER SINCE I CAN remember, I have loved maps and diagrams. I grew up on a dairy farm and spent hours drawing maps of the zoo I planned to build once Mum and Dad left me in charge. My maps made the zoo tangible: I could hear the lions roar and gibbons hoot in paddocks where the cows had once grazed.

When I learned about data visualization, I was naturally drawn to it. For the last thirty years I've been a researcher in this and related fields, most recently investigating the use of new technologies like virtual and mixed reality, and how to provide people who are blind with equitable access to graphical information.

During this time, there has been a dramatic change in attitudes to visualization. Thirty years ago, data visualization was niche and barely worthy of serious scholarly attention. Now it's cool, and visualizations are everywhere. When I started to teach data visualization, I realized there was a lot I didn't know about its history and the reasons for its rise in popularity. While Edward Tufte's books provided a partial answer, as did Michael Friendly's articles and his Milestones Project, I wanted to gain a more holistic understanding—one that took account of the technical and cultural context, and the perceptual and cognitive reasons that made (some) visualizations so effective.

I started writing this book twelve years ago. If I had known how long it would take, I probably wouldn't have started, but the journey has been fascinating. I hope other data visualization researchers will also find what I have discovered of interest. Indeed, I hope anyone who enjoys maps, charts and diagrams will find this history of data visualization engaging and thought-provoking.

Many people have encouraged and supported this project. My friends and colleagues at Monash University, especially Bernd Meyer, Tim Dwyer,

Sarah Goodwin, Michael Wybrow, Benjamin Tag, Matt Butler and Leona Holloway. I also want to thank Dave Barker-Plummer, Alberto Cairo, Stephen Haley, John Richardson and Danielle Szafir, who provided perceptive feedback. Thanks to my research assistant William (Hanmin) Chen, illustrators Kadek Satriadi and Monika Schwarz, and photographers Jacquie Johnstone and Sam Reinders. Thanks to Julie Pinkham for providing invaluable advice as my pro bono literary agent and friend. A special thanks to my editor, Paul Smitz, for his careful reading and editing, and the team at Taylor & Francis: Gerald Bok and Kasturi Ghosh.

I also want to thank the many people who generously provided information and guidance in writing about the use of graphics by Indigenous Australians: Narissa Timbery, Jenny Green, Karl Hampton, Murray Garde and Peter Veth.

I am grateful to my other colleagues, friends outside work and extended family, including Iet, Boy, Andrea, Pete, Ian, Sue, Carlo, Pen, the Min-laws, Singo, Ceridwen, Andy and Claire, who have listened to me talking about this book for over a decade, who reassured me that it was worthwhile.

Most of all, I want to thank my family. My Mum and Dad, who encouraged me but did not get to see the final product. My children, Min and Shasha, who became used to me working on this book whenever I had a chance, and my partner Nicole Beyer. I can't thank Cole enough. She has provided a sounding board for my ideas, been my first reader, and generously supported my obsession. Thank you.

Acknowledgment of Country

THIS BOOK WAS WRITTEN on the lands of the Bunurong people of the Kulin Nation, land that was never ceded. I pay my respects to their Elders, past and present, and to those of other First Nations Australians. I acknowledge First Nations Australians' rich history of graphics use and the critical role it continues to play in Indigenous ways of knowing.

Introduction

R EMEMBER THE COVID-19 PANDEMIC? We pored over graphs showing the number of new cases, trying to make sense of the latest outbreak and understand if our government was bringing the virus under control (see Figure I.1). We saw charts of vaccination rates and the impact of COVID-19 on employment and the economy. We watched animations showing how vaccines would teach our immune systems to fight the virus. We circulated graphics on social media to argue for or against the existence of the pandemic, and about its causes and the effectiveness of vaccines (see Figure I.2).

Graphics played a central role in communicating health directives to reduce risk. Governments released infographics illustrating how to wash your hands to reduce the risk of infection, and how social distancing would curtail the spread of the disease. Government websites showed maps of exposure sites. In Australia and New Zealand, national leaders gave press conferences in which they used charts to explain the imperative to 'flatten the curve' to avoid overloading the health system (see Figure I.3).

Graphics also played a crucial role in fighting COVID-19. Contact tracers drew social networks on whiteboards as they raced against time to identify the origin of new cases. Epidemiologists plotted the results of computer simulations to predict the impact of potential health directives on the spread of the virus. Medical researchers used electron microscopes to scan cryogenically frozen samples of the virus to understand its molecular structure. They shared images and 3D models of the spikes on the virus's surface in a frantic, global effort to determine how these were used to enter

DOI: 10.1201/9781003507642-1

FIGURE I.1   During the COVID-19 pandemic, governments, health authorities and news media crafted a variety of visualizations to illustrate different aspects of the pandemic. This online dashboard from the World Health Organization (WHO) allows the viewer to interactively explore the number of cases, deaths and vaccinations worldwide and country by country.

Source: WHO, August 18, 2023, https://covid19.who.int.

and infect a cell (see Figure I.4). The resulting understanding proved crucial in developing vaccines to protect against COVID-19.

While the number and variety of visualizations used during the pandemic may have been unusual, the use of data visualizations was not. Nowadays, data visualizations are everywhere. Charts fill PowerPoint presentations, webpages and the pages of company reports. Journalists engage their readers with visualizations. Architects and engineers create 3D computer models of houses and space stations. Doctors depend on medical imaging.

It's not only professionals who rely on data visualizations. We all do. We use Google Maps to find our destination, and we look at the rain radar map to see if we will need an umbrella. We turn to visualizations in newspapers and social media to understand current issues. Increasingly, we use graphics to track personal data, such as the state of our bank balance or how much time we have spent exercising or sleeping. People who are blind are accessing tactile equivalents to visual graphics, and smartphones now provide billions of people in developing nations with unprecedented access to data visualizations.

The seventeenth century has been hailed as the Golden Age of Dutch Cartography and the late nineteenth century as the Golden Age of Statistical Graphics. Visualization designer and academic Alberto Cairo

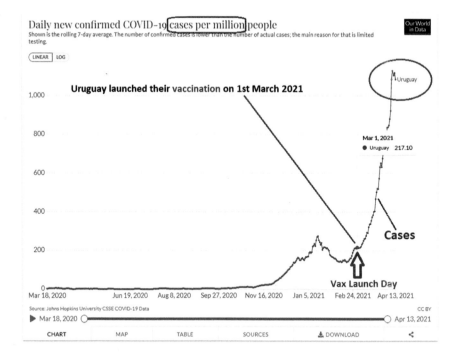

FIGURE I.2   Graphics were used on social media to argue for or against the existence of the pandemic and the effectiveness of vaccines. This chart is from a tweet arguing that vaccinations increase the chances of catching the virus.

Credit: Maxim Lisnic, et al. (2023). (CC BY 4.0).

has identified our era as another Golden Age. The use of data visualization in previous Golden Ages pales into insignificance when compared to our use today. Never before have so many people used so many kinds of data visualizations for so many purposes. Without a doubt, we are living in *the* Golden Age of Data Visualization.

But our Golden Age is only a recent phenomenon. Only a short time ago, graphics were regarded as the poor cousins of spoken and written language. They were seen as childish and preliterate and considered 'boring': too utilitarian and technical. For example, in striking contrast to the use of graphics by politicians during the recent pandemic, *The Guardian* reported on December 6, 1994 that:

> *The Speaker, Betty Boothroyd, rebuked an M.P. for using a cardboard diagram in the Commons to explain overseas aid figures. She said 'I have always believed that all Members of this House should be sufficiently articulate to express what they want to say without diagrams.'*

FIGURE I.3   Then NZ prime minister Jacinda Ardern explains the importance of 'flattening the curve' during the COVID-19 pandemic. These low-tech charts did the trick: New Zealand quickly brought the virus under control.

Credit: Dave Rowland/Stringer via Getty Images.

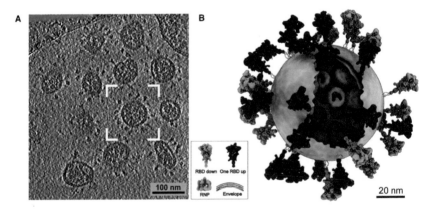

FIGURE I.4   Scientists used digital 3D-imaging techniques (left) to create models of the coronavirus (right) that causes COVID-19. This allowed them to understand how the virus attacks and enters human cells, and led to vaccines that trained the human immune system to attack the spikes on the virus's surface.

Credit: Reprinted from *Cell* 183, no. 3, H Yao et al., 'Molecular Architecture of the SARS-CoV-2 Virus', 730–8, Copyright 2020, with permission from Elsevier.

So how did our current Golden Age of Data Visualization come about? Why has data visualization, which I take to include infographics, become ubiquitous? This is the question that first led me to write this book. To answer it, we will examine the history of information graphics, by which I mean the types of graphics we use to visualize data. Because while data visualizations may contain text, it's their use of information graphics that sets them apart from other forms of communication.

As I researched the history of data visualization, I discovered the many ways in which it has shaped our modern world. This is my second reason for writing this book. You may take data visualization for granted. You may feel that information graphics are eye candy whose only purpose is to increase the visual appeal of the article or video you are viewing. You may even have some sympathy for Betty Boothroyd's views. I want to convince you that data visualization is important, that information graphics are one of our greatest inventions, and that our modern world would not exist without them.

I take a broad-minded view of what counts as an information graphic. As well as maps, graphs, plots and diagrams, I include tables, technical drawings, and scientific and medical images and illustrations. All of these are used in modern data visualizations, and all meet the literal definition of an information graphic: they are intended to show information and they are graphical.

This liberal definition of information graphics accords with what art historian James Elkin calls 'notations'. He distinguishes these from writing and more traditional artworks, which he calls 'pictures'. Writing and notations, like human language, have an unambiguous primary or literal meaning, but pictures do not. The difference between writing and notations is that writing has a single intended reading order. For instance, written English is read from left to right and top to bottom. In contrast, in a notation, the reader may choose to read the graphic elements in a different order and they will still make sense.

It is common to restrict information graphics to graphics drawn on the two-dimensional surface of a piece of paper or a computer display. However, this restriction is problematic because it rules out 3D objects displayed in virtual reality, such as a 3D model of a protein's chemical structure or a 3D scatter plot. Yet I consider these to be information graphics. After all, just like a chemical structural formula or 2D scatter plot they are perceived using vision, and they are designed to communicate information. And once you accept virtual 3D objects as information graphics, you must include physical objects such as architectural models, world globes, even notches on a tally stick. Essentially, I regard the two-dimensionality of most information graphics to be a consequence of the available presentation technologies, not a defining characteristic of an information graphic.

Information graphics are an example of a cognitive artefact. These are devices that we make to aid or enhance reasoning and understanding. They include calendars, textbooks, notepads, calculators, and the alarm you set to remind you to buy milk on the way home from work. As cognitive psychologist Donald Norman says, 'The power of the unaided mind is highly overrated,' and it is our external aids that 'make us smart'. Along with writing and mathematics, information graphics are one of our most valuable cognitive tools.

Like writing and mathematics, information graphics are tools for socially distributed cognition. They allow us to communicate with one another and to work together to solve problems that are beyond the ability of any single individual. Architects and engineers use technical drawings to collaborate on complex projects. Business teams share forecasts and timelines. More generally, visualizations allow journalists to convey complex ideas to their readers and teachers to pass on knowledge to the next generation. They are tools for rhetoric and persuasion. But visualization does more than communicate new ideas. It also plays a crucial role in originating these ideas.

Graphics have frequently been at the heart of scientific discovery. Albert Einstein famously said, 'I rarely think in words at all.' Well-chosen data visualizations can reveal patterns hidden in raw data. The physical, life and social sciences rely on data visualization, as do businesses and governments. And this reliance is only increasing. We are now collecting data at a truly incredible rate, and data visualization remains one of the most effective ways to make sense of this data tsunami.

Information graphics have helped shape how we think about space and time, nationhood, social networks and the balance of trade. Without tally sticks, geometric diagrams and Cartesian coordinates, modern mathematics would not exist. The power of charts and graphs is that they make abstract data and concepts tangible. They provide a visual metaphor that enables us to use visual and spatial intuition to reason about the immaterial.

The story of data visualization began tens of thousands of years ago, long before writing, and it continues in the present day with the latest developments in virtual and mixed reality. In this book, we will investigate how visual notations and conventions—such as maps and charts, contour lines and perspective—have evolved, and how these can be seen as 'visual languages'. But this is only part of the story. It's important to know the cultural context in which these graphics have been used. What needs were they fulfilling, and for whom? What were the prevailing attitudes to graphics and the level of graphic literacy? How did the rise of new professions like architecture and engineering affect graphics use? The technical environment must also be considered. How were graphics produced, and what were the associated limitations and costs? What data was available? If no-one collects information about births and deaths, for example, it is impossible to graph life expectancy. Even more fundamentally, we must understand how data visualizations work and why they are such effective cognitive aids.

This book is for anyone interested in data visualization. I will outline its development from prehistory to the modern day. I do not focus on the individuals who invented the various graphics and notations we now use—although it is impossible not to mention larger-than-life characters such as William Playfair and Florence Nightingale—nor on how to design data visualizations. Instead, I concentrate on how cultural context, production and presentation technologies, and data availability have shaped data visualization and driven the invention of new graphics. I also explore how these graphics leverage the way our visual system works and how our brains reason about the world.

Chapter 1 investigates the use of information graphics in early civilizations. In Chapter 2, we go further back in time and examine their prehistoric precursors and consider to what extent our understanding of maps and drawings is innate.

Chapter 3 examines the history of technical drawings—the kind of drawings created by architects and engineers—looking at how these enabled architecture and engineering to emerge as new professions in the Renaissance by separating design from construction. Chapter 4 is devoted to scientific and medical drawings, exploring their critical role in the birth of modern science and medicine.

In Chapters 5 and 6, we investigate maps. We look at the role they played in the creation of the modern sovereign state and in European exploration and colonization. We also look at how the advent of larger cities and new types of transport such as the train led to increased map use.

Chapters 7 and 8 turn to graphics such as timelines and bar charts that depict abstract data. We investigate their origin in conceptual metaphors and why they became so integral to business, science and government in the nineteenth and early twentieth centuries.

Chapters 9 and 10 take us up to the present day. Chapter 9 examines how scientific imaging and computer graphics revolutionized science and technology in the twentieth century. Chapter 10 investigates the way in which photography, cinema and television created a 'visual culture' in the twentieth century, and how this, in tandem with the arrival of the computer and the internet, led to an explosion in data visualization use in business, media and our private lives—and our current Golden Age.

In Chapter 11, we explore the cognitive benefits of data visualization from a different perspective. Are information graphics still valuable if you cannot see them but can touch them? People who are blind commonly use tactile graphics, a graphical analog to braille. We investigate the differences and similarities between visual and tactile graphics and examine why people who are blind may say they think visually.

Finally, in Chapter 12, we consider the future. How will new technologies such as artificial intelligence and mixed-reality headsets impact our use of data visualization? Will our Golden Age continue?

In the Conclusion, I will return to my two reasons for writing this book, summarizing the factors that have led to the current Golden Age and the many ways in which visualization has shaped our world.

I have written this book for a general audience. As far as possible, I have avoided specialized terms used only by the data visualization community. For the interested reader, these are provided along with notes, references and further reading at the end of each chapter.

NOTES, REFERENCES AND FURTHER READING

Many excellent books have been written about data visualization. The statistician and pioneering data visualization advocate Edward Tufte has written several books showcasing information graphics from the beginning of data visualization to the present day. My two favorites are:

Tufte, Edward R. *Envisioning Information*. Graphics Press, 1990.
Tufte, Edward R. *The Visual Display of Quantitative Information* (2nd ed.). Graphics Press, 2001.

If you want to learn more about how to design your own visualizations, I recommend:

Cairo, Alberto. *The Truthful Art: Data, Charts, and Maps for Communication*. New Riders, 2016.

Or, for a more academic treatment, I suggest:

Munzner, Tamara. *Visualization Analysis and Design*. AK Peters/CRC Press, 2014.

If you like maps and are interested in the cultural context in which they were developed, I recommend Jerry Brotton's book:

Brotton, Jerry. *A History of the World in 12 Maps*. Penguin, 2013.

For a more comprehensive introduction to the cultural context in which information graphics are used, see:

Hentschel, Klaus. *Visual Cultures in Science and Technology: A Comparative History*. Oxford University Press, 2014.

And for a more detailed look at the history of statistical graphics, try:

Friendly, Michael, and Howard Wainer. *A History of Data Visualization and Graphic Communication*. Harvard University Press, 2021.

The website of Michael Friendly and Daniel Denis's Milestones Project provides a comprehensive interactive visualization of the main historical events in data visualization: http://datavis.ca/milestones/.

Visualization and COVID-19

Bao, Huanyu, Bolin Cao, Yuan Xiong, and Weiming Tang. 'Digital Media's Role in the COVID-19 Pandemic.' *JMIR mHealth and uHealth* 8, no. 9 (2020): e20156.

Collins, Francis. 'Structural Biology Points Way to Coronavirus Vaccine.' *NIH Director's Blog*, March 3, 2020. https://directorsblog.nih.gov/2020/03/03/structural-biology-points-way-to-coronavirus-vaccine/

Lisnic, Maxim, Cole Polychronis, Alexander Lex, and Marina Kogan. 'Misleading beyond Visual Tricks: How People Actually Lie with Charts.' In *Proceedings of the CHI Conference on Human Factors in Computing Systems* (2023): 1–21.

Pitt, Sarah. 'How the Leading Coronavirus Vaccines Work.' *The Conversation*, October 7, 2020. https://theconversation.com/how-the-leading-coronavirus-vaccines-work-146969

Zhang, Yixuan, Yifan Sun, Lace Padilla, Sumit Barua, Enrico Bertini, and Andrea G Parker. 'Mapping the Landscape of COVID-19 Crisis Visualizations.' In *Proceedings of the CHI Conference on Human Factors in Computing Systems* (2021): 1–23.

Golden Age of Data Visualization

Cairo, Alberto. 'Uncertainty and Graphicacy: How Should Statisticians, Journalists and Designers Reveal Uncertainty in Graphics for Public Consumption?' In *Power from Statistics: Data, Information, and Knowledge.* Publications Office of the European Union, 2017: 91–102.

Friendly, Michael. 'The Golden Age of Statistical Graphics.' *Statistical Science* (2008): 502–35.

Charles Kostelnick and Miles Kimball also refer to digital data design creating a Second Golden Age (of Statistical Graphics):

Kostelnick, Charles, and Miles Kimball. 'Introduction.' In *Visible Numbers: Essays on the History of Statistical Graphics.* Routledge, 2018: 7.

Disdain for Graphics

The quote from *The Guardian* appeared in:

Scaife, Mike, and Yvonne Rogers. 'External Cognition: How Do Graphical Representations Work?' *International Journal of Human-Computer Studies* 45, no. 2 (1996): 185–213.

What Is an Information Graphic?

Elkins, James. *The Domain of Images.* Cornell University Press, 2018: Chapter 6.

Harris, Robert L. *Information Graphics: A Comprehensive Illustrated Reference.* Oxford University Press, 1999.

Cognitive Artefacts and Socially Distributed Cognition

Hutchins, Edwin. 'Distributed Cognition.' In *International Encyclopedia of the Social & Behavioral Sciences.* Pergamon, 2001: 2068–72.

Norman, Donald A. *Things That Make Us Smart: Defending Human Attributes in the Age of the Machine.* Addison-Wesley, 1993: Preface and Chapter 3. Quotes p.43.

CHAPTER 1

The Beginning

I N THIS AND THE next chapter, we explore the origins of data visualization. We will investigate when information graphics were first used and the reasons why. Our investigation begins in ancient China.

THE MAWANGDUI MANUSCRIPTS

In 1973, a team of Chinese archaeologists excavated three tombs at Mawangdui in south-eastern China. This is one of the most important archaeological finds ever made in China. It is chiefly famous for the rather gruesome, mummified body of a fifty-year-old noblewoman, but equally significant are thirty silk manuscripts found in the tomb of a high-ranking official. While the official was buried in 168 BCE, some of the manuscripts date from before 200 BCE. This means they were written just after China was first unified into a single kingdom under the Han, and at about the time the first stage of the Great Wall of China was completed.

The manuscripts' contents range from philosophical treatises to medical treatments and a sex manual. They reach across the centuries, revealing that the concerns of the ancient Chinese were similar to those we have today. Like us, they wished to be prosperous and healthy. Like us, they wanted to cure hemorrhoids and have a robust libido. The manuscripts also demonstrate that, by 200 BCE, the Chinese were using a wide variety of information graphics.

One of the graphics is a physical exercise chart (see Figure 1.1). It shows forty-four figures in various postures and movements and is accompanied

DOI: 10.1201/9781003507642-2

FIGURE 1.1   One of the Mawangdui manuscripts is a chart illustrating different exercises for improving health and treating pain. This is a reconstruction of the chart.

Credit: Daoyin tu—Wellcome Collection. (CC BY 4.0.)

by text describing the exercises and their benefits. It looks remarkably modern—it could easily adorn the wall of a contemporary school gymnasium.

Another graphic resembles a family tree. This is from a manuscript specifying mourning rituals. While damaged, it is believed to show a male mourner surrounded by his relatives. The relatives are arranged in rows, generation by generation, with lines connecting parents and children. The associated text prescribes the kinds of clothes that should be worn in the mourning period for different relatives, and for how long. This reveals the patriarchal nature of ancient Chinese society. For example, the death of a son's son warrants the second-highest grade of mourning, while that of a daughter's son deserves only the lowest grade.

The Mawangdui manuscripts also contain three maps. One, poorly preserved, shows a city with an inner and outer wall. A second map shows mountain ranges, rivers, roads, and the principal government centers in a region near where the manuscripts were found. The third map (see Figure 1.2) was almost certainly for military use. It details an area near the tombs bordering a reluctant tributary state of the Han, showing the location of army installations and headquarters, rivers, mountains, villages and roads. The map reveals the impact of war, as some towns are marked 'Now nobody' or 'Not yet returned'. The sophistication of the second and third

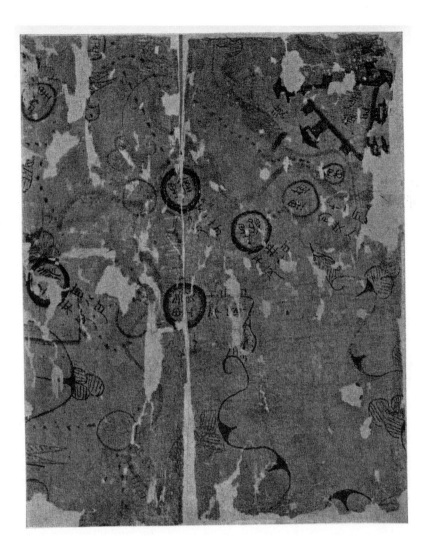

FIGURE 1.2 The Mawangdui tombs contained three maps. One was almost certainly for military use and showed the contested border region near the tombs. The central portion of the map is shown above. Below is a reconstruction of the complete map. (Continued)

Credit: Top: Mawangdui Han Tomb Silk Collection Group. Compilation Briefing On The Garrison Pictures Unearthed From The Han Tomb No. 3. In Mawangdui, *Wen Wu* (1976): pp. 18–23+95–7. Reproduced with permission from the Cultural Relics Publishing House. Bottom: The Han Maps and Early Chinese Cartography, Mei-Ling Hsu, *Annals of the Association of American Geographers*, copyright © 1978 by American Association of Geographers, reprinted by permission of Taylor & Francis Ltd, www.tandfonline.com on behalf of © 1978 by American Association of Geographers.

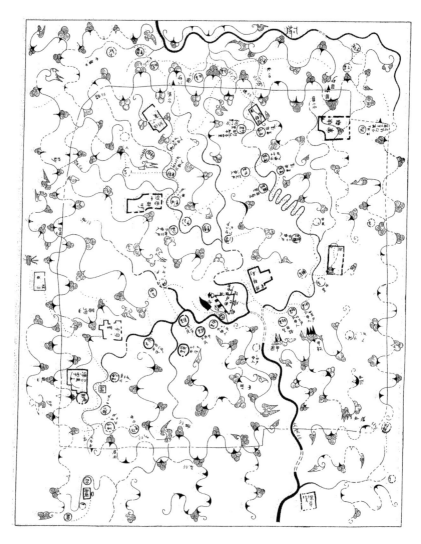

FIGURE 1.2   (Continued)

maps is striking. Each uses a relatively uniform scale and consistent stylized representations of mountains, rivers, villages, forts and watchtowers.

The military map and the following quote from a political and philosophical text written around 200 BCE make it clear that the ancient Chinese regarded maps as indispensable military aids:

> All military commanders must first examine and come to know maps. They must know thoroughly the dangers of winding, gate-like

defiles, streams which may inundate their chariots, famous moun-
tains, passable valleys, arterial rivers, highlands, and hills; where
grow grasses, trees and rushes, the distances of the roads, the size of
the city and suburban walls, famous and deserted towns, and barren
and fertile land. They should thoroughly store up [in their minds] the
relative location of the configurations of the terrain ... In the dispos-
ition [of troops] they will know [what lies] ahead and behind, and
will not lose the advantages of the terrain. This is the constant [value]
of maps.

Maps were also utilized for administration, with ancient Chinese officials using them to manage the regions and towns under their control. They were used to chart natural resources such as mines, settle land disputes, and record the position of tombs on royal burial grounds. Because of their importance, the state strictly controlled the creation and possession of maps. Indeed, they were regarded as symbols of the state. On occasion, they were used as a symbol of defeat, with the conquered side handing over a map of its territory to the victor.

The Mawangdui manuscripts also contain graphics that are unlike anything we use today. One is a schematic map from a medical text. When a child was born, the ancient Chinese would bury the afterbirth in a specific direction from the place of birth, believing that the child's future prosperity crucially depended upon getting this right. The diagram shown in Figure 1.3 guided the choice. There is a square for each birth month. Each square has twelve compass directions, two of which are labeled 'death', a clear indication that this direction is not the best choice. The remaining compass points are 'safe'. These are numbered: the greater the value, the more auspicious the direction. This diagram made it simple to determine where to bury a child's afterbirth. You simply looked at the square relating to the child's birth month and found the compass direction with the greatest value.

Predicting and controlling the future was a significant concern for the ancient Chinese. One manuscript from Mawangdui contains more than 200 drawings of clouds, comets, eclipses, and solar and lunar haloes. Many of these are accompanied by an omen. For instance, the drawing of six concentric circles around a crescent moon has the text: 'When the moon has from six to nine haloes, in Under-heaven (the world) there is a state that perishes.' The ancient Chinese viewed the natural world as symbolic, full of signs and portents that allowed someone with the appropriate understanding to read

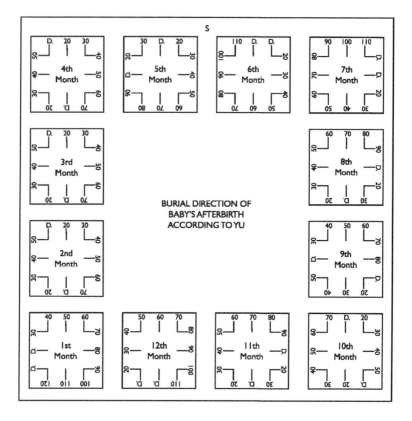

FIGURE 1.3   A translation of one of the more unusual graphics from the Mawangdui manuscripts. It shows the most auspicious direction for burying a child's afterbirth, based on the child's birth month. As with most ancient Chinese maps, south is at the top.

Credit: Adaptation by Monika Schwarz. Original image copyright © 1998. From *Early Chinese Medical Literature: The Mawangdui Medical Manuscripts* by Harper, Donald. Reproduced by permission of Taylor and Francis Group, LLC, a division of Informa plc.

the future. While the drawings in this manuscript are broadly based on what the ancient Chinese saw, they are not observations in the sense of modern science. Indeed, modern scientists have never observed that many haloes around the Moon. Instead, the manuscript is a dictionary or legend with which to decipher the signs of nature: if you happen to see haloes like this, be afraid, very afraid.

The Mawangdui manuscripts capture an exciting time in Chinese intellectualism. Natural philosophers, medical practitioners and occultists were sharing teachings and merging these to give a grand theoretical understanding of nature. This new understanding was built around the duality of yin and yang and the life essence of qi. Fate was no longer the result of capricious spirits. Instead, the world was predictable and controllable, with cosmic cycles and signs that could be understood by those with the necessary knowledge. Manuscripts of the kind uncovered at Mawangdui were crucial in this intellectual revolution, allowing knowledge to be shared and codified. Cosmological diagrams such as the burial chart and the cosmic board (discussed below) played a crucial role in this new worldview. They combined with the written word to reveal a universal plan, as well as being tools for interpreting and controlling cosmic forces.

The discovery of astronomical cycles was the basis for believing that the world was predictable and controllable. For over 1000 years, the Chinese had been observing and recording the position of the planets and eclipses. For instance, an astronomical text found at Mawangdui contains tables detailing the heliacal risings of Jupiter, Saturn and Venus from 246 BCE to 177 BCE. (A heliacal rising is when the planet appears in the east, just before dawn.) From tables like these, Chinese astronomers recognized patterns and cycles, allowing them to predict the arrival of the seasons and the movement of the planets and Moon.

As the heavenly bodies were believed to be manifestations of cosmic forces, it was natural to take their positions—hence, their influence—into account when making decisions. The elite consulted almanacs based on the celestial cycles to identify the most auspicious day on which to marry, make a business decision or go to war. If they were still unsure, they could consult an expert who might use a graphical tool called a cosmic board to precisely calculate the celestial influences (see Figure 1.4). While the Mawangdui tombs did not contain a cosmic board, one was found in a Han tomb dating from about the same time.

The cosmic board has two parts. A round disc representing the heavens sits on top of a larger square plate representing the Earth. These are connected by a pin running through the center of both pieces, allowing the disc to rotate. Reflecting its importance in Chinese cosmology, the Big Dipper constellation is shown at the center of the disc. The Big Dipper's seven stars are depicted as small circles connected by lines. Curiously, it is portrayed as if seen from above rather than from the Earth. The outside of the disc is inscribed with characters for the

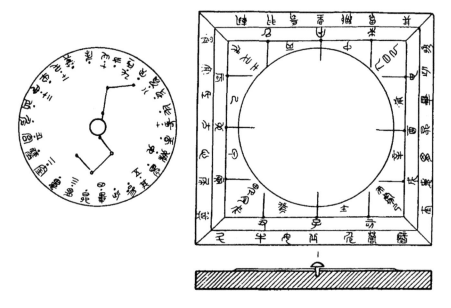

FIGURE 1.4   The ancient Chinese used a variety of graphical tools to divine the future. One was the cosmic board, which consisted of a rotatable disc (left) positioned on top of a square base (right). The disc represented the heavens and was inscribed with the Big Dipper, and the square symbolized Earth.

Credit: Harper, Donald J. 'Warring States Natural Philosophy and Occult Thought.' In *The Cambridge History of Ancient China: From the Origins of Civilization to 221 BC*. © D Harper 1999 published by Cambridge University Press. Reproduced with permission.

twelve months and the twenty-eight lunar mansions, the ancient Chinese equivalent of the signs of the zodiac. The Earth plate is marked with twelve branches referring to both spatial directions and hours in the day. The board was regarded as a working model of the cosmos and used as a tool for astrological calculations. For instance, by rotating the heavens plate, it was possible to determine the position of the handle of the Big Dipper at any time of the day during any season of the year: vital information for any forecaster.

The Mawangdui manuscripts reveal that by the second century BCE, the ancient Chinese were using a wide variety of information graphics—maps, tables, cosmological diagrams and medical illustrations—some of which are remarkably similar to those used today. A natural question to ask is whether the ancient Chinese were unusual in this respect, or whether other early civilizations were producing similar graphics.

GRAPHICS USE IN OTHER EARLY CIVILIZATIONS

The Chinese civilization originated around the Hwang-Ho (Yellow River) in about 2000 BCE. Other civilizations arose somewhat earlier in Mesopotamia and the Nile Valley in Egypt around 3500 BCE and in the Indus Valley in India at about 2500 BCE. Civilizations also independently emerged in the Americas, first in Mesoamerica around 500 BCE and then in South America. Archaeologists have found information graphics from all these ancient civilizations except that of the Indus. This may be because the Indus graphics have perished as India's hot, humid conditions make it unlikely that drawings on organic materials such as palm leaves will have survived. The earliest information graphics I know from India are fragments of an architectural plan of a monastery found on pottery shards dating from around 200 BCE.

The very first civilization arose in Mesopotamia on a flood plain between the Tigris and Euphrates rivers in what is now Iraq. Around 4000 BCE, farmers in small villages banded together to build canals and channels that allowed them to drain marshes and irrigate their crops. This supported a much larger population, and their villages expanded and combined to form cities with hundreds of thousands of inhabitants. By 3000 BCE, the Sumerian and Akkadian empires were born, followed by the Babylonian and Assyrian realms.

The Sumerians invented cuneiform writing, using a stylus to make wedge-shaped indentations in clay tablets. Archaeologists have found tens of thousands of these tablets, as they are relatively durable. About 170 show maps or plans, mostly of fields, agricultural estates and house plots. It is likely these were used to compute taxes and record land ownership. Others are floor plans of houses and temples. A few show canal and irrigation networks. The Mesopotamian canals required regular dredging to remove silt. Canal plans were used to calculate the amount of sediment to be removed and the number of laborers needed to carry out the task. The remaining tablets show city plans and regional maps, one of which was probably for military use as it gives an army camp's location.

As it is difficult to draw on clay, Mesopotamian maps and plans used stylized conventions rather than lifelike renderings of water or mountains; for instance, water was frequently shown by wavy lines. Most maps and plans are uncomplicated, showing only a few geographic features, as the tablets were small and designed to be comfortably held in one hand.

Archaeologists have also found maps and plans from ancient Egypt. However, they are much less common than those from Mesopotamia. This may be because they were drawn on materials that have not survived. Or it may be because archaeologists have focused on excavating religious monuments and tombs rather than the less glamorous villages housing builders and merchants who were more likely to have used maps and plans. Archaeologists have found plans of tombs, and a map that details a 12.5-kilometer stretch of dry riverbed in Egypt's Eastern Desert. This was a significant mining region and a trade route for the ancient Egyptians. The map shows different types of rocks and gravel, a goldmine and a small village.

It is believed that maps were common in Mesoamerica before the Spanish invasion in the sixteenth century. They were drawn on cloth, parchment, animal hides, walls, and a kind of paper made from bark and plant fiber. Most maps were destroyed during colonization. The few that survived, or were created soon after European contact, demonstrate a rich diversity of styles. They were primarily used to record land ownership but also may have been used for trading and military campaigns.

A striking feature of many Mesoamerican maps is that they depict a region's history and social connections in addition to its geography (see Figure 1.5). This mix is exemplified in the community maps created throughout the region. These were an expression of collective identity. They showed the community's territory but also included the story of how the community came into being, pivotal moments in its history, and the genealogy of its ruling families.

Like the ancient Chinese, the ancient Egyptians, Mesoamericans and Mesopotamians created cosmological diagrams: graphics that embodied their worldview. One of the best known is a Babylonian map of the world (see Figure 1.6). The map is not meant to be an accurate geographic representation. Rather, it is a cosmological map incorporating myth and legends to show how the Babylonians saw their place in the world—like most cultures, at its center.

Mesoamerican cosmological diagrams have their own distinctive appearance. They reflect the Mesoamerican belief that the Earth floated on water and that five 'world trees' positioned at the Earth's center and each of its four corners separated the Earth from the sky (see Figure 1.7).

Just as in ancient China, astronomy was valued by the ancient Egyptians, Mesoamericans and Mesopotamians. Each civilization saw patterns in the night sky. In the case of the Egyptians, it was hippopotamuses, crocodiles, lions and tortoises, while the Mesopotamians saw the constellations of the

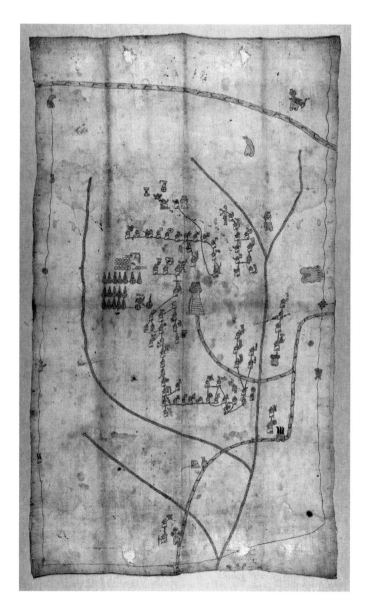

FIGURE 1.5　The Mesoamerican civilizations also made use of maps. This regional sixteenth-century map (*Mapa de Metlaltoyuca*), drawn on hide, shows a town (represented by the stepped pyramid) at the center and the surrounding villages. A thin line on the map's perimeter shows the region's boundary, while the dark, wavy lines represent rivers, and the lighter lines marked with stylized footprints indicate roads. The human figures probably represent the region's ruling families, with cords showing the links between them.

Credit: British Museum Am2006, Ptg.30088. © The Trustees of the British Museum.

FIGURE 1.6   One of the most famous Mesopotamian graphics is a Babylonian world map from 500 BCE, believed to be a copy of a map from two or three hundred years earlier. The horizontal rectangle in the upper central region represents Babylon. The rectangle intersects the river Euphrates, depicted as a vertical rectangle flowing from the curved mountain range at the top to a swamp at the bottom. Around Babylon, labeled circles denote cities and localities. These are encircled by a band of water called the (salt) ocean, around which are triangular regions representing far-off, semi-mythical lands. Note the incised dot at the map's center. This was probably left by the point of a compass that the scribe used to draw the concentric circles.

Credit: British Museum 92687. © The Trustees of the British Museum.

zodiac, which have come down to us via the ancient Greeks and Romans. All these civilizations recorded astronomical events such as eclipses, and tracked the position of stars and constellations through the seasons. They recognized cycles and patterns, allowing them to discover the length of

FIGURE 1.7 The Mesoamericans also drew cosmological diagrams. In this image, four world trees hold up the corners of the sky. They are shown projecting radially from a central square representing the Earth. Like many Mesoamerican maps, this one also shows the passage of time. A calendrical day count arranged in a Maltese cross-like shape separates the trees and the dismembered body parts of the creator god, Tezcatlipoca, illustrating a creation myth.

Credit: Codex Fejérváry–Mayer, before 1521. National Museums Liverpool M12014. © National Museums Liverpool.

the year. This predictability guided the planting of crops, and, again as in China, astronomical events were assumed to be linked to all kinds of events on Earth.

Tables were the primary way of organizing astronomical observations and predictions. They were also used to list stars and constellations. There are also graphics from ancient Egypt and Mesopotamia showing constellations and stars associated with different times of the year. One from the ceiling of an ancient Egyptian tomb shows stars associated with ten-day intervals through the year and the constellations of the northern sky surrounded by twelve circles representing months (see Figure 1.8).

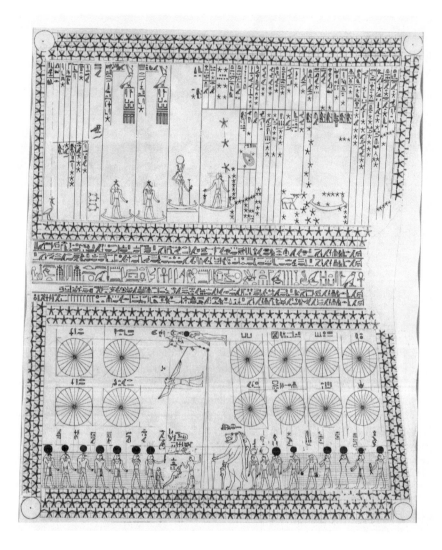

FIGURE 1.8   Drawing of the ceiling of an ancient Egyptian tomb (c. 1470 BCE). The top shows stars associated with ten-day intervals through the year. The bottom is a pictorial representation of the constellations of the northern sky surrounded by twelve circles representing months in the year.

Credit: Charles K Wilkinson. *Astronomical Ceiling.* The Metropolitan Museum of Art, New York, Rogers Fund, 1948.

ORIGINS OF MATHEMATICS AND WRITING

These early graphics from Mesopotamia, Egypt and Mesoamerica clarify that the ancient Chinese were not unusual in using maps and plans, astronomical tables and cosmological diagrams. In addition, graphics played another critical role in these early civilizations: they were central to the invention of both mathematics and writing.

Let's start with mathematics. Ancient mathematics came in two flavors: arithmetic and geometry. The ancient Chinese, Egyptians, Mesopotamians and Mesoamericans developed arithmetic to keep accounts and compute taxes, while geometry allowed them to calculate the area of fields or the volume of a pyramid.

At first glance, it's hard to see what graphics have to do with the development of arithmetic. Like many other animals, humans have an innate sense of quantity. Gazing at a group of three strawberries, we immediately intuit the number of strawberries. With bigger sets, our sense of 'number' is more approximate. Even so, we immediately recognize that a collection of, say, seventy strawberries is greater and preferable to one containing only fifty strawberries.

While basic arithmetic builds upon this innate sense of quantity, it is not an obvious or automatic extension. Not all societies have names for numbers greater than three, and many have never developed techniques for adding or multiplying numbers. Think of how long it takes children to learn to count and perform simple arithmetic calculations.

It is now believed that external counting aids were necessary for us to build an understanding of numbers. Around the world, people count on their fingers. That's why we use a decimal system. Almost certainly, our prehistoric forebears also counted with their fingers. Archaeologists have found bones and pieces of wood with a regular pattern of notches. It's commonly believed these were used for counting, with each cut standing for an object or event (though see the next chapter). We still use tallies like these today; for instance, when scoring points in a game: 卌. Roman numerals (I, II, III) and Chinese characters (一, 二, 三) for 1, 2 and 3 also demonstrate the pervasiveness of tallies. Before they invented written numbers, the ancient Mesopotamians used small clay tokens as counters, and there is some evidence that they used tallies.

External representations such as tallies and clay tokens enabled early humans to build a mental model of numbers. Interacting with these revealed a concept of numerosity independent of the kind of objects being counted. It allowed humans to discover the operations of addition and subtraction, and to 'see' that the number of elements in a group is the same no matter what order you count them in, and that X+Y always equals Y+X. These external representations of numbers are a kind of simple information graphic. But while they are simple, their impact has been profound: they made numbers tangible and manipulable.

Information graphics also play a role in arithmetic calculation. At school, we have to learn our 'times tables'. Early civilizations also used multiplication tables and tables of other useful mathematical functions. When adding numbers, we are taught to place them in a vertical column, carefully aligning their digits to form a grid. We then add the digits column by column from right to left. Early civilizations used similar techniques. The ancient Chinese, for example, arranged counting rods in a grid, with the counting rods in each cell representing a digit. Using these, they could readily add or multiply numbers and even solve systems of linear equations. In fact, our word 'calculate' comes from the Latin 'calculi', for pebble, since the ancient Romans (and Greeks) used small stones arranged in columns on a flat surface for numerical calculations.

The most apparent use of information graphics in early mathematics, however, was for geometry. Geometry is built around two complementary spatial properties: length/distance and angle/direction. While we have an innate understanding of both, we think about them in different parts of our brain. Experiments have shown that children do not combine these into a single integrated representation of a shape's geometry until they are around twelve years old. In one study conducted by Moira Dillon and Elizabeth Spelke, illustrated in Figure 1.9, children were shown the bottom

FIGURE 1.9   In an experiment, children of different ages were shown the bottom two corners of a triangle (left). The corners were then moved apart (right), and the children were asked if the angle of the top corner of the triangle had become smaller, larger or stayed the same.

two corners of a triangle. The corners were then moved apart and the children were asked if the angle at the top of the triangle would change. Nearly 90 per cent of the six-year-old children incorrectly answered that the angle would grow bigger, mistakenly believing that, because the sides of the triangle had grown larger, so would the angle. In comparison, more than 80 per cent of the twelve-year-olds correctly responded that it would not change. Dillon and Spelke have conjectured that exposure to graphics such as maps and geometric diagrams helps children integrate these different aspects of geometry into a single mental representation.

The ancient Chinese, Mesopotamians, Egyptians and Mesoamericans all developed techniques for solving geometric problems, such as finding the area of a field or the volume of a pyramid. Mathematical texts from Mesopotamia, Egypt and Mesoamerica describing these calculations display geometric diagrams next to worked examples (see Figure 1.10). Surprisingly, there are no geometric diagrams in ancient Chinese mathematical manuscripts. No-one knows why, although it has been conjectured that the text may have been accompanied by figures or models.

Early mathematicians focused on the practical applications of arithmetic and geometry. The first texts consisted of examples illustrating how to solve problems such as finding the area of a triangle. Starting in about 500 BCE, however, the ancient Greeks did something rather remarkable. Rather than concentrating on calculations, they focused on reasoning about the abstract properties of numbers, lines, points and geometric shapes. In doing so, they invented modern mathematics.

This new approach to mathematics was exemplified in a text written by Euclid of Alexandria around 300 BCE. His manuscript, *Elements*, is undoubtedly the most influential mathematical work ever written. Starting with a few simple axioms, Euclid showed how geometric theorems could be systematically derived from those proved earlier, building a magnificent mathematical edifice one brick at a time. It is hard to overstate the impact that this rigorous, deductive approach had on the development of Western mathematics and philosophy. For over 2000 years, *Elements* was regarded as the definitive mathematical text and, until recently, was still routinely used to teach geometry.

Geometric diagrams constructed with a ruler and compass are at the heart of Euclid's *Elements* (see Figure 1.11). The diagrams are not an optional decoration. They are an integral part of the argument, with lettered

FIGURE 1.10   Geometric diagrams were used in many early civilizations. These are from the *Rhind Mathematical Papyrus* (1550 BCE), an ancient Egyptian mathematical text. They illustrate how to compute the areas of rectangles and triangles.

Credit: British Museum EA10058. © The Trustees of the British Museum.

labels linking them to the text. Unlike the diagrams in earlier geometry texts, which showed a particular example, such as a rectangular field whose area was being calculated, these diagrams are schematic. A triangle, for example, represents any triangle satisfying the geometric relationships specified in the diagram and text. The ancient Greeks felt that these diagrams were so central to their mathematical proofs that they referred to mathematical propositions and their proofs as 'diagrammata'.

On a given finite straight line to construct an equilateral triangle

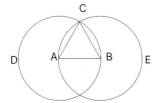

Let AB be the given finite straight line.
Thus it is required to construct an equilateral triangle on the straight line AB.
With center A and distance AB let the circle BCD be described;   [Postulate 3]
again, with center B and distance BA let the circle ACE be described;   [Postulate 3]
and from the point C, in which the circles cut one another, to the points A, B let the
straight lines CA, CB be joined.   [Postulate 1]
Now, since the point A is the center of the circle CDB, AC is equal to AB.   [Definition 15]
Again, since the point B is the center of the circle CAE, BC is equal to BA.   [Definition 15]
But CA was also proved equal to AB; therefore each of the straight lines CA, CB is equal to
AB.
And things which are equal to the same thing are also equal to one another;
therefore CA is also equal to CB.
Therefore the three straight lines CA, AB, BC are equal to one another.
(Being) what it was required to do.

FIGURE 1.11   The ancient Greeks invented modern mathematics. Above is
a translation of the first proposition from Euclid's *Elements*, which was written
in about 300 BCE. Notice how text and labeled diagrams are combined in the
proposition's proof.

**Credit: Adaptation of Table 4, N Miller, *Euclid and His Twentieth Century Rivals*,
© 2007 CSLI Publications.**

Information graphics were also central to the invention of writing. The
ancient Chinese, Mesopotamians, Egyptians and Mesoamericans all had
writing. As their writing systems are very different, they are thought to
have been independent discoveries. Inventing writing would not have been
easy. Reading and writing do not come naturally; consider how long children need to learn these skills.

I previously discussed how writing is distinguished from information
graphics by having a single, fixed order in which the graphical symbols
are intended to be read. This is because writing records speech. Speech
is inherently sequential, as the words in each sentence and the sounds in
each word are uttered one after another. This means that the graphical
symbols representing sounds and words in writing must be read in the
same order to recover what was originally said. However, the precursors to
writing were not intended to directly represent speech. They did not have

a fixed reading order and can therefore be considered a type of information graphic.

We know more about the evolution of writing in Mesopotamia than elsewhere because the use of durable clay tablets has meant that the precursors to writing there have survived. By 4000 BCE, the Mesopotamians were using clay counters called tokens to keep track of goods. Each token represented one unit of a particular commodity. They were 1–2 centimeters in size and came in different shapes. Some resembled the item they represented while others were abstract geometric shapes.

Around 3500 BCE, the clay tokens began to be placed in a clay envelope. To show what was inside the envelope, accountants pressed the tokens onto the surface of the envelope before sealing it. Soon, accountants realized that the tokens inside the envelopes were redundant and that the marks indicating the tokens could simply be applied to solid balls of clay.

The next step was to draw images of the tokens on a clay ball using a stylus rather than impressing the tokens. Then came a stroke of genius. Someone invented written numerals: symbols for one, ten and sixty units of a particular commodity. Scribes no longer had to draw thirty-three symbols, one for each jar of oil, to record thirty-three jars of olive oil. Instead, they could simply inscribe three signs for ten, three signs for one, and the symbol for a jar of oil.

This led to proto-cuneiform—a mix of numerals and symbols that resembled the objects they represented. These symbols, known as pictographs, were used to show commodities, types of transactions, names, titles and professions (see Figure 1.12). This is not true writing; rather, the tablets are a kind of infographic composed of symbols enclosed in rectangular boxes. Each box contained a separate entry. There was no fixed reading order as the boxes, and the signs within them, could be read in different orders without changing their meaning.

It took several more centuries for proto-cuneiform to evolve into authentic writing, with signs becoming more abstract and less pictographic. No longer was it just for administrative records. It was now used to record speech: messages and tales of creation and heroism. The syntax became fixed with regular columns of signs, and these had a fixed reading order: the world's first writing had been invented.

In the case of Mesopotamia, we see that the precursors to cuneiform writing were not intended to mimic speech or perform functions that speech was already ably accomplishing. Instead, they were information graphics designed to record inventories of commodities, something that

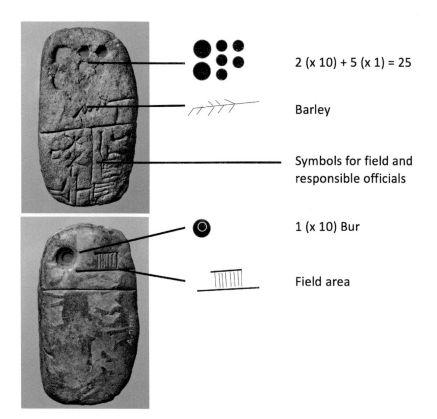

2 (x 10) + 5 (x 1) = 25

Barley

Symbols for field and responsible officials

1 (x 10) Bur

Field area

FIGURE 1.12 Front and rear of a proto-cuneiform tablet (c. 3100 BCE) that describes the amount of barley (25 units) needed to sow an area of 10 *bur* (about 65 hectares).

Credit: Adaptation of Fig. 53, C Woods (ed.) *Visible Language: Inventions of Writing in the Ancient Middle East and beyond.* © 2010 The University of Chicago. Images of front and rear of tablet courtesy of the Institute for the Study of Ancient Cultures of the University of Chicago.

speech is ill-suited for. While we do not know for sure, writing is likely to have developed similarly in other civilizations—at first, fulfilling complementary functions to speech and using information graphics composed of pictographs without a fixed reading order, then evolving to true writing.

We have seen that early civilizations used a variety of information graphics. In the next chapter, we further explore the origins of data visualization and investigate whether the prehistoric forebears of these civilizations also used graphics.

NOTES, REFERENCES AND FURTHER READING

The Mawangdui Manuscripts

Overview of Mawangdui Manuscripts

Harper, Donald. *Early Chinese Medical Literature: The Mawangdui Medical Manuscripts*. Kegan-Paul International, 1998: Section 1, 'Mawangdui Medical Manuscripts'.

Loewe, Michael AN. 'Manuscripts Found Recently in China: A Preliminary Survey.' *T'oung Pao* 6 (1977): 99–136.

Mawangdui Medical Manuscripts, Including the Exercise Chart and Afterbirth Burial Chart

Harper, Donald. *Early Chinese Medical Literature: The Mawangdui Medical Manuscripts*. Kegan-Paul International, 1998: MSV Taichan shu.

Lee, Jen-der. 'Childbirth in Early Imperial China.' *Nan nü* 7, no. 2 (2005): 108–78.

Mawangdui Kinship Diagram

Lai, Guolong. 'The Diagram of the Mourning System from Mawangdui.' *Early China* 28 (2003): 43–99.

Mawangdui Maps and Broader Use of Maps in Ancient China

De Crespigny, RRC. 'Two Maps from Mawangdui.' *Cartography* 11, no. 4 (1980): 211–22.

Hsu, Mei-Ling. 'The Han Maps and Early Chinese Cartography.' *Annals of the Association of American Geographers* 68, no. 1 (1978): 45–60.

Rickett, Allyn W. *Kuan-Tzu: A Repository of Early Chinese Thought. A Translation and Study of Twelve Chapters*. Hong Kong University Press, 1965. Quote from p. 234. The original text is believed to date from about 200 BCE.

Yee, Cordell DK. 'Reinterpreting Traditional Chinese Geographical Maps.' In *The History of Cartography*. University of Chicago Press, 1994: vol. 2, book 2, 35–70.

Yee, Cordell DK. 'Chinese Maps in Political Culture.' In *The History of Cartography*. University of Chicago Press, 1994: vol. 2, book 2, 71–95.

Divination in Ancient China

Harper, Donald. 'Communication By Design: Two Silk Manuscripts of Diagrams (Tu) from Mawangdui Tomb Three.' In *Graphics and Text in the Production of Technical Knowledge in China*. Brill, 2007: 169–89.

Loewe, Michael. *Divination, Mythology and Monarchy in Han China*. Cambridge University Press, 1994: Chapters 3, 9 and 10.

Emergence of New World View
Harper, Donald. 'Warring States Natural Philosophy and Occult Thought.' In *The Cambridge History of Ancient China: From the Origins of Civilization to 221 BC*. Cambridge University Press, 1999: 815–84.

Role of Diagrams in Cosmological Thinking
Bray, Francesca. 'Introduction: The Powers of Tu.' In *Graphics and Text in the Production of Technical Knowledge in China*. Brill, 2007: 1–79.
Henderson, John B. 'Chinese Cosmographical Thought: The High Intellectual Tradition.' In *The History of Cartography*. University of Chicago Press, 1994: vol. 2, book 2, 203–27.

Ancient Chinese Astronomy
Cullen, Christopher. 'Understanding the Planets in Ancient China: Prediction and Divination in the *Wu xing zhan*.' *Early Science and Medicine* 16, no. 3 (2011): 218–51.
Shi, Yunli, and Clive LN Ruggles. 'Ancient Chinese Astronomy: An Overview.' In *Handbook of Archaeoastronomy and Ethnoastronomy*. Springer, 2015: 2031–42.

The Cosmic Board
Harper, Donald J. 'The Han Cosmic Board (Shih).' *Early China* 4 (1978): 1–10.
Harper, Donald J. 'Warring States Natural Philosophy and Occult Thought.' In *The Cambridge History of Ancient China: From the Origins of Civilization to 221 BC*. Cambridge University Press, 1999: 815–84.

Graphics Use in Other Early Civilizations

Use of Graphics in the Indus Civilization

Schwartzberg, Joseph E. 'South Asian Cartography.' In *The History of Cartography*. University of Chicago Press, 1992: vol. 2, book 1, 295–331.

Mesopotamian Maps and Plans
Millard, Alan Ralph. 'Cartography in the Ancient Near East.' In *The History of Cartography*. University of Chicago Press, 1987: vol. 1, 107–16.
Rochberg, Francesca. 'The Expression of Terrestrial and Celestial Order in Ancient Mesopotamia.' In *Ancient Perspectives: Maps and Their Place in Mesopotamia, Egypt, Greece and Rome*. University of Chicago Press, 2012: 9–46.
Wheat, Elizabeth Ruth Josie. *Terrestrial Cartography in Ancient Mesopotamia*. PhD dissertation. University of Birmingham, 2013: Introduction and Chapters 1–6.

Ancient Egyptian Maps and Plans

Harrell, James A, and V Max Brown. 'The World's Oldest Surviving Geological Map: The 1150 BC Turin Papyrus from Egypt.' *The Journal of Geology* 100, no. 1 (1992): 3–18.

O'Connor, David. 'From Topography to Cosmos: Ancient Egypt's Multiple Maps.' In *Ancient Perspectives: Maps and Their Place in Mesopotamia, Egypt, Greece and Rome.* University of Chicago Press, 2012: 47–79.

Shore, AF. 'Egyptian Cartography.' In *The History of Cartography.* University of Chicago Press, 1987: vol. 1, 117–28.

Mesoamerican Maps

Mundy, Barbara E. 'Mesoamerican Cartography.' In *The History of Cartography.* University of Chicago Press, 1998: vol. 2, book 3, 183–256.

Cosmological Diagrams and Maps

Allen, James P. 'Egyptian Cosmology and Cosmogony.' In *Handbook of Archaeoastronomy and Ethnoastronomy.* Springer, 2015: 1471–5.

Brotton, Jerry. *A History of the World in 12 Maps.* Penguin, 2013: Introduction. Observes that the Babylonian world map, like the majority of maps, puts the culture that produced it at the center.

Mundy, Barbara E. 'Mesoamerican Cartography.' In *The History of Cartography.* University of Chicago Press, 1998: vol. 2, book 3, 183–256.

Wheat, Elizabeth Ruth Josie. *Terrestrial Cartography in Ancient Mesopotamia.* PhD dissertation. University of Birmingham, 2013: Chapter 6.

Astronomy

Jones, Philip. *Mesopotamian Cosmic Geography.* Eisenbrauns, 2011: Chapter 7.

Lull, Jose, and Juan Antonio Belmonte. 'Egyptian Constellations.' In *Handbook of Archaeoastronomy and Ethnoastronomy.* Springer, 2015: 1477–87.

Symons, Sarah. 'Egyptian "Star Clocks".' In *Handbook of Archaeoastronomy and Ethnoastronomy.* Springer, 2015: 1495–500.

Vail, Gabrielle. 'Astronomy in the Dresden Codex.' In *Handbook of Archaeoastronomy and Ethnoastronomy.* Springer, 2015: 695–708.

Origins of Mathematics and Writing

Innate Sense of Numbers

Dehaene, Stanislas. *The Number Sense: How the Mind Creates Mathematics.* Oxford University Press, 2011: Chapters 1 and 2.

Núñez, Rafael E. 'Is There Really an Evolved Capacity for Number?' *Trends in Cognitive Sciences* 21, no. 6 (2017): 409–24.

Use of External Representations for Numbers

Damerow, Peter. 'The Origins of Writing and Arithmetic.' In *The Globalization of Knowledge in History*. Max Planck Institute for the History of Science, 2012: 143–60.

Dehaene, Stanislas. *The Number Sense: How the Mind Creates Mathematics*. Oxford University Press, 2011: Chapter 4.

Everett, Caleb. *Numbers and the Making of Us*. Harvard University Press, 2017: Chapter 4.

Giaquinto, Marcus. *Visual Thinking in Mathematics*. Oxford University Press, 2007: Chapter 7.

Hayden, Brian. 'Keeping Count: On Interpreting Record Keeping in Prehistory.' *Journal of Anthropological Archaeology* 63 (2021): 101304.

Ifrah, Georges. *From One to Zero: A Universal History of Numbers* (L Bair, trans.). Viking Penguin, 1985: Chapters 3–6 (original work published 1981).

Lakoff, George, and Rafael Núñez. *Where Mathematics Comes From*. Basic Books, 2000: Chapter 3.

Malafouris, Lambros. *How Things Shape the Mind: A Theory of Material Engagement*. MIT Press, 2013: Chapter 5.

Menninger, Karl. *Number Words and Number Symbols: A Cultural History of Numbers*. MIT Press, 1969: 199–256 (original published 1958; English translation 1969).

Overmann, Karenleigh A. 'Constructing a Concept of Number.' *Journal of Numerical Cognition* 4, no. 2 (2018): 464–93.

Overmann, Karenleigh A. *The Material Origin of Numbers: Insights from the Archaeology of the Ancient Near East*. Gorgias Press, 2019: Chapters 3–5, 8 and 9.

Overmann, Karenleigh A. 'Numerical Origins: The Critical Questions.' *Journal of Cognition and Culture* 21, no. 5 (2021): 449–68.

Calculation Aids

Moon, Parry. *The Abacus: Its History; Its Design; Its Possibilities in the Modern World*. Gordon and Breach, 1971: Chapter 2.

Qiu, Jane. 'Ancient Times Table Hidden in Chinese Bamboo Strips.' *Nature News*, January 7 (2014).

Robson, Eleanor. 'Mesopotamian Mathematics.' In *The Mathematics of Egypt, Mesopotamia, China, India, and Islam: A Sourcebook*. Princeton University Press, 2007: 57–186.

Sugden, Keith F. 'A History of the Abacus.' *Accounting Historians Journal* 8, no. 2 (1981): 1–22.

Volkov, Alexei. 'Chinese Counting Rods: Their History, Arithmetic Operations, and Didactic Repercussions.' In *Computations and Computing Devices in Mathematics Education Before the Advent of Electronic Calculators*. Springer, 2018: 137–88.

Innate Sense of Geometry
Dillon, Moira R, and Elizabeth S Spelke. 'From Map Reading to Geometric Intuitions.' *Developmental Psychology* 54, no. 7 (2018): 1304–16.

Use of Geometric Diagrams in Ancient China, Egypt, Mesopotamia and Mesoamerica
Chemla, Karine Carole. 'Changes and Continuities in the Use of Diagrams Tu in Chinese Mathematical Writings (Third Century to Fourteenth Century) [I].' *East Asian Science, Technology and Society: An International Journal* 4, no. 2 (2010): 303–26.
Katz, Victor J. *History of Mathematics: An Introduction* (3rd ed.). Addison-Wesley, 2009: Chapter 1.
Robins, Gay, and Charles Shute. *The Rhind Mathematical Papyrus: An Ancient Egyptian Text*. British Museum Publications, 1987.
Volkov, Alexei. 'Geometrical Diagrams in Traditional Chinese Mathematics.' In *Graphics and Text in the Production of Technical Knowledge in China*. Brill, 2007: 425–59.
Williams, Barbara J, and María del Carmen Jorge y Jorge. 'Aztec Arithmetic Revisited: Land–Area Algorithms and Acolhua Congruence Arithmetic.' *Science* 320, no. 5872 (2008): 72–7.

Use of Geometric Diagrams in Ancient Greece
Hodgkin, Luke. *A History of Mathematics: From Mesopotamia to Modernity*. Oxford University Press, 2005: Chapter 2.
Netz, Reviel. *The Shaping of Deduction in Greek Mathematics: A Study in Cognitive History*. Cambridge University Press, 1999: Chapter 1.

Evolution of Cuneiform

There remain different views of the purpose and use of clay tokens and how cuneiform evolved. I have tried to present the current view; see:

Bennison-Chapman, Lucy E. 'Reconsidering "Tokens": The Neolithic Origins of Accounting or Multifunctional, Utilitarian Tools?' *Cambridge Archaeological Journal* 29, no. 2 (2019): 233–59.
Cooper, Jerrold S. 'Babylonian Beginnings: The Origin of the Cuneiform Writing System in Comparative Perspective.' In *The First Writing: Script Invention as History and Process*. Cambridge University Press, 2004: 71–99.
Damerow, Peter. 'The Origins of Writing and Arithmetic.' In *The Globalization of Knowledge in History*. Max Planck Institute for the History of Science, 2012: 143–60.

Overmann, Karenleigh A. *The Material Origin of Numbers: Insights from the Archaeology of the Ancient Near East.* Gorgias Press, 2019: Chapters 9 and 10.

Woods, Christopher. 'The Earliest Mesopotamian Writing.' In *Visible Language: Inventions of Writing in the Ancient Middle East and Beyond.* Chicago: Oriental Institute Museum Publications, 2010: 33–50.

Evolution of Writing in Other Cultures

Baines, John. 'The Earliest Egyptian Writing: Development, Context, Purpose.' In *The First Writing: Script Invention as History and Process.* Cambridge University Press, 2004: 150–89.

Bagley, Robert W. 'Anyang Writing and the Origin of the Chinese Writing System.' In *The First Writing: Script Invention as History and Process.* Cambridge University Press, 2004: 190–249.

Damerow, Peter. 'The Origins of Writing and Arithmetic.' In *The Globalization of Knowledge in History.* Max Planck Institute for the History of Science, 2012: 143–60.

Houston, Stephen D. 'Writing in Early Mesoamerica.' In *The First Writing: Script Invention as History and Process.* Cambridge University Press, 2004: 274–309.

CHAPTER 2

The Very Beginning

IN THE PRECEDING CHAPTER, we saw that early civilizations used a variety of graphics, including maps, cosmological diagrams, tables and geometric diagrams. There is no indication that they learned to use these from one another. Hence, their use of graphics appears to have resulted from parallel evolution. The question then is: what did these graphics evolve from? Did the prehistoric societies before these civilizations also use graphics? And if so, what kinds and for what purposes?

PREHISTORIC USE OF INFORMATION GRAPHICS

Modern humans first appeared around 200,000 years ago. They lived in small groups and generally were nomadic hunter-gatherers. However, some may have lived in small villages when permanent food sources, such as year-round fishing or hunting, allowed. The lifestyle was stable, changing very little as humans slowly spread worldwide. Then, about 12,000 years ago, people began to grow crops and raise animals for food. This enabled them to settle in permanent villages, eventually leading to the first civilizations.

It is commonly believed that early humans used maps, tally sticks and drawings of animals to record and share information. However, when I examined the archaeological evidence for this belief, I found it less conclusive and more ambiguous than is commonly realized. Let's start with a critical review of this evidence and then explore other evidence supporting prehistoric human use of information graphics.

DOI: 10.1201/9781003507642-3

Found throughout Eurasia, Africa, America and Australia, cave paintings provide a vivid insight into the life of early humans. Some of the world's oldest and most spectacular cave art is located in the Chauvet Cave in southern France. Many of the paintings were made 37,000 to 33,000 years ago, while Europe was still midway through the last ice age. The striking images bring animals that are now extinct, such as woolly rhinoceroses, mammoths and cave bears, back to life (see Figure 2.1).

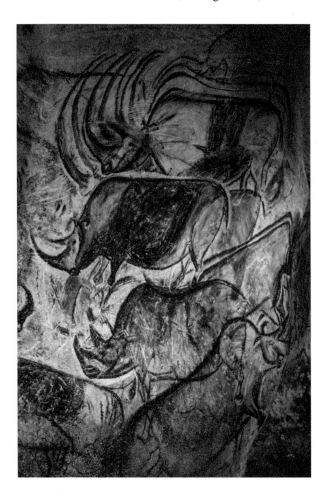

FIGURE 2.1   Are these examples of prehistoric information graphics? Woolly rhinoceroses and other animals adorn the walls of the Chauvet Cave in southern France. Created around 35,000 years ago, this cave art realistically portrays animals of the last ice age. Notice the multiple overlaid images of the rhinoceros at the top, which may have been intended to suggest motion.

Credit: Philippe Psaila/Science Photo Library.

Are these cave art drawings examples of early information graphics? They would be if their primary purpose was to represent information, perhaps to teach hunting skills or animal anatomy. However, the location of the paintings argues against this interpretation. Why would you draw instructional images in a dark, inaccessible cave like Chauvet?

There have been many theories about why the images at Chauvet and similar sites in Europe were created. Many scholars conjecture that they were painted for rituals, perhaps as part of sympathetic hunting magic or initiation ceremonies. It is easy to imagine how awe-inspiring these images would have been when viewed by the light of a flickering torch after crawling through a narrow tunnel to reach them. Did they also play an instructional role in these ceremonies? Unfortunately, we do not know. The current evidence does not allow us to determine why these images were created and for what purpose.

Many cartographers and archaeologists believe that prehistoric humans used maps. However, evidence for early map use in Europe and the Middle East is now being questioned. For many years, a wall painting from Çatal Hüyük in Turkey dating from 6200 BCE has been regarded as a definitive example of early map-making (see Figure 2.2). It was claimed to show a village plan with the twin-peaked volcano Hasan Dağı drawn in the background, erupting and spewing volcanic debris into the sky. This interpretation has been challenged by archaeologist Stephanie Meece. She has argued that it is more likely to be a painting of a leopard skin rather than a volcano, accompanied by a decorative geometric design, not a map. Again, the available evidence is inconclusive.

FIGURE 2.2   Reconstruction of a wall painting from Çatal Hüyük, c. 6200 BCE. Once thought to be a plan of a village with an erupting volcano in the background, it is now believed to be a painting of a leopard skin draped above a geometric pattern.

Credit: James Mellaart. 'Excavations at Çatal Hüyük, 1963, Third Preliminary Report.' *Anatolian Studies* 14 (1964), reproduced with permission.

In another example, in 2009 an archaeological team declared it had found one of the world's oldest maps engraved on a block of stone in the Cave of Abauntz in Spain (see Figure 2.3). Radiocarbon dating of other artefacts in the cave suggests that the engraving was made more than 13,000 years ago. The archaeologists claimed that, as well as showing ibex and other animals, the drawing depicted the landscape—mountain, rivers, paths and a cave—where the rock was found. I am not sure. Nor is Jill Cook, head of the prehistory division at the British Museum, who has called it a 'brave' theory.

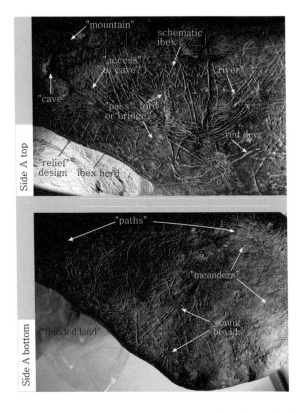

FIGURE 2.3   Is this a 13,000-year-old map? Some archaeologists believe that these engravings, made on a block of stone found in the Cave of Abauntz in Spain show the surrounding landscape.

Credit: Reprinted from *Journal of Human Evolution* 57, no. 2, Utrilla, Pilar, Carlos Mazo, María Cruz Sopena, Manuel Martínez-Bea, and Rafael Domingo. 'A Palaeolithic Map from 13,660 calBP: Engraved Stone Blocks from the Late Magdalenian in Abauntz Cave (Navarra, Spain)', 99–111. Copyright 2009, with permission from Elsevier.

Archaeologists have also found bones and antlers with regular cuts that many believe are prehistoric tally sticks. The oldest is a bone from a baboon leg with twenty-nine notches. It is more than 40,000 years old and was found in a cave on the border of South Africa and the Kingdom of Eswatini. While it is plausible that prehistoric humans were using tallies like these to record, say, the number of days since the last full moon, we really do not know. The notches may have been for decoration. Or perhaps they were cut to make a musical instrument as in many cultures, bones or pieces of wood with serrated surfaces are rasped with a stick to make a noise.

It is fair to say the evidence commonly used to support the use of maps and other kinds of information graphics by prehistoric humans is inconclusive. In the case of graphics from early civilizations, such as the diagrams in the Mawangdui manuscripts, the associated text can clarify their meaning and purpose. This is not the case for prehistoric drawings and artefacts, so identifying early maps and other information graphics remains fraught. Perhaps prehistoric people did use information graphics. However, I do not believe that ancient rock art or artefacts conclusively prove they did.

Another approach for investigating whether prehistoric humans used information graphics is to explore the use of graphics in contemporary societies with a lifestyle similar to our prehistoric forebears. Known as traditional societies, these employ a mix of hunting, gathering and subsistence-level farming. If people from these societies use maps or other information graphics, this suggests our prehistoric ancestors may have done so, too. And the obvious advantage of contemporary traditional societies is that we no longer need to infer what a particular image means or how it is used from the image itself. Instead, we can ask its creator or refer to accounts of traditional customs.

GRAPHICS OF INDIGENOUS AUSTRALIANS

I am writing this book on the lands of the Bunurong people. The Bunurong are one of the hundreds of First Nations peoples who inhabited Australia before it was brutally colonized by the British. Their ancestors arrived in Australia at least 65,000 years ago. Having had limited contact with non-Indigenous Australians, they and the other Indigenous peoples of Australia have one of the oldest continuous cultures on Earth. By talking to Indigenous people with lived knowledge of their culture, and also drawing from accounts of the first European settlers, we can build a picture of graphics use in a traditional culture thousands of years old.

Connection to Country is at the heart of Indigenous Australian culture. The land cares for the people. In turn, the people are responsible for caring for the land by carrying out rituals to maintain its health and through practices such as controlled burning. This deep understanding and connection is based upon the Dreaming, which refers to the complex ways of knowing and being that impact all aspects of Indigenous life.

In many parts of Australia, the Dreaming tells of how ancestral beings emerged from underground at the time of Creation; how they traveled across the landscape and eventually re-entered the earth, where they continue to live. The stories of the Dreaming, often called songlines, are deeply embedded in geography. As they traveled, the ancestral beings shaped the land, populating it with animals, plants and humans. They might have dug a well and left behind a waterhole, left imprints in the rocks as they walked, or metamorphosed into a hill. In a profound sense, the land and all the creatures and plants that inhabit it are manifestations of the ancestral beings. The sites associated with these beings, such as where they emerged or re-entered the earth, are sacred. By visiting these sites and through ceremonies, Indigenous people continue to experience, and have access to, the power of the ancestral beings.

Graphics play an essential role in teaching about the Dreaming. Different communities have their own distinctive visual languages. We will look at two representative examples. The first is the graphics of the Kunwinjku people of western Arnhem Land in Australia's tropical north. The Kunwinjku are famous for their distinctive X-ray style of painting (see Figure 2.4). This uses dotting, hatching and color to show an animal or fish's internal organs, skeleton, and even its eggs and unborn progeny.

Anthropologist Luke Taylor describes how the Kunwinjku use graphics for two interlinked purposes: as instruments for maintaining the health of Country, and as tools for teaching about the ancestral beings. The Kunwinjku believe that the ancestral beings wore cross-hatched geometric designs on their bodies and introduced these sacred designs to the first people, along with the stories, songs and dances to be performed in ceremonies. The designs play a prominent role in ceremonies. They are painted onto the participants' bodies, and may be etched or painted onto the ritual objects used in the ceremony. Even the ground for the ceremony may be sculpted into sacred patterns.

The designs are highly potent. They impart the power of the ancestral being onto the human or ritual object they adorn. They allow participants

FIGURE 2.4   An X-ray-style rock painting of fish at Ubirr, Kakadu National Park. This style has been practiced by the Indigenous peoples of Arnhem Land for around 3000 years. Unlike the images in the Chauvet Cave, we know why these were painted and what they represent because they are part of a living culture.

Credit: Marco Tomasini/Shutterstock.

to encounter an ancestral being and when the designs are used in ceremonies, the power of the ancestral beings is released, ensuring the cycle of the seasons continues, and that plants grow and animals multiply.

Knowledge of the ancestral beings, including the graphic designs and songs used in ceremonies, is carefully controlled. Because of its potency, this knowledge is secret, only for the initiated. However, many of the graphics created by the Kunwinjku are not secret. Images traditionally painted on the bark walls and roofs of huts, and the walls of caves used as shelters in the wet season, are for public viewing. Nowadays, similar designs are painted onto bark or canvas and sold to tourists visiting Arnhem Land and galleries around the world.

These public pictures depict animals, humans, ancestral beings and spirit people, often using the X-ray style. They provide an informal and entertaining basis for the Kunwinjku to instruct children in the habits and characteristics of animals and plants, many of which they will need to hunt or gather in the future. The X-ray paintings of food animals also serve another didactic purpose. They reveal the location of vital organs and bands of fat, which are highly prized delicacies. More than this, the divisions of the animal's body show shared cultural knowledge about named sections of the body, the correct way to butcher the animal, and how particular parts or cuts of meat belong to specific kin of the hunter.

However, the Kunwinjku consider the principal function of these public graphics is to teach children (and tourists) about the ancestral beings. Depictions of the ancestral beings provide children with tangible proof they are real. They also help children visualize the transformation of an ancestral being between its animal and human form, or the metamorphosis of an ancestral being's body part into a geographic feature. These public images prime children for the revelations they will encounter during their induction into various ceremonies. Then, they will discover the secret 'inside' reading of these paintings, one that connects humans, ancestral beings, Country, animals and plants. It is an understanding that links body parts, geometric patterns and geographic features; for instance, that a heart or circle represents a sacred waterhole, and ribs or dotted lines represent streams.

A thousand kilometers south of Arnhem Land in central Australia, the land is arid, totally unlike Arnhem Land's tropical lushness. The Indigenous peoples of this region employ their own distinctive visual language, very different to that of the Kunwinjku people. This features schematic aerial views of sacred sites and the events that occurred there. Its characteristic iconography is the basis for an influential modern art movement that has featured Indigenous artists such as Emily Kame Kngwarreye and Clifford Possum Tjapaltjarri.

The anthropologist Nancy Munn lived with the Warlpiri people of central Australia during the 1950s. She carefully documented their use of graphics. While the designs differ from those of the Kunwinjku, they fulfill similar functions: instruments to ensure the health of Country, tools to teach the Dreaming, and sources of entertainment. Like the Kunwinjku, the Warlpiri regard some designs as secret, while others can be viewed by anyone.

The designs often portray an event or journey of an ancestral being. This is shown from above using iconic symbols. Concentric circles or a spiral, for example, usually represent a campsite. People sleeping next to the camp are shown by short lines, while a 'U' shape depicts someone sitting—its form suggesting the impression left by their buttocks. A series of circles connected by lines might signify a journey, with each circle denoting a camping spot. While the layout is based on the underlying geography, the position of campsites and other symbols may be rearranged so that the design is symmetric or laid out in a grid.

Warlpiri women use a similar iconography when telling 'sand stories'. The linguist Jennifer Green writes about how sand stories are a regular part of daily life across central Australia and are used by the women to exchange the latest gossip or entertain children with stories of the Dreaming (see Figure 2.5). Unlike the designs used in sacred rituals, the graphics used in sand stories are intended for public viewing.

When a woman decides to tell a story, she will sit down and clear and flatten the sand in front of her. Children and adults will then rapidly assemble to hear the story. The woman begins by drawing the setting, perhaps a camp

FIGURE 2.5 The use of the ground for illustrative and explanatory purposes is pervasive throughout central Australia, where there is ample inscribable terrain. Here, an Eastern Anmatyerr woman is telling a sand story about two sisters who set out to vanquish a monster. The two sticks represent the sisters and the spiral shows their path.

Credit: Jennifer Green, *Drawn from the Ground Sound, Sign and Inscription in Central Australian Sand Stories* ©Jennifer Green 2014 published by Cambridge University Press, reproduced with permission. Color image courtesy Jennifer Green.

or a group of men out hunting. She may use sticks and leaves to embellish the drawing. As the story progresses, she sketches on the sand, and uses gestures and a singsong voice to clarify what is happening. The drawing is an animation: she adds signs for characters when they appear, using her fingers to impress the tracks of people and animals in the sand as they move across the scene. And if the story changes location, she erases the drawing and replaces it with the new setting—just like a scene change in a TV show or movie.

However, unlike stories shown on TV or at the cinema, sand stories show the action viewed from above. Also, like a map on your smartphone, the layout is oriented to the surrounding geography, not the narrator or audience's position. Geographic features are aligned with their position in the surrounding environment. And if the prevailing winds come from the west, the drawing will show the windbreak on the western side of the camp.

It's not only Indigenous women who draw in the sand when telling stories. Throughout central Australia, both men and women use the sand as a handy 'notepad' to keep notes or explain complex subjects. The first Europeans to visit central Australian communities wrote about how Indigenous people, when asked for directions, would use a stick to sketch a map on the ground.

More recently, Laurent Dousset, an anthropologist studying kinship in the Ngaatjatjarra community in central Australia, described how the people he was quizzing would use drawings in the sand to explain their multifaceted relationships. The left-hand diagram in Figure 2.6 was drawn by a woman explaining the structure of her immediate family. The family is enclosed in a circle, signifying they are 'all from one place'. She is represented by the single, 'lonely' vertical line at the circle's center. Above her are four vertical lines representing her biological children. The horizontal line beneath them indicates they were born in the same community—they stand on the same ground. Below her, standing on different ground, are three lines representing her adopted or fostered children.

The right-hand diagram in Figure 2.6 is by a man. He is the dot at the bottom. The dots at the top are—from left to right—his wife, his wife's father, and a woman who promised him a daughter, though he did not marry her. The lines connecting them depict the relationships between them. But the diagram also has a spatial reading. The position of the dots is based on locations associated with the people they represent, such as their birthplace. The lines therefore also represent tracks between these locations.

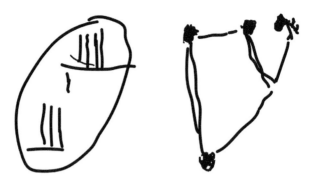

FIGURE 2.6   People from the Ngaatjatjarra community drew these diagrams in the sand as part of their answers to questions about kinship. A woman drew the picture on the left to show her family; a man drew the diagram on the right to show his wife, her father and the relationships between them.

Credit: Adaptation by Kadek Satriadi. Original images from Dousset, Laurent. 'Indigenous Modes of Representing Social Relationships: A Short Critique of the "Genealogical Concept". *Australian Aboriginal Studies.* **Copyright 2003 Aboriginal Studies Press, reproduced with permission.**

Early Europeans also recorded the use of 'message sticks' by Indigenous Australians. These were used to invite people to ceremonies, consolidate alliances, declare war or request trade. They were engraved with crisscrossed lines and simple geometric shapes. Notched tallies were frequent. For instance, for a ceremony, at the top of the stick there might be a notch for each Elder sending the message, with notches on the side representing the people invited.

The message stick was carried by an envoy. It was a symbol of authority, establishing the envoy's credentials and providing them with safe passage to the destination. The stick may also have been a mnemonic aid for the envoy, who would verbally deliver the message when they arrived. In some cases, the message could be deciphered from the stick without the need for interpretation.

GRAPHICS USE IN TRADITIONAL SOCIETIES

This brief introduction to the use of graphics by the Indigenous peoples of Australia establishes that they have long employed information graphics for various purposes. But while Indigenous Australians have been more prolific graphics users than most other traditional societies, their use of information graphics is definitely not unusual.

Graphics are frequently used in traditional societies to envisage cosmological beliefs about their origin and place in the world. Such cosmological diagrams are not passive. Around the world, they are regarded as potent instruments of change and form an integral part of ceremonies to maintain health and cure sickness.

We saw how the Kunwinjku and the Warlpiri in Australia use sacred designs to conceptualize and teach about Country. Cosmological diagrams are also common throughout North America. In the south-west, the Navaho and Hopi created elaborate sand paintings. On the central plains, the Skiri drew celestial maps onto animal skins, while in other parts of the continent, shamans painted sacred designs onto drumheads and animal skins.

In the Andes, participants in 'mapping rituals' arrange amulets representing geographic features and villages around a holy object considered to be a portal to the spirit world. In Africa, cosmological representations range from simple geometric diagrams to schematic maps. In West Africa, for instance, the Bozo depict the surface and underground flow of waters that they believe maintain the health of the rivers they rely on for fishing.

In traditional societies, cosmology blurs into oral history. Cosmological diagrams frequently serve as records and aids for remembering historical events. In central Africa, for example, the Mbudye court historians called 'men of memory' were responsible for guarding and disseminating oral histories of the kings of the Luba people. During their recitations, the historian 'read' the history of the king from a *lukasa* memory board (see Figure 2.7). This was a hand-sized carved board covered with beads and cowrie shells. The beads and cowrie shells represented the travels of the king, the location of sacred lakes and trees, and the tombs of divine kings.

Worldwide, tallies have been used in traditional societies to record and communicate quantities and spans of time. In Australia, tallies were notched onto message sticks or drawn on the sand. In the Amazon, the Jarawara etch triangles onto the edge of a thin strip of wood to show the estimated number of days of an upcoming trip. If the Siuai people of Papua New Guinea are holding a feast, the host will send each guest a palm frond with one leaf for each day to pass until the banquet; the host and guests will tear off a leaf each day until the day of the feast arrives. In North America, tallies frequently formed part of pictorial messages that Native Americans

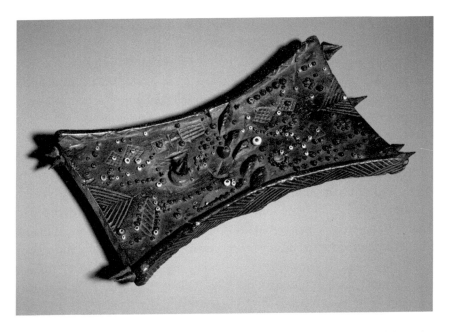

FIGURE 2.7   The *lukasa* memory board was used by court historians of the Luba people of central Africa. Covered in shells and beads, these record the history and important places for a specific Luba king.

Credit: Luba. *Lukasa Memory Board,* **late nineteenth or early twentieth century. Wood, metal, beads, 25.4 × 14.6 × 5.7 cm. Brooklyn Museum, Gift of Marcia and John Friede, 76.20.4. Creative Commons-BY.**

left on tanned skin, birch bark, or the exposed wood of a tree that had been blazed (had its bark removed) (see Figure 2.8).

Knotted strings were also widely used in the Americas, Asia and Pacific Islands to record information. They functioned as tallies and as mnemonic aids for lists of data such as genealogies and locations along ancestral migration routes. The best-known example is the Incan *khipu*, a shawl-like collection of knotted strings hanging from a primary cord. Information was recorded by varying the type of knot, its position, and the thread color. The *khipu* was not a true writing system. Most recorded numerical data such as censuses and the amount and kind of tribute paid to the Incan ruler. These fulfilled a similar administrative function to the Mesopotamian proto-cuneiform tablets. *Khipus* are also said to have recorded songs, genealogies and historical narratives, but, as yet, we do not know how.

In the Pacific, charts played a crucial role in teaching children how to navigate between far-flung islands. The Micronesian and Polynesian peoples

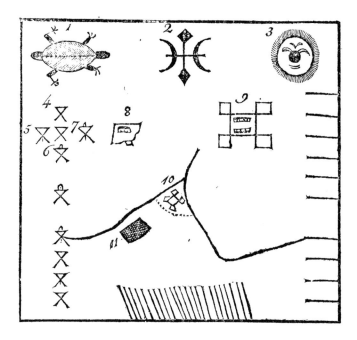

FIGURE 2.8   Annotated sketch of a 'war mark' left by a Delaware warrior on a blazed tree (c. 1781). Its message is that he is a redoubtable warrior who is angry with the European invaders, and he is on his way with a band of warriors to do something about it. The river turtle icon (1) indicates that the warrior is from the turtle clan of the Delaware; (2) is his personal mark; and (3) is the sun. The ten horizontal stripes below the sun are a tally of the number of times the warrior has been on a war expedition. The tallies under the turtle (4–7) record the number of prisoners he has captured and the number of scalps. The remaining symbols (8–11) depict American forts. The smallest (10) shows Fort Pitt, which is situated at the confluence of the Monongahela and Allegheny rivers and near the town of Pittsburgh (11). The strokes at the bottom represent the number of warriors with him when he made this infographic.

Credit: William Bray. 'XXII. Observations on the Indian Method of Picture-Writing by William Bray, Esq. in a Letter to the Secretary.' *Archaeologia* 6. © William Bray 1782, published by Cambridge University Press, used with permission.

settled islands throughout the Pacific starting some 3500–4000 years ago. When European sailors first explored the Pacific, they were astounded to discover that virtually all of the larger islands were inhabited by people with a similar language and culture who regularly traveled between the islands using outrigger canoes. These intrepid sailors often had to sail for days out of sight of land to reach their destination. They used the wind, stars and swell patterns for navigation. They looked for signs revealing the presence of an island below the horizon, such as reflections in the clouds or flocks of birds.

We know most about navigation on the Caroline and Marshall islands, as traditional methods were used there until recently. Islanders from both locations used diagrams. These were not taken on board the craft like Western nautical charts but rather were used to teach navigation skills to novice sailors and as a mnemonic aid when preparing for a journey.

The Caroline Islands, a widely scattered collection of about 500 small landmasses, are located about 2000 kilometers north-east of Papua New Guinea. Caroline Islanders once primarily used the stars to navigate between the islands. They memorized the point they needed to sail to on the horizon in terms of rising and setting points of 'landmark' stars and constellations. This was taught using a 'star compass' made by the instructor from objects at hand. For instance, lumps of coral might be arranged in a circle or square around some coconut leaves. The leaves represented the canoe, while the coral pieces represented the thirty-two cardinal directions associated with the landmark stars and constellations. After learning the directions and associated stars or constellations, the novice navigator was required to memorize the points of interest around each island, such as reefs and other islands. Again, a chart constructed from materials at hand might have been used as part of the instruction.

In the Marshall Islands, navigation relied on observing swell patterns rather than the stars. This was probably because complex seasonal currents made it difficult to correct for drift when using navigation techniques based solely on heading in the right direction. The Marshall Islands consist of thirty-four main coral atolls and islands arranged in two parallel chains, stretching across 1000 kilometers. When sailing between these low-lying islands, canoes could need to travel for several days out of sight of land. They would set off in squadrons with an experienced navigator, who would start them off in the correct direction and then track and correct the squadron's progress by monitoring wave patterns. Unseen islands disrupted ocean swells and currents to create distinctive wave patterns, which allowed the experienced navigator to orient themself with respect to these islands.

The Marshallese used a novel navigation chart to teach these wave and swell patterns (see Figure 2.9). This had three variants. The basic principles of how an island disrupted the swell was introduced with the *mattang* stick

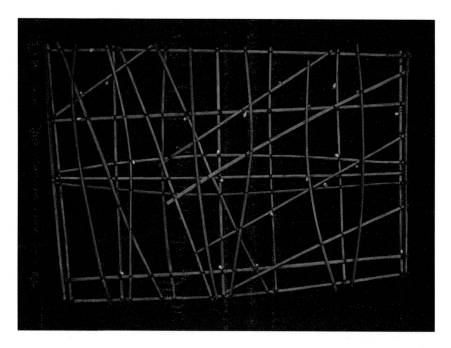

FIGURE 2.9   A traditional Marshall Island *rebbelib* chart. It shows how ocean swells bend around two island chains. The chart is made from wooden sticks and cowrie shells. A horizontal and vertical grid of sticks provides support for the other elements. The cowrie shells represent islands, while the curved and diagonal sticks show the swells.

Credit: British Museum Oc1904,0621.34. © The Trustees of the British Museum.

chart, while the *meddo* and *rebbelib* charts showed the direction of the principal deep ocean swells and how they curved around specific islands and intersected around actual islands. The *meddo* was a detailed map of a relatively small part of the island chains; the *rebbelib* chart was a less detailed map of one or both chains of islands.

The indigenous peoples of northern North America and Eurasia's arctic and subarctic regions also made maps. They frequently left maps as part of messages painted or etched on birch bark or blazed tree trunks (see Figure 2.8). They also used maps when planning hunts or raids and journeys outside their usual territory. The North American explorer Gilbert Malcolm Sproat describes how, in 1855, Nootka warriors from Vancouver Island drew a map on the sand to plan a raid on the village of Ky-yoh-quahts 150 kilometers to the north:

The meeting adjourned to a smooth untrodden sand-beach in the neighbourhood. Here Quartsoppy ... was directed [by the chief] to describe on the sand the Island of Ocktees on which the village of Ky-yoh-quahts was placed. He immediately set to work and drew an outline of the island, then showed the coves, beaches, tracks; next the village with the different houses, divisions and sub-divisions—referring now and then to other natives who also knew the locality. Small raised piles of sand represented houses, one of which was Nancie's, the chief of the Ky-yoh-quahts; another belonged to Moochinnick, a noted warrior; others to chiefs of inferior repute. Quartsoppy, referring to his drawing, also showed or otherwise informed his audience of the usual number of men in each division of the camp.

There are also frequent accounts of people from traditional societies in the Arctic, North America, Africa and the Pacific Islands sketching maps to guide European explorers. However, maps are not found in all traditional societies. After all, maps are unnecessary if you only travel within the region you grew up in, as by adulthood you will have built a detailed mental map of this area.

THE ORIGINS OF INFORMATION GRAPHICS

So let's return to our original question: did prehistoric people use information graphics? We have seen that cosmological diagrams, tallies and maps are relatively common in contemporary traditional societies. However, in 30,000 years, there will be few archaeological records of this. Most of these graphics are drawn on the ground or body and erased after use, or they are drawn on decomposable materials such as birch bark and animal skins. And, even if they did survive, for many of these graphics, such as the cosmological diagrams of Indigenous Australians and the stick charts of the Marshallese, it would be virtually impossible to determine their meaning and function.

Given this, it is not surprising that we have not found conclusive evidence that prehistoric people used information graphics. However, the prevalence of graphics use in contemporary traditional societies suggests that many prehistoric societies may have done so. It therefore seems likely that information graphics used in the first civilizations evolved from those used in the traditional societies preceding them.

There are nonetheless significant differences between information graphics used in traditional societies and those used in early civilizations.

Compare the ancient Chinese military map with that used by the Nootka to plan a raid. The Nootka map was a one-off map quickly drawn using the materials at hand, and specifically for planning that raid. In contrast, the Chinese map was the product of a bureaucracy. It integrated information from multiple sources and was drawn on relatively durable material. It was intended to be a general resource for the local military commanders that would remain useful for several years.

The Chinese map was also designed to be used independently, without needing a verbal explanation from its creator. This was possible because of the invention of writing. Writing allowed the graphic's creator to provide additional information using labels, and contextual text explaining how to understand and use the graphic. In traditional societies, however, graphics are almost always part of a multimodal dialogue in which speech or song supplements the graphic, helping to clarify and augment its meaning. For instance, Quartsoppy verbally stated the number of people in each camp. No doubt he would also have given a running commentary explaining what he was drawing; for example, that this line is the shoreline, not a track.

The larger populations and more complex social and administrative structures of the first civilizations introduced new needs, some of which were met by new kinds of graphics. These included maps recording property boundaries and diagrams to teach geometry. On the other hand, the invention of writing did away with the need for graphics such as *lukasas* whose primary function was to act as a mnemonic for oral histories and genealogies. In early civilizations, we also see that graphics use became a more specialist skill associated with scribes and scholars, reflecting the emergence of different professions and trades.

Given that humans have likely been using graphics such as maps, cosmological diagrams and tallies for tens of thousands of years, the next question is: how did this come about?

It is instructive to compare our use of graphics with language and writing. No matter where people live, they talk. They ask for information, listen to stories, gossip about colleagues, and flirt. Language is an example of what anthropologists call a human universal—a behavior that at least some members of all human societies, past and present, exhibit. Other human universals include gestures, sexual jealousy, tool-making, shelter building, use of fire, religion and art.

Our ability to speak is innate. We don't need to be formally taught to talk; we simply copy those around us. We need to speak. Communities of children who are deaf will spontaneously develop sign language to talk among themselves. We have specialized brain areas for understanding and composing speech, and there is little doubt that we have evolved to speak. As Steven Pinker says, we have a 'language instinct'.

On the other hand, reading is definitely not a human universal. It is a recent invention that takes children many years of schooling to learn. We do not have an inbuilt ability to read, and we have not evolved specialized brain areas for reading, or writing. Instead, brain imaging reveals that reading repurposes neurons originally designed for recognizing facial features. Reading takes advantage of the pre-existing capabilities of the human brain, and the design of writing systems has been constrained by the brain's ability to repurpose these inbuilt capabilities.

Our use of information graphics sits somewhere between these two extremes. While not all societies utilize what we would recognize as an information graphic, the use of cosmological diagrams, tallies and maps is considerably more widespread than writing. It is also apparent that statistical graphics such as bar charts are a recent invention and that our ability to understand them is definitely not innate.

Visual mark-making is a human universal. Around the world, people draw. They decorate the things they make and their own bodies. They draw on cave walls and on the ground. John Willats has talked about our 'drawing instinct'. Young children like to draw. When given pencils and paper, they take great pleasure in placing marks on the paper. At first, they make scribbles. Then, around three years of age, they draw faces and other objects: the drawings have become representational. This joy in making marks on paper is not limited to humans. Chimpanzees also like to draw and paint. However, unlike three-year-old children, there is no evidence that their drawings are intended to represent anything.

While it seems unlikely that we have evolved to draw, I think it is a consequence of how our visual system works and our innate desire to make tools and manipulate our environment. For whatever reason, we enjoy creating geometric shapes and patterns.

When the first humans started to draw, it would have been enough to make pleasing patterns, to scribble like a child. Prehistoric rock art is full of lines, handprints, spirals, labyrinths and geometric shapes. At some point, these would have brought other ideas to mind. Perhaps a shape resembled a bison or a person. Our prehistoric artist would have played with the drawing, accentuating the resemblance or metaphor. Their scribble had become symbolic and was well on the way to becoming an information graphic.

Geographers David Stea and James Blaut and their colleagues conjecture that mapping is universal. By this, they mean 'the thinking and action involved in reading, making and using map-like models', where a map-like model is an artefact such as a drawing, model or aerial photograph that represents a 'geographical landscape in the traditional map-like way reduced in scale and depicted as though viewed from overhead'. This hypothesis is supported by their studies demonstrating that children from a wide variety of cultures understand that aerial photographs and map-like models are symbolic representations of physical spaces.

This hypothesis is backed by the finding that people from a wide range of traditional cultures create sketch maps—for instance, to guide European explorers—even if map use is not required in their day-to-day lives. Further support comes from a study showing that chimpanzees also recognize that map-like models represent space. This study found that chimpanzees have a similar skill level to three-year-old children when matching features in a model with those in the environment.

So, if mapping is a human universal, is there a biological basis? Mapping builds upon our innate sense of space. In Chapter 5, we will see that humans, like other mammals, form mental maps of their environment and use these for wayfinding. This is undoubtedly a biological adaptation, as it relies on specialized neurons and brain regions. Maps reify and externalize these cognitive maps. They depend on imagining the appearance of geographic features when viewed from above. We know that humans seek high vantage points to inspect their environment and integrate this information into their cognitive map. It seems a small step for them to imagine and draw the contents of their cognitive map as if viewed from an imaginary vantage point.

So, is mapping a human universal? Like Stea and Blaut, I believe the answer is yes if we understand what is meant by a map more broadly. There is evidence that humans from all cultures can, when necessary, create sketch maps or models of their environment and use these to refine their cognitive maps. Nevertheless, the conventions used in maps are mediated by culture. Modern maps—that is, maps utilizing a consistent scale and formalized in terms of map projections—are undoubtedly a recent invention.

While mapping and drawing may be human universals, I do not believe we evolved to use maps, drawings or any other information graphic. Unlike language, we do not have specialized brain regions for understanding information graphics. Instead, our ability to use these graphics has emerged from a combination of pre-existing cognitive and perceptual capabilities. And, as we shall explore in the rest of this book, information graphics have evolved to make the best use of these inbuilt capabilities.

NOTES, REFERENCES AND FURTHER READING

Prehistoric Use of Information Graphics

Early Humans

Bergström, Anders, Chris Stringer, Mateja Hajdinjak, Eleanor ML Scerri, and Pontus Skoglund. 'Origins of Modern Human Ancestry.' *Nature* 590, no. 7845 (2021): 229–37.

Cave Art

Bahn, Paul G. 'Religion and Ritual in the Upper Palaeolithic.' In *The Oxford Handbook of the Archaeology of Ritual and Religion*. Oxford University Press, 2011: 344–57.

Conkey, MW. 'Images without Words: The Construction of Prehistoric Imaginaries for Definitions of "Us".' *Journal of Visual Culture* 9, no. 3 (2010): 272–83.

David, Bruno. *Cave Art*. Thames & Hudson, 2017: Chapters 2 and 6.

Nowell, April. 'Learning to See and Seeing to Learn: Children, Communities of Practice and Pleistocene Visual Cultures.' *Cambridge Archaeological Journal* 25, no. 4 (2015): 889–99.

Robb, John. 'Art (Pre) History: Ritual, Narrative and Visual Culture in Neolithic and Bronze Age Europe.' *Journal of Archaeological Method and Theory* 27, no. 3 (2020): 454–80.

Whitley, David S. 'Rock Art, Religion and Ritual.' In *The Oxford Handbook of the Archaeology of Ritual and Religion*. Oxford University Press, 2011: 307–26.

Prehistoric Maps

Bates, Claire. 'Oldest Map in Western Europe Found Engraved on 14,000-Year-Old Chunk of Rock.' *Mail Online*, August 6, 2009. www.dailymail.co.uk/sciencetech/article-1204539/Oldest-map-western-Europe-engraved-14-000-year-old-chunk-rock.html. Contains quote from Jill Cook.

Meece, Stephanie. 'A Bird's Eye View of a Leopard's Spots: The Çatalhöyük "Map" and the Development of Cartographic Representation in Prehistory.' *Anatolian Studies* 56 (2006): 1–16.

Utrilla, Pilar, Carlos Mazo, María Cruz Sopena, Manuel Martínez-Bea, and Rafael Domingo. 'A Palaeolithic Map from 13,660 calBP: Engraved Stone Blocks from the Late Magdalenian in Abauntz Cave (Navarra, Spain).' *Journal of Human Evolution* 57, no. 2 (2009): 99–111.

Utrilla, Pilar, Carlos Mazo, Rafael Domingo, and Manuel Bea. 'Maps in Prehistoric Art.' In *Making Scenes: Global Perspectives on Scenes in Rock Art*. Berghahn Books, 2021: 207–22.

Prehistoric Tally Sticks

The notched baboon bone was found in the Border Cave in the Lebombo Mountain Range and is known as the 'Lebombo bone' after the range.

Hayden, Brian. 'Keeping Count: On Interpreting Record Keeping in Prehistory.' *Journal of Anthropological Archaeology* 63, no. 1 (2021): 101304.

Wikipedia. 'Lebombo Bone.' https://en.wikipedia.org/wiki/Lebombo_bone

Graphics of Indigenous Australians

First Australians

Clarkson, Chris, et al. 'Human Occupation of Northern Australia by 65,000 Years Ago.' *Nature* 547, no. 7663 (2017): 306–10.

Hayes, Elspeth H, et al. '65,000-Years of Continuous Grinding Stone Use at Madjedbebe, Northern Australia.' *Scientific Reports* 12, no. 11747 (2022).

Connection to Country, Songlines and the Dreaming

Morphy, Howard. *Aboriginal Art*. Phaidon, 1998: Chapter 3.

Neale, Margo. 'Everything Starts and Finishes with Country.' In *Songlines: The Power and Promise*. Thames & Hudson Australia, 2020: 35–44.

Neale, Margo. 'Knowledge in Country and the Third Archive.' In *Songlines: The Power and Promise*. Thames & Hudson Australia, 2020: 45–66.

Graphics of the Kunwinjku

David, Bruno. *Cave Art*. Thames & Hudson, 2017: Chapter 7.

Taylor, Luke. *Seeing the Inside: Bark Painting in Western Arnhem Land*. Oxford University Press, 1996: Chapters 5–10.

Taylor, Luke. 'Bodies Revealed: X-Ray Art in Western Arnhem Land.' In *The Oxford Handbook of the Archaeology and Anthropology of Rock Art*. Oxford University Press online publication, 2017.

Graphics of Central Australia

Dousset, Laurent. 'Indigenous Modes of Representing Social Relationships: A Short Critique of the "Genealogical Concept".' *Australian Aboriginal Studies* 1 (2003): 19–29.

Green, Jennifer. *Drawn from the Ground: Sound, Sign and Inscription in Central Australian Sand Stories*. Cambridge University Press, 2014: Chapters 2 and 7.

Munn, Nancy D. *Walbiri Iconography: Graphic Representation and Cultural Symbolism in a Central Australian Society.* Cornell University Press, 1973: Chapters 2–7.

Sutton, Peter. 'Icons of Country: Topographic Representations in Classical Aboriginal Traditions.' In *The History of Cartography.* University of Chicago Press, 1998: vol. 2, book 3, 353–86.

Sutton, Peter. 'Aboriginal Maps and Plans.' In *The History of Cartography.* University of Chicago Press, 1998: vol. 2, book 3, 387–416.

Message Sticks

Hamlyn-Harris, Ronald. 'On Messages and "Message Sticks" Employed among the Queensland Aborigines.' *Queensland Museum Memoirs* 6 (1918): 13–36.

Hayden, Brian. 'Keeping Count: On Interpreting Record Keeping in Prehistory.' *Journal of Anthropological Archaeology* 63, no. 1 (2021): 101304.

Howitt, Alfred William. 'Notes on Australian Message Sticks and Messengers.' *The Journal of the Anthropological Institute of Great Britain and Ireland* 18 (1889): 314–32.

Kelly, Piers. 'Australian Message Sticks: Old Questions, New Directions.' *Journal of Material Culture* 25, no. 2 (2020): 133–52.

Graphics Use in Traditional Societies

Cosmological Diagrams

Bassett, Thomas J. 'Indigenous Mapmaking in Intertropical Africa.' In *The History of Cartography.* University of Chicago Press, 1998: vol. 2, book 3, 24–48.

Gartner, William Gustav. 'Mapmaking in the Central Andes.' In *The History of Cartography.* University of Chicago Press, 1998: vol. 2, book 3, 257–300.

Lewis, G Malcolm. 'Maps, Mapmaking, and Map Use by Native North Americans.' In *The History of Cartography.* University of Chicago Press, 1998: vol. 2, book 3, 51–182.

Lukasa Memory Board

Bassett, Thomas J. 'Indigenous Mapmaking in Intertropical Africa.' In *The History of Cartography.* University of Chicago Press, 1998: vol. 2, book 3, 24–48.

Roberts, Mary Nooter, and Allen F Roberts. 'Memory: Luba Art and the Making of History.' *African Arts* 29, no. 1 (1996): 23–35, 101–3.

Tallies

Everett, Caleb. 'A Closer Look at a Supposedly Anumeric Language.' *International Journal of American Linguistics* 78, no. 4 (2012): 575–90.

Green, Jennifer. *Drawn from the Ground: Sound, Sign and Inscription in Central Australian Sand Stories.* Cambridge University Press, 2014: 61.

Howitt, Alfred William. 'Notes on Australian Message Sticks and Messengers.' *The Journal of the Anthropological Institute of Great Britain and Ireland* 18 (1889): 314–32.

Oliver, Douglas L. *A Solomon Island Society: Kinship and Leadership among the Siuai of Bougainville.* Harvard University Press, 2013: 98.

Knotted Records

Barthel, Thomas S. 'Pre-Contact Writing in Oceania.' In *Linguistics in Oceania.* De Gruyter Mouton, 1971: 1165–86.

Birket-Smith, Kaj. 'Circumpacific Distribution of Knot Records.' *Folk* 8–9 (1966–67): 15–24.

Silverman, Eric Kline. 'Traditional Cartography in Papua New Guinea.' In *The History of Cartography.* University of Chicago Press, 1998: vol. 2, book 3, 423–42.

Urton, Gary. 'From Knots to Narratives: Reconstructing the Art of Historical Record Keeping in the Andes from Spanish Transcriptions of Inka Khipus.' *Ethnohistory* 45, no. 3 (1998): 409–38.

Urton, Gary. 'Recording Measure(ment)s in the Inka Khipu.' In *The Archaeology of Measurement: Comprehending Heaven, Earth and Time in Ancient Societies.* Cambridge University Press, 2010: 54–68.

Micronesian and Polynesian Navigation

Finney, Ben. 'Nautical Cartography and Traditional Navigation in Oceania.' In *The History of Cartography.* University of Chicago Press, 1998: vol. 2, book 3, 443–94.

Genz, Joseph, Jerome Aucan, Mark Merrifield, Ben Finney, Korent Joel, and Alson Kelen. 'Wave Navigation in the Marshall Islands: Comparing Indigenous and Western Scientific Knowledge of the Ocean.' *Oceanography* 22, no. 2 (2009): 234–45.

Hutchins, Edwin. *Cognition in the Wild.* MIT Press, 1995: Chapter 2.

Map Use

Barton, Phillip Lionel. 'Maori Cartography and the European Encounter.' In *The History of Cartography.* University of Chicago Press, 1998: vol. 2, book 3, 493–536.

Bassett, Thomas J. 'Indigenous Mapmaking in Intertropical Africa.' In *The History of Cartography.* University of Chicago Press, 1998: vol. 2, book 3, 24–48.

Finney, Ben. 'Nautical Cartography and Traditional Navigation in Oceania.' In *The History of Cartography.* University of Chicago Press, 1998: vol. 2, book 3, 443–94.

Lewis, G Malcolm. 'Intracultural Mapmaking by First Nations Peoples in the Great Lakes Region: A Historical Review.' *The Michigan Historical Review* 32, no. 1 (2006): 1–17.

Lewis, G Malcolm. 'Maps, Mapmaking, and Map Use by Native North Americans.' In *The History of Cartography*. University of Chicago Press, 1998: vol. 2, book 3, 51–182. The quote from Sprout is on p. 112.

Okladnikova, Elena. 'Traditional Cartography in Arctic and Subarctic Eurasia.' In *The History of Cartography*. University of Chicago Press, 1998: vol. 2, book 3, 329–49.

The Origins of Information Graphics

Language and Writing

Dehaene, Stanislas. *Reading in the Brain: The New Science of How We Read*. Penguin Group, 2010: Chapters 1–4 and 8.

Dehaene, Stanislas. 'Reading in the Brain Revised and Extended: Response to Comments.' *Mind & Language* 29, no. 3 (2014): 320–35.

Pinker, Steven. *The Language Instinct: How the Mind Creates Language*. Harper Collins, 1994.

Human Universals

Antweiler, Christoph. *Our Common Denominator: Human Universals Revisited*. Berghahn Books, 2016: Chapters 2, 4 and 7.

Brown, Donald E. *Human Universals*. Temple University Press, 1991: Introduction, and Chapters 2–4 and 6.

Pinker, Steven. *The Blank Slate: The Modern Denial of Human Nature*. Penguin Books, 2002: Appendix—DE Brown's List of Human Universals.

The Drawing Instinct

Pinker, Steven. *The Blank Slate: The Modern Denial of Human Nature*. Penguin Books, 2002: Appendix, DE Brown's List of Human Universals.

Saito, Aya, Misato Hayashi, Hideko Takeshita, and Tetsuro Matsuzawa. 'The Origin of Representational Drawing: A Comparison of Human Children and Chimpanzees.' *Child Development* 85, no. 6 (2014): 2232–46.

Willats, John. *Art and Representation: New Principles in the Analysis of Pictures*. Princeton University Press, 1997. Quote from p. 318.

Emergence of Representational/Symbolic Drawings

Fein, Sylvia. *First Drawings: Genesis of Visual Thinking*. Exelrod Press, 1993.

Malafouris, Lambros. 'Mark Making and Human Becoming.' *Journal of Archaeological Method and Theory* 28, no. 1 (2021): 95–119.

Mapping as a Human Universal

Antweiler, Christoph. *Our Common Denominator: Human Universals Revisited.* Berghahn Books, 2016: Chapter 4.

Blaut, James M, David Stea, Christopher Spencer, and Mark Blades. 'Mapping as a Cultural and Cognitive Universal.' *Annals of the Association of American Geographers* 93, no. 1 (2003): 165–85. Quotes p. 1.

Kuhlmeier, Valerie A, and Sarah T Boysen. 'Chimpanzees (Pan Troglodytes) Recognize Spatial and Object Correspondences between a Scale Model and Its Referent.' *Psychological Science* 13, no. 1 (2002): 60–3.

Pinker, Steven. *The Blank Slate: The Modern Denial of Human Nature.* Penguin Books, 2002: Appendix, DE Brown's List of Human Universals.

Plester, Beverly, Mark Blades, and Christopher Spencer. 'Children's Understanding of Environmental Representations: Aerial Photographs and Model Towns.' In *Children and Their Environments: Learning, Using and Designing Spaces.* Cambridge University Press, 2006: 42–56.

Stea, David, James M Blaut, and Jennifer Stephens. 'Mapping as a Cultural Universal.' In *The Construction of Cognitive Maps.* Springer, 1996: 345–60.

Uttal, David H. 'Seeing the Big Picture: Map Use and the Development of Spatial Cognition.' *Developmental Science* 3, no. 3 (2000): 247–64.

CHAPTER 3

Drawing Buildings and Machines

W̶E HAVE SEEN THAT early civilizations used a variety of information graphics, including cosmological diagrams, maps, tables and geometric diagrams. However, very few information graphics are more than 1000 years old, suggesting that while they were used, this was relatively rare. For instance, you might expect the Romans to have left a legacy of maps, plans, and medical and scientific drawings. As long as you weren't a slave, the Roman Empire was an excellent place to live. There was clean water, plentiful food, well-planned cities and extensive infrastructure, including libraries serving a literate elite. Yet, only a handful of information graphics survive from Roman times. It is now believed that Roman manuscripts contained very few information graphics, primarily tables, geometric diagrams and a few simple drawings. Few Romans would have noticed if these graphics had suddenly disappeared, and daily life would have continued unchanged.

The contrast to the extensive use of information graphics in our modern world is stark. So how did this come about? How and why did Western civilization move from a society with relatively infrequent use of information graphics to one with absolute dependence upon them? In this and the following three chapters, we will see that the European Renaissance was a pivotal moment in the development of information graphics. This chapter focuses on the evolution of technical drawings. These are the kind

DOI: 10.1201/9781003507642-4

of drawings used by architects and engineers. The techniques developed in the Renaissance for these drawings continue to be used today and provide the basis for computer algorithms for rendering 3D objects and scenes (see Chapter 10). I'll also reveal how these drawings enabled us to move away from craft methods of construction practiced in the Middle Ages to modern-day methods of mass production.

THE RENAISSANCE

The European Renaissance began at the end of the fourteenth century in Florence (see Figure 3.1). At the time, Italy was split into numerous city-states, of which Florence was one of the most powerful. From there, the Renaissance spread through Italy and the rest of Europe. It marks the transition from the Middle Ages to what historians call the Modern Era, the period in which we now live.

The Renaissance was a time of profound change. The sovereign state emerged as European rulers consolidated their power. European exploration and colonization led to European empires. The invention of printing provided the intellectual elite with unprecedented access to knowledge. And the expansion of trade and manufacturing led to a new middle class of shopkeepers, merchants and bankers.

The Renaissance was built upon inventions originating in China: gunpowder, the compass, paper and woodblock printing. It also benefitted from the rediscovery by Western Europe of ancient Greek and Roman texts, such as Euclid's *Elements*, that had been lost to Europe after the fall of the Roman Empire in the fifth century. These returned to Europe in the

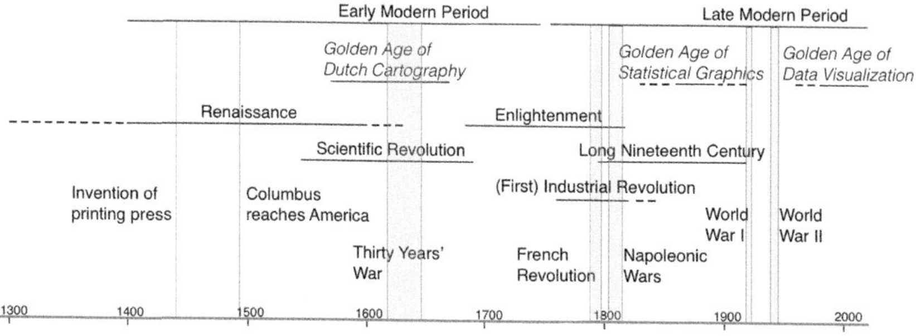

FIGURE 3.1   Like me, you may have a sketchy knowledge of Western history. Above is a summary of the events and historical periods I will refer to in subsequent chapters. For some periods, such as the Renaissance, there is a lack of agreement on the beginning and end dates. This is indicated by dashes.

late Middle Ages via a vast Islamic Empire bordering Western Europe. The Empire was the result of the Islamic conquest of the Middle East, the Persian Empire, North Africa and Spain during the Middle Ages. Relatively tolerant of Jews, Christians and other non-believers, the Islamic Empire became a center for learning, and Greek texts on natural philosophy, medicine and mathematics were translated into Arabic. It was also via Islam that the aforementioned Chinese inventions and the Hindu-Arabic number system reached Europe.

However, while the Renaissance was based upon Greek and Roman literature and philosophy and the various extensions developed by Islamic and European scholars in the Middle Ages, it had an unheralded emphasis on vision and graphics. While the classical texts were still revered, scholars increasingly trusted what they saw with their own eyes, and they believed that graphical representations were integral to communicating what they had seen.

There is no better place to see this emphasis on the visual than in the notebooks of Leonardo da Vinci, that great scientist, artist and engineer of the early Renaissance (see Figure 3.2). They contain a wealth of images: depictions of machines and human anatomy as well as maps and drawings for engineering projects. Da Vinci exuberantly writes:

> *O writer, with what letters will you describe with such perfection all that is depicted here in drawing? Because of your lack of information, you write confusingly and give little notion of the true shape of things, with which, deceiving yourself, you believe you can fully satisfy your listener.*

In Leonardo's words and drawings, we see the transition from antiquity to the Renaissance and its new focus on the visual. Little wonder the Renaissance was the birthplace of Western visual arts, technical and scientific drawing, and modern map-making.

PAPER AND PRINTING

This focus on the visual was supported by the introduction of paper and woodblock printing from China. Before paper, a variety of media had been used in Europe and the Middle East. Clay tablets were used in Mesopotamia, although these were fragile, ill-suited to damp environments, and didn't allow fine details. Ancient Egypt, then Greece and Rome, used papyrus. From the first century, parchment gradually replaced

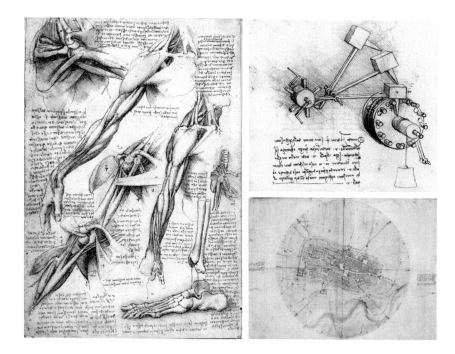

FIGURE 3.2   The drawings of Leonardo da Vinci epitomize the visual culture of the Renaissance. Leonardo was interested in human anatomy (left), machinery (top right), and drew maps and plans for his engineering projects (bottom right).

Credit: Left and bottom right—RCIN 919013 and RCIN 912284 Royal Collection Trust / © His Majesty King Charles III, 2023; top right: MSS/8937 Image taken from the holdings of the Biblioteca Nacional de España.

papyrus. It was longer-lasting, reusable, and did not need to be imported from Egypt. However, it required careful preparation, and many animal hides were needed for even a single book.

Sometime before the first century, paper was invented in China, replacing bamboo and silk. The use of paper slowly spread from China, reaching Europe in the twelfth century where, because of its lower cost, it quickly replaced parchment. At last, Europeans had a (relatively) inexpensive and durable medium on which they could draw or print finely detailed graphics.

The second technology introduced to Europe from China was woodblock printing. This had been invented in the first half of the seventh century, though it was not widely used in China until the tenth century. It arrived in Europe soon after the introduction of paper.

The impact of printing on graphics use was immense. Before printing, all illustrations had to be laboriously created by hand, meaning they were costly. Even more of a problem, copying by hand was error-prone. Before printing, it was simply impossible to reliably copy complex images. This was the main reason ancient Greek and Roman scholars did not use graphics in their manuscripts. For instance, the distinguished Roman naturalist and philosopher Pliny the Elder advised authors of botanical texts to limit themselves to written descriptions of plants. He wrote that:

> not only is a picture misleading when the colors are so many, particularly as the aim is to copy Nature, but besides this, much imperfection arises from the manifold hazards in the accuracy of copyists.

Perhaps even stranger to modern sensibilities, the two most eminent geographers of the ancient world, Strabo and Ptolemy, forbade copying of maps. Instead, they advocated that, if a map was required, the reader should draw their own by following instructions in the text. Indeed, Ptolemy, regarded as the father of geography, employed latitude and longitude as a simple method for precisely specifying location using only text. Thus, his great work *Geographica* contained written descriptions of the shape of lands and seas and the coordinates of more than 8000 places. Any associated maps were not intended to be copied; instead, they were to be drawn anew, using only the text for guidance.

Woodblock printing was initially used for printing items such as tarot and playing cards. It was also used to print books, though it was not well suited to this because the fine detail required for text was challenging and time-consuming to carve. Around 1440, Johannes Gutenberg invented the printing press and moveable metal type. This revolutionized the production of books, allowing printers to cater to the rising demand by scholars. By 1500, around ten million books had been printed. These included the works of ancient Roman and Greek scientists and philosophers, many of which had just become available in the West, as well as new works by Renaissance scholars. Never before had so much information been available to scholars. Never before had they been able to communicate so extensively.

Soon enough, woodblock illustrations were combined with printing to create illustrated books. Among the first was Robert Valturius's *De re militari* (*On the Military Arts*). Published in 1472, it contained numerous woodcuts depicting military devices such as machine guns and their use.

By the middle of the sixteenth century, there were illustrated books on architecture, technology, mathematics, botany, zoology and anatomy.

Woodblock printing was gradually replaced by copperplate printing (see Figure 3.3). By about 1600, this had become the method of choice for technical illustrations and maps because it allowed finer detail. In woodblock

FIGURE 3.3 This 1705 hand-colored copperplate print from *Metamorphosis insectorum Surinamensium* (*Metamorphosis of Surinamese Insects*) by the scientist Maria Sibylla Merian shows the White Witch Moth (*Thysania Agrippina*). Merian's observations and meticulously drafted illustrations of insect metamorphosis helped refute the contemporary belief that insects were 'born of mud' by spontaneous generation.

printing, the raised parts of the woodcut are coated with ink and pressed onto the paper to create the print. This means that the non-printed parts of the image must be carefully carved away to leave only the desired image. In copperplate printing, this process is reversed: it is the incised lines and recessed areas that hold the ink when printing, and so it is the image itself that is etched into copper. Etching allowed the printer to use fine lines to show shading and texture, similar to pencil drawings.

The nineteenth century saw a transformation in printing technologies. First came lithography, in which the printing plate is chemically treated so that ink adheres to some parts but not others. Then came photography, photoengraving and half-tone printing. These automated the production of the printing plate. No longer was there a need for skilled and expensive engraving or etching; instead, the plate could be generated photo-mechanically. New processes for making paper reduced its cost, and the invention of the steam press meant that, by 1860, it was possible to print thousands of copies an hour. These new technologies also provided affordable color printing. This was a breakthrough as before then, coloring was almost always done by hand, making colored graphics rare and expensive.

By the beginning of the twentieth century, graphics had never been so easy or cheap to produce. Drawings, maps and charts were commonplace in architecture, engineering, medicine and science. Paper and printing enabled this surge in use. However, they were not the underlying reason for the surge. To understand what happened, we must examine the fundamental changes occurring in society as our modern world emerged in the European Renaissance.

EARLY TECHNICAL DRAWINGS

To understand these changes, let's start with technical drawings, the types of graphics that architects and engineers use to depict buildings and machines. While we do have examples of plans for buildings from ancient China, Mesopotamia and Egypt, these are very rare. Early buildings had simple designs and were built using a 'craft' construction style. Because the builder and architect were one and the same person, there was no need for a detailed plan before construction started. In craft construction, design and making are inseparable. Details of the final design are determined on the fly as the builder measures and shapes new components to fit the current structure.

However, this does not mean that drawings were not used. We know that floor plans for Gothic cathedrals were paced out and marked on the ground; templates were used for repetitive decorative patterns; and the details of piers, arches and windows were worked out using full-scale drawings on 'tracing floors'. We also know that stonemasons used rulers, set squares and compasses to calculate how to shape stones for complex structures like vaulted ceilings.

Such construction drawings were created on the building site and often drawn on the construction materials themselves. They were usually full-scale and used to refine a design or by the master builder to specify to other workers on the site what needed to be done. While they may seem make-shift, the utility of construction drawings should not be underestimated. They continue to be widely used in construction (see Figure 3.4), and, since the invention of sewing patterns in the nineteenth century, they have become essential in home dressmaking.

Almost no technical drawings survive from Roman times. Our knowledge of Roman building and engineering practices is primarily based upon medieval copies of *De architectura* (*On Architecture*), the only architectural text surviving from antiquity. It was written in the first century by

FIGURE 3.4 The use of construction drawings did not stop in the Renaissance. Here, contractors have drawn on my neighborhood pavement to guide their repairs.

Vitruvius, a Roman architect and engineer who, when a young man, served in the army of Julius Caesar as a military engineer. Vitruvius describes Roman building and architectural practices, including surveying and building materials, as well as civil and military machines. His book was one of the first technical books to be printed. It had an enormous influence on Renaissance architects who regarded it as the bible of architectural style.

Vitruvius advocated three kinds of architectural drawings: floor plans, elevations (that is, depictions of the building's sides), and a type of perspective drawing of the front of the building. However, perhaps because of his awareness of the difficulties in accurately copying complex images, or because of a desire to make his work look more scholarly, it is believed that the original *De architectura* contained very few illustrations, and that these showed geometric shapes and constructions rather than actual buildings or machines. As a result, no-one really knows what Vitruvius meant by a perspective drawing. The current guess is that it depicted the front of the building face-on and showed one side in a receding view with its horizontal lines converging to a point in the distance.

We have a better record of technical drawings from the Middle Ages. The French draftsman Villard de Honnecourt left a folio of thirty-three sheets of parchment covered with some 250 illustrations. Dating from around 1230, these contain drawings and plans of buildings as well as sketches of machines he had seen or invented, including a perpetual motion machine. While not an architect or engineer, Villard was clearly both interested in and knowledgeable about technical matters, and his sketches likely reflect the technical drawing conventions of that period.

Villard's floor plans and side and front views of buildings look familiar. However, today, most people will have difficulty understanding his drawings of machines. These show the complete device, but the components are illustrated using a variety of viewpoints, with Villard utilizing the one that he thinks best depicts the part. To the modern eye, Villard's drawing of the water-powered saw in Figure 3.5 looks like the machine has been squashed onto the page by a steamroller. It is difficult to understand how the different components of the saw fit together and virtually impossible to figure out how it works unless you are already familiar with similar devices. (As the water wheel turns, the axle's rotating spindle pulls the saw downwards, cutting the wood and bending the sapling downwards. At the bottom of the stroke, the saw disengages from the spindle and, as the sapling straightens, the saw is pulled upwards.)

Villard's drawings demonstrate the challenge faced by early technical illustrators: how to draw buildings and machines in a way that reveals

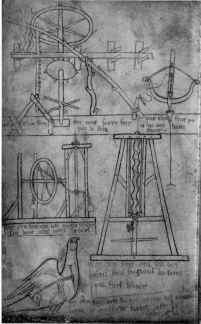

FIGURE 3.5   Drawings from the Workbook of Villard de Honnecourt, c. 1230. On the left is an elevation for a chapel of the Rheims Cathedral. On the right are drawings of various machines including that of a water-powered saw, one of the most complex machines used in the Middle Ages.

Credit: Bibliothèque nationale de France, MS Fr 19093 Folio 31r and 22v.

their three-dimensional structure and shape in a precise yet understandable manner. For more complex machinery and buildings, this also means showing their internal structure. The problem, of course, is that paper is two-dimensional. In Edward Tufte's memorable phrase, drawing techniques that allow us to 'escape flatland' are required. Developing these was the great challenge that Renaissance architects and engineers addressed.

DRAWING BUILDINGS

The invention of these new technical drawing conventions and the emergence of architecture as a new profession are indivisible. During the Renaissance, building practices profoundly changed, with a shift from craft models of building to one in which design was recognized as a separate activity to construction. The architect was now responsible for designing the building, using models and drawings to share his design with clients and the builders. Technical drawings underpinned this change. As

Wolfgang Lefèvre writes: 'Drawings and the practice of drawing funda-mentally shaped the activity and profession of Renaissance architects', and the 'importance of drawings, and of the practice of drawing, can hardly be overemphasized'.

The introduction of paper enabled this change. Parchment had been too expensive for everyday use. Paper was cheaper and provided an ideal medium for designers to sketch and play with initial designs and then com-municate these designs to clients and builders. Printing also played a role. For the first time, designers had access to detailed drawings of buildings and machines. Unlike Villard, they no longer had to travel to see these themselves. Instead, they could consult printed books, such as illustrated copies of *De architectura*. Soon, architectural texts such as Sebastiano Serlio's *I sette libri dell'architettura*, with its detailed drawings of columns, facades and other 'architectural patterns', fueled the spread of the Italian Renaissance architectural style throughout Europe.

Over the course of the Renaissance, architects developed distinctive new ways to depict buildings. The invention and mathematical formulation of linear perspective is one of the crowning achievements of the Renaissance. The architect, engineer and sculptor Filippo Brunelleschi is usually credited with its discovery. In about 1420, he amazed his contemporaries with two demonstration paintings of iconic Florentine buildings. These used linear perspective to create an image that could scarcely be distinguished from the actual object.

Earlier technical drawings, like those of Villard de Honnecourt, fre-quently show objects from multiple viewpoints and utilize ad hoc rules for showing depth. Linear perspective provides a systematic procedure for depicting a building or machine from a single vantage point. The drawing canvas is positioned between the viewpoint and the scene. Conceptually, it is a window that the observer is looking through, and the drawing is constructed by imagining the line of sight between each point in the scene and the viewpoint, and recording where the line intersects the canvas (see Figure 3.6). These lines are called projec-tion lines.

Over the next two centuries, architects and artists, including Leon Battista Alberti, Leonardo da Vinci and Albrecht Dürer, formalized and refined Brunelleschi's 'geometry of vision'. They invented tools to create perspective drawings and they devised geometric rules that enabled them to draw a building from its plan and elevation.

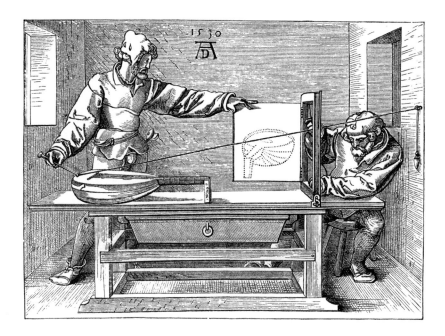

FIGURE 3.6   Linear perspective is an inherently geometric understanding of vision. It provides geometric rules for drawing a scene as it appears from a single viewpoint. The above woodcut is a copy of one by Albrecht Dürer. It shows (using linear perspective, of course) an artist employing a simple tool to create a linear perspective drawing.

Credit: iStock.com/wynnter.

Renaissance architects, who had frequently trained as artists, quickly utilized linear perspective in their drawings and began to use perspective drawings instead of wooden models (see Figure 3.7). They believed that Vitruvius had recommended the use of perspective, and they found these drawings were ideal for showing prospective designs to clients as the sketches were readily understood and confirmed the technical proficiency of the architect. It was their ability to draw in perspective and a knowledge of classical architecture gained from reading Vitruvius that allowed architects to distinguish themselves from stonemasons and woodworkers, who were viewed as 'mere' craftsmen, not genuine creative artists like architects.

Nonetheless, linear perspective was not ideal for all purposes. The limitation was that it was impossible to determine the precise dimensions of a building from a perspective drawing. This meant that perspective

FIGURE 3.7   Renaissance architects were quick to use linear perspective in their drawings. Drawing of a small commemorative tomb at the church of San Pietro in Montorio from a sixteenth-century Italian manuscript.

Credit: Codex Coner: Perspective of the Tempietto by Bramante at S. Pietro in Montorio Vol 115/33 © Sir John Soane's Museum, London.

drawings were not a particularly useful way of recording the design of an existing building or of communicating a new design to builders. Renaissance architects needed a way to create a scaled drawing of a building, so they invented multiview orthographic projections—the core of modern architecture and engineering drawings. These are believed to derive from geometric techniques used by stonemasons, who would draw the desired final shape on the faces of a rectangular block of stone before cutting it.

Orthographic projections are the kind of 'flat', scaled drawings that we now associate with architectural plans. Like linear perspective, orthographic projection is based on drawing projection lines from an object and computing where they intersect the drawing canvas. In linear perspective, the projection lines meet at the viewpoint. Because they radiate out at different angles, objects further away appear smaller on the canvas, and the angles between objects are distorted. In an orthographic projection, however, the lines run in parallel, as if the object is being viewed from infinitely far away. The effect is to 'squash' the object onto the drawing canvas, which is positioned parallel to one of the object's surfaces. If the surface is the side or front of a building, the result is an elevation; if it is the bottom of a building, it is a ground plan. Because the projection lines are parallel, the scale is the same regardless of how far an object is from the canvas. This makes it straightforward to precisely reconstruct the shape and dimensions of a building from orthographic views.

While architects had been drawing elevations for centuries, these were not proper orthographic projections. Genuine orthographic projections are flat and do not show depth. However, like Villard (see Figure 3.5), early Renaissance architects found it almost impossible not to use some type of perspective to show depth when drawing the sides or front of a building with angled or curved sides.

In 1450, Leon Battista Alberti railed against the use of linear perspective by his fellow architects:

> Between the drawing of a painter and that of an architect there is
> the difference that the former seeks to give the appearance of relief
> through shadow and foreshortened lines and angles. The architect
> rejects shading and gets projection from the ground plan. The dis-
> position and image of the facade [front] and side elevations he shows
> on different [sheets] with fixed lines and true angles as one who does
> not intend to have his plans seen as they appear [to the eye] but in
> specific and consistent measurements.

Alberti's position is striking because, in his earlier texts about painting, he had been responsible for one of the first formulations of linear perspective. However, in his architectural treatise *De re aedificatoria* (*On the Art of Building*), Alberti strongly advocated architects use what we now call orthographic projections instead of linear perspective.

At first Alberti was ignored, but by the middle of the sixteenth century, Renaissance architects such as Palladio and Antonio da Sangallo the Younger routinely used multiview orthographic projections (see Figure 3.8).

FIGURE 3.8   Later in the Renaissance, architects realized the value of multiview orthographic projections. This drawing (c. 1537) is by Antonio da Sangallo the Younger and shows a design for the church of Santa Maria de Monte Moro in Montefiascone, Florence. It provides a plan, elevation and cross-section.

Credit: Gabinetto Fotografico delle Gallerie degli Uffizi, Arch. 173.

They drew a ground plan, elevation and often a cross-section. The use of cross-sections to show the interior of the building and its relationship to the exterior was another technique that allowed Renaissance architects to escape the tyranny of 'flatland'.

DRAWING MILITARY FORTS

While Renaissance architects were perfectly happy to use linear perspective and orthogonal projection, Renaissance military engineers were not.

The Renaissance was a time of almost continual conflict, with the various city-states of Italy, the Papal States, France, Spain, England, Scotland and the Holy Roman Empire all fighting it out. In 1495, France captured the kingdom of Naples by utilizing a new kind of bronze cannon that could demolish traditional high-walled fortifications in only a few days. The Italian military responded by engaging engineers and architects to design a new style of fort that would be safe from this deadly new weapon.

These new forts had much lower walls than the old kind of fort. Instead of using high walls for protection, large ditches were dug around the fortress. Gun platforms called bastions protruded from the walls, carefully placed so that every square foot of the ditches was within range (see Figure 3.9), ensuring that attacking troops would be annihilated by deadly fire as they attempted to cross the ditches and reach the fort.

The design of this new kind of fort was a challenge that occupied some of the best architects, engineers and military minds of the Renaissance, including Leonardo da Vinci and Michelangelo. A fort could be the size of a small town. Determining the position of bastions, guns, walls and ditches required the designer to carefully analyze sightlines and possible lines of fire. They had to ensure the fort would not be vulnerable to cannon fire from higher points around it. And on top of these considerations, they also needed to minimize the amount of earth moved. To achieve this, they created detailed drawings and models of potential designs based on a carefully measured survey of the site. Figure 3.2, for instance, shows a plan of the Italian city of Imola created by Leonardo da Vinci while working as a military architect and engineer for Cesare Borgia.

Multiview orthogonal projections were not well suited to fort design. Analysis of vulnerability to enemy cannon fire required careful consideration of both position and height, something that separate ground plans and elevations made difficult. Drawings made with linear perspective were even less helpful because of the distortion introduced by viewing the potential battlefield from a single viewpoint. Rather, the military commander required an eagle-like perspective that allowed them to understand the position and height of the fortress's components and surrounds.

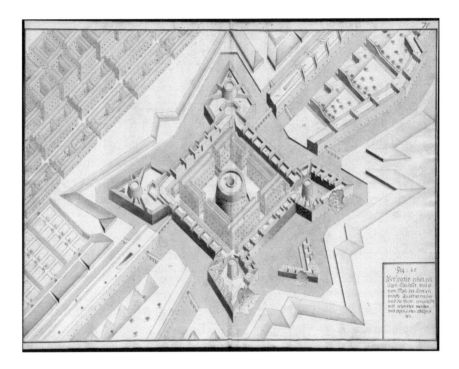

FIGURE 3.9 Renaissance military engineers invented a new type of fort in which gun platforms protruded from the walls to protect from attack. These were designed using drawings employing military perspective, such as that shown above, and handmade models.

Credit: Ernst Friedrich von Borgsdorff. *Die befestigte Stütze eines Fürstenthumbs.* 1686: 153. Copyright: ÖNB Vienna: Cod. 10.811, fol. 70v–71r.

To achieve this eagle-like view, military engineers invented 'military perspective'. Like orthogonal projection, it was a kind of parallel perspective, but unlike orthogonal projection, it showed the top, front and sides of a building in a single drawing (see Figure 3.9). Since antiquity, mathematicians had used parallel projection to draw three-dimensional geometric forms and it was also used in Renaissance drawings of machines. Military perspective is likely to have been based on these conventions.

A great advantage of military perspective was that it was easy to draw. You started with a ground plan and then drew vertical lines to show height. Because it is a parallel projection, military perspective provided many of the advantages of orthographic projection while still showing a fort's three-dimensional structure in a single, readily understandable drawing. However, despite its benefits, military perspective was ignored by Renaissance architects. It was not until the twentieth century and the modernism movement in architecture that it was revived as 'axonometric projection'.

DRAWING MACHINES

During the Renaissance, there was little separation between architecture, engineering and the visual arts. At the time, science meant theoretical knowledge, while art was the technical skill required to make things, be they paintings, buildings or machines. Leonardo da Vinci, for instance, was a visual artist and engineer, and Filippo Brunelleschi was an architect, sculptor and engineer. So it is unsurprising that drawing conventions invented to draw buildings were also used to draw machines.

Early Renaissance texts about machines share the same structure: a single image of the device accompanied by a technical description. The beautifully illustrated 'Theatre of the Machine' manuscripts are particularly striking (see Figure 3.10). These were the Renaissance equivalent of a hi-tech company's glossy brochure. They were intended for the broader public, especially potential patrons. Like today's glossy brochures, they focused on the usefulness of each device and its real-world application. And, also like today's brochures, 'Theatre of the Machine' showcased the author's ingenuity, often containing drawings of new inventions, and in an early type of patent, inventors could apply for the exclusive right to use their design in a particular region for several years.

Besson's drawings in *Theatrum instrumentorum et machinarum* used linear perspective because they were intended for the general public, and linear perspective drawings looked more realistic and artistically proficient. However, when technicians drew for themselves or other technicians, they frequently used parallel projection, often a type of cavalier perspective (see Figure 3.16). As discussed, in parallel projections, the projection lines run in parallel, meaning the scale in each dimension is consistent regardless of the distance from the viewer. This makes it easier to understand the relative size of the components and the way they fit together.

Early drawings of machines show a single view of the machine. However, devices such as pumps and winches have multiple interlocked components, some of which may be hidden from sight. For such machinery, a single view cannot show how all the components fit together. Renaissance technicians invented new visual techniques to reveal the workings of these more complex devices. They combined an overview with detailed views of selected components and emphasized essential details such as transmission

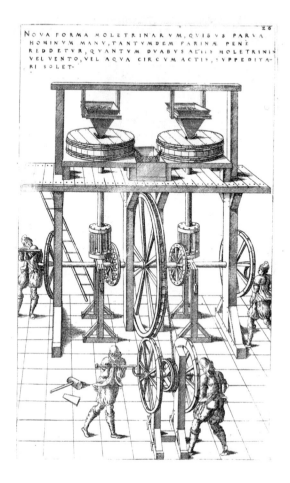

FIGURE 3.10 'Theatre of the Machine' publications were intended to demonstrate the engineering prowess of the writer. This (slightly wonky) linear perspective drawing of a grain milling machine is from Jacques Besson's *Theatrum instrumentorum et machinarum* (1578).

Credit: Smithsonian Libraries CC0.

mechanisms. They used cutaway views, transparent faces and exploded views to show the machine's internal structure (see Figure 3.11). When combined with parallel perspective, these conventions provided a powerful new visual language for depicting machinery. While we now take these visual conventions for granted, imagine the excitement of a Renaissance technician seeing these for the first time: it was as if they had X-ray vision and could see inside a machine.

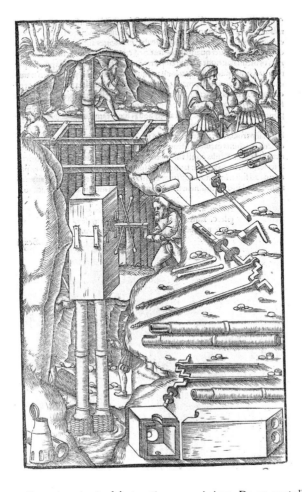

FIGURE 3.11   Georgius Agricola's treatise on mining, *De re metallica* (*On the Nature of Metals*), was printed in 1556 and was the primary text on all things to do with mining for two centuries. The woodcut above shows a duplex suction pump. On the left, Agricola utilizes a cutaway view to show the pump in action. On the right, he presents the pump and its parts. The pump is drawn with a transparent casing to show its internal structure, and there are detailed drawings of each component. The components were labeled A, B, etc., for reference in subsequent editions.

Credit: Library of Congress, Rare Book and Special Collections Division.

Unlike buildings, scaled plans and orthographic projections were rarely used to show machines in the Renaissance. They were simply not required. While a designer would provide initial drawings of the device, craft construction methods continued to be used. It was the responsibility of the skilled tradesmen building the machine to determine its precise dimensions.

Mills were the first machines to be designed using scaled plans. This began early in the sixteenth century and was probably because orthographic architectural drawings were used to plan the buildings housing the mills.

Naval ships were next, with scaled plans introduced in Elizabethan England (see Figure 3.12). The oldest known plans for an English warship date from 1586 and show the ship's side, top and cross-section. For the first time, ship design was clearly separated from ship construction. Naval architects were required to produce a complete ship plan in an office before construction began in the shipyard. Warships were the fighter jets of their time. They were notoriously difficult to design and very expensive to build—a massive burden for a country like England that needed a large navy. Plans reduced wastage, allowed construction by less-skilled workers, and reduced construction time as multiple ships could be made from the same plan.

It was not until the Industrial Revolution that orthographic projections began to be more widely used in mechanical engineering. The Industrial Revolution began around 1760, starting in Great Britain and spreading to other European countries and the United States. It was a time of considerable technological and social change. Steam engines powered pumps, factories, trains and steamboats. Iron was used to build machines, bridges and buildings. Factory production using machines and unskilled labor gradually replaced traditional hand-manufacturing methods, resulting in a

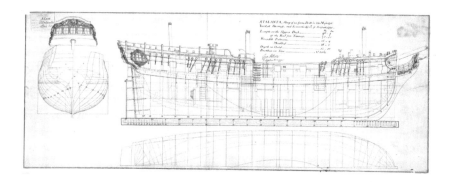

FIGURE 3.12   Ships were one of the first machines to be designed with scaled plans. This is for the fourteen-gun sloop *HMS Atalanta*, launched in 1775.

Credit: © National Maritime Museum, Greenwich, London.

mass movement of workers to the cities and the rise of an educated middle class, but also of a poor underclass of factory workers.

The use of modern engineering drawings is tied to these changes. They allowed an object's dimensions to be precisely specified, settling design issues before construction and removing discretion from the shop floor. This enabled the specification of more complex machines, the use of factories and less-skilled workers, and components to be manufactured in different locations.

The first factory for building steam engines pioneered the use of modern engineering drawings. This was established by Mathew Boulton and James Watt in 1775 near Birmingham in England. At the time, each steam engine was different and had to be housed in a bespoke building. Their design was complex and time-consuming. Boulton and Watt carefully specified the dimensions of each new engine using engineering drawings, which were then used as the basis of the contract with the client. Their detailed drawings enabled them to precisely stipulate the dimensions of engine parts to be manufactured outside the factory and that of the building housing the steam engine.

Like architectural drawings, engineering drawings use a multiview orthographic projection. They typically show a side, bottom and front projection (see Figure 3.13). These use the same scale and are arranged so that the views are aligned. Construction lines are used to emphasize important alignments between components and to provide dimensions. The drawing may also include cross-sections, auxiliary views from different angles and detailed views of sub-components if these are required to clarify the design.

Multiview orthographic projections, however, are difficult to understand. It takes engineering students years to learn how to fuse the different views into a single representation. So engineers continued using linear perspective in marketing brochures to show new products to their best advantage. They also continued to use parallel perspective. A particular kind of parallel perspective, 'isometric projection', was introduced in the early nineteenth century. This places the viewing canvas so that the three axes are treated symmetrically and drawn 120 degrees apart. Isometric projection is now routinely used in engineering textbooks and design documentation as an adjunct to multiview plans.

Isometric projection was popularized by William Farish, a professor at Cambridge University (see Figure 3.14). Farish formalized its geometric properties and construction rules, which were probably based on existing

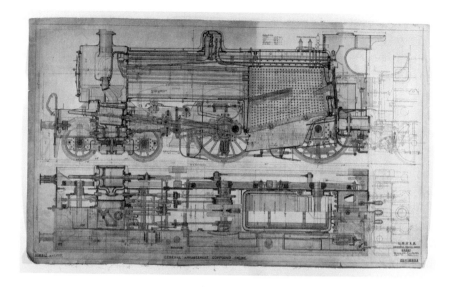

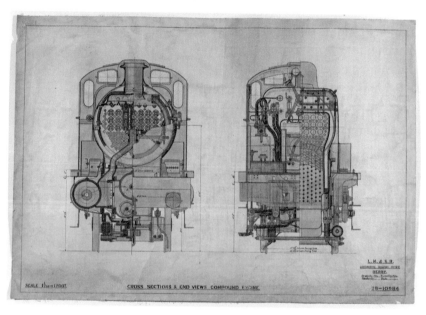

FIGURE 3.13 During the Industrial Revolution, engineers utilized multiview orthographic projections to detail the design of new types of machinery, such as the steamship and locomotive. The drawings above are of the LMS Compound 4-4-0, a steam locomotive designed at the London Midland and Scottish Railway Derby Works in 1928.

Credit: National Railway Museum © Science Museum Group.

FIGURE 3.14   William Farish formalized isometric projection, which he used to record the mechanical models he used in his lectures.

Credit: William Farish. 'On *Isometrical Projection*.' *Transactions of the Cambridge Philosophical Society*, vol. 1, 1822. **Courtesy University of Toronto—Gerstein Science Information Centre.**

drawing conventions. He must have been an engaging lecturer. He created a Meccano-like set of mechanical parts, including pulleys, gears, belts and bars, from which he and his assistants would assemble models for his lectures to clarify mechanical concepts. After each lecture, the models would be pulled apart and the parts reused in models for the next lecture. Farish developed isometric projection as a way of recording his models, so that his assistants could reassemble them when needed.

WHY DO DRAWINGS WORK?

The need for isometric projection raises an interesting question. Why do we think a picture of a machine or building drawn using linear perspective or isometric perspective looks more realistic than one drawn using an orthographic projection? In fact, why do we believe that any drawing looks realistic? This may seem like a stupid question, but as philosophers of art have pointed out, visual resemblance is not as straightforward as it first appears. The drawings of Besson and Farish, for instance, actually share few visual features with the objects they depict: they are simply black lines drawn on a white background.

In 1968, the philosopher Nelson Goodman argued that realism in art was not innate but purely a result of cultural convention. He asserted that pictures, like words, are symbolic, and there is no privileged correspondence between them and the objects they represent. He wrote: 'Realistic representation, in brief, depends not upon imitation or illusion or information but upon inculcation. Almost any picture may represent anything … realism is a matter of habit.' He did not believe that linear perspective was inherently realistic, stating that 'perspective provides no absolute or independent standard of fidelity'.

Goodman's view was supported by anecdotal evidence from European anthropologists and early cross-cultural studies reporting that indigenous Africans with no prior exposure to pictorial representations found it difficult to comprehend (black and white) photographs or outline drawings.

'But hang on,' I hear you say. 'This is ridiculous. Surely, the drawings created by architects and engineers resemble the objects they depict, and this resemblance is innate, not a question of cultural convention.' I agree. So do most psychologists, and they have collected evidence to back this belief. In an experiment unlikely to obtain ethics approval today, two American researchers raised their son without direct exposure to pictures until he was nineteen months old. Despite an unfamiliarity with pictorial conventions, the child could name familiar objects when shown pictures of them for the first time. Chimpanzees are also able to understand photographs and line drawings. They recognize other chimpanzees and objects, and they can imitate actions shown in illustrations. Furthermore, they appear to realize that these are representations, not the actual things themselves.

Today, we know that, while a technical drawing may not visually resemble an object, it *perceptually* resembles the object. Even though the drawing is not a faithful reproduction of the object's visual appearance, viewing it triggers many of the same low-level neural pathways as viewing the original object. One of the first steps in visual processing is identifying contours, the borders between regions of different color or distance from the viewer. As a line has a different color from its background, it is also recognized as a contour. This is why lines used to show the edges of an object are intrinsically understandable by the human visual system.

It also turns out that our visual system understands linear perspective. Inferring depth is one of the most challenging tasks facing our visual system. Unlike bats, which can use sonar to directly sense their distance from objects in their environment, we must infer this from the two-dimensional image projected onto each eye. The visual system uses an eclectic collection of rules of thumb to do this. Information from these depth cues is combined to make educated guesses about the shape and location of objects.

Some of these clues arise from the geometry of vision. Closer objects obscure those behind them. Things that are smaller or closer to the horizon are further away. If you know an object's actual height, you can roughly tell how far away it is by its apparent size. Parallel lines also provide information, appearing closer at greater distances and eventually converging to a point. Shading and shadows give yet more clues to an object's shape. These pictorial depth cues are why linear perspective drawings look realistic.

However, drawings also provide depth cues that tell the brain they are flat. When you move your head, objects do not move relative to one another. You cannot rotate a picture to see around the corner of a building. Furthermore, the image falling on each eye is identical. With actual objects, the image falling on each eye is slightly different, and our brain uses these slight differences to see depth. That's how 3D movies, TVs and computer displays work: they present each eye with a slightly different image, giving the illusion of depth. However, drawings on paper do not, which is one of the reasons why they feel flat.

Despite this, perspective drawings look realistic. The visual system deals with inconsistencies between the pictorial cues used to show depth in the picture and the other depth cues indicating that the paper is flat. It has little difficulty handling any disparity between the viewer's actual viewpoint and the viewpoint suggested by linear perspective. This is true even when the use of parallel perspective indicates that the reader is infinitely far away. This is because our visual system has evolved to opportunistically combine information from different cues. This flexibility allows it to deal with the inconsistent depth cues provided in technical drawings.

Subsequent, more critical reviews of the earlier cross-cultural comparisons of pictorial perception are revealing. Drawings of a single familiar object are almost always recognized regardless of prior exposure to pictures. However, recognition of more complex scenes drawn using linear perspective improves with experience. This is perhaps unsurprising. As I have identified, a drawing presents conflicting depth cues reflecting its dual nature: as an object, it is flat, two-dimensional; but as a representation, it is three-dimensional. With experience, we learn that we should focus on the pictorial depth cues. However, this is not obvious when we are shown pictures for the first time. Even more fundamentally, we must first learn the function of a picture—that it is a representational device, and only the markings on its surface are pertinent.

There is little doubt that Goodman was wrong. Our understanding of technical drawings and Renaissance artworks is not simply a matter of cultural convention; they really do (perceptually) resemble the objects they represent. Nonetheless, he was right in believing that experience and familiarity with drawing conventions play a role. One cross-cultural study showed a picture of a bird whose flight path was represented by a curved line of dots emanating from its tail. Unsurprisingly, viewers unfamiliar with this convention found it challenging to understand, interpreting it as a trail of blood or water. Likewise, architects and engineers must learn that dashed lines represent hidden edges in multiview orthographic drawings, and how to combine information from the drawing's different views.

THINKING THROUGH DRAWING

It is no exaggeration to say that, if technical drawings had not been invented, our modern world of skyscrapers, airplanes, cars and refrigerators would not exist. Technical drawings enabled modern design and manufacturing techniques to replace craft construction methods. They permitted design to be separated from making. This separation occurred gradually. During the Middle Ages, design and construction were indivisible. During the Renaissance, an architect or engineer would sketch the intended arte-fact, perhaps build a model, and provide drawings detailing any unusual design aspects. However, it was only during construction that skilled artisans working with the designer would determine the final design and dimensions. By the start of the twentieth century, the separation was com-plete. Architects and engineers committed the entire design to paper before construction began, and the shop floor played no role in design.

Separating design from construction permitted production to be split into separate pieces with confidence that the pieces would fit together. It was now possible to construct more complex artefacts such as skyscrapers or aircraft that would be too big for a single team led by a master builder to make on their own. It also reduced costs: less-skilled labor was required during construction, and there was less wastage of materials. Separation of design from production was a prerequisite for mass production. Pioneered by bicycle and then car manufacturers in the late nineteenth and early twentieth centuries, mass production took factory production methods of the Industrial Revolution to the next level. Unskilled workers were organized in an assembly line and used machinery to make identical copies of a product at a low cost. For better or worse, mass production and our modern consumer culture are a product of technical drawings.

The act of design was also fundamentally changed by drawing. Drawing encouraged creativity and innovation. When sketching on paper, a designer is free to dream and ignore the mundane reality of construction. There is no cost in exploring alternatives or making drastic changes to a design. For both engineers and architects, free-hand sketching is their primary design tool (see Figure 3.15). They use sketches to try new ideas and to capture fleeting ideas on paper. Design is a kind of dialogue with these sketches. Gabriela Goldschmidt writes how 'sketching does not follow ideas but instead, precedes them'. Creating a sketch allows the architect to see the consequences and unexpected implications of their design decision.

FIGURE 3.15   Since the Renaissance, free-hand sketching has been synonymous with design thinking. On the left are the architect Renzo Piano's first sketches of The Shard, now a London landmark (shown on the right). He sketched the design using a green felt-tip pen on a restaurant napkin when meeting with a property developer in 2000.

Credit: Left: Renzo Piano Building Workshop © Renzo Piano; Right: The Shard from the Night Sky © User:Colin / Wikimedia Commons / CC BY-SA 4.0.

The use of sketches by designers epitomizes the role of visualizations as external cognitive aids. The designer's thinking is built around the sketch, and mental transformations of it are central to design. They imagine changing elements in the current drawing before sketching their next idea. More-experienced designers use mental animation to think about functional behavior, such as imagining the sightlines in a building or traffic flow in an urban plan. Sketches are typically drawn quickly and may be vague or ambiguous. Vagueness is frequently intentional. It allows the designer to visually imagine different ways of resolving ambiguity and to mentally regroup graphic elements in the sketch in ways that encourage new interpretations.

Drawing enabled not only more creativity but also the design of more complex artefacts. It allowed the designer to record tentative conclusions about one part of the design before working on another aspect. It let designers work in teams. Modern buildings such as The Shard and planes like the Boeing 777X are too complex to be designed by a single person.

The ethnographer Kathryn Henderson spent more than a year observing engineering design teams. She identified the central role that sketches and drawing play in collaborative design, and how all other forms of knowledge and communication—verbal, mathematical or tacit—are built on top of these visual representations:

> In the world of engineers and designers, sketches and drawings are the basic components of communication, words are built around them. Visual representations are so central that people assembled in meetings wait while individuals fetch drawings from their office or sketch facsimiles on whiteboards. Coordination and conflict take place over, on, and through drawings. Visual representations shape the structure of the work and determine who participates in that work and what its final products will be. They are a central component of a social organization based on collective ways of knowing.

Designers don't only use mental animation to think about a design. Because technical drawings completely specify an object's dimensions and geometry, designers can use physics to reason about it and predict its behavior before it is built. During the Renaissance, military engineers drew firing lines on their plans of fortresses, checking that all approaches to the fort were protected. Naval architects computed a ship's displacement from its plan. This allowed them to check that its ports could open safely without letting water in when the vessel was fully laden. At first, the properties that could be calculated were limited because there was no mathematical theory of materials or mechanical structures. This gradually changed. In the late seventeenth century, Christopher Wren used the new science of statics when designing St Paul's Cathedral. And at the end of the nineteenth century, engineers were using structural mechanics to calculate the forces acting on the components of a new bridge or skyscraper to check that it would not collapse.

By the early twentieth century, drawings were used at all stages of design and construction. The architect or engineer would sketch the initial design, then use drawings and perhaps a model to pitch it to their client. The final design would be conveyed to the builder using detailed blueprints specifying every facet of the design. A complex object such as an engine might have hundreds of drawings. This was a stunning change from the Middle Ages, when the use of drawings was rare and largely confined to construction drawings.

We have seen that this change was the consequence of three factors. The first was technological. Paper and printing fundamentally changed graphics production and presentation. Paper provided Renaissance designers with an affordable medium on which to draw. Printed technical books enabled designers to learn from one another.

The second factor was cultural. The emergence of architecture and engineering as new professions during the Renaissance drove the use of drawings in design. In both disciplines, drawing was central to professional practice and identity, and architects and engineers learnt their trade by studying drawings and plans of buildings and machines. The first academy for the arts (including architecture) was established in Florence in the late sixteenth century. The first specialized schools for engineering were established in France in the eighteenth century. In both, drawing was central to the curriculum.

The final factor was the invention of a comprehensive visual language for representing three-dimensional objects on paper, one that met the new needs of designers and allowed them to escape from flatland. In particular, the invention and formalization of different kinds of projection—linear and parallel perspectives, including multiview orthographic projections— was a remarkable triumph (see Figure 3.16). These fulfilled complementary cognitive needs. The pictorial depth cues in a linear perspective drawing made it easy to understand the three-dimensional structure of a building or machine but impossible to determine its precise dimensions. Conversely, while it was cognitively challenging to understand a three-dimensional

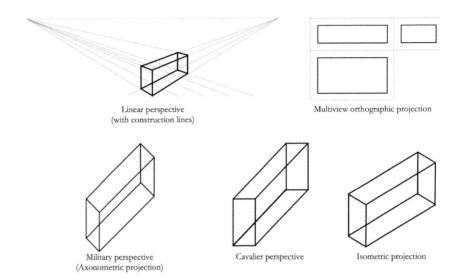

Linear perspective
(with construction lines)

Multiview orthographic projection

Military perspective
(Axonometric projection)

Cavalier perspective

Isometric projection

FIGURE 3.16   The invention and formulation of visual conventions to draw three-dimensional objects on paper was one of the outstanding contributions of the Renaissance. These underpinned technical drawing and European visual art for 500 years. They rely on projecting points in three-dimensional space onto points on a two-dimensional canvas. In linear perspective, the projection lines converge on a fixed viewpoint. In the other four projections, the projection lines run in parallel. Multiview orthogonal projections project the object onto canvases parallel to the object's surfaces. Military perspective draws the object based on its ground plan, cavalier perspective from its front or side view and isometric projection (formalized after the Renaissance) places the canvas so that the object's three axes are shown symmetrically.

shape from a multiview orthogonal projection, a uniform scale made it simple to determine the shape's exact dimensions. And military perspective and isometric projection provided a compromise solution. Even today, these techniques remain our primary tool for depicting three-dimensional objects on a two-dimensional surface.

Design was not the only activity fundamentally changed by drawing. In the next chapter, we will investigate how scientific illustrations played a crucial role in the emergence of science during the Renaissance.

NOTES, REFERENCES AND FURTHER READING

The Renaissance

For an accessible introduction to the Renaissance, I recommend:

Brotton, Jerry. *The Renaissance Bazaar: From the Silk Road to Michelangelo*. Oxford University Press, 2003.

Jardine, Lisa. *Worldly Goods: A New History of the Renaissance*. Macmillan, 1996.

Origins of the Renaissance

Brotton, Jerry. *The Renaissance Bazaar: From the Silk Road to Michelangelo*. Oxford University Press, 2003: Introduction and Chapter 1.

Lindberg, David C. *The Beginnings of Western Science: The European Scientific Tradition in Philosophical, Religious, and Institutional Context, Prehistory to AD 1450* (2nd ed.). University of Chicago Press, 2010: Chapter 9.

Merriman, John. *A History of Modern Europe: From the Renaissance to the Present* (4th ed.). WW Norton & Company, 2019: Chapters 1–3.

Emphasis on the Visual

Smith, Pamela H. 'Art, Science, and Visual Culture in Early Modern Europe.' *Isis* 97, no. 1 (2006): 83–100.

But also see

Jay, Martin. *Downcast Eyes: The Denigration of Vision in Twentieth-Century French Thought*. University of California Press, 1993: Chapter 1.

Leonardo da Vinci's Drawings

Ackerman, James S. *Origins, Imitation, Conventions: Representation in the Visual Arts*. MIT Press, 2002: Chapter 6.

Galuzzi, Paolo. 'Art and Artifice in the Depiction of Renaissance Machines.' In *The Power of Images in Early Modern Science*. Birkhäuser Basel, 2003: 47–68. The quote from Leonardo da Vinci is from pp. 67–8.

Paper and Printing
History of Paper and Printing

Brotton, Jerry. *The Renaissance Bazaar: From the Silk Road to Michelangelo*. Oxford University Press, 2003: Chapter 2.

Eisenstein, Elizabeth L. *The Printing Revolution in Early Modern Europe* (2nd ed.). Cambridge University Press, 2005: Chapters 1 and 2.

Febvre, Lucien, and Martin Henri-Jean. *The Coming of the Book: The Impact of Printing 1450–1800*. Verso, 1997: Chapters 1, 2 and 8.

Koeman, C. 'The Application of Photography to Map Printing and the Transition to Offset Lithography.' In *Five Centuries of Map Printing*. University of Chicago Press, 1974: 137–55.

Lyons, Martyn. *Books: A Living History*. J. Paul Getty Museum, 2011: Chapters 1 and 2.

Pan, Jixing. 'On the Origin of Printing in the Light of New Archaeological Discoveries.' *Chinese Science Bulletin* 42, no. 12 (1997): 976–81.

Ristow, Walter W. 'Lithography and Maps, 1796–1850. Copperplate Printing.' In *Five Centuries of Map Printing*. University of Chicago Press, 1974: 77–112.

Robinson, Arthur H. 'Mapmaking and Map Printing: The Evolution of a Working Relationship.' In *Five Centuries of Map Printing*. University of Chicago Press, 1974: 1–23.

Twyman, Michael. *The British Library Guide to Printing: History and Techniques*. Toronto Press, 1998.

Verner, Coolie. 'Copperplate Printing.' In *Five Centuries of Map Printing*. University of Chicago Press, 1974: 51–75.

Woodward, David. 'The Woodcut Technique.' In *Five Centuries of Map Printing*. University of Chicago Press, 1974: 25–50.

Maria Sibylla Merian

Etheridge, Kay. 'Maria Sibylla Merian and the Metamorphosis of Natural History.' *Endeavour* 35, no. 1 (2011): 16–22.

Lack of Graphics in Greek and Roman Texts, and Impact of Printing on Reproducibility

Carpo, Mario. *Architecture in the Age of Printing: Orality, Writing, Typography, and Printed Images in the History of Architectural Theory*. MIT Press, 2001: Chapter 2.

Eisenstein, Elizabeth L. *The Printing Revolution in Early Modern Europe* (2nd ed.). Cambridge University Press, 2005: Chapter 2.

Ivins, William M, Jr. *Prints and Visual Communication*. MIT Press, 1953: Chapters 1 and 2.

Pliny the Elder. *Naturalis Historia* (H Rackham, WHS Jones and DE Eichholz, trans.). Harvard University Press and William Heinemann, 1949–54. The quote is from Book 25.

Early Technical Drawings
Craft Construction and Construction Drawings

Carpo, Mario. *Architecture in the Age of Printing: Orality, Writing, Typography, and Printed Images in the History of Architectural Theory*. MIT Press, 2001: Chapter 3.

McGee, David. 'Ships, Science and the Three Traditions of Early Modern Design.' In *The Power of Images in Early Modern Science*. Birkhäuser Basel, 2003: 28–46.

Turnbull, David. 'The Ad Hoc Collective Work of Building Gothic Cathedrals with Templates, String, and Geometry.' *Science, Technology, & Human Values* 18, no. 3 (1993): 315–40.

Walsh, Margaret. 'The Democratization of Fashion: The Emergence of the Women's Dress Pattern Industry.' *The Journal of American History* 66, no. 2 (1979): 299–313.

Vitruvius

Carpo, Mario. *Architecture in the Age of Printing: Orality, Writing, Typography, and Printed Images in the History of Architectural Theory.* MIT Press, 2001: Chapter 2.

Medieval Technical Drawings and Villard de Honnecourt

Ackerman, James S. *Origins, Imitation, Conventions: Representation in the Visual Arts.* MIT Press, 2002: Chapter 2.

Carpo, Mario. *Architecture in the Age of Printing: Orality, Writing, Typography, and Printed Images in the History of Architectural Theory.* MIT Press, 2001: Chapter 3.

Drawing Buildings
Escaping Flatland

Tufte, Edward R. *Envisioning Information.* Graphics Press LLC, 1990: Chapter 1.

The Emergence of Architects in the Renaissance

Ackerman, James S. *Origins, Imitation, Conventions: Representation in the Visual Arts.* MIT Press, 2002: Chapter 2.

Carpo, Mario. *Architecture in the Age of Printing: Orality, Writing, Typography, and Printed Images in the History of Architectural Theory.* MIT Press, 2001: Chapters 4–6.

Ettlinger, Leopold D. 'The Emergence of the Italian Architect During the Fifteenth Century.' In *The Architect: Chapters in the History of the Profession.* University of California Press, 2000: 96–123.

Lefèvre, Wolfgang. 'Architecture on Paper: The Development and Function of Architectural Drawings in the Renaissance.' In *Creating Place in Early Modern European Architecture.* Amsterdam University Press, 2022: 41–69. Quote from p. 45.

Wilkinson, Catherine. 'The New Professionalism in the Renaissance.' In *The Architect: Chapters in the History of the Profession.* University of California Press, 2000: 124–60.

Linear Perspective

Edgerton, Samuel Y. *The Mirror, the Window, and the Telescope: How Renaissance Linear Perspective Changed Our Vision of the Universe.* Cornell University Press, 2009: Chapters 1 and 6–8.

Hentschel, Klaus. *Visual Cultures in Science and Technology: A Comparative History.* Oxford University Press, 2014: Section 5.1.

Kemp, Martin. *The Science of Art: Optical Themes in Western Art from Brunelleschi to Seurat.* Yale University Press, 1990: Chapter 1.

Lefèvre, Wolfgang. 'Architecture on Paper: The Development and Function of Architectural Drawings in the Renaissance.' In *Creating Place in Early Modern European Architecture.* Amsterdam University Press, 2022: 41–69.

Orthogonal Projection

Ackerman, James S. *Origins, Imitation, Conventions: Representation in the Visual Arts.* MIT Press, 2002: Chapter 2. The quote by Leon Battista Alberti is on p. 28.

Davies, Paul. 'Antonio da Sangallo, His Workshop, and the Drawings for S. Maria di Monte Moro in Montefiascone.' In *Antonio da Sangallo il Giovane: Architettura e Decorazione da Leone X a Paolo III.* Officina libraria, 2018: 120–32.

Lefèvre, Wolfgang. 'The Emergence of Combined Orthographic Projections.' In *Picturing Machines 1400–1700.* MIT Press, 2004: 209–44.

Lefèvre, Wolfgang. 'Architecture on Paper: The Development and Function of Architectural Drawings in the Renaissance.' In *Creating Place in Early Modern European Architecture.* Amsterdam University Press, 2022: 41–69.

Drawing Military Forts

Alonso-Rodríguez, Miguel Ángel, and José Calvo-López. 'Prospettiva Soldatesca: An Empirical Approach to the Representation of Military Architecture in the Early Modern Period.' *Nexus Network Journal* 16 (2014): 543–67.

Ferguson, Eugene S. *Engineering and the Mind's Eye.* MIT Press, 1994: Chapter 3.

Galindo Díaz, Jorge. 'The Dissemination of Military Perspective through Fortification Treatises between the Sixteenth and Eighteenth Centuries.' *Nexus Network Journal* 16 (2014): 569–85.

Henninger-Voss, Mary. 'Measures of Success: Military Engineering and the Architectonic Understanding of Design.' In *Picturing Machines 1400–1700.* MIT Press, 2004: 143–69.

Scolari, Massimo. *Oblique Drawing: A History of Anti-Perspective.* MIT Press, 2012: Chapters 1, 4 and 8.

Drawing Machines

Engineering Drawings in the Renaissance

Ferguson, Eugene S. *Engineering and the Mind's Eye*. MIT Press, 1994: Chapters 4 and 5.

Kostelnick, Charles, and Michael Hassett. *Shaping Information: The Rhetoric of Visual Conventions*. Southern Illinois University Press, 2003: Chapter 1.

Lefèvre, Wolfgang. 'The Limits of Pictures: Cognitive Functions of Images in Practical Mechanics, 1400 to 1600.' In *The Power of Images in Early Modern Science*. Birkhäuser Basel, 2003: 69–88.

Leng, Rainer. 'Social Character, Pictorial Style, and the Grammar of Technical Illustration in Craftsmen's Manuscripts in the Late Middle Ages.' In *Picturing Machines 1400–1700*. MIT Press, 2004: 85–111.

Pacey, Arnold. *The Maze of Ingenuity: Ideas and Idealism in the Development of Technology*. MIT Press, 1992: Chapter 5.

Popplow, Marcus. 'Why Draw Pictures of Machines? The Social Contexts of Early Modern Machine Drawings.' In *Picturing Machines 1400–1700*. MIT Press, 2004: 17–48.

Use of Orthographic Projections in Mill Design

Lefèvre, Wolfgang. 'The Limits of Pictures: Cognitive Functions of Images in Practical Mechanics, 1400 to 1600.' In *The Power of Images in Early Modern Science*. Birkhäuser Basel, 2003: 69–88.

Use of Orthographic Projections in Ship Design

Baynes, Ken, and Francis Pugh. *The Art of the Engineer*. Lutterworth Press, 1981: Chapter 3.

Booker, Peter Jeffrey. *A History of Engineering Drawing*. Northgate Publishing, 1963: Chapter 7.

McGee, David. 'Ships, Science and the Three Traditions of Early Modern Design.' In *The Power of Images in Early Modern Science*. Birkhäuser Basel, 2003: 28–46.

The Industrial Revolution

Merriman, John. *A History of Modern Europe: From the Renaissance to the Present* (4th ed.). WW Norton & Company, 2019: Chapters 10 and 14.

The Emergence of Multiview Orthographic Engineering Drawings

Baynes, Ken, and Francis Pugh. *The Art of the Engineer*. Lutterworth Press, 1981: Chapter 2.

Booker, Peter Jeffrey. *A History of Engineering Drawing*. Northgate Publishing, 1963: Chapter 14.

Ferguson, Eugene S. *Engineering and the Mind's Eye*. MIT Press, 1994: Chapter 4.

Hentschel, Klaus. *Visual Cultures in Science and Technology: A Comparative History*. Oxford University Press, 2014: Section 8.1.

Isometric Projection

Booker, Peter Jeffrey. *A History of Engineering Drawing*. Northgate Publishing, 1963: Chapter 11.

Why Do Drawings Work?
Cross-Cultural Understanding of Images

Bovet, Dalila, and Jacques Vauclair. 'Picture Recognition in Animals and Humans.' *Behavioural Brain Research* 109 (2000): 143–65.

Deregowski, Jan B. 'Real Space and Represented Space: Cross-Cultural Perspectives.' *Behavioral and Brain Sciences* 12 (1989): 51–119.

Gilman, Daniel. 'Pictures in Cognition.' *Erkenntnis* 41, no. 1 (1994): 87–102.

Goodman, Nelson. *Languages of Art: An Approach to a Theory of Symbols*. Bobbs-Merrill, 1968: Part I. Quotes are from pp. 38 and 19, respectively.

Hagen, Margaret A, and Rebecca K Jones. 'Cultural Effects on Pictorial Perception: How Many Words Is One Picture Really Worth?' In *Perception and Experience*. Plenum Press, 1978: 171–212.

Hudson, William. 'Pictorial Depth Perception in Sub-Cultural Groups in Africa.' *The Journal of Social Psychology* 52, no. 2 (1960): 183–208.

Miller, Robert J. 'Cross-Cultural Research in the Perception of Pictorial Materials.' *Psychological Bulletin* 80, no. 2 (1973): 135–50.

Serpell, Robert, and Jan B Deregowski. 'The Skill of Pictorial Perception: An Interpretation of Cross-Cultural Evidence.' *International journal of Psychology* 15, nos 1–4 (1980): 145–80.

Perceptual Resemblance

Cavanagh, Patrick. 'The Artist as Neuroscientist.' *Nature* 434, no. 7031 (2005): 301–7.

Livingstone, Margaret. *Vision and Art: The Biology of Seeing*. Abrams, 2014: Chapters 5, 12 and 13.

Mather, George. *The Psychology of Visual Art: Eye, Brain and Art*. Cambridge University Press, 2014: Chapter 5.

Depth Cues

Schwartz, Bennett L, and John H Krantz. *Sensation and Perception* (2nd ed.). Sage Publications, 2019: Chapter 7.

Ware, Colin. *Information Visualization: Perception for Design* (4th ed.). Elsevier, 2021: Chapter 7.

Thinking through Drawing

From Craft Manufacturing to Modern Design and Production

Hounshell, David. *From the American System to Mass Production, 1800-1932: The Development of Manufacturing Technology in the United States*. Johns Hopkins University Press, 1985: Introduction and Chapters 5 and 6.

Jones, John Chris. *Design Methods: Seeds of Human Futures* (2nd ed.). Von Nostrand Reinhold, 1992: Chapter 2.

McGee, David. 'Ships, Science and the Three Traditions of Early Modern Design.' In *The Power of Images in Early Modern Science*. Birkhäuser Basel, 2003: 28–46.

Wilkinson, Catherine. 'The New Professionalism in the Renaissance.' In *The Architect: Chapters in the History of the Profession*. University of California Press, 2000: 124–60.

Thinking with Sketches

Goldschmidt, Gabriela. 'On Visual Design Thinking: The Vis Kids of Architecture.' *Design studies* 15, no. 2 (1994): 158–74. The quote is from p. 162.

Henderson, Kathryn. *On Line and on Paper: Visual Representations, Visual Culture, and Computer Graphics in Design Engineering*. MIT Press, 1999: Chapters 3 and 4. The quote is from p. 1.

Jones, John Chris. *Design Methods: Seeds of Human Futures* (2nd ed.). Von Nostrand Reinhold, 1992: Chapter 2.

Lamont, Tom. 'Renzo Piano: My Inspiration for the Shard.' *The Observer*, December 30, 2012. www.theguardian.com/artanddesign/2012/dec/30/shard-renzo-piano-inspiration

Schön, Donald A. *The Reflective Practitioner: How Professionals Think in Action*. Basic Books, 1991: Chapter 3.

Suwa, Masaki, Barbara Tversky, John Gero, and Terry Purcell. 'Seeing into Sketches: Regrouping Parts Encourages New Interpretations.' In *Visual and Spatial Reasoning in Design II*. KCDCC, 2001: 207–19.

Predicting Behavior from Technical Drawings

Addis, WA [Wren, Sir Christopher]. *A Biographical Dictionary of Civil Engineers in Great Britain and Ireland: 1500-1830*. Thomas Telford, 2002: vol. 1, 799–802.

Henninger-Voss, Mary. 'Measures of Success: Military Engineering and the Architectonic Understanding of Design.' In *Picturing Machines 1400-1700*. MIT Press, 2004: 143–69.

Kurrer, Karl-Eugen. *The History of the Theory of Structures: Searching for Equilibrium*. Ernst & Sohn, 2008: Sections 4.4 and 5.2.

Lefèvre, Wolfgang. *Minerva Meets Vulcan: Scientific and Technological Literature-1450-1750*. Springer International Publishing, 2021: Section 2.7.

McGee, David. 'Ships, Science and the Three Traditions of Early Modern Design.' In *The Power of Images in Early Modern Science*. Birkhäuser Basel, 2003: 28–46.

Emergence of Architecture and Engineering as Professions, and the Importance of Drawing

Ferguson, Eugene S. *Engineering and the Mind's Eye*. MIT Press, 1994: Chapter 3.

Hentschel, Klaus. *Visual Cultures in Science and Technology: A Comparative History*. Oxford University Press, 2014: Section 8.1.

Jack, Mary Ann. 'The Accademia del Disegno in Late Renaissance Florence.' *The Sixteenth Century Journal* 7, no. 2 (1976): 3–20.

Formalizing Different Types of Perspective and Projections

Maynard, Patrick. *Drawing Distinctions: The Varieties of Graphic Expression*. Cornell University Press, 2005: Chapter 2.

CHAPTER 4

Drawing Nature

S CIENCE UNDERPINS OUR MODERN world. It has proven to be an extraordinarily effective way of understanding nature. Modern technologies, medicine and the management of the economy all rely on science. And it is through science that we comprehend the universe and our place in it.

Modern science was invented in what is now called the Scientific Revolution. This began in the second half of the Renaissance when natural philosophers, the precursors to scientists, developed a new methodology for understanding nature. Rather than relying on the wisdom of ancient scholars like Aristotle or the authority of the Bible, they studied the world first-hand. They carefully observed nature and conducted experiments to better comprehend it.

Graphics played—and continue to play—a crucial role in this way of understanding nature. Sociologist Michael Lynch has spent decades observing how scientists work. He writes about how 'visual displays are more than a simple matter of supplying pictorial illustrations for scientific texts. They are essential to how scientific relationships are revealed and made analyzable.'

THE RISE OF SCIENCE

Modern science has its origins in ancient Greece. The Greeks studied mathematics and geometry, optics, mechanics, geography, astronomy and meteorology, natural history and medicine. Islamic scholars preserved and extended their findings, and it was through Islam that many Greek and

DOI: 10.1201/9781003507642-5

Roman texts eventually made their way back to Western Europe in the late Middle Ages. The most influential writings include Pliny's *Natural History*; Euclid's *Elements*; Aristotle's works on philosophy, logic and natural history; Galen's works on medicine and anatomy; and Ptolemy's treatises on astronomy (*Almagest*) and geography (*Geographia*).

The invention of printing allowed the widespread distribution of these ancient teachings among European scholars during the fifteenth century. However, the authority of Aristotle, Pliny, Ptolemy and the Church was challenged by European exploration. A wealth of new data about geography, climate, animals, plants and human societies dramatically revealed their shortcomings. Aristotle was clearly wrong: the regions around the equator were not too hot to inhabit. And there were two new continents to the west, vast new realms that had been unsuspected by Ptolemy or any other ancient geographer. Natural philosophers were forced to evaluate accepted truths more critically, to privilege direct observation over ancient teachings. Step by step, modern science was born.

The year 1543 is regarded as a watershed moment in this birth, with the publication of Nicolaus Copernicus's *De revolutionibus orbium coelestium* (*On the Revolutions of the Heavenly Spheres*) and Andreas Vesalius's anatomical text *De humani corporis fabrica* (*Of the Structure of the Human Body*). Both contain multiple illustrations.

Copernicus uses a simple diagram near the start of his book to explain his radical idea that the Earth and the other planets orbit the Sun (see Figure 4.1). It communicates his heliocentric theory clearly and powerfully. It is a worthy contender for being the most influential diagram of all time, one that fundamentally changed how human beings understand the universe and (literally) our place in it.

Copernicus used nearly 150 geometric diagrams to argue the case for his theory. This was not unusual. At the time, astronomy was viewed as a sub-discipline of mathematics, and Ptolemy's *Almagest*, for example, also contained many geometric diagrams. What changed in the Scientific Revolution was that mathematics, especially geometry, began to play a critical role in reasoning about other aspects of the physical world. Aristotle had previously argued that, because mathematics deals with abstract entities, it cannot be used to reason about the imperfect objects that form our world. The Scientific Revolution overturned this, with the great Renaissance scientist Galileo Galilei arguing that mathematics and geometry were central to science:

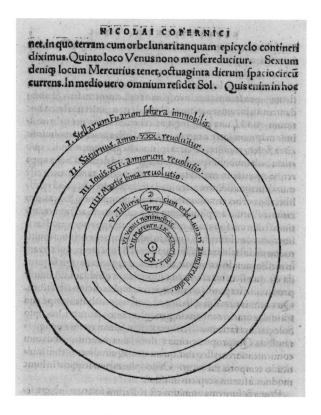

FIGURE 4.1   Copernicus used this diagram to explain his heliocentric theory in *De revolutionibus orbium coelestium.*

Credit: Library of Congress, Rare Book and Special Collections Division.

It [natural philosophy] is written in the language of mathematics, and its characters are triangles, circles, and other geometric figures, without which it is humanly impossible to understand a single word of it; without these, one is wandering around in a dark labyrinth.

Galileo is regarded as the father of physics. He investigated the behavior of falling bodies, famously concluding that lighter objects fell at the same speed as heavier objects in a vacuum. This was in direct contrast to Aristotle, who had claimed that heavier bodies fell faster. Galileo's investigation of falling bodies was not idle curiosity. Determining the angle at which to fire a cannon so that the projectile reached its target was a practical problem facing Renaissance gunners. Unfortunately for the gunners, for most of the Renaissance, science was of little help.

At that time, the theory of motion was based on the ideas of Aristotle. He distinguished between violent and natural motion. In his theory, a cannonball's trajectory was initially violent, followed by a natural component during which the ball falls to Earth (see Figure 4.2). However, it was apparent to the gunners, and to anyone else who knew anything about cannons, that this theory did not match the facts. It was clear that projectiles fired from a gun followed smooth curves without abrupt bends. It was also evident that the maximum range was not reached by firing the cannon horizontally, although this was what Aristotelian physics predicted.

Drawings of trajectories and geometric diagrams were crucial in developing a mathematical understanding of ballistics that agreed with these real-life observations. Early scientists thought about the problem visually, sketching possible curves in their notebooks. Galileo took this one step further. He investigated the trajectories of falling objects by rolling balls down ramps inclined at different angles, or off the tops of tables at different speeds and heights, then drew the results in his notebook. This led to Galileo's discovery that, if wind resistance is ignored, cannonballs and other projectiles follow a parabolic trajectory (see Figure 4.2), a key step in the development of Newtonian mechanics.

Experiments such as those of Galileo were a defining characteristic of science's new methodology. New scientific instruments such as the thermometer and barometer also drove scientific discovery. Scientists published drawings of novel experiments and equipment, allowing other scientists to replicate the experiment or to use the equipment in new experiments (see Figure 4.3).

Illustrations of experiments and equipment had a less obvious but no less important function. They were implicit evidence that the experiments had taken place. They assisted scientists in imagining an experiment from its description, allowing them to 'virtually witness' the investigation.

Now let's consider the second scientific masterpiece, published in 1543: Vesalius's De humani corporis fabrica. Vesalius uses drawings for quite another purpose than Copernicus. His book contains more than 200 detailed drawings of the human body: muscles and bones, the heart and lungs, digestive organs, the brain and the nervous system (see Figure 4.4). Their accuracy eclipses that of previous anatomical texts, and Vesalius's book remained the premier anatomical reference for centuries. While it contains some errors, Vesalius is regarded as the founder of modern anatomy because of his empirical approach. His book was based on

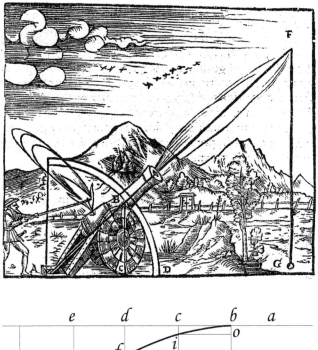

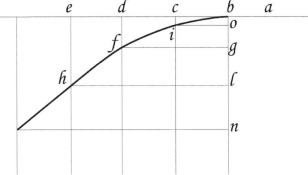

FIGURE 4.2   Above is an illustration of the Aristotelian theory of projectile motion, published in 1561. Below is the geometric argument given by Galileo that a projectile will follow a parabolic trajectory if wind resistance is ignored. Galileo realized that the vertical downward movement of the projectile would accelerate due to gravity, but that while it was being pulled to Earth, it would continue to move at the same speed horizontally.

Credit: Top: Daniel Santbech. *Problematum astronomicorum et geometricorum.* 1561. Courtesy Biblioteca Universitaria de Granada. BHR/A-009-044. Bottom: De Angelis, A. (2021). Day Four. In: Galileo Galilei's "Two New Sciences". *History of Physics.* Springer, Cham. https://doi.org/10.1007/978-3-030-71952-4_4. With permission Springer Nature. Redrawn by Kadek Satriadi.

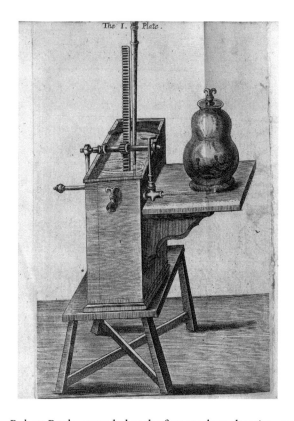

FIGURE 4.3   Robert Boyle, regarded as the first modern chemist, used an innovative air pump to investigate the properties of air. The pump allowed Boyle to extract the air from a glass container and observe the effect on its contents. This figure shows the result of an experiment demonstrating that animals need air to survive—you can see the poor asphyxiated mouse lying dead at the bottom of the Jar.

Credit: Robert Boyle. *A Continuation of New Experiments, Physico-Mechanical, Touching the Spring and Weight of the Air, and Their Effects.* R Davis, 1669. Library of Congress, Rare Book and Special Collections Division.

first-hand observations he made during his systematic dissection of dozens of human cadavers. Where these contradict the anatomical theories of Galen, which were based on the dissection of apes and other animals rather than humans because of Roman strictures against human dissection, his observations prevail. And drawings are the primary way in which Vesalius communicates his detailed observations; without them, the book could not exist.

FIGURE 4.4   Illustration from Vesalius's *De humani corporis fabrica* (1543). While the background and pose look a little strange, even macabre, Vesalius's intent was to show the human body as it appears in life, not in death.

Credit: The Metropolitan Museum of Art, New York: Gift of Dr. Alfred E Cohn, in honor of William M. Ivins Jr., 1953.

Accurate anatomical drawings, such as those of Vesalius, were the bedrock of modern medicine. They provided the facts on which early scientists developed new theories of blood circulation and the nervous system. Furthermore, because drawings such as those of Vesalius were published and widely available, there could be an ongoing discourse about their correctness. When scientists conducted their own dissections and saw something that did not match a drawing, they could challenge the drawing's accuracy and correct the error.

Other early Renaissance scientific drawings were of plants. These were in books known as herbals that described the medicinal properties of plants. One of the first printed books with illustrations was based on a Roman herbal widely copied during the Middle Ages. Despite the strictures of Pliny and Galen against images, the original herbal had been illustrated. But manual copying meant that, by the Renaissance, the drawings had been simplified, losing all detail.

At the start of the Scientific Revolution, however, herbals such as Leonhart Fuchs's *De historia stirpium* (*History of Plants*) boasted finely detailed drawings based on first-hand observation (see Figure 4.5). Fuchs made it clear that he disagreed with Pliny and Galen and believed that only pictures, not words, could adequately describe the appearance of a plant:

Who, I ask, in their right mind would condemn a picture which, it is clear, expresses things much more clearly than they can be described with any words of the most eloquent men? … It is certain that there are many plants which cannot be described by any words so as to be recognised, but which, being placed before the eyes in a picture, can be recognised immediately at first sight.

It took a little longer for drawings of animals to reach the same level of scientific rigor as those of anatomy and plants. Medieval Europe had a tradition of bestiaries—books full of fabulous and mythical creatures. The first printed books continued this tradition, mixing drawings of mythical creatures with those of real animals. The mythical creatures slowly disappeared as Renaissance scientists grew more skeptical of traditional authorities such as Aristotle or Pliny. They were replaced by drawings of new types of animals that European explorers encountered in Asia, Africa, the Americas and the Pacific.

Scientific illustrations enabled scientists to escape Europe and see animals and plants from around the globe. But this was only the beginning. Dutch spectacle-makers are credited with inventing the microscope and the telescope sometime around 1600. Each device provided scientists with the ability to see a new world, one that earlier generations had never imagined existed. Again, it was scientific drawings that allowed other scientists, and the public, to experience these new worlds.

Alii porno. Alii Polypleron.
Nafcitur in paludibus plurimum & pratis.
AD CAPITIS DOLOREM.
Herbae Plātagis radix collo fufpēfa dolorē mire
tollit. AD VENTRIS DOLOREM.
Herbae Plantaginis fucus tepefaĉtus fometādo
uentris dolorē tollit mire: & fi tumor fuerit: tu/
fa & impofita tollet tumorem.

SILIQVASTRVM
MAIVS ET MINVS

Calechutifcher Pfffa.
Pepper-wort

FIGURE 4.5   The first printed herbals contained only crude drawings of plants, such as the illustration of the plantain on the left. The plantain was prescribed as an antidote to snakebite and scorpion stings, which is why these two animals appear in the illustration. By the beginning of the Scientific Revolution, however, printed herbals contained finely detailed drawings, such as the pepperwort shown on the right.

Credit: Left: Pseudo-Apuleius Platonicus. *Herbarium.* Johannes Philippus de Lignamine, 1483–84. The Metropolitan Museum of Art, New York: The Elisha Whittelsey Collection, The Elisha Whittelsey Fund, 1944. Right: Leonhart Fuchs. *De historia stirpium.* 1542 M0002892: Public Domain Mark. Wellcome Collection.

The microscope permitted scientists to observe small objects like snowflakes, human hairs, and tiny insects like the flea. Carefully drawn images of these objects in the book *Micrographia* (1665) by Robert Hook captivated the public at the time, and continue to do so today. But what really gobsmacked scientists was discovering that our immediate environment was teeming with bizarre organisms such as bacteria and rotifers (see Figure 4.6)—tiny creatures that no-one had any clue existed because they

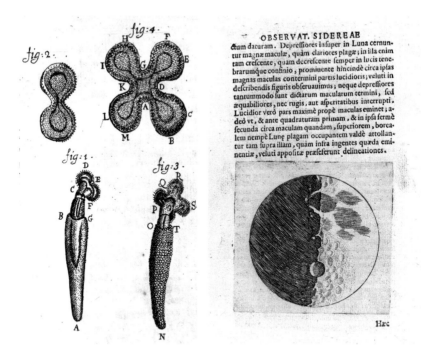

FIGURE 4.6 The microscope and the telescope introduced new worlds to scientists. Scientific drawings allowed other scientists and the public to also experience these strange new domains. On the left is an illustration by Antonie van Leeuwenhoek of the rotifers he observed in pond water. On the right is an illustration of the Moon made by Galileo using a telescope.

Credits: Left: Antonie Van Leeuwenhoek. 'A Letter to the Royal Society, from Mr. Anthony Van Leeuwenhoek ...', *Philosophical Transactions of the Royal Society* 24 (1705): 1784–93. Courtesy The Royal Society. Right: Galileo Galilei. *Sidereus nuncius*. 1610. Library of Congress.

were too small to be seen with the naked eye. A century and a half later, the microscope helped reshape medicine when Robert Koch used it to identify the bacteria causing anthrax. His drawings and photographs provided the first visual proof that microorganisms cause diseases, paving the way for our modern understanding of illness.

And with the invention of the telescope, we return full circle (!) to one of the topics that ignited the Scientific Revolution: Copernicus's heliocentric theory. When Galileo heard about the Dutch discovery, he quickly made his own telescope and turned it to the night sky. He published his findings in his groundbreaking astronomical treatise *Sidereus nuncius* (*Starry Messenger*). Written in 1610 and with only thirty pages, it was the first astronomical work to contain highly detailed illustrations of heavenly bodies rather than simple figures.

In his book, Galileo drew the different phases of the Moon, clearly showing that the Moon's surface was not smooth but covered in mountains and craters (see Figure 4.6). He also drew four previously unknown stars that he had observed circling Jupiter in a smaller model of the heliocentric theory. These posed considerable challenges to the Aristotelian belief (adopted by the Church) that, while the Earth was changeable and imperfect, objects in the heavens above were unchanging and perfect.

Then, in 1623, Galileo dealt a death blow to the Ptolemaic theory that planets circled the Earth. He observed the phases of Venus, confirming that these were just like those of the Moon. However, unlike the Moon, he noticed the diameter of Venus changed with each phase—it was smallest when the phase was full and grew larger as the phase waxed or waned. As shown in Figure 4.7, this accorded with Copernicus's theory that Venus would appear smallest and fully illuminated when it was on the opposite side of the Sun to the Earth, and that it would be fully dark when it was closest to Earth and positioned between the Earth and the Sun. While Copernicus's simple diagram succinctly described his theory, it was Galileo's observations and drawings that convinced astronomers Copernicus was correct.

VISUAL LANGUAGES OF SCIENCE

Until the mid-nineteenth century, most scientific illustrations were the joint product of a scientist, an artist who did the drawing or painting under instruction, and the engraver or etcher who transferred the image to the printing plate. Or, in the case of scientists such as Galileo who had the artistic skills to create their own illustrations, they had probably trained as an artist. Unsurprisingly, early scientific illustrations resemble Renaissance artworks. The artists employed by scientists strove to create a lifelike image of whatever they were asked to draw. To achieve this, they employed the same techniques—linear perspective and shadows—they would use to draw a portrait or landscape.

Scientists soon realized that this was not what they wanted. They did not want a photorealistic image of a single specimen. They wanted an image that was 'true to nature', an image that captured the typical specimen and its characteristic features.

Fuchs's images of plants illustrate this change. The herbals immediately preceding the *De historia stirpium* contain beautifully rendered perspective drawings of a single specimen, complete with shadows and withered

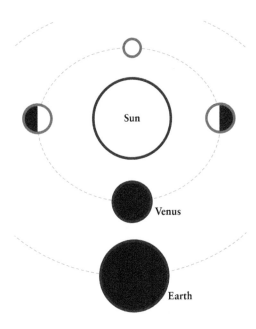

FIGURE 4.7   Galileo's observations of the phases of Venus refuted the Ptolemaic theory that the planets orbited the Earth. He observed that the diameter of Venus changed with each phase, being smallest when the phase was full and growing larger as the phase waxed or waned. This was exactly what Copernicus's theory predicted.

Credit: Kadek Satriadi.

or insect-eaten leaves. Fuchs's illustrations, however, are generalizations from multiple examples. They show an idealized plant unobscured by foreshortening, shadows or inconvenient foliage. Sometimes Fuchs drew flowers and fruit on the plant, even though these would never occur together. His goal was to precisely represent the individual components of the plant—leaves, flowers and fruit—rather than convey a realistic image of a particular plant. Fuchs writes how:

we have purposely and deliberately avoided the obliteration of the natural form of the plants by shadows and other less necessary things by which the delineators sometimes try to win artistic glory

Similarly, the illustration by Maria Sibylla Merian (see Figure 3.3) of the White Witch Moth is drawn from multiple observations and depicts the moth in various stages of its life cycle.

As botany matured, it became usual to only illustrate a plant's significant or identifying features rather than provide a complete drawing. In
fact, the use of illustrations in scientific botanical works decreased in the
seventeenth century. By this time, botanists had created a precise technical
language for specifying differentiating characteristics of plant morphology
and no longer needed illustrations to show these. Paradoxically, this was a
result of the success of the detailed botanical illustrations of the previous
century. They had allowed botanists to develop a mutual understanding
and vocabulary; without shared images, this would have been impossible.
Of course, botanical illustrations did not disappear. They continued to be
found in encyclopedias and other less technical texts for gardeners and
armchair naturalists. They also played a crucial role in teaching aspiring
botanists how to 'see' plant morphology.

As with botany, other scientific disciplines developed distinctive visual
languages and ways of seeing that the aspiring scientist needed to learn as
part of their craft. Like Fuchs's images of plants, Vesalius's detailed anatomical drawings were generalizations from multiple observations. Unlike
Fuchs, Vesalius also faced the problem of showing the internal organs
clearly, without their details being obscured by other organs.

This problem was similar to that faced by Renaissance engineers when
drawing the inner workings of machinery. As a consequence, the two fields
influenced one another. For instance, Leonardo da Vinci's studies of human
anatomy saw him reapplying many of the techniques he had previously
developed for drawing machines. Hidden organs are shown using transpar-
ency, and he uses exploded views and enlarged drawings to reveal details of
small bones. While these drawings were not published until long after his
death, he shared some with his contemporaries. It is likely his techniques
influenced later illustrators, including Vesalius. In turn, borrowing the idea
from Vesalius, Agricola was the first to use cutaway views in mechanical
drawings.

However, despite their accuracy, the drawings of Vesalius are, to our
eyes, a strange mixture of art and science. The cadavers replicate the poses
found in artworks and are even shown frolicking in ornate landscapes
(see Figure 4.4). In subsequent centuries, anatomical illustrations became
less artistic and more diagrammatic. This dry style was perfected in what
is undoubtedly the most popular anatomical textbook of all time. First
published in 1858, Henry Gray's *Anatomy* remains in print today (see
Figure 4.8).

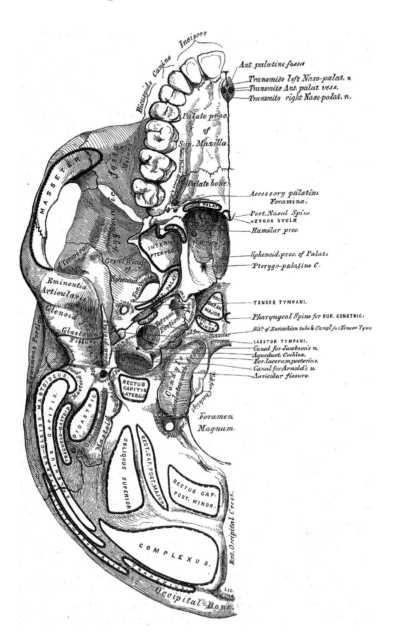

FIGURE 4.8   Nowadays, anatomical textbooks, such as the above illustration from Henry Gray's *Anatomy: Descriptive and Applied* (1887), often use indication lines to link labels to parts of an image.

Credit: State Library Victoria.

Another difference between the drawings of Vesalius and Gray is the way in which anatomical features are labeled. Labeling different parts of a diagram so that the labels did not obscure the drawing but it was still clear which part they were identifying, was a challenge facing early authors of both engineering and scientific drawings. While we take good labeling for granted today, this is only because Renaissance illustrators invented the conventions we now use.

Labeling is a particular problem in anatomical illustration because labels can be long, and the body parts to be labeled may be small and close together. Vesalius used alphabetic keys, with an explanation of the key in the text. This was also used in Renaissance illustrations of machines and is probably based on the use of text labels in geometric diagrams. Nowadays, it is more common to use 'indication lines' to link labels with their corresponding regions. Gray's *Anatomy*, for example, uses a mix of direct labeling and indication lines (see Figure 4.8).

Geology is another scientific discipline that invented its own distinctive visual language. Like anatomists, geologists are interested in visualizing the interior of a complex three-dimensional object—the Earth. But unlike astronomy, physics, biology and chemistry, which had their origins in Greek and medieval natural philosophy, geology arose as a genuinely new science. Its subject of study, geological processes, and the Earth's geological history would have been considered nonsensical in the Middle Ages or early Renaissance. At that time, it was clear to all right-minded Christians that the Earth was only a few thousand years old and had been created by God over six days. Determining the exact time of creation was a serious scholarly activity but did not require studying rock strata or fossils. In 1650, James Ussher, archbishop of Ireland, laid the matter to rest. After careful study of the Bible, he calculated that the world began on October 23, 4004 BCE.

The emergence of geology resulted from the new kind of thinking that had arisen in the Scientific Revolution. It required rejecting a literal reading of the Bible and recognizing that the Earth was considerably older than 6000 years. Scientific illustrations of fossils and rock strata were crucial to this acceptance. They forced geologists to stare into the 'abyss of time' and realize that the Earth was some 4.5 billion years old—nearly a million times older than Ussher had calculated.

Martin Rudwick has detailed how the emergence of geology as a new science in the first half of the nineteenth century was tightly coupled with the invention of a new visual language for showing the Earth's three-dimensional structure. In the late eighteenth century, geological articles and books contained few illustrations. By 1830, however, they included numerous maps and diagrams. One reason for this was the nineteenth-century printing transformation, which significantly reduced the cost of illustrations. But the main reason is that text by itself is ill-suited to describing landforms and the arrangement of rock strata. By this time, geologists had realized that the various rock strata and the fossils they contained gave them a remarkable window into the Earth's past. For geology to advance, it was necessary to invent a new language of discourse in which images of landforms and strata were an integral and complementary component to text.

This new visual language had its origins in technical drawings, the maps of mineral surveyors and mining engineers, as well as the drawings of geological formations and landscapes by 'traveler naturalists'. It included geological maps and geological sections showing the different rock strata making up the Earth's crust (see Figure 4.9). In combination, these allowed geologists to record observations, and to depict hypotheses about rock strata distribution and theories of rock formation and erosion.

Chemists also created their own visual language. At the start of the nineteenth century, they invented the formulas we know from high school, those that list the component elements and compounds in a chemical substance and their relative proportions. For instance, butane has the formula C_4H_{10}, indicating it is made of four carbon atoms and ten hydrogen atoms. However, this formula reveals little about the arrangement of these atoms. Chemical structural formulas were invented five decades later to address this (see Figure 4.10).

Structural formulas showed the individual atoms in the molecule and the chemical bonds between them. They provided a 'paper tool' for chemists to reason about the arrangement of atoms in a molecule. They also made it obvious that molecules composed of precisely the same number and type of atoms could have very different structures.

Early structural formulas were flat and showed only a two-dimensional layout. They were later extended to show a three-dimensional structure when chemists realized this affected chemical behavior. However, it is impossible to fully capture the three-dimensional shape of complex molecules such as DNA in a structural formula. For this reason, since the

FIGURE 4.9   In the early nineteenth century, geologists invented a visual language for showing the three-dimensional structure of the Earth's crust. Geologic maps and sections provided a multiview orthographic visualization of the location and extent of different types of rock strata. English surveyor William Smith created one of the first geologic maps. Published in 1815, it showed the surface distribution of various rock strata across England, Wales and southern Scotland, and included a geologic section. An enlarged view of the section is shown below.   (Continued)

Credit: 'A Delineation of the Strata of England and Wales with part of Scotland' by William Smith (1815). Reproduced by permission of the Geological Society of London.

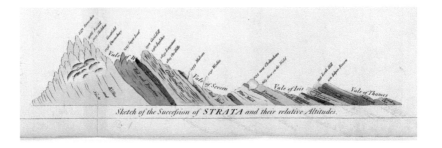

FIGURE 4.9 (Continued)

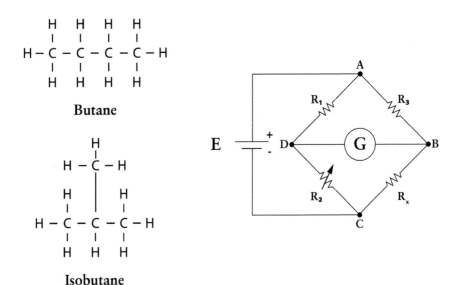

FIGURE 4.10 Chemical structural formulas like those on the left allowed chemists to reason about the spatial arrangement of atoms in a molecule; the lines show bonds between the atoms. Structural formula clarified why compounds with the same chemical formula, such as butane and isobutane, could have different chemical properties. Circuit diagrams evolved from realistic drawings of electrical circuits. The circuit diagram on the right shows the Wheatstone bridge, a simple circuit that allows the resistance of an electrical component with unknown resistance (R_x) to be measured.

Credit: Kadek Satriadi.

late nineteenth century, chemists have also extensively used 3D models to reason about molecular structure.

While chemical structural formulas appear rather abstract, their spatial layout still mirrors that of the molecule they represent. This is not true of electrical circuit diagrams (see Figure 4.10). These were invented around the same time as chemical structural formulas and are composed of iconic symbols depicting electrical components such as batteries, switches, resistors and capacitors. These are connected by wires typically drawn using horizontal and vertical line segments.

The first drawings of electrical circuits depicted the actual physical circuit, the wire connecting the components, the batteries, and the wires wound around wooden pins to form resisters. However, the components' position and the wires' route do not affect the circuit's behavior. All that matters is whether or not components are connected.

That's why scientists invented a new notation for electrical circuits, one that abstracted from the irrelevant details of where the components were placed and their appearance. These electrical circuit diagrams made it easier to reason about the fundamental electrical properties of a circuit because they allowed the designer to position elements and lines where they liked in the diagram, enabling them to use standard layouts for common sub-components to highlight the circuit's functionality and logical structure.

These examples of branches of science developing their own visual languages are not unusual. We see the invention of new kinds of drawings and diagrams in discipline after discipline. Often, the first illustrations are lifelike renderings of the phenomena of interest. Then, as the field matures, scientists develop more specialized representations that abstract away from unimportant details and enable scientists to immediately see salient information. And this has not stopped. For instance, in 1948, the Nobel Prize-winning physicist Richard Feynman invented a graphical method of representing the interactions of subatomic particles. Christened 'Feynman diagrams', these revolutionized quantum electrodynamics.

ESCAPING DEADLAND

Escaping flatland was one of the most demanding challenges facing technical and scientific illustrators in the Renaissance. But scientists and engineers also faced another problem: escaping 'deadland'. Nature and machines are not static. It is necessary to show motion and how things change over time if you are to understand natural processes such as cell division or the operation of machinery such as Villard's saw. The difficulty is that paper only allows static images.

In the Scientific Revolution, scientists had three techniques for showing motion, which are still widely used today. The first is to draw the trajectory of an object as a line. From the time of the ancient Greeks, astronomers have used lines to show the orbits of heavenly bodies. Renaissance scientists used lines to indicate the course of projectiles fired from a cannon, and lines were used by early choreographers to show the movement of ballroom dancers on the dance floor. This technique probably has its genesis in tracing a journey on a map. In Chapter 2, for instance, we saw how the Warlpiri use tracks and lines to show the paths of ancestral beings.

Another technique for escaping deadland is to use a sequence of snapshots to show an object or scene as it changes over time. Galileo used this technique to depict the movement of Jupiter's satellites. He also used it to show how sunspots progress across the Sun's surface. He made a drawing of the Sun's surface at the same time each day for more than a month, arranging these into a sequence. Galileo's rival, the Renaissance astronomer Christopher Scheiner, also used this technique to present his first observations of sunspots (see Figure 4.11).

One graphical convention now commonly used to indicate motion, the arrow, is conspicuously absent from Renaissance technical and scientific diagrams. Arrows appear on Renaissance maps, but only to show compass directions. Somewhat later they were used to show wind direction (see Figure 8.6), water flow and direction of movement on maps. They have since become ubiquitous in diagrams, indicating not only direction or motion but also forces, dependency and other asymmetric relationships in node-link diagrams, as well as guiding visual attention.

THINKING VISUALLY

Scientists use graphics in different ways. They use them to record what they have seen or done, and as evidence to convince other scientists of their claims. They also use graphics to explain science to the public. And, like architects and engineers, they use them for thinking. Many scientists are famous for their visual imagery. These include the physicists James Clerk Maxwell and Michael Faraday, and the chemist August Kekulé who, in a moment of inspired mental imagery, realized that the six carbon atoms in benzene are arranged in a ring with alternating single and double bonds.

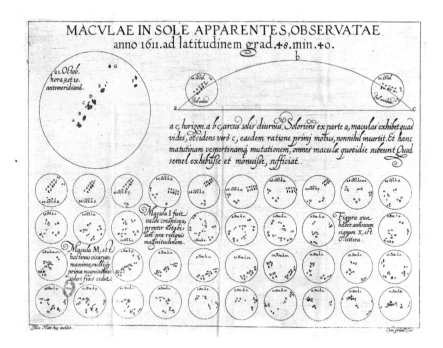

FIGURE 4.11 Renaissance astronomer Christopher Scheiner used a variety of techniques to show motion in his publications on sunspots. In the topmost part of this graphic, Scheiner uses a curved line to show the Sun's trajectory over a day. In each of the four rows below, he uses a sequence of snapshots to track the changing appearance and position of a particular configuration of sunspots.

Credit: Christopher Scheiner. *De maculus solaribus (On Solar Spots).* 1612. Bibliothèque nationale de France.

Another example of inspired visual thinking is the discovery of continental drift and tectonic plates. At the end of the nineteenth century, most geologists believed that the Earth's geography was fixed and that mountain ranges resulted from the crust crumpling as the Earth slowly contracted due to cooling. In 1912, Alfred Wegener proposed a radically different theory, continental drift, after looking at how the different continents could fit together (see Figure 4.12). He claimed that the continents had originally formed a single supercontinent, Pangaea, which had broken up as the continents drifted apart. While not the first to notice the close fit between Africa and the Americas, he argued that his theory also explained the distribution of similar geological structures and plant and animal species, such as marsupials, in widely separated continents.

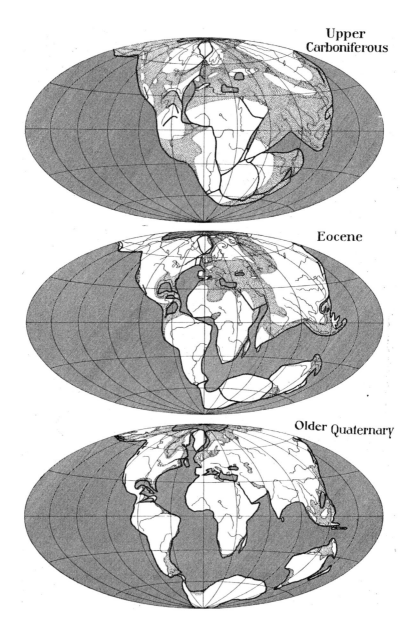

FIGURE 4.12   The geologist Alfred Wegener proposed his theory of continental drift in 1912. He suggested that the continents had originally formed a single supercontinent, Pangaea, which had broken up as the continents drifted apart. His radical idea was based on a jigsaw fit of the continents. Note the use of snapshots to show change over time.

Credit: Alfred Wegener, *The Origins of Continents and Oceans*, Methuen, 1924. State Library Victoria.

It was not until the late 1960s that Wegener's theory led to a paradigm shift in geology and a refined version of continental drift became the new orthodoxy. The arguments for its acceptance relied on maps and diagrams, with the clinching evidence provided by maps of the ocean floors. The oceans were systematically surveyed for the first time after World War II, and the results were totally unexpected. The deepest water was not found in the center of the oceans but close to land, where deep trenches ran alongside the continental shelf. And, in the middle of the ocean, ridges were discovered with 'rift valleys' running along their centers. This led to the sea-floor spreading version of continental drift in which continents were hypothesized to move along the oceanic crust as molten material welled up at the mid-oceanic ridges, pushing the oceanic crust and continents on either side of the ridge further apart, while at the trenches, the continental 'plates' collided, with the ocean crust pushed under the continental shelf.

Albert Einstein is also famous for his visual thinking. He wrote how words did not seem to play any role in his thought processes and that his insights into time and space resulted from mental images of 'thought experiments'. For instance, his theory of special relativity was the result of imagining what an observer would see if they were traveling at near light speed next to a ray of light moving in the same direction. Electromagnetics told Einstein that light is a series of waves. He imagined a point on the light wave next to the observer. The laws of classical physics predicted that as the observer approached the speed of light, the point would appear to slow down until, at the speed of light, the observer would be traveling at the same rate, and the point would appear to be stationary. However, Einstein's intuition told him that light behaves the same way regardless of the observer's speed, and so the wave should not slow down. His mental model allowed him to see that these two seemingly contradictory views could be reconciled if time slows down for the observer, allowing the point to maintain the same speed from the observer's viewpoint. A few equations later and the theory of special relativity was born.

Mental images stored and manipulated in working memory underpin this kind of visual thinking. Suppose you are asked which is redder, a cherry or a tomato. You will almost certainly bring an image of each to mind, then mentally compare their colors. If you are holding a map with north at the top but you are facing south, you may mentally rotate the streets on the map to match your orientation. These two images illustrate different types of visual thinking. Some visual thinkers are good at visualizing objects and can vividly imagine their appearance. Others are better at picturing the spatial relationships between objects using more schematic and abstract images. Unsurprisingly, the first kind of visual thinker tends to be found in the visual arts, while the second kind is found in science and mathematics. Einstein's thought experiments and Wegener's grouping of continents, for instance, are examples of spatial thinking.

Regardless of the type of mental image, visual reasoning utilizes working memory. This is the brain's hardware for supporting reasoning. It holds the objects we are currently thinking about. Working memory is short term. Unless we consciously try to remember something, it will fade after a few seconds. This is what distinguishes working from long-term memory. Long-term memory is responsible for storing information for extended time periods, from minutes to a lifetime, while working memory is our window on the present.

The nature of mental imagery in memory led to fierce debate among cognitive scientists, artificial intelligence researchers, and philosophers in the 1980s. One side of the debate argued that all information in the brain, including visual images, was stored in a language-like format consisting of propositions like 'X is red' or 'X is to the left of Y'. The other side argued that mental images are represented similarly to external visual images and that this representation is distinct from that used by the brain to store propositional knowledge. Support for this view came from experiments showing that reasoning with mental images was similar in terms of behavior to reasoning with external visual images. For example, mental images can be mentally rotated, and the larger the rotation, the longer it takes to turn them. Likewise, the time taken to imagine zooming in or out of a mental image is proportional to the change in scale. Subsequent neuroimaging studies also provided support for this view. They showed that mental imagery activates many of the same parts of the brain as viewing an external image, strongly suggesting that internal images are represented similarly to external visual images.

However, while most researchers now believe that mental images are not represented as propositions, they are not precisely pictures either. Typically, mental images are sketchy and contain less detail than an external graphic. They also include some degree of interpretation. In a study conducted in Canada, fifteen people were shown an outline of Texas rotated anticlockwise by 90 degrees and asked to memorize it. They were then requested to imagine the sketch and mentally rotate their image clockwise by 90 degrees. Next, they were asked to identify the 'familiar geographic form'. None could. Finally, they were asked to draw the rotated image on paper. More than half recognized it as Texas. This is because it is harder to reinterpret the mental image than the drawing because our memory of a visual image is not a photograph. We actually remember the effect of the image on the visual system, including the visual image's original interpretation, which is why our brain finds it challenging to reinterpret the image after mental rotation.

Mental images are powerful tools for scientific reasoning because they are linked to mental models, which scientists such as Wegener and Einstein used in their thought experiments. It's not only genius scientists who use mental models and imagery. Philip Johnson-Laird has persuasively argued that human reasoning is built around mental models. These are integrated representations of scenes or events constructed from what we perceive, remember or imagine. They are not propositional representations; instead, they are rich, structured representations frequently visualized and manipulated through mental images in working memory.

Carefully read the following sentences:

The fork is on the left of the plate.
The knife is to the right of the plate.
The salt is behind the knife.
The fork is in front of the pepper.
Where is the pepper relative to the salt?

How did you answer the question? Like me, you probably created a mental model of the objects' positions, updating this as you read each sentence. From this model, it is immediately apparent that the pepper is to the left of the salt. You almost certainly used a mental picture when constructing the model, with images of the various items and the surface they sit upon.

However, working memory has a severe limitation. Unlike long-term memory, working memory can only remember a few things at a time—somewhere between three and seven items. This means that mental models are necessarily simple. If I had asked you to imagine more things on the table, you would have found this cognitively overwhelming. Furthermore, mental models are concrete. When you mentally visualize a table setting with a knife, fork and plate, the relative position of the elements is fixed. Johnson-Laird has shown that we find it challenging to reason if more than one model is consistent with what we have been told. We tend to focus on a single model, ignoring other possible models.

The limited capacity of working memory is one reason graphics are so beneficial. They provide an external representation of a mental model, allowing us to reason with more complex models and keep track of multiple models. Graphics are also valuable because they can teach new visual languages, allowing us to imagine new types of mental models. Once a chemist has seen a chemical structural formula, they can use this notation to mentally picture the spatial arrangement of atoms in a molecule. Once a physicist has seen a Feynman diagram, they have a new way to visualize particle interactions in quantum mechanics.

VISUAL CULTURES OF SCIENCE AND MEDICINE

We have looked at the origins of modern science in the late European Renaissance and seen how the Scientific Revolution is inextricably associated with scientific drawings. Without illustrations, it would have been impossible for early scientists to share their observations of nature and human anatomy. They would have been unaware of the new kinds of animals and plants encountered by European explorers and the new worlds visible through the telescope and microscope. Scientific illustrations also allowed scientists to depict new experimental equipment and procedures. Geometric diagrams played a fundamental role in the mathematization of science. And, for many scientists, mental imagery was a powerful tool for understanding nature.

The use of graphics in early science was enabled by several factors. One was the introduction of paper and printing, which allowed scientific illustrations to be quickly and accurately reproduced for the first time. Equally important were the Renaissance's focus on first-hand visual experience and the technical expertise of its artists. Early scientific illustrations were typically a collaboration between scientists and artisans. Linear perspective, previously developed by artists and architects, provided the initial language for scientific graphics, allowing realistic representations of observations and equipment. As science progressed, more specialized languages evolved that highlighted relevant information. Still, fundamentally, scientific illustrations were a product of the drawing techniques invented by the Renaissance artists and technicians detailed in the preceding chapter.

Graphics were not only necessary for the birth of science in the Scientific Revolution. Changes in scientific culture have meant that they have become increasingly central to scientific practice. One of these changes was the introduction of the scientific journal. At the beginning of the Scientific Revolution, scientific journals did not exist. Printing meant that would-be scientists had access to the works of Greek and Roman authorities and to monographs such as those by Copernicus or Vesalius. However, publishing a book was a risky and expensive undertaking, and so handwritten letters remained a common way for scientists to communicate discoveries to their peers. For instance, the astronomer and scholar Nicolas-Claude de Peiresc had nearly 500 correspondents across Europe.

The first scientific academies and journals appeared in the middle of the seventeenth century. They quickly became the primary forums for the pursuit and communication of science. One of the first academies was the Royal Society of London. Created in 1662, the society recognized the importance of scientific graphics. Its founding document stipulated that it retain an official engraver, and the society's prestigious journal *Philosophical Transactions* included engraved plates (e.g., see Figure 4.6).

Lisa Best has charted the steady increase of graphics in *Philosophical Transactions* (see Figure 4.13). At first, about 15 per cent of articles contained scientific illustrations. By 1900, this had increased to nearly 90 per cent. One reason for this was the decreasing cost of graphics: we can see a sharp rise in the use of illustrations in the nineteenth century when new printing techniques were introduced.

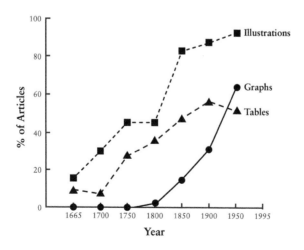

FIGURE 4.13   Lisa Best found a steady increase in the use of different kinds of graphics in the Royal Society of London's *Philosophical Transactions* journal.

Credit: Lisa A Best, (2006). Redrawn by Kadek Satriadi.

The articles in *Philosophical Transactions* were intended for scientists. During the Scientific Revolution, scientists and other intellectuals wrote for one another, not the public. This changed in the eighteenth century during the European Enlightenment. Directly following the Scientific Revolution, the Enlightenment was a time of radical inquiry. The scientific methods and critical analysis developed in the Scientific Revolution to analyze nature and the cosmos were now applied to philosophy and the study of government and society. Philosophers expounded on intellectual freedom and the use of reason in the search for progress and knowledge. Some argued that slavery and censorship were wrong, that religion was a social construct, and that a monarch's duty was to rule for the good of their subjects. Such ideas helped set the stage for the French Revolution, bringing the Enlightenment to a bloody end.

During the Enlightenment, intellectuals were no longer content to only talk to one another. They wanted to educate the literate public. Nothing epitomizes this desire more than the mammoth 28-volume *Encyclopédie, ou dictionnaire raisonné des sciences, des arts et des métiers* (*Encyclopedia, or a Systematic Dictionary of the Sciences, Arts, and Crafts*). Edited by Denis Diderot and Jean le Rond d'Alembert, the *Encyclopédie* was published between 1751 and 1765. Around 25,000 copies were sold, bringing science and technology to the educated middle class all over Europe.

Diderot and d'Alembert recognized the need for graphics when communicating science and technology to non-scientists, and the *Encyclopédie* contained more than 3000 illustrations. From this time on, graphics would be an essential component of science education.

Science education was also linked to education reform. During the nineteenth century, many countries introduced compulsory schooling, and there were heated battles over what should be taught. On the one hand, the traditionalists believed schools should continue to provide the humanist curriculum devised in the Renaissance: Ancient Greek and Latin, rhetoric, and Euclidean geometry. On the other hand, the new guard argued that everybody required a basic knowledge of science and scientific thinking. The new guard won the argument, and scientific graphics became more common in the classroom—not only in textbooks but also on wall charts and blackboards, two new tools that had been introduced to support mass education.

Graphics also play a central role in medicine and medical training. Contemporary medicine is inextricably linked to the life sciences. Our understanding of anatomy, the circulatory and nervous systems, and the cause of disease relies on science. As we have seen, illustrations were crucial in obtaining this understanding. The use of graphics in modern medicine is also built on traditions derived from the Middle Ages. Illustrated manuscripts detailing medical procedures, surgical instruments and medicinal plants were common then. This may be because medieval monasteries were responsible for both producing manuscripts and caring for the sick.

One variety of graphics that did not appear in medieval or Renaissance medical texts is illustrations designed to help doctors recognize different diseases. While there were illustrations of diseases and other medical conditions, these were of rarities and curiosities. No texts, for instance, systematically illustrated the typical appearance of different skin ailments. The first such pathological atlases did not appear until the end of the eighteenth century. But by the mid-nineteenth century, these, together with anatomical texts, had become an indispensable tool for medical practitioners (see Figure 4.14).

The introduction of pathological atlases was linked to the emergence of modern clinical medicine during the Enlightenment and a more scientific understanding of disease and evidence-based diagnosis. During the Renaissance, medical diagnosis was based on what the patient told the doctor about their condition and lifestyle. By the beginning of the nineteenth century, diagnosis relied on the physical examination of the patient using new medical practices such as listening to the patient's heart and lungs with a stethoscope. For the first time, doctors routinely performed autopsies after death to confirm their diagnosis. Medical education became less subjective and moved to practice-based training in hospitals where doctors studied anatomy and pharmacology as well as pathology.

In this chapter, we have focused on scientific and medical illustrations, as these were central to the development of early science and medicine. However, nowadays, scientists and medical practitioners also use many other types of graphics, such as tables, maps, graphs, photographs and scans.

For example, Best's analysis of graphic use in the *Philosophical Transactions* shown in Figure 4.13 reveals that tables have become more common. In 1665, about 10 per cent of articles contained them, which rose to about 50 per cent in 1900. The importance of printed tables to science and mathematics should not be underestimated. Printing allowed error-free reproduction of tables of observations such as those of the astronomer

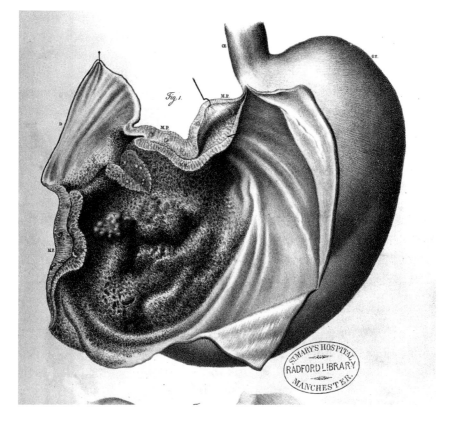

FIGURE 4.14   Illustration of a diseased stomach, from Jean Cruveilhier's *Anatomie pathologique* (*Pathological Anatomy*) (1829–42). One of the first comprehensive illustrated atlases of pathology, it contained about 230 folio plates and was published from 1829 to 1842 in forty instalments. Cruveilhier deliberately chose to use lithographic printing to make the work more affordable for medical students.

Credit: *Anatomie pathologique du corps humain, ou descriptions ... des diverses altérations morbides dont le corps humain est susceptible* / [J. Cruveilhier]. Wellcome Collection.

Tycho Brahe, and tables of logarithms and other mathematical functions used for calculation.

Best's analysis also shows a rapid rise in the use of scientific graphs after they first appeared in the middle of the eighteenth century. Again, the importance of charts to modern science cannot be overstated. They reveal patterns and anomalies that remain hidden when data is presented in tables.

In subsequent chapters, we will consider these different types of graphics. However, first let's turn our attention back to China. In Chapter 1, we saw that by 200 BCE, the Chinese were using a variety of information graphics. We also know that paper and woodblock printing were invented in China before making their way to Europe. Given this, we might expect the Chinese to have developed similar techniques to those employed in European technical and scientific drawings, perhaps before they appeared in the Renaissance.

To some extent, this is true. Since the eleventh century, the Chinese had printed books about technology, science and medicine. Many were illustrated (see Figure 4.15). Some Chinese illustrations employ techniques reinvented in the Renaissance: exploded views, transparent exteriors to show the inside of machinery, and component labeling. However, these techniques occur in only one or two books and are then forgotten.

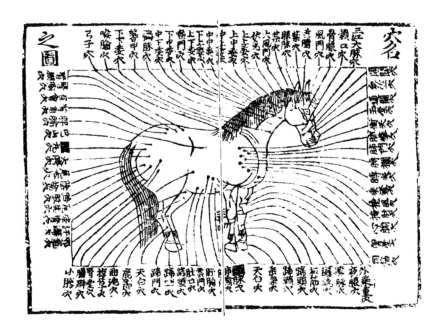

FIGURE 4.15   Reproduction of a drawing from a Chinese veterinary text, c. 1399, illustrating acupuncture points for the treatment of horses.

Credit: Copyright (© 2002) From *Celestial Lancets: A History and Rationale of Acupuncture and Moxa* by Gwei-Djen Lu, Joseph Needham. Reproduced by permission of Taylor and Francis Group, LLC, a division of Informa plc.

Unlike Europe, China did not develop a distinct tradition of technical drawing with specialized conventions and techniques. Text had primacy over illustrations. There was not the same focus on first-hand observation and geometric accuracy that drove Renaissance technicians and scientists to continuously improve the precision and effectiveness of their illustrations. While Chinese texts had images of human anatomy and medicinal plants, none were as detailed or precise as those of Vesalius or Fuchs and their successors.

I suspect that this difference between the visual cultures of Europe and China is part of the reason why China did not experience a Scientific Revolution or Industrial Revolution while Europe did. It is certainly not the whole story. Other factors such as greater respect for ancient authorities in China, and the absence of a merchant class and capitalist economy, are also important. Nonetheless, the differences reinforce the critical role that technical and scientific illustrations played in the invention of modern science and technology.

NOTES, REFERENCES AND FURTHER READING

A number of beautifully illustrated books showcase images and diagrams that have shaped modern science:

Barrow, John D. *Cosmic Imagery: Key Images in the History of Science*. The Bodley Head, 2008.

Ford, Brian J. *Images of Science: A History of Scientific Illustration*. The British Library, 1992.

Robin, Harry. *The Scientific Image: From Cave to Computer*. Harry N. Abrams Inc., 1992.

Chapter Introduction

Lynch, Michael. 'The Externalized Retina: Selection and Mathematization in the Visual Documentation of Objects in the Life Sciences.' *Human Studies* 11, no. 2 (1988). Quote is from 201–2.

The Rise of Science

The Scientific Revolution

Goodman, David. 'Europe's Awakening.' In *The Rise of Scientific Europe 1500–1800*. Hodder & Stoughton, 1991: 1–31.

Henry, John. *The Scientific Revolution and the Origins of Modern Science* (3rd ed.). Palgrave Macmillan, 2008: Chapters 1 and 2.

Wootton, David. *The Invention of Science: A New History of the Scientific Revolution*. Harper Collins, 2015: Chapters 1–3.

Copernicus's De revolutionibus orbium coelestium
Russell, Colin. 'Copernicus and His Revolution.' In *The Rise of Scientific Europe 1500–1800*. Hodder & Stoughton, 1991: 33–61.

Importance of Mathematics to the Scientific Revolution
Galilei, Galileo, and Maurice Finocchiaro. *Essential Galileo*. Hackett, 2008. The quote is from p. 183.
Henry, John. *The Scientific Revolution and the Origins of Modern Science* (3rd ed.). Palgrave Macmillan, 2008: Chapter 3.
Kossovsky, Alex Ely. *The Birth of Science*. Springer Nature, 2020: Chapter 17.
Wootton, David. *The Invention of Science: A New History of the Scientific Revolution*. Harper Collins, 2015: Chapter 5.

Mathematical Understanding of Ballistics
Büttner, J, P Damerow, J Renn, and M Schemmel. 'The Challenging Images of Artillery.' In *The Power of Images in Early Modern Science*. Birkhäuser Basel, 2003: 3–27.
Kossovsky, Alex Ely. *The Birth of Science*. Springer Nature, 2020: Chapters 18–22.

Role of Illustrations of Experimental Apparatus and Experiments
Henry, John. *The Scientific Revolution and the Origins of Modern Science* (3rd ed.). Palgrave Macmillan, 2008: Chapter 3.
Robin, Harry. *The Scientific Image: From Cave to Computer*. Harry N. Abrams Inc., 1992: Chapter 3.
Shapin, Steven. 'Pump and Circumstance: Robert Boyle's Literary Technology.' *Social Studies of Science* 14, no. 4 (1984): 481–520.
Wootton, David. *The Invention of Science: A New History of the Scientific Revolution*. Harper Collins, 2015: Chapter 5.

Vesalius's De humani corporis fabrica
Herrlinger, Robert. *History of Medical Illustration, from Antiquity to 1600*. Pitman Medical & Scientific Publishing, 1970: Vesalius.
Wootton, David. *The Invention of Science: A New History of the Scientific Revolution*. Harper Collins, 2015: Chapter 7.

Botanical Illustrations

Ford, Brian J. *Images of Science: A History of Scientific Illustration.* The British Library, 1992: Chapter 4.

Hentschel, Klaus. *Visual Cultures in Science and Technology: A Comparative History.* Oxford University Press, 2014: Section 6.1.

Kusukawa, Sachiko. 'Leonhart Fuchs on the Importance of Pictures.' *Journal of the History of Ideas* 58, no. 3 (1997): 403–27. The quote from Fuchs is taken from p. 411.

Morton, Alan G. *History of Botanical Science.* Academic Press, 1981: Chapters 3–5.

Robin, Harry. *The Scientific Image: From Cave to Computer.* Harry N. Abrams Inc., 1992: 24.

Zoological Illustrations

Ford, Brian J. *Images of Science: A History of Scientific Illustration.* The British Library, 1992: Chapter 3.

George, Wilma. 'Sources and Background to Discoveries of New Animals in the Sixteenth and Seventeenth Centuries.' *History of Science* 18, no. 2 (1980): 79–104.

The Microscope

Bardell, David. 'The Invention of the Microscope.' *Bios* 75, no. 2 (2004): 78–84.

Blevins, Steve M, and Michael S Bronze. 'Robert Koch and the "Golden Age" of Bacteriology.' *International Journal of Infectious Diseases* 14, no. 9 (2010): e744–e751.

Ford, Brian J. *Images of Science: A History of Scientific Illustration.* The British Library, 1992: Chapter 8.

The Telescope

Goodman, David. 'Crisis in Italy.' In *The Rise of Scientific Europe 1500–1800.* Hodder & Stoughton, 1991: 91–116.

Kossovsky, Alex Ely. *The Birth of Science.* Springer Nature, 2020: Chapter 26.

Wootton, David. *The Invention of Science: A New History of the Scientific Revolution.* Harper Collins, 2015: Chapter 6.

Visual Languages of Science
True to Nature vs. Photorealism

Daston, Lorraine, and Peter Galison. *Objectivity.* MIT Press, 2007: II Truth-to-Nature.

Evolution of Botanical Drawings

Ogilvie, Brian W. 'Image and Text in Natural History, 1500–1700.' In *The Power of Images in Early Modern Science*. Birkhäuser Basel, 2003: 141–66.

Saunders, Gill. *Picturing Plants: An Analytical History of Botanical Illustration* (2nd ed.). KWS Publishers, 2009.

Evolution of Anatomical Drawings

Galuzzi, Paolo. 'Art and Artifice in the Depiction of Renaissance Machines.' In *The Power of Images in Early Modern Science*. Birkhäuser Basel, 2003: 47–68.

Ghosh, Sanjib Kumar. 'Evolution of Illustrations in Anatomy: A Study from the Classical Period in Europe to Modern Times.' *Anatomical Sciences Education* 8, no. 2 (2015): 175–88.

Herrlinger, Robert. *History of Medical Illustration, from Antiquity to 1600*. Pitman Medical & Scientific Publishing, 1970: Leonardo, Vesalius.

Smith, Sean B. 'From Ars to Scientia: The Revolution of Anatomic Illustration.' *Clinical Anatomy* 19, no. 4 (2006): 382–8.

Visual Language of Geology

Oldroyd, David R. *Thinking about the Earth: A History of Ideas in Geology*. The Athlone Press, 1996: Chapters 2, 5 and 6.

Playfair, John. 'Biographical Account of the Late Dr James Hutton, FRS Edin.' *Earth and Environmental Science Transactions of the Royal Society of Edinburgh* 88, no. 3 (1805): 39–99. Published online by Cambridge University Press, 2013. The quote 'abyss of time' comes from p. 73.

Rudwick, Martin. 'The Emergence of a Visual Language for Geological Science 1760–1840.' *History of Science* 14, no. 3 (1976): 149–95.

Rudwick, Martin. 'Cuvier and Brongniart, William Smith, and the Reconstruction of Geohistory.' *Earth Sciences History* 15, no. 1 (1996): 25–36.

Chemical Structural Formula and 3D Models of Molecules

Hentschel, Klaus. *Visual Cultures in Science and Technology: A Comparative History*. Oxford University Press, 2014: Sections 1.7 and 3.2.

Klein, Ursula. 'The Creative Power of Paper Tools in Early Nineteenth-Century Chemistry.' In *Tools and Modes of Representation in the Laboratory Sciences*. Kluwer, 2001: 13–34.

Ritter, Christopher. 'An Early History of Alexander Crum Brown's Graphical Formulas.' In *Tools and Modes of Representation in the Laboratory Sciences*. Kluwer, 2001: 35–46.

Electrical Circuit Diagrams

Gregory, Richard Langton. *The Intelligent Eye.* Weidenfeld & Nicolson, 1970: Chapter 9.

Mishra, Punyashloke. 'The Role of Abstraction in Scientific Illustration: Implications for Pedagogy.' *Journal of Visual Literacy* 19, no. 2 (1999): 139–58.

Escaping Deadland

Techniques for Showing Motion

de Souza, José Marconi Bezerra, and Mary C Dyson. 'An Illustrated Review of How Motion Is Represented in Static Instructional Graphics.' Paper presented at First Global Conference on Visual Literacies: Exploring Critical Issues. Oxford, July 2007.

Galileo and Scheiner's Drawings of Sunspots

Tufte, Edward R. *Envisioning Information.* Graphics Press, 1990: Chapter 1.

Van Helden, Albert. 'Galileo and Scheiner on Sunspots: A Case Study in the Visual Language of Astronomy.' *Proceedings of the American Philosophical Society* 140, no. 3 (1996): 358–96.

Arrows

Horn, Robert E. *Visual Language: Global Communication for the 21st Century.* MacroVu Inc., 1998: Chapter 4.

Mijksenaar, Paul, and Piet Westendorp. *Open Here: The Art of Instructional Design.* Thames & Hudson, 1999: Chapter 3.

Tversky, Barbara, Jeff Zacks, Paul Lee, and Julie Heiser. 'Lines, Blobs, Crosses and Arrows: Diagrammatic Communication with Schematic Figures.' In *Theory and Application of Diagrams (Diagrams).* Springer, 2000: 221–30.

Thinking Visually

Scientific Imagery

Le Grand, HE. 'Is a Picture Worth a Thousand Experiments?' In *Experimental Inquiries.* Springer Netherlands, 1990: 241–70.

Miller, Arthur I. *Imagery in Scientific Thought: Creating 20th-Century Physics.* Birkhäuser, 1984: Chapter 3.

Oldroyd, David R. *Thinking about the Earth: A History of Ideas in Geology.* The Athlone Press, 1996: Chapter 11.

Shepard, Roger N. 'Externalization of Mental Images and the Act of Creation.' In *Visual Learning, Thinking, and Communication.* Academic Press, 1978: 133–89.

Visual Thinking: Object vs. Spatial Relations

Blazhenkova, Olesya, and Maria Kozhevnikov. 'Visual-Object Ability: A New Dimension of Non-Verbal Intelligence.' *Cognition* 117, no. 3 (2010): 276–301.

Kozhevnikov, Maria, Stephen Kosslyn, and Jennifer Shephard. 'Spatial Versus Object Visualizers: A New Characterization of Visual Cognitive Style.' *Memory & Cognition* 33, no. 4 (2005): 710–26.

Working Memory

For simplicity, I have not distinguished between short-term and working memory.

D'Esposito, Mark, and Bradley R Postle. 'The Cognitive Neuroscience of Working Memory.' *Annual Review of Psychology* 66 (2015): 115–42.

Goldstein, E Bruce. *Cognitive Psychology: Connecting Mind, Research and Everyday Experience*. Nelson Education, 2019: Chapter 5.

Postle, Bradley R. 'Working Memory as an Emergent Property of the Mind and Brain.' *Neuroscience* 139, no. 1 (2006): 23–38.

Mental Images

Pearson, Joel, and Stephen M Kosslyn. 'The Heterogeneity of Mental Representation: Ending the Imagery Debate.' *Proceedings of the National Academy of Sciences* 112, no. 33 (2015): 10089–92.

Reisberg, Daniel, and Deborah Chambers. 'Neither Pictures nor Propositions: What Can We Learn from a Mental Image?' *Canadian Journal of Psychology/Revue Canadienne de Psychologie* 45, no. 3 (1991): 336–52.

Reisberg, Daniel. 'Mental Images.' In *The Oxford Handbook of Cognitive Psychology*. Oxford University Press, 2013: 374–87.

Mental Models

Johnson-Laird, Philip. *How We Reason*. Oxford University Press, 2006: Chapter 2.

Visual Cultures of Science and Medicine

Letter Writing

Grayling, Anthony C. *The Age of Genius: The Seventeenth Century and the Birth of the Modern Mind*. Bloomsbury Publishing, 2016: Chapter 12.

Early Scientific Societies and Journals

Best, Lisa A. 'An Examination of Drawings in Philosophical Transactions (1665 to Present).' *International Journal of the Book* 3, no. 3 (2006): 45–54.

Jardine, Lisa. *Ingenious Pursuits: Building the Scientific Revolution*. Little, Brown & Co., 1999: Chapter 2.

Roberts, Gerrylynn K. 'Scientific Academies across Europe.' In *The Rise of Scientific Europe 1500-1800*. Hodder & Stoughton, 1991: 227–52.

The Enlightenment and the Encyclopédie

Merriman, John. *A History of Modern Europe: From the Renaissance to the Present* (4th ed.). WW Norton & Company, 2019: Chapter 9.

Use of Scientific Graphics in Education

Bucchi, Massimiano. 'Images of Science in the Classroom: Wallcharts and Science Education 1850–1920.' *British Journal for the History of Science* 31, no. 2 (1998): 161–84.

Carl, Jim. 'Industrialization and Public Education: Social Cohesion and Social Stratification.' In *International Handbook of Comparative Education*. Springer, 2009: 503–18.

DeBoer, George. *A History of Ideas in Science Education*. Teachers College Press, 1991.

Wylie, Caitlin Donahue. 'Teaching Nature Study on the Blackboard in Late Nineteenth-and Early Twentieth-Century England.' *Archives of Natural History* 39, no. 1 (2012): 59–76.

History of Pathological Illustrations

Meli, Domenico Bertoloni. *Visualizing Disease: The Art and History of Pathological Illustrations*. University of Chicago Press, 2018: Chapters 1–3, 6 and 7.

Spray, EC. 'Health and Medicine in the Enlightenment.' In *The Oxford Handbook of the History of Medicine*. Oxford University Press, 2011.

Importance of Printed Tables

Eisenstein, Elizabeth L. *The Printing Revolution in Early Modern Europe* (2nd ed.). Cambridge University Press, 2005: Chapters 2 and 7.

What Was Happening in China?

Bray, Francesca. 'Introduction: The Powers of Tu.' In *Graphics and Text in the Production of Technical Knowledge in China*. Brill, 2007: 1–79.

Golas, Peter J. *Picturing Technology in China: From Earliest Times to the Nineteenth Century*. Hong Kong University Press, 2014: Introduction, Chapters 3 and 6, and Closing Remarks.

Olerich, Rebecca L. *An Examination of the Needham Question: Why Didn't China Have a Scientific Revolution Considering Its Early Scientific Accomplishments?* MArts Thesis. City University of New York, 2017: Chapters 1 and 3.

CHAPTER 5

Mapping the World

W E NOW TURN OUR attention to another type of information graphic: the map. Maps are an indispensable tool for visualizing spatial data, such as the spread of COVID-19. They shape how we think about space and geography, about our place in the world. More than this, they appeal to our imagination: they entice and encourage us to daydream about foreign countries and the people who live there.

Not only do maps of the real world draw us in, but so do maps of imaginary worlds. How could you not be enthralled by the map of Middle Earth in the *Lord of the Rings*, or the Marauders Map in the Harry Potter movies? And it's not only readers of fiction who are captivated by maps of imaginary lands, but also the writers. The author Orson Scott Card writes: 'I began this book [*The Lost Gate*] as I have begun so many others—with a map. It was 1997. I doodled it and then began naming the places in it ...'

It is hard to imagine writing a book after doodling a bar chart or line graph. Maps have a unique power to engage our imagination and instill belief in an imaginary world.

But before we get too enthusiastic about how delightful maps are, there is a dark side to their power. Think of the Berlin Conference that took place from November 1884 to February 1885, when German chancellor Otto von Bismarck invited representatives from Europe, the United States and the Ottoman Empire to divide up Africa 'in accordance with international law'. Indigenous Africans, of course, were not invited to the meeting. Maps were central to this plundering of a continent and the division of spoils (see

DOI: 10.1201/9781003507642-6

FIGURE 5.1   In 1885, leaders from Europe, the United States and the Ottoman Empire met to partition Africa. The meeting was dominated by a map of Africa, 5 meters high, on which the borders of the new colonies would soon be drawn.

Credit: Illustration from the *Allgemeine Illustrierte Zeitung*. Wikimedia commons: Kongokonferenz.jpg.

Figure 5.1). Lines of longitude and latitude, rivers and mountain ranges shown on European maps became the borders separating the new colonies.

So how did maps become so important? When did they become widely used? While we saw in Chapter 1 that humans have been drawing maps for thousands of years, it was not until the Renaissance that map use really took off. Between 1400 and 1472, just before the first printed map appeared, there were only a few thousand maps in circulation. This number rose to 56,000 by 1500, and by 1600, millions of maps were in circulation. By the end of the Renaissance, maps were widely available and a source of pleasure to the educated elite. The English writer Richard Burton records in *The Anatomy of Melancholy* (1652) that:

> *Methinks it would please any man to look upon a geographical map … What greater pleasure can there now be, than to view those*

elaborate maps of Ortelius, Mercator, Hondius, &c.? To peruse those books of cities, put out by Braunus and Hogenbergius?

Maps also had more pragmatic uses, such as navigation at sea, property management and military campaigns. Map use continued to increase, and by the beginning of the twentieth century, they had become pervasive in Western culture. They were found at school in the form of wall maps and in atlases, and in newspapers and other popular media. They had become an indispensable tool for wayfinding; atlases and street maps were found in most homes. Unlike technical and scientific drawings, maps were used and understood by virtually everyone. In this and the next chapter, we will explore how and why this happened.

MAPPING THE WORLD: EUROPEAN EXPLORATION AND EXPLOITATION

Modern maps, with their focus on physical geography and political boundaries, were an invention of the Renaissance. They reflect a profound change in European understanding of space and geography, and a worldview very different from that of the Middle Ages.

Medieval world maps, known as mappae mundi, look nothing like modern maps. The largest and most famous mappa mundi is the Hereford Mappa Mundi (see Figure 5.2). Made in about 1290, it shows the three continents of the inhabited world known to Europeans at that time—Europe, Africa and Asia—arranged in a T-shape surrounded by ocean. Like most medieval maps, east is at the top—that is why we use the word 'orientation' to refer to the direction of a map, as 'orientem' is Latin for 'east'. This means Asia is above Africa and Europe. The Mediterranean, which runs vertically, separates Europe on the left from Africa on the right. The Nile separates Africa from Asia, and the Don divides Europe from Asia. In a rather significant oversight, the mapmaker has switched the names of Europe and Africa.

The Hereford Mappa Mundi reflects a deeply Christian understanding of the world. At the top of the map, Christ presides over the Last Judgment: sinners are shown entering Hell to the right, while the saved are received in Heaven to the left. Directly below is the walled Garden of Good and Evil. This is depicted as a circular earthly paradise in which Adam and Eve can be seen taking the forbidden fruit. Jerusalem is at the very center of the map, with Christ's crucifixion shown immediately above. The map is

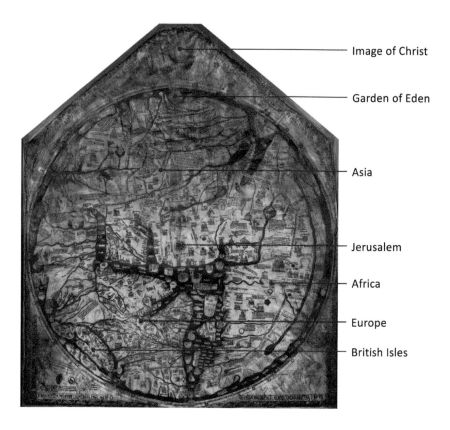

Image of Christ

Garden of Eden

Asia

Jerusalem

Africa

Europe

British Isles

FIGURE 5.2   The thirteenth-century Hereford Mappa Mundi. Measuring 1.3 meters by 1.6 meters, it is the product of a profoundly Christian worldview.

Credit: © Hereford Cathedral.

liberally covered with text and drawings, many of which illustrate creatures and beliefs from Greek and Roman authorities, such as satyrs and what might be a rhinoceros.

The Hereford Mappa Mundi shows how medieval Europeans saw their place in the world: in the present, past and future. The map bears only a loose relationship to actual physical geography. Its medieval maker did not wish to show the precise location and shape of cities, rivers, countries or continents. Instead, like the cosmological diagrams of the Mesoamericans and Indigenous Australians, it is intended to provide a richer, more complete explanation of the world, one that explicitly encodes the cultural and religious beliefs of the mapmaker.

Our maps owe far more to ancient Greek cartography than medieval mappae mundi. Europeans became reacquainted with the geographical knowledge of the Greeks when a copy of *Geographia* (*Geography*) was brought to Florence in 1397. *Geographia* had been written in the second century by Claudius Ptolemy. A Greek living in the great Roman city of Alexandria in Egypt, his writing was built upon a long tradition of Greek cosmological thinking. *Geographia* is a mapmaker's manual. Ptolemy describes how the Earth is a sphere and provides an estimate of its circumference. He explains how to specify locations on the Earth's surface using latitude and longitude.

Ptolemy also describes map projections. Like linear perspective or parallel projections, map projections depict a three-dimensional shape—in this case, the surface of the Earth—on a flat surface such as a piece of paper. He compares terrestrial globes with flat maps, and points out the inherent difficulty of projecting the Earth's curved surface onto a flat surface without distortion. He describes and recommends two map projections of his own invention, both of which resemble an unfolded cone with the top cut off.

Most of *Geographia* is devoted to the geography of the Roman world. Ptolemy describes the shapes of land and seas and gives the latitude and longitude of 8000 places in Eurasia and northern Africa. As previously discussed, this detailed written description was provided so the reader could draw their own maps directly from the text without the need for error-prone manual copying of any associated maps. While we do not definitively know if Ptolemy originally included maps in *Geographia*, most scholars now believe he did not.

Geographia was one of the earliest printed books. It was first printed without maps in 1475, then two years later with maps (see Figure 5.3). Over the next three centuries, more than fifty editions were published. They had a profound impact on Renaissance cartography.

However, while translations of *Geographia* provided the theoretical foundation for Renaissance cartography, its development and acceptance was linked to the practices of Renaissance architects and engineers. Leon Battista Alberti, Leonardo da Vinci and Albrecht Dürer explored new ways of representing landscapes and cities using panoramas, bird's-eye views and plans (see Figure 3.2). Italian military engineers, in particular, helped drive the use of maps. During the sixteenth century, they were hired throughout Europe by rulers who wished to modernize their fortifications. Once employed, they taught the local military and nobility how to read and use

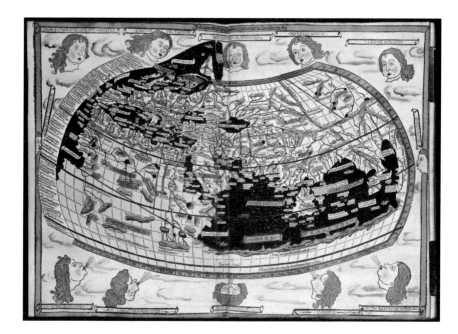

FIGURE 5.3   World map from a copy of Ptolemy's *Geographia* made in 1482. In addition to this overview map, *Geographia* contained twenty-six more detailed regional maps.

Credit: akg-images.

measured plans as they constructed these new defenses. These mapping skills were then deployed for non-military uses.

European exploration and the increasing use of nautical charts to navigate the open sea were other drivers of Renaissance cartography. The so-called 'Age of Exploration' had its origins in the late Middle Ages. At this time, the Mediterranean was a multicultural mosaic of different empires. Muslims, Jews and Christians traded and mixed together, especially in the Iberian Peninsula, most of which was part of the Islamic Empire. The pre-eminent sea power of the Mediterranean was Venice. It had grown from its humble beginning as a cluster of fishing villages built on stilts to a rich and mighty seaport connecting Europe with the Byzantine Empire and the Arab trade routes. Through these trade routes, highly prized goods from Asia, such as spices, silk and porcelain, made their way to Europe. This is probably also how the magnetic compass made its way to the Mediterranean.

By the late thirteenth century, the magnetic compass was being used by Mediterranean sailors. Before then, ships had generally hugged the coastline. There was no need for nautical charts, as written or oral itineraries, occasionally supplemented by drawings of coastal features, were all that were required for navigation. The compass enabled a new kind of navigation in which a ship sailed directly to its destination by following a constant bearing with respect to the needle. It permitted ships to sail directly between ports, out of sight of land and away from shallow water, dangerous shoals and pirates. This new kind of navigation was supported by an innovative type of map: the portolan chart.

Drawn on vellum with colored ink, portolan charts are designed for the seafarer. They show coasts and headlands in detail, and placenames are written perpendicularly on the interior side of the coastline to keep the seaward side clear. They are the first map known to contain an explicit scale. But the defining feature of the portolan chart is the crisscrossing lines called rhumb lines that radiate from compasses drawn on the map's perimeter. With these, the map reader can immediately see the correct compass bearing for travel between ports, islands and other destinations on the map.

Portolan charts were first used for sea travel in the Mediterranean (see Figure 5.4). They were then used to record discoveries in Africa, America, Asia and the Pacific as European ships sailed further afield in the early Renaissance. This exploration began with the Portuguese and the Spanish, who had recently freed themselves from Muslim control.

During the fifteenth century, the Portuguese systematically explored the western coast of Africa. Voyage after voyage set sail, each going a little

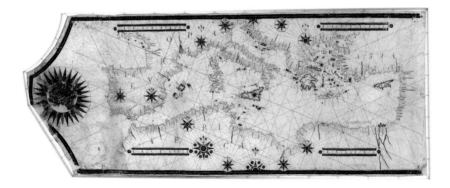

FIGURE 5.4   A sixteenth-century portolan chart of the Mediterranean Sea. The crisscrossing lines show the sailor the compass bearing to reach their desired destination.

Credit: Library of Congress, Geography and Map Division.

further, each claiming a little more of the African coast for Portugal. When an expedition returned, new information was integrated into official charts. Exploration was highly lucrative—the Portuguese ships returned home laden with gold and enslaved Africans. The Portuguese were building a global empire, one built on seaborne trade.

In 1487, Bartolomeu Dias sailed from Portugal. Blown off course by a massive storm, he rounded the southern tip of Africa, becoming the first European to see the Indian Ocean. He had made the unexpected and momentous discovery that Ptolemy was wrong (see Figure 5.3): Africa was not joined to a large southern continent. Recognizing the implications, Vasco da Gama set sail in 1497 to find a way to Asia. After rounding Africa, he was guided by Arab pilots from Mozambique to the west coast of India. Soon, with the aid of Arabian charts, Portuguese ships were supplying Europe with spices from the small group of Indonesian islands known as the Moluccas or 'Spice Islands'. Venice went out of business, while the Portuguese rapidly accumulated wealth and power by providing Europe with pepper, cloves, nutmeg and mace.

Maps based on *Geographica* were extended and modified to include these new findings. Clearly, Ptolemy had not known everything. But his authority was about to take an even larger blow. In 1492, Christopher Columbus set sail with three ships. Hired by the Spanish court to find a new sea route to Asia, he mistakenly believed that he could reach his destination after only a few months at sea by sailing westwards from Europe rather than around the bottom of Africa, then eastwards. Columbus would have seen maps based on Ptolemy's *Geographia* printed a few years earlier, which promulgated two significant errors made by Ptolemy. The first was to underestimate the Earth's circumference; the second was to overestimate the width of Asia. These fueled Columbus's conviction and convinced his Spanish backers that Japan was less than 5000 kilometers to the west of Spain. In fact, it is more than four times this distance, far further than Columbus could have sailed without taking on more supplies. Luckily for the explorer, a vast, totally unexpected continent blocked his way. He made landfall in the West Indies after two months at sea. Columbus had arrived in America, though he never realized this—for the rest of his life, he believed he had reached Asia.

Then, in 1522, the world was circumnavigated. The epic sea voyage began in 1519, soon after America had been recognized as a new continent. While the expedition was Spanish, it was led by a Portuguese explorer,

Ferdinand Magellan. He had convinced the king of Spain, Charles V, that sailing westwards around the tip of South America would provide a faster route to Asia and the Moluccas than the Portuguese route around Africa. Like Columbus, Magellan based this on Ptolemy's miscalculations of the Earth's circumference and the size of Asia.

In just three decades, the voyages of da Gama, Columbus and Magellan enlarged the worldview of Renaissance Europe. Europeans now had a direct sea route to Asia, and they had learned of a vast new continent and successfully circumnavigated the Earth. Ironically, while cartography played a decisive role in this early European exploration, it was because of errors in early maps and globes. If these had not severely underestimated the distance between Europe and Asia, neither Columbus nor Magellan would have set sail.

The first world maps showing these new discoveries used map projections based on those of Ptolemy. We can see this on the world's most valuable map (see Figure 5.5)—the US Library of Congress bought the map, which has been called the birth certificate of America, for US$10 million in 2003. It was published in 1507 by Martin Waldseemüller and was the first map to name America, showing it as a separate landmass. Waldseemüller based his map on Ptolemy's second projection (also used in Figure 5.3). However, Ptolemy's projection was designed to show the Roman world, not the more extensive world of da Gama and Columbus. Waldseemüller had to increase the map's width to incorporate America, while the bottom of Africa extends below the rest of the map. The result is profoundly unsatisfying and led to considerable distortion on the edges of the map.

Navigators were also running into problems with portolan charts. Perfectly adequate for the Mediterranean, they distorted distances and angles for regions spanning large differences in latitude. This meant they could not be used to reliably compute bearings for the longer voyages that sailors were now making when crossing the Pacific or Atlantic.

Globes of the Earth were one way of showing the new discoveries without distortion, and these were popular among the rich. However, they were expensive to make, bulky to store, and it was impractical to make them large enough to show sufficient detail for navigation. A new map projection was required, one that could show the entire world on a flat piece of paper but which did not distort the shape of continents too much; one that, like the portolan chart, allowed sailors to compute the bearing to their destination.

FIGURE 5.5 *Universalis cosmographia secundum Ptholomaei traditionem et Americi Vespucii aliorumque lustrationes (The Universal Cosmography According to the Tradition of Ptolemy and the Discoveries of Amerigo Vespucci and Others)*. Published in 1507 by Martin Waldseemüller, this is the first map to name America and show it as a separate landmass.

This problem perplexed Renaissance mapmakers. Many different map projections were devised, but it was not until 1569 that Gerard Mercator solved the problem by inventing the projection that now bears his name. In 1569, he published a massive, wall-mounted world map engraved on eighteen sheets (see Figure 5.6). The map used a rectangular grid of meridians (lines showing longitude) and parallels (lines showing latitude). The actual distance between meridians is greatest at the equator, then decreases until they meet at the north and south poles. However, the meridians remain the same distance apart on Mercator's map, regardless of latitude. This means the horizontal scale of Mercator's map increases as you move away from the equator. The clever part of Mercator's projection was to also increase the vertical scale away from the equator so that the vertical and horizontal scales remain equal. This is why the parallels on the map are further apart as you move north or south from the equator, even though they are actually evenly spaced apart. By fixing the vertical scale to the horizontal scale, Mercator ensured that the local region around each point retained its shape, as the scale was the same in all directions. Even better, his projection guaranteed that a straight line drawn between two locations on the map gave the correct bearing to travel between them. He had solved the problem of how to draw a nautical chart that always showed rhumb lines as straight lines no matter how large the region covered by the chart.

Mercator invented his map near the end of the Renaissance. By this time, maps of the world looked very much like modern maps. The differences between Mercator's map and the Hereford Mappa Mundi, made less than three centuries earlier, are profound.

The first noticeable change was the method of production: the Mappa Mundi was hand-drawn, while the map of Mercator's was a print from a finely etched copperplate. Unlike the Mappa Mundi, Mercator's map could be accurately reproduced and widely distributed.

Another obvious difference was that by the time of Mercator, Europeans knew much more about Earth's geography; only the North Pole and southern regions remained uncharted. A more subtle change was that Mercator allowed his map to contain empty white space, exposing the limits of his knowledge. A more scientific viewpoint had emerged in cartography. Maps were permitted to include unfilled areas and unfinished coastlines and clearly display the current limitations of geographic knowledge.

More fundamentally, the shape and placement of the geographic features shown on Mercator's map correlated to their actual form and location. In contrast, the relationship between elements on the Mappa Mundi and

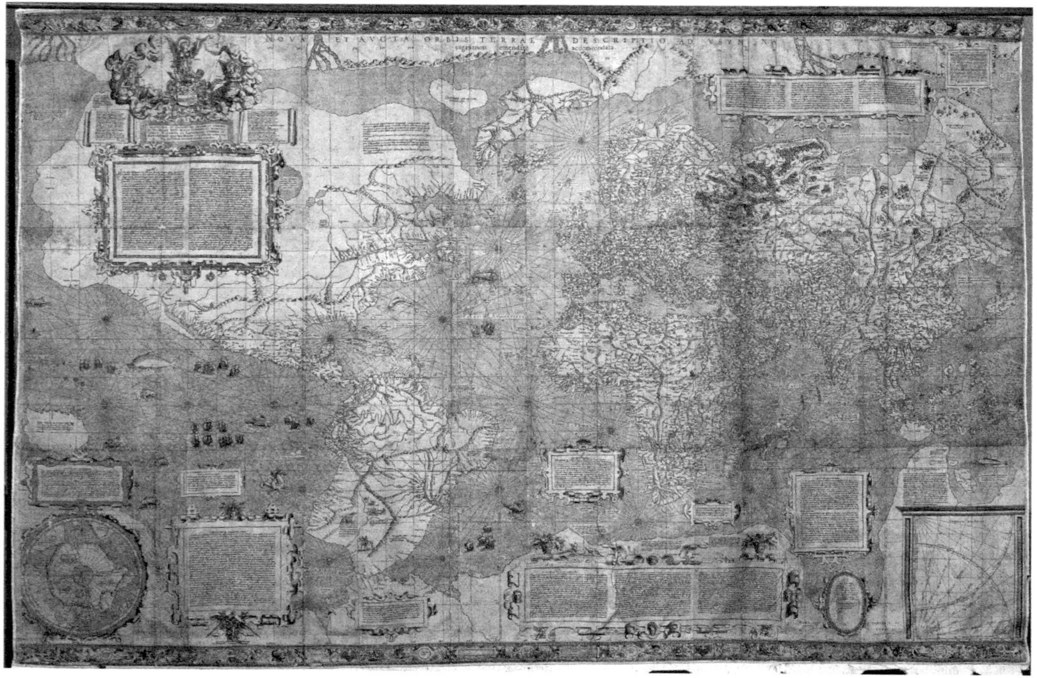

FIGURE 5.6 Gerard Mercator's world map from 1569 showcased his new map projection. His map is based on the observations of Renaissance explorers. However, the geography of the north polar region (shown as an inset in the bottom left corner) is based on the writings of a fourteenth-century monk. The monk claimed to have sailed to the North Pole and discovered it was a circular landmass broken into quarters by sea passages.

Credit: Bibliothèque Nationale de Cartes et Plans. Paris, France. Photo © Tom Graves Archive/Bridgeman Images.

the geographic features they represented was looser and more schematic. Mercator used well-defined geometric rules to project locations on the Earth to positions on the map. The parallels and meridians running across the map revealed this mapping, allowing viewers to determine the latitude and longitude of each feature shown on the map, and thereby its position on the Earth's surface.

Another critical difference was that the objects and features shown on Mercator's map were synchronous in time. The Hereford Mappa Mundi mixed locations from the past, present and future to tell the story of Christianity and Christian Europe. By the time of Mercator, Renaissance mapmakers distinguished between current and historical geography. A map only showed features from the same period in time. This is not to say that historical geography was unimportant in the Renaissance. Interest in the ancient Greek and Roman worlds meant maps of ancient Rome were extremely popular, as were historical maps of the Holy Land. What was different was that a map was now implicitly understood to be a geographic snapshot taken at a particular point in time.

These differences reveal a transformation in the way mapmakers and map-readers thought about space and place. In the Middle Ages, the map was feature-centered, focused on cities and other objects of interest: the space between these was not of interest. Furthermore, the map had a carefully chosen and meaningful center: Jerusalem. By the end of the Renaissance, latitude and longitude specified an object's position in a uniform, abstract space. The focus was on how the map projection transformed the Earth's surface onto the map. No location was more important than any other, and geographic space was the fundamental entity being mapped. Modern cartography had arrived.

THE IMPOSSIBLE DREAM: THE PERFECT MAP PROJECTION

Notwithstanding its benefits for navigation, Mercator's map projection has two considerable drawbacks. The scale varies across the map, and regions at high latitude are disproportionately large: it is not even possible to show the north or south poles. Despite this, the Mercator projection has become *the* standard map projection. It is used on most maps, including those of Google. Because of the Mercator projection's deficiencies, many people still believe that Greenland is the same size as South America when, in fact, Greenland's surface area is only an eighth of South America's.

The fundamental problem facing all cartographers was identified by Ptolemy: there is no perfect map projection. It is impossible to flatten the

Earth's surface onto a piece of paper without introducing distortion. If you peel an orange, there is no way to flatten the peel without deforming or tearing it. Nonetheless, the quest for a better map projection continued long after Mercator invented his. Hundreds of map projections have been devised, each with advantages and disadvantages (see Figure 5.7).

After the Renaissance, mathematicians clarified the inherent limitations of map projections. They proved that it was impossible to preserve both the local shape of regions and their area. Mercator's projection maintains local shape but distorts area. Conversely, mathematicians and cartographers invented projections that kept the relative size of regions but distorted their shape. More recently, cartographers have vied to find the best compromise projection. These are the Goldilocks choice: they ensure that area distortion is not too bad and local shape distortion is also not too bad. Often, the map is elliptical rather than rectangular to reduce distortion at the poles.

The choice of map projection and the consequent distortion inevitably affects the reader's understanding. It also reflects the biases of the mapmaker. In 1973, the German historian Arno Peters introduced a new world map based on a projection that he claimed removed the Euro-bias of Mercator's projection. His projection preserved areas, thereby increasing the size of the tropical regions, where most developing countries lay, relative to the temperate zones, where most developed nations lay. The media and progressive political and religious organizations, including UNESCO, immediately championed his map.

The response from the traditional cartographic community, however, was scathing. One leading cartographer claimed that Peters's map stretched the landmasses to 'look like wet, ragged long winter underwear hung out to dry on the Arctic Circle'. Peters's case was not helped by the fact that his projection was not as novel as he claimed. It turned out to be a rediscovery of the James Gall projection invented more than a century earlier.

Nonetheless, Peters's essential argument is well made. The choice of map projection is one of the more insidious ways in which our worldview is shaped. The Mercator projection does inflate the size of temperate countries relative to tropical countries, implicitly increasing their importance. In 1989, the Committee on Map Projections of the American Cartographic Association released a resolution strongly advocating against the use of rectangular world maps, including the Mercator projection, because of the serious, erroneous conceptions they create. The take-home message is that the use of the Mercator projection should not be automatic. While it is familiar, unless you need to sail around the world, it is almost certainly not the best choice of map projection.

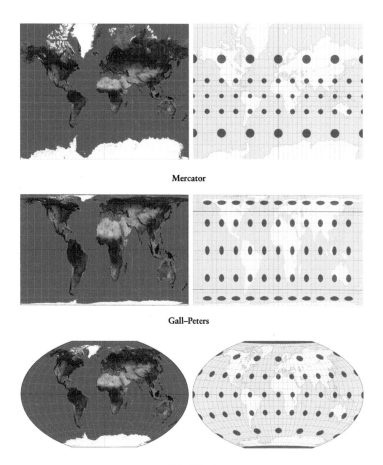

Mercator

Gall–Peters

Winkel Tripel

FIGURE 5.7   Sadly for cartographers, there is no perfect map projection. The Mercator projection shown at top left preserves the local shape but severely distorts area. The figure to its right reveals the distortion by overlaying the map with the projection of a grid of equally sized circles drawn on the globe. You can see that the Mercator projection does not change the shape of the circles but varies their size dramatically. The Gall–Peters projection in the middle was independently invented by James Gall in 1855 and Arno Peters in 1973. It preserves area but distorts shape. At the bottom is the Winkel tripel projection. Invented in 1921 by Oswald Winkel, this is a compromise projection that tries not to distort area or shape too much.

Credit: Wikimedia Commons. Left: Mercator projection Square (modified) CC BY-SA 3.0; Gall–Peters projection SW CC BY-SA 3.0; Winkel tripel projection SW CC BY-SA 3.0. All by Daniel R Strebe. Right: Mercator with Tissot's Indicatrices of Distortion (modified) CC BY-SA 4.0; Gall–Peters with Tissot's Indicatrices of Distortion CC BY-SA 4.0; Winkel tripel with Tissot's Indicatrices of Distortion CC0 1.0. All by Justin Kunimune.

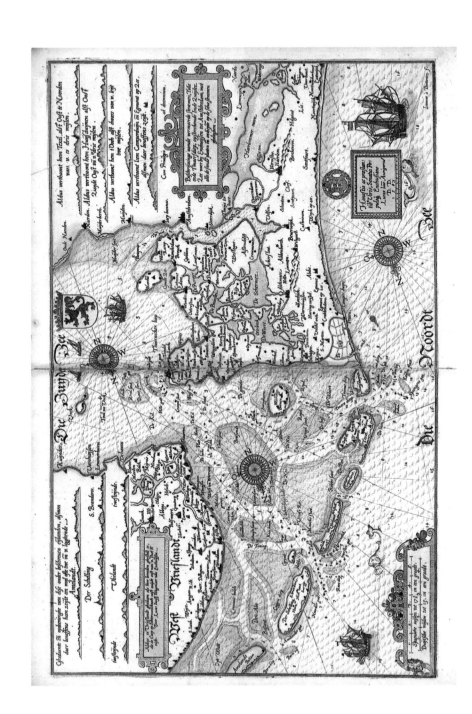

ALL AT SEA

In the fifteenth and sixteenth centuries, Portugal and Spain built empires spanning the world. The Dutch Republic, France and England soon followed. European powers colonized America, Asia, Africa and the Pacific and built global trade networks. European slave traders bought people in Africa and sold them to European colonizers in America to work in mines and plantations. Silver, tobacco, sugar, then cotton were brought back to Europe. The silver paid for spices, tea and other goods from Asia, while textiles, guns and ammunition manufactured in Europe were traded for enslaved Africans. Colonization of the Americas and the associated trade networks were the basis for the emergence of European nations as the world's first global superpowers.

All of this trade relied on faster and safer sea travel, which in turn relied on the development of new navigation techniques and more accurate navigation charts (see Figure 5.8). In the late fifteenth century, Portuguese sailors used portolan charts developed for navigation in the Mediterranean. They developed new ways of navigating out of sight of land. By measuring the height above the horizon of the Pole Star or the noonday Sun, they could compute how far north or south they had come: their latitude. This led to a new way of conceptualizing navigation. Previously, pilots had thought of their location in terms of routes, calculating their position by estimating the bearing and the distance they had traveled since leaving their last port. Celestial navigation encouraged pilots to think more spatially, to conceptualize location in terms of latitude and longitude and the ship's position on the Earth's surface. Portolan charts assisted this change in perception, and latitude began to be marked on them.

In the seventeenth century, longitude as well as latitude began to be shown on nautical charts. By this time, it was straightforward for sailors to determine their latitude at sea. Accurately determining their longitude,

FIGURE 5.8 (Facing page) Coastal chart from *Spieghel der zeevaerdt* (*Mariner's Mirror*). Written by the Dutchman Lucas Waghenaer and published in 1584, this was the first printed sea atlas. It contained nautical charts, profile views of the coast, and navigation instructions for western and north-western European waters. Waghenaer's sea atlas was translated into Latin and English and became known as the sailors' bible.

Credit: Kaart van Noord-Holland, Friesland, De Noordzee, De Zuiderzee en De Waddeneilanden. Uit de atlas 'Spieghel der zeevaerdt', 1584. Lucas Janszoon Waghenaer (kaartenmaker) Christoffel Plantijn (uitgever), Leiden / collectie Het Scheepvaartmuseum.

however, was a much more challenging task, one that would perplex navigators and scientists until the late eighteenth century. Until then, it was common to sail northwards or southwards to the desired latitude, then head east or west to reach the destination. The ship's speed would then be measured and used to estimate the distance traveled.

Finding a way to determine longitude was a problem that absorbed European scientists. In principle, it is easy to compute if you know the local time on the ship and the time at some fixed reference longitude, say that of Greenwich. A difference of 15 degrees in longitude gives rise to a time difference of one hour. A navigator could readily use the Sun to establish the local time; the difficulty was determining the reference time.

Two approaches eventually proved successful. The first was to measure the angular distance between the Moon and the Sun or some fixed star. The time at the reference location could then be found by looking up an astronomical table giving the time this event had been calculated to occur. The difficulty lay in predicting the Moon's path, and it was not until 1761 that the first accurate tables of lunar positions were published. By coincidence, 1761 is also when the world's first marine chronometer was built. The size of a fob watch, this was a highly accurate timepiece that was robust enough to withstand the rigors of sea travel. It provided a far more straightforward way of computing longitude: the navigator simply read the reference time from the chronometer.

Once sailors had access to reliable methods for computing their longitude at sea, they could sail directly to their destination, no matter how far away it was. This also meant they could accurately record the position of rocks, atolls and other navigational hazards they encountered on their way. Hence, nautical charts became increasingly trustworthy, further improving the safety of sea travel.

A study by ethnographer Edwin Hutchins provides an insight into the crucial role charts play in nautical navigation. He spent four months in the 1980s studying navigation practices on the US Navy vessel *Palau*, discovering that navigation centered around a chart sitting on top of the chart table in the chart house. When navigating near the coast, the navigation team took the bearings of landmarks shown on the chart. This was called a 'fix'. They plotted a line on the chart for each landmark, indicating the ship's possible position based on its bearing. The intersection of these lines gave the ship's location. They then computed the ship's speed and trajectory from this and the previous fix, and calculated the probable position of the vessel at the following two fixes. These were recorded on the chart, and the navigators checked for potential hazards.

Like engineering design, nautical navigation is an example of socially distributed cognition built around an information graphic. The chart is a shared representational and computational device. Without it, the navigation team would have been all at sea.

THE GOLDEN AGE OF DUTCH CARTOGRAPHY

Mercator and Waghenaer were both prominent figures in the Golden Age of Dutch Cartography, which ran from about 1570 up to the 1670s. As well as navigation charts and sea atlases, Dutch mapmakers fashioned large wall maps for display in palaces, grand homes and public buildings. Very few of these wall maps have survived, though they can be seen in paintings from this period. They were chosen as backgrounds to emphasize the power and influence of the person sitting for the portrait, as well as that of their great seafaring nation, the Dutch Republic. In fact, it wasn't only the rich and powerful who had maps on their walls. Printed maps like the one shown in Figure 5.9 adorned the homes of the growing middle class of traders and shopkeepers too.

Mapmakers also printed sumptuous atlases for the wealthy. Highly revered and expensive, these cost about the same as a portrait by a fashionable painter like Rembrandt. One of the first atlases, produced by Mercator, comprised 107 maps and was published shortly after the mapmaker's death in 1594. The front cover depicted the Titan Atlas from Greek mythology, who was condemned to carry the world upon his shoulders. This is why we now call a collection of maps an 'atlas'.

The Golden Age of Dutch Cartography was intimately tied to the Golden Age of Dutch Painting. Painters were regularly employed to color maps, and some artists were also mapmakers. The resulting maps were beautiful, decorated in the baroque style with ships, people and cityscapes. In turn, maps informed art. Dutch artists pioneered new genres: the panoramic landscape and the cityscape. Unlike Italian Renaissance paintings, which focused on biblical or classical narratives, geography was the subject of these paintings.

Mapmakers in the Dutch Golden Age of Cartography were not only concerned with geography but also made maps of the stars (see Figure 5.10). European astronomy had been revitalized by the translation of classical Greek and Roman astronomical and astrological texts from Greek or Arabic into Latin during the late Middle Ages. This included Ptolemy's *Almagest*, which gave the positions and magnitude of 1022 stars. Ptolemy's

FIGURE 5.9 The Dutch artist Johannes Vermeer frequently included images of maps in his artworks. In this painting, a map of the Netherlands takes pride of place on the wall behind the flirting couple.

Credit: *Officer and Laughing Girl*, c. 1657 Oil on canvas, 19 7/8 × 18 1/8 in. (50.5 × 46 cm) The Frick Collection, New York Photo: Joseph Coscia Jr. Copyright The Frick Collection.

catalog formed the basis for the first printed star map, which was created by Albrecht Dürer in 1515.

Over the next three centuries, celestial maps became increasingly accurate and detailed as the telescope revealed more of the night sky, and new stars came into view as explorers traveled further south. Mapmakers vied to produce ever more comprehensive sky atlases, with constellations taking centerstage in their sumptuous illustrations.

FIGURE 5.10 The cartographer Andreas Cellarius was born in Germany but moved to Holland, where he created one of the most beautiful celestial atlases ever made. The *Harmonia macrocosmica* (1661) contains twenty-nine double-page plates. The one shown here depicts the stars of the Northern Hemisphere.

Credit: Rare Books Division, J Willard Marriott Library, University of Utah.

During this time, there was a rapid growth in the number of constellations, as astronomers and mapmakers grouped the new stars. Many took this as an opportunity to reward their patrons and demonstrate their patriotism. It was not until 1922 that the International Astronomical Union removed the Scepter of the French King Louis XIV and the Harp of King George III of England from our night sky. Disappointingly, they also removed Bufo, the toad, and Limax, the slug. By then, constellations no longer had astronomical credibility: they were simply a convenient mechanism for partitioning the sky into regions.

FINDING YOUR WAY AROUND

However helpful nautical charts are for mariners, and celestial maps are for astronomers, for most of us, navigation on land is the primary reason we use maps. We rely on Google Maps, metro and railway maps, and shopping mall maps for navigation and wayfinding. Surprisingly, this is a relatively recent function for maps.

Until the late seventeenth century, written itineraries were all that were required for land travel. These listed the locations the traveler needed to pass through on the way to their destination. They gave overnight stops and travel distances or times, indicated river or frontier crossings, and provided advice on tolls and possible dangers. Itineraries were well suited to travel by foot or horse because travel was slow, with travelers covering no more than 50 kilometers a day. At this speed, there was ample time to hire local guides or to ask other travelers or locals encountered en route about how to reach the next stop on the itinerary.

Written itineraries were circulated in medieval times and then, with the arrival of printing, published in almanacs and road books. Renaissance almanacs and road books intended for the professional traveler did not include maps. One type of Renaissance book, however, in which we do find travel maps is that describing journeys made by pilgrims and explorers. These were primarily bought by armchair travelers.

One of the first printed books with illustrations was *Peregrinatio in terram sanctam* (*Pilgrimage to the Holy Lands*). Published in 1486, this describes the pilgrimage by Bernhard von Breydenbach from Germany to Jerusalem by way of Venice. At the time, Jerusalem was the ultimate travel destination for all European Christians. However, the trip was long and arduous, so few made the trip. Originally published in Latin and German, the book was an immediate bestseller, reprinted many times and translated into French, Dutch and Spanish. It featured fold-out tourist maps and city panoramas, one of which was a map of the Holy Land with a magnified view of the City of Jerusalem at its center. This map shows pilgrims disembarking from a ship, and the major cities and religious sites encountered on the way to Jerusalem. No wonder the book was popular—the reader could feel virtuous, taking in the sights of the Holy Land while remaining safe and comfortable at home.

Von Breydenbach's fold-out map shows Jerusalem and the Holy Land as if seen from an elevated position out to sea. This view was standard in early Renaissance city maps, with cities drawn as if observed from a high vantage point, such as the top of a hill. However, the disadvantage was that buildings at the front obscured those behind. Later in the Renaissance, mapmakers took a leap of imagination and elevated the viewpoint so that the reader had a bird's-eye view, allowing them to see the entire city in perspective.

An alternative to the bird's-eye view was the planimetric view, which showed the city directly from above. Renaissance engineers used these when designing fortifications. However, a bird's-eye view was generally preferred by Renaissance mapmakers for two reasons. First, it was difficult and time-consuming to accurately survey medieval towns, with their complex networks of small, winding streets. A bird's-eye view allowed the cartographer to focus on the prominent landmarks and fudge other details. Second, a bird's-eye view was readily understood by the intended audience, who were not trained engineers or architects and so unfamiliar with plans.

By the end of the Renaissance, however, this all began to change (see Figure 5.11). Survey data of cities was increasingly available, and the educated public had become more familiar with plans. Furthermore, cities such as Paris and London had become too large to show clearly via a bird's-eye view. They were now depicted using either a genuine planimetric view or a kind of oblique bird's-eye plan that showed the city from directly above but the sides of the buildings as if seen from a lower vantage point.

Maps of towns and cities were wildly popular during the Renaissance. Only thirty city maps or plans date from before 1490; a century later, there were too many to count. They were proudly displayed by monarchs and civil authorities, and were included in illustrated Bibles, news-sheets and books about travel, as well as atlases. Between 1572 and 1617, Georg Braun and Frans Hogenberg published the monumental *Civitates orbis terrarum* (*Atlas of Cities of the World*). Printed in six volumes, this contained 546 images of cities and towns from all over Europe. It sold well, and other printed collections of town views followed. These were intended for the armchair traveler and would not have been terribly helpful for actual travel as they contained multiple errors. In fact, it was not uncommon for the publisher to save costs by reusing the same illustration for different towns.

It was not until the end of the Renaissance that town maps began to be included in books intended for genuine travelers. These early tourist guidebooks contained bird's-eye views showing the locations of famous sights. However, at this time, tourism was only for the very rich and relied on the services of local guides. Mass tourism did not start until after the Napoleonic Wars. In 1836, John Murray III published the first modern

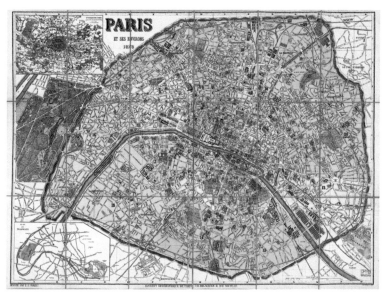

FIGURE 5.11   Early maps of towns and cities used a bird's-eye view. Then, as cities increased in size and the public became used to plans, they were shown as if seen from directly above, using a planimetric view. These two maps of Paris illustrate this change. The top map dates from 1615 and employs a bird's-eye view. The bottom map is from 1878 and shows a much larger Paris using a planimetric view.

Credit: Top: Musée Carnavalet, Histoire de Paris. Bottom: Library of Congress, Geography and Map Division.

guidebook, designed for the independent middle-class traveler. A plethora of guidebooks followed the *Murray Handbooks for Travellers*, as each generation reinvented the guidebook. But the *Baedekers*, *Blue Guides*, *Frommers*, *Michelin*, *Rough Guides* and *Lonely Planet* guides all had one thing in common: maps to guide the tourist.

As cities grew in size, maps became increasingly necessary. Catherine Delano-Smith and Roger Kain analyzed the number of new maps of London produced between 1550 and 1850. The increase is astounding. From 1550 to 1649, only seven maps are known to have been created: on average, a new map every fourteen years. But between 1800 and 1849, a new map was produced on average every three months. These new maps were needed not only by tourists and commercial travelers but also by residents, as London rapidly expanded because of the Industrial Revolution and an influx of workers from the countryside.

Travelers began using road maps for navigation in the late seventeenth century. Until then, written itineraries had been adequate because European travelers had been forced to use tracks and the remains of the old Roman road network, making travel slow and challenging, with plenty of time to ask for directions. During the mid-seventeenth century, European nations began modernizing road networks to transport goods, people and mail. Britain, for instance, built toll roads called turnpikes and post roads linking large towns and cities with London. The number of people traveling by stagecoach and on the postal service, which conveyed passengers as well as mail, multiplied rapidly.

In 1675, John Ogilby published *Britannia*, a road atlas for Britain (see Figure 5.12). Weighing a hefty 8 kilograms, it contained 200 pages of written descriptions and 100 sheets of strip maps detailing the post roads. Ogilby's strip maps were sophisticated graphical aids for navigation. Drawn as if on a scroll, they provided subtle hints on how to follow the strip map: the vertical strips were read from left to right, starting from the bottom. These maps showed the streams, bridges, intersections, towns (in plan) and landmarks (in profile) the traveler would encounter on the route. Hill symbols indicated an ascent, while an inverted hill indicated a descent. Distances were accurately surveyed and given in 'statute' miles rather than the variable-length local miles used in Britain at that time. Ogilby also used a uniform scale of 1 inch to the mile, as well as compass roses to show the direction of the road. The line type for the road indicated whether it was 'open' or 'closed'. This was important to know. Open roads were unfenced and unhedged, providing the traveler with room to skirt obstacles such as

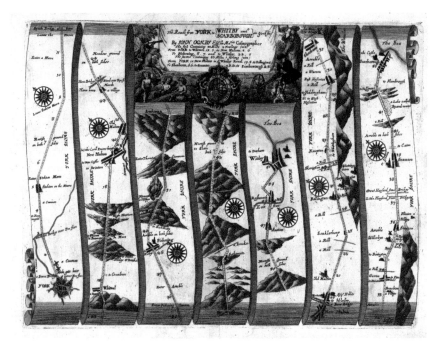

FIGURE 5.12   Some of the earliest road maps were strip maps showing individual routes. This strip map is a copy of that from *Britannia* (1675) by John Ogilby. It details the path from York to Whitby and Scarborough in York.

Credit: Map Collection, Local and Family History, Leeds Libraries.

mud, deep ruts and fallen trees, and to escape highway robbers. Closed roads, however, were dangerous and could be impassable after rain, snow or a storm.

The bulk of Ogilby's road atlas meant that it was impractical for travelers to carry it on the road. This, and the cost, limited his market to wealthy armchair travelers. However, individual sheets and pocket-sized editions of his strip maps were published a few years later. These proved popular and may have been used for wayfinding when traveling. Similar strip maps also appeared in Italy, Germany, France and the United States.

Two years after Ogilby published *Britannia*, John Adams published a very different kind of road map (see Figure 5.13). This showed a network of straight lines connecting 780 towns and cities. Locations were linked if they were joined by roads, with the mileage between them written on the link. While county boundaries and some topographical information (rivers and some forests and highlands) were shown in the background, the map was

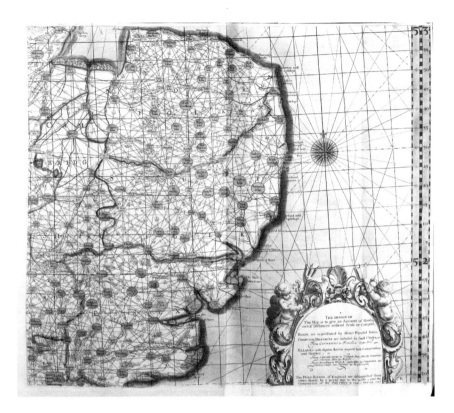

FIGURE 5.13   A number of early road maps showed the routes between cities and towns as an abstract network of lines. Above is detail from *Anglia totius tabula cum distantiis notioribus in itinerantium usum accomodata* (*A Map of the Whole of England with the More Important Distances Arranged for the Use of Travelers*), John Adams's verbosely named route map of the English post roads, published in 1677.

Credit: Royal Geographical Society.

designed to help travelers find the best route between two locations before travel. Adams's map was popular and widely imitated.

These two road maps exemplify the two main types of maps that have been developed for navigation. On the one hand, maps like that of John Adams, modern road maps and urban transit maps show complete networks of routes. These tend to be smaller-scale and allow the traveler to plan and compare different routes before travel. Depending upon the detail, they may also be used for wayfinding when traveling. Ogilby's strip maps, on the other hand, are an example of a route-specific map. These are a visual analog of the written itinerary. They are designed to help the traveler navigate along one particular route and are usually larger-scale maps providing detailed directions and showing landmarks. Each kind of map has advantages and disadvantages, which is why Google Maps, for instance, provides both.

However, it was not until the nineteenth century that travel maps for personal wayfinding really took off. This was driven by new, faster modes of transport. First came steam-powered trains, then a bicycle craze in the late nineteenth century. This was followed by electrified urban light railways, buses, automobiles, and airplanes in the early twentieth century. With these new modes of transport, it was no longer feasible to wander along a street or path and ask passersby for directions. Travelers required maps to plan their route and for navigation when taking it. Differences in technology meant that each mode of transport developed its own distinctive travel maps. For instance, maps for travel by bicycle showed elevation changes and warning signs for dangerous slopes and corners.

The level of abstraction also depended upon the transport mode. When the traveler had to personally navigate the route, maps tended to be more detailed and less schematic, such as the strip maps of Ogilby. When the traveler was being conveyed along the route, travel maps were more schematic, such as the network maps used to show railways.

The most famous schematic travel map is undoubtedly Harry Beck's map of the London Underground (see Figure 5.14). Early transit maps for the city showed train or subway lines overlaid on a map of London. However, as urban transport networks grew more extensive, the resulting maps became cluttered and less and less legible. To remedy this, graphic designers removed streets, parks and other topographical information. This process of simplification and abstraction culminated in Beck's 1933 map.

Beck's transit map has been copied worldwide, from Melbourne in Australia to São Paulo in Brazil. Eschewing all geographic features except the River Thames, the stations in Beck's map are evenly spaced along the transit lines. These are drawn using horizontal, vertical and diagonal segments. The lines are differentiated using color, and interchanges and stations are clearly signposted. Beck said that he was inspired by engineering diagrams of the sewage system.

Beck's map is ideal for planning a subway trip. However, this clarity comes at a price. The variable scale confuses even experienced subway travelers. They discount their own experience and will choose a route that appears shorter on the schematic map even though the actual distance and travel time are longer. This highlights why so many different types of maps have evolved. Just as for technical drawings, there is no single best

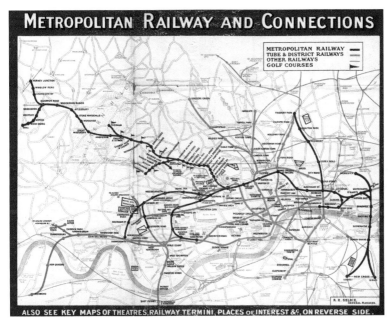

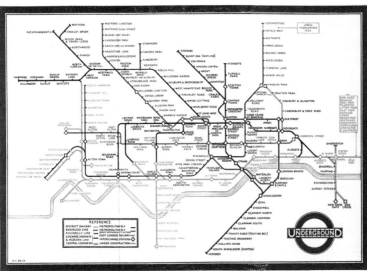

FIGURE 5.14   These two maps of the London Underground show the evolution of the modern urban transit map. When the Metropolitan Railway opened in 1863, the first maps, such as that at the top, showed the tracks printed over existing street maps. As the Underground grew more extensive, graphic designers removed topographical information to reduce clutter, showing only the lines and stations. This culminated in Harry Beck's 1933 transit map, shown at the bottom.

Credit: © TfL from the London Transport Museum collection.

representation. Different maps provide different cognitive benefits and so are suited to different tasks.

WHY DO MAPS WORK?

Before the start of the Renaissance, Europeans hardly used maps. But by the early twentieth century, maps had become indispensable tools for navigation at sea and on land. We saw in Chapter 1 that the ability to understand and create maps is widespread. It is so widespread that map understanding is conjectured to be a human universal. Why is it that maps work so well? Fundamentally, this is because they complement and enhance our innate ability for wayfinding: choosing a route and then following it.

Human wayfinding is built around a mental representation of space called a cognitive map. We use this to continuously track our position and orientation, providing an instinctive sense of direction and place.

Cognitive maps are not unique to humans. In fact, most of our knowledge is drawn from studies of rats whose ability to navigate in mazes has been tested for decades. These have revealed that humans and rats navigate in similar ways. Rats can learn a route through a maze as a series of turns: turn left, then right. Humans also navigate in this way: turn left, walk to the fountain, then turn right. Rats also use the relative position of visual landmarks and the destination or knowledge of the environment's geometry, such as the shape of the enclosure, to guide them to the destination. Likewise, humans use landmarks such as buildings and environmental geometry such as an encircling mountain range to determine where they are.

These different ways of navigating correspond to different reference frames. In an egocentric representation, the position and orientation of objects are specified relative to the self. Instructions for following a route and strip maps implicitly use an egocentric reference frame. On the other hand, allocentric representations encode the positions of objects relative to the environment. This may be in terms of landmarks, boundaries, or an external coordinate system such as latitude and longitude. Network travel maps, such as Adams's route map or urban transit maps, utilize an allocentric reference frame.

Our cognitive map is an allocentric representation. It allows us to plan a shortcut or a detour around an unexpected obstacle. However, it is not a precise map with a well-defined scale. Instead, it resembles a patchwork collection of sketch maps at different levels of scale and detail, loosely organized into a hierarchy. For instance, you probably have distinct cognitive maps for your neighborhood, the house or apartment in which you live, and each enclosed area in this house or apartment. These are stitched together, creating a sort of cognitive 'collage'. Each map contains a simplified, schematic representation of the space's shape and geometry, landmarks, paths, routes, and (some) angles and distances between these. And, like physical maps, our internal cognitive maps have a particular orientation.

Our cognitive maps exhibit various systematic distortions. People overestimate the distance between two locations if there is an obstacle in the way or if there are frequent intersections or turns between them. And, bizarrely, people's estimates of the distance between two locations need not be symmetric. When asked how far it is to a prominent landmark from a particular location, people tend to give a smaller value than when asked how far that location is from the landmark.

The hippocampus, located at the base of the brain, is responsible for creating cognitive maps. Striking evidence of this comes from London. In 2000, researchers compared the size of the hippocampus in London taxi drivers with those in non-taxi drivers. They found that the hippocampus was considerably larger in taxi drivers. In a subsequent study, they compared taxi drivers to bus drivers. Unlike taxi drivers, bus drivers follow the same route and so do not need to have a mental model of the complex network of London streets. Again, they found that the hippocampus was larger in the taxi drivers, providing compelling evidence that it plays a crucial role in storing their cognitive map of London.

The hippocampus is also responsible for storing memories of events we have experienced, indicating the primary role that spatial location plays as an index for such memories. That is why spatial indexing can be used as a memory aid. In the BBC TV series *Sherlock*, Holmes uses his 'mind palace' as a mnemonic prompt. He imagines a mansion and then places the things he wishes to remember at different locations in it. To recall an item, he simply pictures walking through the rooms to the object's location. This mental trick has been used for thousands of years—in ancient Greece and Rome, it was taught as part of the orators' art.

Remarkably, there is emerging evidence that the hippocampus is also used to encode maps of time; that is, the order in which events occur. It even stores maps of social status and other, more abstract concepts. In a real sense, spatial thinking underpins reasoning with abstract concepts like time and status.

Like other animals, active exploration of our environment is the most direct way we build a cognitive map. But, unlike other animals, we also use physical maps to inform our cognitive maps. Maps enhance our understanding of the layout of larger spaces such as our neighborhood, areas we can walk through but which can't be seen from a single vantage point. And maps are invaluable for understanding the geography of countries, continents and the entire world—regions that are simply too large for us to ever comprehend from personal travel.

Various studies have demonstrated that maps allow us to quickly build a cognitive map of a new space or refine an existing cognitive map. A Canadian study found that providing student nurses with a short tour and a floor plan of an unfamiliar hospital with a complex design gave them a better understanding of the layout than that of student nurses who had worked in the hospital for two years.

But maps do more than this. There is evidence that prior exposure to maps affects how children build a cognitive map and leads to more geometrically accurate representations. David Uttal writes how:

Maps provide a cognitive tool that helps children extend their reasoning about space in a new way. Over time children can internalize the tool and think about space in map-like ways, even if they are not looking at a map at the time.

As discussed in Chapter 1, other studies have suggested that maps encourage children to think about the geometry of space in terms of angles and distances. Physical maps reify our internal cognitive maps, making us aware of their existence and so allowing us to consciously reason about their content. More fundamentally, modern maps rely upon an abstract conception of space; they implicitly assume that space exists independently of the objects contained in that space. Maps encourage us to think about space as an entity in its own right, something that can be described and measured.

Put simply, maps enhance our ability to create accurate cognitive maps of our environment. It is therefore unsurprising that we use maps to understand the world's physical geography and for wayfinding. However, maps are now used for much more. In the next chapter, we will investigate the link between maps and the rise of the modern state.

NOTES, REFERENCES AND FURTHER READING

Maps are the superstars of the information graphics world. There are dozens of popular books about maps and mapmakers; old maps are valuable collector items; and the academic journal *Imago Mundi* is devoted to the history of maps. More has been written about maps than all the other kinds of information graphics put together.

It is impossible to write a history of maps without referring to the multi-volume History of Cartography Project, based at the University of Wisconsin. Begun by JB Harley and David Woodward four decades ago, it has shaped the modern understanding of the history of maps by broadening the definition of 'map' to include all 'graphic representations that facilitate a spatial understanding', and emphasizing the need to understand maps in terms of their social context.

Three books I relied on were:

Brotton, Jerry. *A History of the World in Twelve Maps*. Penguin, 2012.
Thrower, Norman JW. *Maps & Civilization: Cartography in Culture and Civilization* (3rd ed.). University of Chicago Press, 2008.
Wilford, John Noble. *The Mapmakers* (rev. ed.). Vintage, 2000.

Jerry Brotton's book provides an engaging and accessible introduction to the history of cartography, while the other two provide more academic but still very accessible introductions.

Chapter Introduction

Burton, Richard. *The Anatomy of Melancholy* (6th ed.). 1652. www.gutenberg.org/files/10800/10800-h/10800-h.htm. Quote pp. 3324–5.
Card, Orson Scott. *The Lost Gate*. Macmillan, 2011: Afterword.
Fischer, Hilke. '130 Years Ago: Carving Up Africa in Berlin.' *DW*, February 25, 2015. www.dw.com/en/130-years-ago-carving-up-africa-in-berlin/a-18278894
Pastoureau, Mireille. 'French School Atlases: Sixteenth to Eighteenth Centuries.' In *Images of the World: The Atlas through History*. McGraw-Hill, 1997: 109–35.
Patton, Jeffrey C. 'The American School Atlas: 1784–1900.' *Cartographic Perspectives* 33 (1999): 4–32.
Woodward, David. 'Cartography and the Renaissance: Continuity and Change.' In *The History of Cartography*. University of Chicago Press, 2007: vol. 3, Part 1, 3–24.

Mapping the World: European Exploration and Exploitation
Medieval Mappae Mundi

Brotton, Jerry. *A History of the World in Twelve Maps*. Penguin, 2012: Chapter 3.
Edson, Evelyn. *The World Map, 1300–1492: The Persistence of Tradition and Transformation*. JHU Press, 2007: Chapter 1.
Harvey, Paul DA. *Mappa Mundi: The Hereford World Map*. Hereford Cathedral & The British Library, 1996.
Woodward, David. 'Medieval Mappaemundi.' In *The History of Cartography*. University of Chicago Press, 1987: vol. 1, 286–370.

Ptolemy's Geographia

Brotton, Jerry. *A History of the World in Twelve Maps*. Penguin, 2012: Chapter 1.

Thrower, Norman JW. *Maps & Civilization: Cartography in Culture and Civilization* (3rd ed.). University of Chicago Press, 2008: Chapters 2 and 5.

Role of Renaissance Architects and Engineers

Buisseret, David. *The Mapmakers' Quest: Depicting New Worlds in Renaissance Europe*. Oxford University Press, 2003: Chapters 2 and 5.

Portolan Charts

Astengo, Corradino. 'The Renaissance Chart Tradition in the Mediterranean.' In *The History of Cartography*. University of Chicago Press, 2007: vol. 3, Part 1, 174–262.

Campbell, Tony. 'Portolan Charts from the Late Thirteenth Century to 1500.' In *The History of Cartography*. University of Chicago Press, 1987: vol. 1, 371–463.

Nicolai, Roel. *The Enigma of the Origin of Portolan Charts: A Geodetic Analysis of the Hypothesis of a Medieval Origin*. Brill, 2016.

Portuguese and Spanish Exploration

Alegria, Maria Fernanda, Suzanne Daveau, João Carlos Garcia, and Francesca Relaño. 'Portuguese Cartography in the Renaissance.' In *The History of Cartography*. University of Chicago Press, 2007: vol. 3, Part 1, 975–1068.

Brotton, Jerry. *Trading Territories*. Reaktion Books, 1997: Chapters 2 and 4.

Renaissance Maps of the World

Brotton, Jerry. *A History of the World in Twelve Maps*. Penguin, 2012: Chapters 5–7.

Thrower, Norman JW. *Maps & Civilization: Cartography in Culture and Civilization* (3rd ed.). University of Chicago Press, 2008: Chapter 5.

Differences between Medieval and Renaissance World Maps

Edson, Evelyn. *The World Map, 1300–1492: The Persistence of Tradition and Transformation*. JHU Press, 2007: Conclusion.

Woodward, David. 'Cartography and the Renaissance: Continuity and Change.' In *The History of Cartography*. University of Chicago Press, 2007: vol. 3, Part 1, 3–24.

The Impossible Dream: The Perfect Map Projection

Plethora of Map Projections

Snyder, JP. *Flattening the Earth: 2,000 Years of Map Projections*. University of Chicago Press, 1993.

The Gall–Peters Map Projection

Brotton, Jerry. *A History of the World in Twelve Maps*. Penguin, 2012: Chapter 11.
Wilford, John Noble. *The Mapmakers* (rev. ed.). Vintage, 2000: Chapter 6. Quote by
cartographer Arthur Robinson p. 101.

All at Sea

Global Trade

Fernández-Armesto, Felipe. 'Exploration and Navigation.' In *The Oxford Handbook
of Early Modern European History, 1350-1750: Volume II—Cultures and
Power*. Oxford University Press, 2014: 173–99.

Harley, C Knick. 'Trade: Discovery, Mercantilism and Technology.' In *The
Cambridge Economic History of Modern Britain: Volume 1—Industrialisation
1700-1860*. Cambridge University Press, 2004: 175–203.

Romaniello, Matthew P. 'Trade and the Global Economy.' In *The Oxford Handbook
of Early Modern European History, 1350-1750: Volume II—Cultures and
Power*. Oxford University Press, 2014: 307–33.

Portuguese Navigation and Charts

Alegria, Maria Fernanda, Suzanne Daveau, João Carlos Garcia, and Francesc
Relaño. 'Portuguese Cartography in the Renaissance.' In *The History of
Cartography*. University of Chicago Press, 2007: vol. 3, Part 1, 975–1068.

Ash, Eric H. 'Navigation Techniques and Practice in the Renaissance.' In *The History
of Cartography*. University of Chicago Press, 2007: vol. 3, Part 1, 509–27.

Fernández-Armesto, Felipe. 'Maps and Exploration in the Sixteenth and Early
Seventeenth Centuries.' In *The History of Cartography*. University of Chicago
Press, 2007: vol. 3, Part 1, 738–70.

Determining Longitude

Sandman, Alison. 'Longitude and Latitude.' In *The History of Cartography*,
University of Chicago Press, 2019: vol. 4, 1384–432.

Wilford, John Noble. *The Mapmakers* (rev. ed.). Vintage, 2000: Chapters 8–10.

Navigation as Socially Distributed Cognition

Hutchins, Edwin. *Cognition in the Wild*. MIT Press, 1995: Chapters 1 and 2.

The Golden Age of Dutch Cartography

Golden Age

Alpers, Svetlana. *The Art of Describing: Dutch Art in the Seventeenth Century*.
University of Chicago Press, 1983: Chapter 4.

Brotton, Jerry. *A History of the World in Twelve Maps*. Penguin, 2012: Chapter 8.

Sutton, Elizabeth A. *Capitalism and Cartography in the Dutch Golden Age*.
University of Chicago Press, 2015: Chapter 2.

Mapping the Stars

Kanas, Nick. *Star Maps: History, Artistry, and Cartography*. Springer, 2012: Chapters 3–6 and 10.

Finding Your Way Around

Lack of Map Use by Travelers in the Middle Ages and Renaissance

Delano-Smith, Catherine. 'Milieus of Mobility: Itineraries, Route Maps, and Road Maps.' In *Cartographies of Travel and Navigation*. University of Chicago Press, 2006: 16–68.

Renaissance Travel Books

Von Breydenbach wrote his book to encourage people to make the pilgrimage to Jerusalem and to support calls for another crusade to rescue Jerusalem from the Ottoman Empire. However, in actuality, few of his readers would ever make the pilgrimage.

Dym, Jordana. 'Mapping Travel: The Origins and Conventions of Western Journey Maps.' *Brill Research Perspectives in Map History* 2, no. 2 (2021): Sections 3–5, 1–135.

Ross, Elizabeth. *Picturing Experience in the Early Printed Book: Breydenbach's Peregrinatio from Venice to Jerusalem*. Penn State Press, 2014.

Renaissance City Maps

Ballon, Hilary, and David Friedman. 'Portraying the City in Early Modern Europe: Measurement, Representation, and Planning.' In *The History of Cartography*. University of Chicago Press, 2007: vol. 3, Part 2, 680–704.

Buisseret, David. *The Mapmakers' Quest: Depicting New Worlds in Renaissance Europe*. Oxford University Press, 2003: Chapter 6.

Tourist Maps after the Renaissance

Frangenberg, Thomas. 'Chorographies of Florence: The Use of City Views and City Plans in the Sixteenth Century.' *Imago Mundi* 46, no. 1 (1994): 41–64.

Garfield, Simon. *On the Map: Why the World Looks the Way It Does*. Profile Books, 2012: Chapter 16.

Use of City Maps after the Renaissance

Delano-Smith, Catherine, and Roger JP Kain. *English Maps: A History*. British Library, 1999: Chapter 6.

Construction of Road Networks in the Seventeenth Century, and Ogilby and Adams's Road Maps

Delano-Smith, Catherine. 'Milieus of Mobility: Itineraries, Route Maps, and Road Maps.' In *Cartographies of Travel and Navigation*. University of Chicago Press, 2006: 16–68.

Different Kinds of Travel Maps

Akerman, James R. In *Cartographies of Travel and Navigation*. University of Chicago Press, 2006: Introduction, 1–15.

New Kinds of Transport in the Nineteenth and Early Twentieth Centuries and Use of Travel Maps

Akerman, James R. In *Cartographies of Travel and Navigation*. University of Chicago Press, 2006: Introduction, 1–15.

Vance, James E. *Capturing the Horizon: The Historical Geography of Transportation since the Sixteenth Century*. Johns Hopkins University Press, 1990: Chapters 3–7.

Urban Transit Maps

While I have focused on Beck's 1933 transit map, the 1931 transit map of Berlin's S-Bahn uses similar conventions.

Guo, Zhan. 'Mind the Map! The Impact of Transit Maps on Path Choice in Public Transit.' *Transportation Research Part A: Policy and Practice* 45, no. 7 (2011): 625–39.

Ovenden, Mark. *Transit Maps of the World*. Penguin Books, 2007: Introduction, Berlin, London.

Why Do Maps Work?

Cognitive Maps

Burgess, Neil. 'Spatial Memory: How Egocentric and Allocentric Combine.' *Trends in Cognitive Sciences* 10, no. 12 (2006): 551–7.

Dudchenko, Paul A. *Why People Get Lost: The Psychology and Neuroscience of Spatial Cognition*. Oxford University Press, 2010: Chapters 3 and 4.

Lew, Adina R. 'Looking beyond the Boundaries: Time to Put Landmarks Back on the Cognitive Map?' *Psychological Bulletin* 137, no. 3 (2011): 484–507.

McNamara, Timothy P. 'Spatial Memory: Properties and Organization.' In *Handbook of Spatial Cognition*. American Psychological Association, 2013: 173–90.

Nadel, Lynn. 'Cognitive Maps.' In *Handbook of Spatial Cognition*. American Psychological Association, 2013: 155–71.

Tversky, Barbara. 'Distortions in Cognitive Maps.' *Geoforum* 23, no. 2 (1992): 131–8.

Hippocampus
Eichenbaum, Howard. 'Time (and Space) in the Hippocampus.' *Current Opinion in Behavioral Sciences* 17 (2017): 65–70.
Maguire, Eleanor A, David G Gadian, Ingrid S Johnsrude, Catriona D Good, John Ashburner, Richard SJ Frackowiak, and Christopher D Frith. 'Navigation-Related Structural Change in the Hippocampi of Taxi Drivers.' *Proceedings of the National Academy of Sciences* 97, no. 8 (2000): 4398–403.
Tavares, Rita Morais, Avi Mendelsohn, Yael Grossman, Christian Hamilton Williams, Matthew Shapiro, Yaacov Trope, and Daniela Schiller. 'A Map for Social Navigation in the Human Brain.' *Neuron* 87, no. 1 (2015): 231–43.

Mind Palace
Yates, Frances A. *Art of Memory*. Routledge, 1966.

Map Use by Adults
Kitchin, Rob, and Marc Blades. *The Cognition of Geographic Space*. I.B. Tauris, 2002: Chapter 3.
Moeser, Shannon Dawn. 'Cognitive Mapping in a Complex Building.' *Environment and Behavior* 20, no. 1 (1988): 21–49.
Zhang, Hui, Ksenia Zherdeva, and Arne D Ekstrom. 'Different "Routes" to a Cognitive Map: Dissociable Forms of Spatial Knowledge Derived from Route and Cartographic Map Learning.' *Memory & Cognition* 42, no. 7 (2014): 1106–17.

Map Use by Children
Davies, Clare, and David H Uttal. 'Map Use and the Development of Spatial Cognition.' In *The Emerging Spatial Mind*. Oxford University Press, 2007: 219–47.
Dillon, Moira R, and Elizabeth S Spelke. 'From Map Reading to Geometric Intuitions.' *Developmental Psychology* 54, no. 7 (2018): 1304–16.
Plester, Beverly, Mark Blades, and Christopher Spencer. 'Children's Understanding of Environmental Representations: Aerial Photographs and Model Towns.' In *Children and Their Environments: Learning, Using and Designing Spaces*. Cambridge University Press, 2006: 42–56.
Uttal, David H. 'Seeing the Big Picture: Map Use and the Development of Spatial Cognition.' *Developmental Science* 3, no. 3 (2000): 247–64. Quote p. 249.

CHAPTER 6

Mapping the State

I N THE PREVIOUS CHAPTER, we saw how maps recorded the expanding
worldview of Europe during the Renaissance, and how nautical charts
underpinned European trade networks and the colonization of Africa, Asia
and the Americas. These were the obvious functions of maps during the
Renaissance. But they played another less prominent but equally consequential role: the creation of the modern state. It is a role that has only
recently been appreciated by historians and cartographers.

VISUALIZING THE STATE

Like the modern map, the modern state arose during the Renaissance. In
country after country, we find that map-making went hand in hand with the
introduction of the modern state. Maps were instrumental in this change
from medieval sovereignty, in which a sovereign ruled a people, to our
current understanding, in which a sovereign rules a territory with sharp,
well-defined borders within which sovereignty is complete and uniform.

In France, the change began in 1254 when the royal chancellery stopped
referring to the monarch as 'King of the Franks' and instead described
him as 'King of France'. Even so, the medieval conception of territory
differed significantly from our modern understanding. A state's territory
was a collection of locations rather than a contiguous region. Borders
were unclear and overlapping, with state authority strong at the center
and weaker at the periphery. In medieval peace treaties, territories were

described using textual lists of placenames, with each location's associated rights and privileges carefully detailed.

We see this overlap of boundaries in a report made by the engineer Claude de Chastillon in 1608, when the French king sent him to survey and map France's frontier. De Chastillon describes how he found that the château of Passavant belonged to the neighboring Duchy of Lorraine but that the surrounding towns and wood were French. Nearby was a village that paid tax to the King of France but owed allegiance to Lorraine. Inevitably, once rulers mapped their territory, they wanted to simplify the borders and impose uniform rights and responsibilities across their dominion.

The other critical change during the Renaissance was to transition from a feudal culture based on mutual obligation, in which loyalty was personal and given to one's lord, family and community, to one in which loyalty was given to an impersonal, abstract state. The difficulty was in convincing the state's citizens that the state was real and that it deserved their commitment. Maps achieved this by providing a way of depicting the state. Without maps, the modern state cannot be visualized and so remains unimaginable. On the map, a state becomes concrete. It is the homeland, a geographic region with well-defined borders that must be defended.

Given the map's unparalleled power to represent the state, it is unsurprising that Renaissance rulers fell in love with maps. Map collecting became a source of pleasure and joy for many heads of state. They commissioned maps for their palaces and government offices that were artful tools of national propaganda, calculated to awe the viewer by emphasizing the extent of the state's territories. The wealthy followed suit, and during the sixteenth century it became the height of fashion to decorate a residence's halls and entrances with painted maps and panoramic city views.

Renaissance rulers created specialized cartographic offices and commissioned maps to help them better govern their territories. Charles V, the sponsor of Magellan and ruler of Spain and the Holy Roman Empire, was particularly enthused by maps. Before he attacked southern France in 1536, Charles V is said to have studied his maps of the Alps and Provence so passionately that he convinced himself that he already possessed the land in the same way he owned the map. (Unfortunately for Charles V, the invasion was unsuccessful.)

Henry VIII, King of England, was another early Renaissance ruler who recognized the usefulness of maps. The initial impetus for their use was the expansion and modernization of England's defenses, which started with a survey of the nation's coastal fortifications. But Henry soon realized that maps could be used to enhance his royal authority and power by fostering a growing national self-awareness. Map use intensified during the reign of his son Edward VI and daughter Elizabeth I. It was during Elizabeth's reign that Christopher Saxton published his famous atlas of county maps that helped shape the English view of their country (see Figure 6.1)

By the end of the Renaissance, European rulers had realized the value of accurate maps for administration. Over the next three centuries, they commissioned surveys to produce ever more detailed maps of their homelands and colonial territories.

This did not always go to plan. In 1679, the French King Louis XIV directed Jean Picard and Philippe de la Hire, distinguished members of the newly created Académie des Sciences, to map France's coastline. For the first time, the longitude of locations on the coast could be computed

FIGURE 6.1   Map of Dorset from the *Atlas of the Counties of England and Wales* (1579). Published by Christopher Saxton, this was the first atlas of any country. Elizabeth I supported the production. In part, this was because she required an accurate survey of England's coastal defenses to prepare against invasion by foes such as Spain—which, in fact, did attack with its armada a few years after the publication of the atlas.

Credit: Marzolino/Shutterstock.com.

accurately (by observing the moons of Jupiter). To the horror of Louis XIV, this revealed that France was some 20 per cent smaller than had been shown on previous maps. It would be another fifty years before a French ruler was courageous enough to ask for another survey. By then, the French Government had realized it needed a detailed map of France to plan how to fortify the country and modernize its network of roads and canals.

In 1733, Jacques Cassini was asked to accurately survey all of France. This ended up taking another sixty years and required three generations of Cassinis. The resulting map of France, known as the *Carte de Cassini*, was groundbreaking. Comprising 182 sheets, it was nearly 12 meters high and 11 meters wide. It demonstrated a new level of accuracy and detail in national mapping (see Figure 6.2).

The accuracy of the *Carte de Cassini* was due to the Cassinis' systematic use of the surveying technique known as triangulation. Their first step was to create a baseline of precisely measured length whose endpoints had the same latitude. From this, it was possible to compute the position of a third point, such as a distant church spire, relative to the endpoints of the baseline. All the Cassinis needed to do was measure the angle between the point

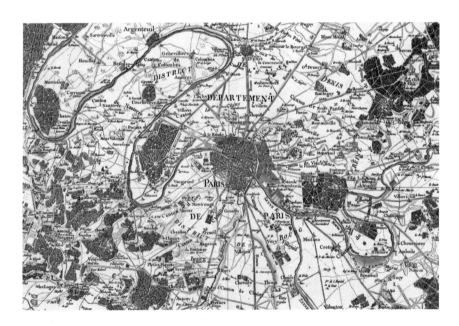

FIGURE 6.2   Detail from the *Carte de Cassini* showing Paris and its surrounds.

Credit: Library of Congress, Geography and Map Division.

and baseline from each of the baseline's endpoints. They and their survey team repeated this process, again and again, to compute a triangular grid of points across France whose location was known precisely. The position of other features, such as villages and forests, was then calculated from the points on this grid.

Other countries quickly saw the value of a detailed survey like the *Carte de Cassini* for national defense, natural resource management, and planning canals, roads and other engineering works. Britain was the first to act, with the Ordnance Survey of England and Wales being initiated in 1791. Other countries followed, using triangulation to accurately map lakes, rivers, forests, mountains, cities, towns, roads and canals. Now known as topographic maps, these national series of large-scale, general-purpose maps have become invaluable tools for government and industry, and the basis for myriad other types of specialized maps.

Shortly after the *Carte de Cassini*'s creation, Europe's three-century transition from medieval regimes with porous and indistinct borders to modern nation-states was completed. By 1815, as a consequence of the post-Napoleonic treaties, Europe was divided into territorial states that could be readily drawn on a map. There were now clear linear boundaries between the states, and very few enclaves. There was an understanding that each state had exclusive and complete authority within all parts of its territory.

By this time, maps had also became a powerful construct for uniting the diverse groups inhabiting each nation. Topographic map series like the *Carte de Cassini* and the British Ordnance Survey were powerful expressions of nationalism that reinforced the homogeneity of the territory ruled by the state. Jerry Brotton observes how Parisian French is used throughout the Cassinis' map rather than regional dialects or the many other languages—such as Occitan, Breton and Flemish—spoken in France at the time. He also describes how the map uses the same standardized visual vocabulary of signs and symbols to show features, including administrative boundaries, across the whole of France. The country is shown as a unified whole, encouraging individual citizens to see themselves as part of one nation.

Nationalism was also driven by map use at schools. During the eighteenth and nineteenth centuries, many countries introduced national schooling systems. These fostered a sense of national identity by teaching a shared history, language and culture. Children learned about history and geography from globes, wall maps and atlases. The clear boundaries and uniform color of each state on these maps reinforced the importance of territorial sovereignty and the homogeneity of each state. The children learned that they belonged to a particular region on the map. Indeed, by the time they finished school, the students knew the outline of this region so well that its shape was immediately recognizable and had become an iconic symbol for their nation.

DEFENDING THE STATE

National defense was one of the main reasons for investing the considerable resources and time required to create accurate, large-scale topographic map series. The British Ordnance Survey, for example, was a direct response to the Jacobite Uprising by the Scots in 1745 and the French Revolutionary War. The link between maps and war is not new. In Chapter 2, for instance, we saw how Nootka warriors sketched a map in the sand to plan a raid. As warfare has become more complex, involving larger and larger forces dispersed over greater and greater areas, the military need for maps has only increased.

To understand how modern military map use has developed, we must return to the Renaissance. War was the normal state of affairs during this period, ranging from local skirmishes between city-states in Italy to the Thirty Years' War of 1618–48 that devastated Europe. Armies grew massively in size. For instance, France increased its military under Louis XIV from 80,000 to 400,000 fighters. Other states fearful of France followed. Rather than employing mercenaries or conscripting citizens through feudal obligations only when needed, states formed professional standing armies. Military academies were set up to train officers, and troops were drilled in the use of pikes and firearms and provided with uniforms. Weapons, particularly guns, and also warships improved. Command was no longer about personal bravado but optimizing the use of troops on the battlefield and taking advantage of the terrain.

Maps were part of this modernization. Their primary use was for planning national defense. In Chapter 3, we saw that Italians developed a new defensive structure for their cities to defend against mobile cannons based on protruding bastions along the city's defensive wall, so that soldiers firing from them could protect the wall and other bastions from attack. Other Renaissance rulers, such as Henry VIII of England, hired Italian military engineers to build bastioned fortifications along their nation's frontiers and coastlines.

The Italian engineers soon taught the local military how to plan these fortifications using a mixture of site plans, bird's-eye views and three-dimensional models. If required, the engineers also fashioned smaller-scale regional maps showing mutually supportive fortifications, so the military commander could plan how to supply the forts with men and provisions and explore different attack scenarios.

Maps were not only used for defense. Both Charles V and Henry VIII used maps to plan their military campaigns. In *The Art of War* (1520), Niccolò Machiavelli advises the military leader that, when advancing into enemy territory:

> *the first thing he ought to do, is to have all the country through which he marches described and depicted, so that he will know the places, the numbers, the distances, the roads, the mountains, the rivers, the marshes, and all their characteristics.*

By the eighteenth century, maps were used in military academies as part of officer training (see Figure 6.3). As the size of armies increased, military commanders began using battlefield maps during the clash itself to direct troops. During the Napoleonic Wars, both Napoleon Bonaparte and the Duke of Wellington keenly appreciated the value of maps. Bonaparte and his aides carried copies of the *Carte de Cassini*, while one reason that Wellington won the Battle of Waterloo was that he had previously mapped the region, guessing this might be where he would fight Napoleon. Wellington's detailed topographic map allowed him to skillfully position his troops before the fighting began, helping him win one of the most critical battles of the nineteenth century (see Figure 6.4).

Maps proved even more essential in World War I. By this time, maps were familiar to most of the population in the Western world. National schooling meant that many children had encountered maps at school, while organizations such as the Boy Scouts taught map-making and reading, and the general populace routinely used maps for travel planning and navigation.

Maps were used in virtually all aspects of campaigns during the First World War. They were used to plan the movement of troops and supplies so that they arrived at their destinations unscathed by enemy forces. They were used on the battlefield for planning and to record the conflict, including the timing and movement of troops, allowing the military

FIGURE 6.3   By the eighteenth century, maps were used in military academies as part of officer training. This illustration from 1726—Hans Friedrich von Fleming's *Der vollkommene teutsche Soldat* (*The Perfect German Soldier*)—depicts instructors at a German academy discussing how best to assault the seaport shown on the map at the front of the hall.

Credit: Heinrich Heine Universität Düsseldorf, Universitäts—und Landesbibliothek CC 0.

to learn from a post-battle analysis and better train new soldiers. It is estimated that a staggering 1.5 billion maps were printed for military use during World War I.

This explosion in map use was driven by a new kind of warfare. World War I was an artillery war. For the first time, sudden, precisely targeted barrages from powerful, unseen guns were used to catch the enemy unawares. Such scientific gunnery relied on field troops having access to large-scale topographic maps detailing the exact location of the enemy forces and the trenches to be shelled.

FIGURE 6.4   Map of the Battle of Waterloo, prepared from a sketch by British Captain Thornton, Royal Engineers, c. 1815. Thornton made his sketch of the battle on top of a pre-existing map drawn the previous year at the instruction of Wellington. It shows how Wellington carefully placed his main troops on a ridge, protected on one flank by a village and on the other by a large house. Notice the abstract representation of the troops using colored blocks. Early military maps showed individual soldiers, but by the end of the Renaissance, troops were usually shown using stylized conventions explained in a key.

Credit: Royal National Archives. Catalog reference: WO 78/1006/25.

Both sides in the war quickly realized the need for surveyors on the front line who could rapidly produce maps using the latest information about the position of enemy troops, trenches and gun batteries. The surveyors developed innovative methods to pinpoint the location of the enemy guns, as they were out of eyeshot, far to the rear of the trenches. One approach was to use reconnaissance flights, which led to a significant innovation in map-making: aerial photogrammetry—the production of maps from aerial photographs.

Map use was not confined to the military. There was also unprecedented use by the popular media. Magazines and newspapers such as London's *Daily Mail* published compilations of maps and wall maps so their readers could follow the war at home (see Figure 6.5). Larger wall maps were installed on billboards and outside newspaper offices. Crowds gathered to watch as small, moveable flags were repositioned to show the locations of new battles on the map. Maps were also a standard part of war reporting in newsreels, displaying the latest advance or retreat accompanied by an analysis of what this meant for the war effort.

Map production in World War II vastly surpassed even that in World War I. This was memorably communicated to me during a visit to the

FIGURE 6.5   Since the Renaissance, maps have been used to tell the public about the latest military wins and defeats. The map above is the cover of a map compilation published by London's *Daily Mail* in 1915 for purchase by their readers to follow the progress of World War I.

Credit: *Daily Mail War Panorama: 20 Birds-Eye Views and Maps of the World Wide War.* Daily Mail, London, 1915. Rare Books Collection, State Library Victoria.

Churchill War Rooms Museum, which lies under the Treasury building in London. It contains the Cabinet War Rooms, an underground bunker built just before World War II. It was from here that Winston Churchill and his chiefs of staff directed the war against Hitler. The War Rooms is a rabbit warren of offices, conference rooms, kitchens and bedrooms. At its heart is the Map Room, which contains dozens of reference maps; graphs showing the production of military equipment; and large, wall-mounted maps showing the location of troops and convoys with pins, string and small, typed notes. During the war, the room was staffed day and night by the 'Glamour Boys', who were responsible for updating the maps when new information arrived. It was with these maps that Churchill and his chiefs of staff planned the war. And it was on these maps that they saw the fate of the Allied troops, planes and ships, as the Glamour Boys repositioned or removed their markers based on the latest news from the front line.

UPS AND DOWNS

A characteristic feature of the military maps produced in World War I was the use of contours—lines connecting adjacent points of equal height. Knowing how the land slopes and changes height—its relief—has long been critical information for military commanders when planning fortifications and campaigns. During World War I, accurate elevation information was imperative because of long-range artillery. When calculating the angle to fire their guns, gunners needed to know the exact differences in height between themselves and their hidden targets. And during peacetime, knowledge of the land's 'ups and downs' was also crucial for administrators and engineers when planning roads, canals, railways and dams.

Nowadays, contours are so commonly used to display land elevation on topographic maps that they have become a topographic map's defining feature. However, early topographic maps like the *Carte de Cassini*, while they showed hills and mountains, did not use contours. It was not until the mid-nineteenth century that these began to be used on topographic maps.

At the beginning of the Renaissance, maps showed hills and mountains using colored strips (see Figure 5.3) or stylized shapes (see Figure 6.1). Later, mountains were drawn using a bird's-eye view (see Figure 6.6) in a similar style to that used to depict cities and fortifications. While beautiful and easily understandable, the bird's-eye view is at odds with the planimetric view in which the map region is shown as if seen from directly

FIGURE 6.6   Detail from a copy of a 1566 woodcut engraving of Zürich Canton, Switzerland by Joseph Murer. This is an elegant example of the way Renaissance mapmakers used a bird's-eye view to show mountain ranges.

Credit: *Eigentliche Verzeichnuss der Städten, und Graffschaften und Herrschaften, welche in der Stadt Zürich-Gebiet und Landschaft gehörig sind.* Zürich: bey Johannes Hofmeister, an der Rosengass, [1765?]. Zentralbibliothek Zürich. Wak 11. https://doi.org/10.3931/e-rara-77818 / Public Domain Mark.

above. Furthermore, the mountains hide features behind them, and the bird's-eye view does not give precise information about elevation changes.

After the Renaissance, mapmakers such as the Cassinis invented new techniques for showing relief that were better suited to a planimetric view. In the *Carte de Cassini*, tiny strokes show the orientation and steepness of slopes (see Figure 6.2). This is called hachuring. The strokes are drawn in the direction of the steepest gradient, with short, thick lines indicating a steep slope and long, thin lines a gentle slope. It is common to use heavier lines to show the shadows that the hills and mountains would cast if illuminated obliquely from one side of the map. But while hachuring gives an immediate impression of terrain, it cannot provide precise information about the actual elevation, so spot heights are also commonly included.

In 1791, just after the Cassinis finished the *Carte de Cassini*, a much smaller map of France was produced by the French engineer Jean-Louis Dupain-Triel. This was the first map of a large region to use contours to show height. As well as showing elevation, contours have since proved to be one of the most helpful ways to display data such as air pressure or average temperature that, like elevation, change value smoothly across the map region.

Dupain-Triel was not the first to use contour lines, however. They originated in the sixteenth century and were initially used to indicate water depth, not elevation. When you think about it, this is not surprising. Knowing the depth of water under a keel in shallow waters is essential if you're a sailor. In contrast, knowing your precise elevation above sea level is unnecessary for most purposes. Furthermore, it is considerably easier to measure water depth than height above sea level: you simply drop a weighted sounding line.

I'm unsure why contours began to appear on topographic map series such as the British Ordnance Survey in the mid-nineteenth century (see Figure 6.7). It may be linked to industrialization. British towns and cities were growing rapidly, and since the invention of the steam locomotive a few decades earlier, railways also had been spreading. Town planners and engineers required precise land height information when planning new civic infrastructure such as railway lines.

The military also drove the use of contours on topographic maps. We saw that accurate elevation information was necessary during World War I for long-range artillery attacks. And with the introduction of aerial photogrammetry, obtaining elevation data was much quicker and cheaper, enabling the widespread use of contours on topographic maps after the war.

MAPPING LAND AND PROPERTY

In Australia, where I live, each state has an official register of property titles. This includes a map showing the property's boundary, dimensions and location. While maps like this may not be as exciting as world maps, they, too, have shaped our modern world.

Property maps are not new. In Chapter 1, we saw that the Mesopotamians left behind numerous plans of properties and buildings. We also know that the Romans used maps to record property boundaries and compute taxes. During the Middle Ages, however, maps were replaced by written surveys. These recorded a property's boundary by listing the features along it, such as trees, hedges and stones. It is not until the Renaissance that we again see widespread use of property maps.

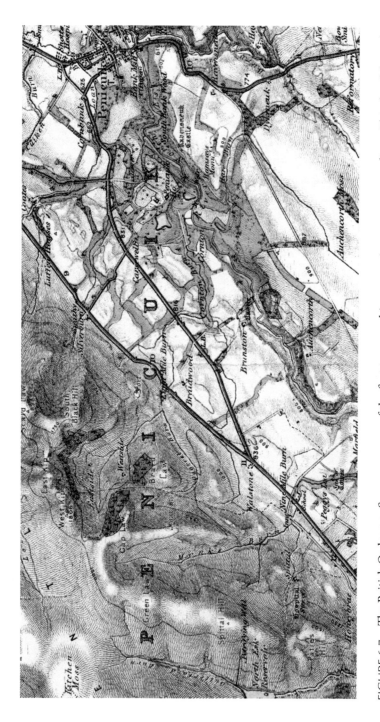

FIGURE 6.7 The British Ordnance Survey was one of the first topographic map series to use contour lines. This detail from the *One-inch-to-the-mile Scotland* (3rd ed., 1902), Sheet 32—Edinburgh, uses both hachuring and contour lines to show relief.

Credit: Reproduced with the permission of the National Library of Scotland Map Images CC-BY (NLS).

By the start of the seventeenth century, estate managers in England had maps of their estates drawn up to document their boundaries before possible disputes, and as a tool for land management (see Figure 6.8). During the next two centuries, the use of estate maps spread to other European countries. The change was partly due to increased familiarity with maps and the growing culture of map use. Just as Renaissance rulers enjoyed looking at maps of their territories, so did the landed gentry, often hanging beautifully decorated estate maps in their study or in the entrance hall of their manor. But a more fundamental reason for this was the rise of capitalism and the commodification of land.

In the Middle Ages, land ownership was understood in terms of various rights of the lord and farmers—rights to use the land in different ways and rights to its produce. Just as maps drove the rise of the modern state, they also helped Europe move from this feudal system of land ownership to one in which the land itself was the commodity. In this more modern understanding, land is simply a physical resource that can be bought and sold. Estate maps, in which properties were shown as regions with crisp borders, undoubtedly contributed to this view of land as a commodity with

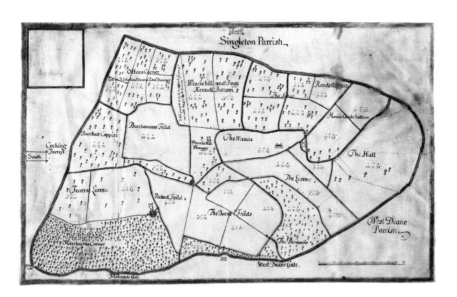

FIGURE 6.8   Estate map c. 1630–70 of Downley Park, comprising 658 acres in the Chichester district of West Sussex, England, belonging to Lord Lumley.

Credit: West Sussex Record Office Add Mss 18014.

clear boundaries and acreage—a view by which ownership conferred uniform, exclusive rights over the entire area.

The commodification of land was linked to population growth. As the population grew, land prices and rent rose rapidly. In England, for instance, rents rose by 900 per cent between 1510 and 1630. This provided a compelling incentive for even the most map-averse landowners to accurately measure their estates and ensure their tenants were charged for every square inch of land they used.

Land commodification went hand in hand with land improvement and resource management. This was part of an agricultural revolution in Europe during which country after country transitioned from medieval strip farming to enclosed fields. By 1750, maps were routinely used throughout Europe for planning and recording land reorganization and enclosures. In England, for instance, acts of parliament in the nineteenth century required common land to be surveyed and mapped before enclosure and division.

Maps were also used to plan land drainage schemes and irrigation schemes. During the Renaissance, Italy, Germany, England and, of course, the Netherlands drained large areas of swampland and built dykes around low-lying land to protect it from flooding. Unsurprisingly, given their map-making prowess, the Dutch were among the first to use maps for this purpose. By the start of the Renaissance, their local communities had been organized into self-governing polder boards (low-lying land enclosed by dykes is known as a polder). These boards were responsible for the drainage and reclamation of land from low-lying coastal areas and shallow lakes. As the scale of the Dutch land-reclamation projects increased, so did the map use. Not only were maps used for planning, they were also employed to advertise land-reclamation projects to potential investors.

The Dutch polder authorities also used maps to compute what was known as the 'dyke tax'. Paid by each village in the district for the upkeep of the polders, the dyke tax was usually based on the area of the town, with the inhabitants then sharing the cost between them. However, there were often anomalies in the amount paid by the villages, leading to unrest. Many of the first polder maps were drawn in response to court cases about the dyke tax. By the end of the Renaissance, maps were commonly used by the polder authorities to record property boundaries and compute the dyke tax. This is the first general use of cadastral maps we know of in modern Europe—the name comes from the French word *cadastre*, meaning a property register.

The use of cadastral maps gradually spread through Europe. After the Thirty Years' War finished in 1648, many European states found themselves on the edge of financial ruin. They needed to raise money to pay for a standing army to protect the nation, its roads and canals, and the swelling bureaucracy required to run an increasingly complex government. But simply increasing existing taxes led to civil unrest. Country after country reformed their taxation system from idiosyncratic medieval taxes and levies that varied from estate to estate, to modern, more equitable tax systems. This change included moving from taxes on produce to property taxes based on land area and use. Cadastral surveys and maps were introduced by the Netherlands and the Swedish Baltic provinces to transparently assess and record these land taxes. Other European nations followed suit.

In France, unrest due to taxation was one of the main reasons for the French Revolution in 1789. After the revolution, a new land tax was introduced, and once in power, Napoleon instigated a cadastral survey to compute it. This was initially conducted in France and then extended to the Netherlands, Luxembourg and Belgium, which France had annexed. Switzerland and Prussia were next, and by the late nineteenth century, most European countries were using cadastral maps to compute some variant of land tax.

Another important use for maps is urban planning, which began in the Renaissance. At first, this was for fortifications, then for urban renewal. For example, from 1853 to 1870, the newly crowned Emperor Napoleon III tasked Georges-Eugène Haussmann with rebuilding Paris to reduce congestion, improve sanitation and increase its grandeur. Napoleon III is said to have installed a large map of Paris in his office and drawn colored lines to show where he wanted new boulevards to be built. The medieval center of Paris was reshaped and opened up with wide boulevards and parklands, creating the imposing cityscape that is now the heart of the French capital.

By the start of the twentieth century, urban planning had emerged as a new profession. The tremendous growth of London and other European cities due to the Industrial Revolution had led to slums—environments fostering crime and disease among the working poor forced to live there. Better planning was recognized as the answer. Local authorities introduced planning codes and required new developments to be designed on paper and approved before construction began. The shape of our modern urban landscape is the product of the lines drawn on these maps by administrators, urban planners and engineers.

MAPPING EMPIRE

I now want to return to the image in Figure 5.1, of the delegates at the Berlin Conference in 1884–85. Maps have long been tools of European conquest and legitimization. During the Berlin Conference, they gave the authority for colonial powers to claim lands with the stroke of a pen. This monumental hubris was not restricted to the nineteenth century. We also saw it in the Spanish and Portuguese territorial disputes in the early Renaissance that resulted in the 1494 Treaty of Tordesillas. Undoubtedly, the indigenous inhabitants of Africa, Asia and America would have been horrified to learn that this treaty split ownership of their continents between Spain and Portugal. The treaty was intrinsically cartographic. A north–south line, drawn 370 leagues west of the Cape Verde Islands, divided the two empires. Lands to the east of the line, including Africa and lands bordering the Indian Ocean, belonged to the Portuguese, and those to the west, discovered by Columbus, belonged to Spain.

The Treaty of Tordesillas was only the start of European colonization. In 1500, European powers controlled only 7 per cent of the world's land. By 1914, they controlled 84 per cent. Maps made European colonization possible. Nautical charts allowed European steamships to move colonists, troops and manufactured goods to the colonies and to bring back the raw materials needed to fuel Western industrialization. Topographic maps facilitated settlement and trade by providing Europeans with precise information about the location of villages, roads, rivers and natural resources. And maps were tools of control, with military mapmakers carefully preparing maps for future campaigns in case of rebellion.

But more than making it possible, maps made empire-building imaginable and desirable (see Figure 6.9). Blank spaces at the heart of maps of Africa, North America and Australia invited Europeans to see the land as empty, terra nullius, theirs for the taking. Maps omitted indigenous peoples and nations but depicted European settlements and imposed European placenames. This was central to empire-building. As Thomas Bassett said, 'More than a mere reflection of conquest, maps helped to produce empire by enabling and legitimizing the process of colonization.'

In Europe, cadastral maps were an instrument for equitable taxing. In European colonies, however, they played a more sinister role. For instance, the Down survey of Irish property in 1654 resulted in nearly half of Ireland

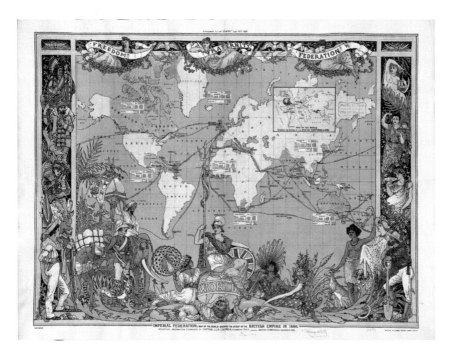

FIGURE 6.9   Maps such as the *Imperial Federation: Map Showing the Extent of the British Empire in 1886*, glorified and legitimized European colonization.

Credit: Published by Maclure & Co. as a supplement to *The Graphic*, July 24, 1886. Map reproduction courtesy of the Norman B Leventhal Map & Education Center at the Boston Public Library.

being taken by English colonists. In the United States, maps played a central role in the settlement of the vast tracts of land the government took from indigenous Americans and Mexicans during the Mexican–American War of 1846–48. After the War of Independence, the new nation legislated that land should be surveyed before settlement. The statute further stipulated that townships and properties should be organized using a rectilinear grid whose basic unit was the square-mile section. Consequently, the human geography of the United States, like that of Australia and Canada, is the product of government officials and administrators who conjured a nation into existence by drawing railways, roads and towns onto the blank spaces on their maps.

While maps have been powerful tools for European colonization, they have also become a tool for decolonization. In Australia, the British Government justified its seizure of land from Indigenous Australians using the legal fiction of terra nullius: that before their arrival, the land had belonged to no-one. In 1992, the Supreme Court of Australia recognized the absurdity of this assertion. It determined that Indigenous Australians had owned their lands before colonization, and, in certain situations, they continued to own them. The subsequent *Native Title Act* clarified that, for native title to exist, the claimants had to establish an ongoing connection to the land under traditional laws and customs. Maps are now being used to prove this connection.

The *Ngurrara Canvas II* (see Figure 6.10) is a renowned example. In 1997, the Ngurrara peoples argued for native title of their lands in the arid north-western region of Australia. English was not their first language, and they struggled to articulate their connection to Country. Instead of talking, they decided to explain this graphically. Over fifty artists collaborated to create the monumental, 80 square meter *Ngurrara Canvas II*. Each artist was responsible for painting their traditional land on a section of the canvas. The result is not a Western map. It is a cosmological diagram that

FIGURE 6.10   The *Ngurrara Canvas II* was a central part of the Ngurrara people's evidence that they had an ongoing connection to their traditional lands.

Credit: Photo by K Dayman (Ngurrara Artists and Mangkaja Arts Resource Agency).

combines traditional and contemporary design to depict the Ngurrara, their Country, its stories, and the fundamental connection between these. When the Ngurrara argued their case to the Native Title Tribunal, each artist stood on their section of the map. In turn, they spoke passionately, in their own language, about their connection to Country. The map licensed them to do so. As each artist stood on their map section, they were standing on Country, empowering them with the confidence and authority to speak about it. This performance proved central to the Ngurrara argument for native title, which was officially granted in 2007.

More than any other information graphic, maps have been responsible for our transition from the medieval world to the modern state and economy. They were essential to the evolution of the contemporary nation-state, providing a tangible representation of this rather abstract notion. Since then, topographic and cadastral maps have become indispensable tools for infrastructure and urban planning, resource management, taxation and government administration. Maps also played a significant part in the globalization of trade and European colonization, which gave Western nations access to the natural resources that fueled the Industrial Revolution. It is difficult to comprehend how our modern world could have come into existence without maps, or how it would function if there were no maps.

NOTES, REFERENCES AND FURTHER READING
Visualizing the State
Emergence of the Modern State Based on Territory and the Role of Maps

Branch, Jordan. 'Mapping the Sovereign State: Technology, Authority, and Systemic Change.' *International Organization* 65, no. 1 (2011): 1–36.

Buisseret, David. 'The Cartographic Definition of France's Eastern Boundary in the Early Seventeenth Century.' *Imago Mundi* 36, no. 1 (1984): 72–80.

Elden, Stuart. *The Birth of Territory.* University of Chicago Press, 2013: Chapters 8 and 9, Coda.

Wood, Denis. *Rethinking the Power of Maps.* Guilford Press, 2010: Chapter 1.

Renaissance Rulers' Love of Maps

Barber, Peter. 'England I: Pageantry, Defense and Government: Maps at Court to 1550.' In *Monarchs, Ministers, and Maps: The Emergence of Cartography as a Tool of Government in Early Modern Europe.* University of Chicago Press, 1992: 26–56.

Barber, Peter. 'England II: Monarchs, Ministers, and Maps, 1550–1625.' In *Monarchs, Ministers, and Maps: The Emergence of Cartography as a Tool of Government in Early Modern Europe*. University of Chicago Press, 1992: 57–98.

Kagan, Richard, and Benjamin Schmidt. 'Maps and the Early Modern State: Official Cartography.' In *The History of Cartography*. University of Chicago Press, 2007: vol. 3, Part 1, 661–79.

Parker, Geoffrey. 'Maps and Ministers: The Spanish Habsburgs.' In *Monarchs, Ministers, and Maps: The Emergence of Cartography as a Tool of Government in Early Modern Europe*. University of Chicago Press, 1992: 124–52.

Mapping France and the Carte de Cassini

Brotton, Jerry. *A History of the World in Twelve Maps*. Penguin, 2012: Chapter 9.

Pelletier, Monique. 'Carte de France.' In *The History of Cartography*, 2019: vol. 4, 239–44.

Pelletier, Monique. 'Cassini Family.' In *The History of Cartography*, 2019: vol. 4, 251–8.

Wilford, John Noble. *The Mapmakers* (rev. ed.). Vintage, 2000: Chapter 8.

Topographic Maps

Thrower, Norman JW. *Maps & Civilization: Cartography in Culture and Civilization* (3rd ed.). The University of Chicago Press, 2008: Chapters 6 and 7.

Wilford, John Noble. *The Mapmakers* (rev. ed.). Vintage, 2000: Chapter 8.

Maps and Nationalism

Biggs, Michael. 'Putting the State on the Map: Cartography, Territory, and European State Formation.' *Comparative Studies in Society and History* 41, no. 2 (1999): 374–405.

Black, Jeremy. *Maps and History: Constructing Images of the Past*. Yale University Press, 2000: Chapter 3.

Black, Jeremy. *Maps and Politics*. University of Chicago Press, 2000: Chapter 5.

Branch, Jordan. 'Mapping the Sovereign State: Technology, Authority, and Systemic Change.' *International Organization* 65, no. 1 (2011): 1–36.

Ramirez, Francisco O, and John Boli. 'The Political Construction of Mass Schooling: European Origins and Worldwide Institutionalization.' *Sociology of Education* 60, no. 1 (1987): 2–17.

Wintle, Michael. 'Emergent Nationalism in European Maps of the Eighteenth Century.' In *The Roots of Nationalism: National Identity Formation in Early Modern Europe, 1600-1815*. Amsterdam University Press, 2016: 271–87.

Defending the State
The Military Revolution in the Renaissance
Black, Jeremy. *Maps of War: Mapping Conflict through the Centuries.* Bloomsbury Publishing, 2016: Chapter 2.

Buisseret, David. *The Mapmakers' Quest: Depicting New Worlds in Renaissance Europe.* Oxford University Press, 2003: Chapter 5.

Grayling, Anthony C. *The Age of Genius: The Seventeenth Century and the Birth of the Modern Mind.* Bloomsbury Publishing, 2016: Chapter 18.

Hale, John. 'Warfare and Cartography, ca. 1450 to ca. 1640.' In *The History of Cartography.* University of Chicago Press, 2007: vol. 3, Part 1, 719–36.

Machiavelli, Niccolò. *The Seven Books on the Art of War.* 1520. https://archive.org/details/MachiavelliNiccoloTheSevenBooksOnTheArtOfWarEN152089P./mode/2up: Quote p. 62.

Use of Maps in the Napoleonic Wars
Black, Jeremy. *Maps of War: Mapping Conflict through the Centuries.* Bloomsbury Publishing, 2016: Chapter 4.

Buisseret, David. *The Mapmakers' Quest: Depicting New Worlds in Renaissance Europe.* Oxford University Press, 2003: Chapter 5.

Smart, Lez. *The Battle of Waterloo.* In *Maps that Made History.* The National Archives, 2004: 128–33.

Use of Maps in World War I
Black, Jeremy. *Maps of War: Mapping Conflict through the Centuries.* Bloomsbury Publishing, 2016: Chapter 5.

Chasseaud, Peter. *Mapping the First World War.* Collins, 2013: Introduction.

Churchill's Map Room
Black, Jeremy. 'Maps and Navigation in the Second World War.' *The RUSI Journal* 163, no. 5 (2018): 62–74.

Churchill War Rooms. IWM. www.iwm.org.uk/visits/churchill-war-rooms

Ups and Downs
Early Representations of Relief
Andrews, JH. *Maps in Those Days: Cartographic Methods before 1850.* Four Courts Press, 2009: Chapter 12.

Imhof, Eduard. *Cartographic Relief Presentation.* Walter de Gruyter GmbH & Co KG, 1982; reprinted 2007, ESRI Press: Chapter 1.

Thrower, Norman JW. *Maps & Civilization: Cartography in Culture and Civilization* (3rd ed.). The University of Chicago Press, 2008: Chapter 6.

Industrialization and the Introduction of Contours on the British Ordnance Survey

Delano-Smith, Catherine, and Roger JP Kain. *English Maps: A History*. British Library, 1999: Chapter 7.

Rodrigue, Jean-Paul. *The Geography of Transport Systems* (5th ed.). Routledge, 2020: Chapter 1.

Thrower, Norman JW. *Maps & Civilization: Cartography in Culture and Civilization* (3rd ed.). The University of Chicago Press, 2008: Chapter 7.

Use of Contours in Military Maps

Chasseaud, Peter. *Mapping the First World War*. Collins, 2013: Introduction.

Zentai, László. 'The Transformation of Relief Representation on Topographic Maps in Hungary: From Hachures to Contour Lines.' *The Cartographic Journal* 55, no. 2 (2018): 150–8.

Mapping Land and Property

Pre-Renaissance Property Maps

Kain, Roger JP, and Elizabeth Baigent. *The Cadastral Map in the Service of the State: A History of Property Mapping*. University of Chicago Press, 1992: Chapter 1.

Kain, Roger JP. 'Maps and Rural Land Management in Early Modern Europe.' In *The History of Cartography*. University of Chicago Press, 2007: vol. 3, Part 1, 719–36.

Commodification of Land, Land Enclosure and Resource Management

Abel, Wilhelm. *Agricultural Fluctuations in Europe: From the Thirteenth to Twentieth Centuries*. Routledge, 1980: Chapter 4, in particular Figure 27.

Kain, Roger JP. 'Maps and Rural Land Management in Early Modern Europe.' In *The History of Cartography*. University of Chicago Press, 2007: vol. 3, Part 1, 719–36.

Kain, Roger JP, and Elizabeth Baigent. *The Cadastral Map in the Service of the State: A History of Property Mapping*. University of Chicago Press, 1992: Chapter 9.

Dutch Polder Authorities

Kain, Roger JP, and Elizabeth Baigent. *The Cadastral Map in the Service of the State: A History of Property Mapping*. University of Chicago Press, 1992: Chapter 2.

Cadastral Map Usage in Europe after the Renaissance

Black, Jeremy. 'Government, State, and Cartography: Mapping, Power, and Politics in Europe, 1650–1800.' *Cartographica: The International Journal for Geographic Information and Geovisualization* 43, no. 2 (2008): 95–105.

Kain, Roger JP, and Elizabeth Baigent. *The Cadastral Map in the Service of the State: A History of Property Mapping*. University of Chicago Press, 1992: Chapters 4, 6 and 9.

Modernization of Paris

Kirkland, Stephane. *Paris Reborn: Napoléon III, Baron Haussmann, and the Quest to Build a Modern City*. St Martin's Press, 2013: Chapters 5 and 7.

Pinkney, David H. 'Napoleon III's Transformation of Paris: The Origins and Development of the Idea.' *The Journal of Modern History* 27, no. 2 (1955): 125–34.

Urban Planning

Shell, Jacob. 'Planning, Urban and Regional.' In *The History of Cartography*. University of Chicago Press, 2015: vol. 6, 1157–62.

Sutcliffe, Anthony. *Toward the Planned City: Germany, Britain, the United States, and France 1780–1914*. Basil Blackwell, 1981: Chapter 1.

Mapping Empire

Treaty of Tordesillas

Brotton, Jerry. *A History of the World in Twelve Maps*. Penguin, 2012: Chapter 6.

Nineteenth-Century Empire-Building

Bassett, Thomas J. 'Cartography and Empire Building in Nineteenth-Century West Africa.' *Geographical Review* (1994): 316–35.

Merriman, John. *A History of Modern Europe: From the Renaissance to the Present* (5th ed.). WW Norton & Company, 2019: Chapter 21.

The story behind the *Imperial Federation* map (Figure 6.9) is more nuanced than the map first suggests. The creator is believed to be Walter Crane, who was in favor of imperialism as a vehicle for social reform but against imperialism's exploitation of workers:

Biltcliffe, Pippa. 'Walter Crane and the Imperial Federation Map Showing the Extent of the British Empire (1886).' *Imago Mundi* 57, no. 1 (2005): 63–9.

Cadastral Mapping in Ireland and the United States

Kain, Roger JP, and Elizabeth Baigent. *The Cadastral Map in the Service of the State: A History of Property Mapping*. University of Chicago Press, 1992: Chapters 8 and 9.

Thrower, Norman JW. *Maps & Civilization: Cartography in Culture and Civilization* (3rd ed.). The University of Chicago Press, 2008: Chapter 8.

Maps and Decolonization: The Ngurrara Canvas II

Anker, Kirsten. 'The Truth in Painting: Cultural Artifacts as Proof of Native Title.' *Law Text Culture* 9 (2005): 91–124.

Geissler, Marie. 'Contemporary Indigenous Australian Art and Native Title Land Claim.' *Arts* 10 (2021): 32. Multidisciplinary Digital Publishing Institute.

Reilly, Alexander. 'Cartography and Native Title.' *Journal of Australian Studies* 27, no. 79 (2003): 1–14.

CHAPTER 7

Seeing the Unseeable

I N THE PREVIOUS FOUR chapters, we have investigated maps and technical and scientific drawings and their origins in the Renaissance. These information graphics portray physical objects and are intrinsically based on the object's physical geometry and visual appearance. Now, we will discuss a very different kind of information graphic, one that does not depict physical objects but instead uses a variety of visual metaphors to represent abstract relationships and quantities. In this and the following chapter, we explore the evolution of these graphics—diagrams, charts and plots—and the way in which they have shaped how we think about abstract concepts like time, numbers and social connection.

THE IMPORTANCE OF METAPHOR

Over the past five decades, linguists and cognitive scientists have discovered that metaphor is a fundamental reasoning mechanism. It allows us to leverage our direct experiences of the world to reason about more abstract concepts like time, emotion and possession. This discovery is part of a revolution in psychology. The human brain is no longer considered a disembodied computing device like a laptop or PC. Instead, psychologists now recognize that it is intrinsically embedded in the external world, the world it has evolved to understand and manipulate.

George Lakoff and Mark Johnson argue that subconscious conceptual metaphors are a routine part of everyday speech and underlie how we think about abstract concepts. The *understanding-is-seeing* metaphor is one

DOI: 10.1201/9781003507642-8

example that appeals to me because of my enthusiasm for data visualization. This metaphor is revealed in phrases such as 'Now I *see* what you are getting at' and 'We need to *look* closely at the details'.

Cognitive scientists believe that a handful of metaphors based on places, paths, motion, force and agency underlie the meaning of tens of thousands of words and constructions, not only in English but in all languages. A striking example is the use of spatial metaphors when thinking and speaking about time. One that is commonly used is the *events-in-time-are-a-sequence-in-space* metaphor. For instance:

> *The meeting with Lin is before the meeting with Tom.*
> *Your birthday is close to Christmas.*

Similar constructions are found in other languages, and the use of spatial metaphors to reason about time appears to be a human universal. Experiments have shown that spatial reasoning interacts with temporal reasoning but not vice versa, suggesting that spatial reasoning underpins temporal reasoning. However, while we have the predisposition to think of time spatially, this is mediated by culture. When asked to arrange objects from oldest to newest, English speakers place them left to right, Arabic speakers right to left, Mandarin speakers may position them vertically, and the Pormpuraaw people of northern Australia arrange them east to west regardless of their own orientation.

Conceptual metaphors not only underlie how we talk about abstract information but also how we visualize it. The timeline is an obvious example. It is a direct graphical representation of the *events-in-time-are-a-sequence-in-space* metaphor. Joseph Priestley was one of the first to position historical events on a timeline. Before then, chronological data had been presented in lists and tables. Priestley's *A Chart of Biography* (see Figure 7.1), published in 1765, showed the lifespan of historical figures using horizontal lines. Then, in a companion graphic, Priestley created a 'space–time' map charting the rise and fall of empires through the ages.

Priestley's charts were an immediate hit. They captured the Zeitgeist of the Enlightenment, the cluster of names at the right reflecting and reinforcing the belief that modern European nations, with their rational, scientific outlook, were the culmination of history. Priestley clearly explains the benefits of his visual metaphor:

> *As no image can be formed of abstract ideas, they are, of necessity represented by particular but variable ideas … Thus the abstract idea*

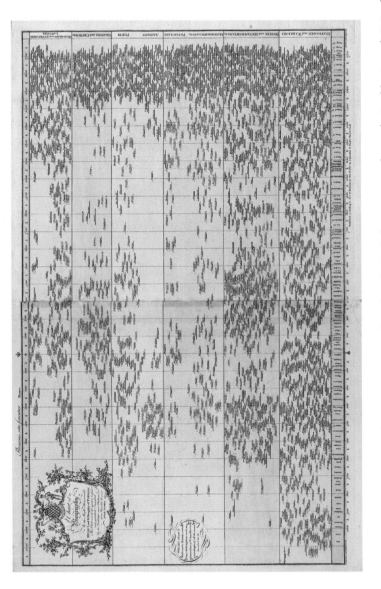

FIGURE 7.1   Timelines of historical events were introduced in the Enlightenment and popularized by Joseph Priestley. In his *A Chart of Biography* (1765), shown above, he used horizontal lines to show the lifespans of more than 2000 historical figures grouped by profession.

Credit: Library Company of Philadelphia.

of time, though it not be the object of any of our senses, and no image can properly be made of it, yet because it has real quantity, and we can say a greater or less space of time, it admits of a natural and easy representation in our minds by the idea of a measurable space, and particularly that of a line; which, like time, may be extended in length, without giving any idea of breadth or thickness. And thus a longer or a shorter space of time may be most commodiously and advantageously represented by a longer or a shorter line.

Just like linguistic metaphors, visual expressions of conceptual metaphors fundamentally shape our understanding of abstract ideas. The timeline underpins how Westerners think about time. We have previously seen how the *state-is-a-region* visual metaphor was critical in the invention of the modern state. We shall now explore how visual metaphors have shaped our understanding of other kinds of abstract concepts and relationships, such as kinship and numbers.

VISUALIZING RELATIONSHIPS

One of the oldest visual metaphors I know of is based on the *genealogy-is-a-tree* conceptual metaphor. This metaphor underlies phrases such as 'different *branches* of the family' and the visual metaphor of the family tree (see Figure 7.2). Family trees have been drawn for thousands of years: we saw an example from ancient China in Chapter 1. They were also used in ancient Rome. Roman writers describe how the central reception area of upper-class Roman family townhouses were decorated with portraits of the owners' ancestors connected by 'garlands' of ribbons.

Medieval manuscripts also contain family trees. These were visual aids for students wishing to remember complicated genealogies such as the ancestry of Christ, whose mother, Mary, was believed to descend from King David. Others showed the origin of noble families, reinforcing a family's ties to royalty.

Medieval scholars also used tree diagrams to classify and structure knowledge. This reflects the *knowledge-is-a-tree* metaphor, which has led to phrases such as 'the *root* of all knowledge' or 'different *branches* of science'. By the end of the Renaissance, the tree had become the primary metaphor for organizing and classifying knowledge. The introduction to Denis Diderot and Jean le Rond d'Alembert's *Encyclopédie*, for instance, featured a tree classifying different kinds of knowledge.

FIGURE 7.2 The *genealogy-is-a-tree* conceptual metaphor underlies the visual metaphor of the family tree. This family tree from 1641 shows the lineage of the kings of Portugal, from King Alfonso I to King João IV.

Credit: National Library of Portugal. E. 909 A.

These two different uses of the tree diagram—to show genealogy and to visualize hierarchical classification schemes—were brought together by Charles Darwin in the evolutionary tree (see Figure 7.3). Darwin was a meticulous draftsman who carefully drew natural specimens to record their similarities and differences and diagrams to think about geological and biological processes. His notebooks reveal how early versions of the evolutionary tree helped shape his understanding of natural selection. His seminal 1859 work *On the Origin of Species* contains only a single figure, that of an evolutionary tree. This formed the core of Darwin's argument. It shows how species have evolved from common ancestors. The more similar the species, the less time since they diverged from their shared ancestor. Thus, the tree shows both the genealogy of today's living species and a taxonomy for grouping them.

Family trees also exemplify the more general conceptual *social-relationship-is-a-physical connection* metaphor. We say that we feel

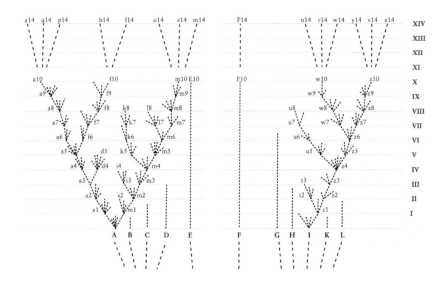

FIGURE 7.3 Evolutionary tree from Charles Darwin's *On the Origin of Species* (1859). The vertical axis shows time, with each horizontal line indicating 1000 generations. The letters A–L at the bottom represent ancestral species. The dotted lines show how three species—A, F and I—evolved into the species at the top. Reading across a horizontal line gives the species you would expect to find in the fossil record for that time period. Thus, the diagram resembles geological diagrams showing rock strata but also provides an explanation for the fossils found in each layer.

Credit: Redrawn by Kadek Satriadi.

connected to a friend or that there are *links* or *ties* between two families. In the Mesoamerican map shown in Figure 1.5, cords depict connections between ruling families. This metaphor also underpins diagrams showing social networks. Known as sociograms, these are widely used in the social sciences to show how people or other entities, such as companies, interact and influence one another.

Sociograms were introduced by Jacob Moreno in 1934 in his book *Who Shall Survive?* (see Figure 7.4). He used them to investigate how social

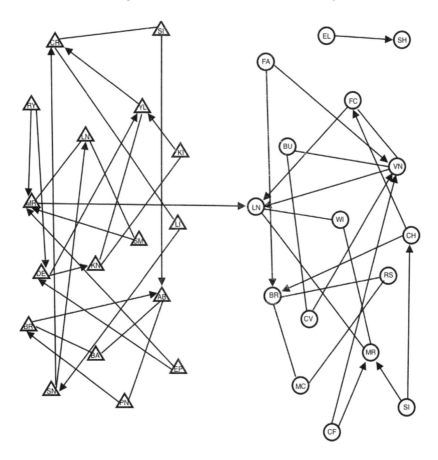

FIGURE 7.4   Sociograms were introduced by Jacob Moreno. He used them to show social interaction and influence between students in different grades. This example shows the relationships between fourth graders. Triangles denote boys and circles represent girls. The diagram reveals little interaction between the two genders at this age.

Credit: Jacob Levy Moreno. *Who Shall Survive? A New Approach to the Problem of Human Interrelations.* Nervous and Mental Disease Publishing Co., 1934. Redrawn by the author.

interaction at school changed as students grew older. He identified visual patterns that revealed different kinds of interaction and social roles, such as stars, who are the nucleus of a social group.

Commonly regarded as the founder of social network analysis, Moreno was, to say the least, an unusual figure. Born Jacob Levy in Bucharest in 1889, he lied about his origins, heard voices, and was encouraged by his mother to believe he was God. While undoubtedly brilliant, he was an extremely jealous man and happy to take credit for other people's work. Indeed, it is thought that while Moreno takes credit as the sole author of *Who Shall Survive?*, it was, in fact, a collaboration between Moreno and his partner at the time, Helen Jennings.

Sociograms are an example of a node-link diagram. These use nodes to represent the objects in the network and links or edges to represent relationships between the nodes. Node-link diagrams are not a modern invention. In the Middle Ages, they were used when teaching logical reasoning. Philosophers have long been interested in whether an argument is valid. The ancient Greeks investigated what you can validly conclude from two premises of the form: *Every X is Y, Some X are Y, No X is Y* and *Some X are not Y*. Medieval scholars used a simple node-link diagram called a square of opposition as a visual mnemonic to show the logical relationship between any two of these premises, which are called syllogisms (see Figure 7.5).

Node-link diagrams play an essential role in the mathematical theory of graphs. Graph theory began with the great Swiss mathematician Leonhard Euler's solution to the Königsberg bridges problem (see Figure 7.6). The town of Königsberg was built on either side of a river containing two large islands connected by seven bridges. The problem was to find a walk through the city that crossed each bridge exactly once. Euler abstracted the puzzle into what mathematicians now call a graph. This had four nodes, one for each side of the river and islands, connected by seven edges, one for each bridge. By considering the paths in this graph, Euler proved that it was impossible to find such a walk.

While Euler did not draw an abstract graph, subsequent mathematicians soon did, using node-link diagrams to visualize and understand them. Nowadays, graph theory underpins the mathematical analysis of social networks, biological networks and many other types of network.

Euler did use diagrams to teach logical reasoning to Princess Friederike Charlotte of Brandenburg-Schwedt and her younger sister Louise in a

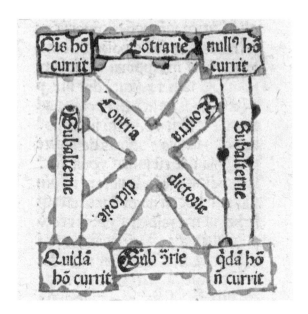

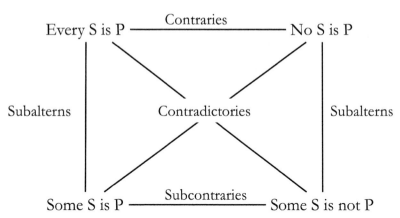

FIGURE 7.5 The top square is from a fifteenth-century publication by Nicolas d'Orbelles. The bottom square is an explanation. If two premises are contrary to one another, then at most one can be true, though neither may be true. If two premises are contradictories, then exactly one of them must be true. If two premises are subcontrary, then both may be true, but at most one is false. Finally, subaltern means that the top premise implies the bottom premise; that is, if the top premise is true, then so is the bottom one.

Credit: Top: Nicolas d'Orbelles. (1478). *Commentaries on Aristotle.* Columbia Digital Library Collections [Columbia University Libraries]. Bottom: Kadek Satriadi.

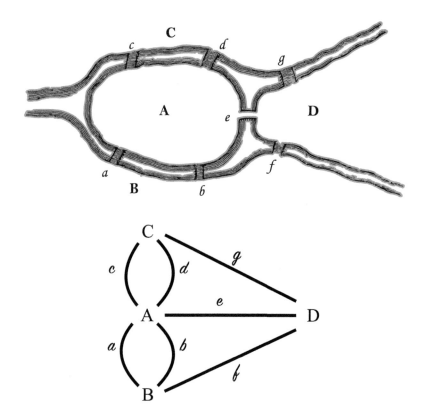

FIGURE 7.6   The Königsberg bridges problem. On top is Euler's original illustration of the problem and below is a modern representation using a node-link diagram.

Credit: Top: Leonhard Euler, 'Solutio problematis ad geometriam situs pertinentis.' *Commentarii Academiae Scientiarum Imperialis Petropolitanae*, vol. 8 (1736): 128–40. Courtesy The Euler Archive. Redrawn by Kadek Satriadi. Below: Author.

series of letters he wrote from 1760 to 1762. Now known as Euler diagrams, these use the region inside a geometric shape, usually a circle, to represent a set or class, with crosses or dots drawn in the region representing objects in the set or class; we saw in Figure 2.6 that a Ngaatjatjarra woman used a similar representation to show membership in the same family. Such diagrams provide a direct visual realization of the *classes-are-containers* conceptual metaphor that underlies reasoning about categories. This metaphor is revealed through phrases such as 'the class Mammalia *lies within* the Chordata phylum'.

The great power of this visual metaphor is that spatial containment and intersection exactly reflect mathematical set containment and intersection, allowing the novice logician to immediately see inferences flowing from the initial premises. As an example, consider the statements:

No cat is a dog.
All poodles are dogs.

If we look at the Euler diagram representing these premises, it is immediately apparent that no cat is a poodle.

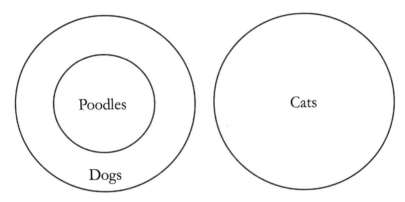

While Euler is often credited with inventing these diagrams, other logicians were already using them at the start of the eighteenth century, and their use may even date back to the Middle Ages.

VISUALIZING NUMBERS

While many of us remember Euler's and other types of mathematical diagrams from our school days, many professional mathematicians disparage their usefulness. This attitude dates from the late nineteenth century, by which time diagrams were felt to be misleading. For instance, the renowned mathematician and philosopher Bertrand Russell wrote in 1901, 'In the best [mathematical] books there are no figures at all.' I will now show that, despite the antipathy of Russell, diagrams have been integral to the development of mathematics. Math-phobic readers may wish to skip this section.

We have previously seen that geometric diagrams were central to the mathematics of the ancient Greeks and Renaissance scientists such as Galileo. More generally, diagrams have allowed mathematicians to visualize abstract concepts such as the real and complex number systems and mathematical functions. George Lakoff and Rafael Núñez have argued that mathematics is grounded in our experience of the world around us and that conceptual metaphors link mathematical concepts with these experiences. They claim that these metaphors provide mathematicians with the subconscious and conscious mental models that underlie mathematical reasoning.

In Chapter 1, we saw how tangible objects such as pebbles and clay tokens underpinned the development of arithmetic. Lakoff and Núñez call this the *arithmetic-is-object-collection* metaphor. They also discuss two other metaphors we use to understand numbers. The first is the *number-is-a-length* metaphor. Schoolchildren are introduced to this metaphor by the brightly colored, variable-length wooden rods named after their inventor, Georges Cuisenaire. The second metaphor is *numbers-are-a-sequence-in-space*. We see this conceptual metaphor in phrases such as 'four comes *before* five' and 'eight is *between* six and twelve'.

These metaphors come together in the number line. The earliest drawing of a number line I know of is from the seventeenth century, but rulers and measuring rods have been used for thousands of years. Nowadays, number lines, like Cuisenaire rods, are widely used to teach arithmetic. For instance, to add two numbers, you start at the point on the line representing the first number and then move right by the number of steps—that is, length—corresponding to the second number.

Number lines are not only used to teach basic arithmetic but also to introduce negative numbers. Extending the number line to the left of zero gives one a natural visual metaphor for negative numbers. This may have helped their acceptance by European mathematicians in the seventeenth century, who were quite uncomfortable with the idea of negative quantities.

The *numbers-are-a-sequence-in-space* metaphor is deeply entrenched. Experiments have found that English speakers unconsciously associate numbers with spatial location: smaller numbers with their left-hand side and larger numbers with their right-hand side. In one experiment, people were asked to indicate whether a number flashed on a screen was bigger or smaller than an initial number. They were asked to respond by pressing one of two response keys held in their left and right hands. People who held the 'less than' response key in their left hand and the 'larger than' response key in their right hand were quicker at responding and made fewer errors than those for which the response keys were swapped. This suggests that we reason about numbers as if they are mentally arranged in increasing order from left to right. Further experiments have corroborated our innate disposition to visualize numbers on a mental line. However, they have also revealed that orientation and spacing of numbers on this line depend on cultural factors such as reading direction and prior exposure to number lines.

The next great leap in visual metaphors for mathematics was to place two number lines at right angles to one another, creating the Cartesian coordinate system (the graphs with 'x' on the horizontal axis and 'y' on the vertical axis). This idea dates back to the late Middle Ages. At this time, philosophers were trying to understand rates of change, such as the velocity of moving objects or the variation in temperature along a bar heated at one end. Scholars at Merton College at Oxford realized that if an object moves with uniformly accelerating motion, then the distance it travels is equal to that covered by an object moving at a constant speed midway between the start and end velocity of the first body. The philosopher Nicole Oresme had the inspired idea of drawing a chart showing how the velocity varied over time (see Figure 7.7). He drew points indicating

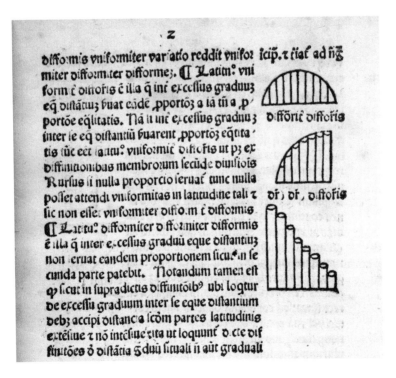

FIGURE 7.7 The medieval philosopher Nicole Oresme used a precursor to Cartesian coordinates to visualize different ways in which quantities such as velocity can vary over time.

Credit: Nicole Oresme, *De latitudinibus formarum* (1486). 88404. The Huntington Library, San Marino, California. This is an abridgement of his fourteenth-century work.

instances of time along the horizontal axis. Then he drew a vertical line for each point whose length gave the velocity. The resulting diagram for a body with uniformly accelerating motion provided a geometric justification for the Merton rule.

While Oresme did not express it like this, he had used two orthogonal axes to show the values of a mathematical function. His invention was ahead of its time—it was not until the mid-seventeenth century that mathematicians began to systematically use Cartesian coordinates for this purpose. This was when the mathematician and philosopher René Descartes and the gifted mathematician Pierre de Fermat invented analytic geometry by linking geometric curves with algebraic expressions. While Cartesian coordinates are named after Descartes, he did not use them. Fermat was probably the first to draw a function on a Cartesian plane when he sketched a linear equation as a line segment.

Analytic geometry underpinned the invention of differential and integral calculus by Isaac Newton and Gottfried Wilhelm Leibniz. Analytic geometry allowed mathematical functions to be visualized as curves on the Cartesian plane. Tangents to the curve and the area under the curve provide geometric intuition for differentiation and integration. Diagrams were at the heart of the first proof of the fundamental theorem of calculus: namely, if you take a function and compute the derivative—that is, tangents—of the area under the function, this equals the original function (see Figure 7.8).

Cartesian coordinates also played an essential part in the acceptance of complex numbers. These were introduced in the sixteenth century to allow all polynomial expressions, such as $x^2 = -1$, to have a solution, in this case the imaginary number i. But mathematicians were afraid of these new numbers: what on Earth did i mean? It was not until the introduction of the complex plane in the early nineteenth century that mathematicians felt comfortable using complex numbers. This provided a straightforward geometric interpretation of these hitherto unimaginable numbers. Now, a complex number was understood to be a point on a plane where the horizontal position gave its real part, and the vertical position gave its imaginary part.

Not only were diagrams important in mathematics, they also played a critical role in the development of modern economics. Alfred Marshall

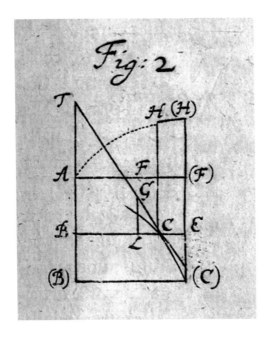

FIGURE 7.8   Geometric diagrams such as this one by Gottfried Wilhelm Leibniz from *Acta Eruditorum* (1693) were central to the invention of calculus in the seventeenth century.

Credit: Gottfried Wilhelm Leibniz Bibliothek—Niedersächsische Landesbibliothek, Hannover, Aa-A 35: 1693, p. 386.

wrote in the preface of his influential textbook *Principles of Economics*, first published in 1890, that:

> *The use of [diagrams] requires no special knowledge, and they often express the conditions of economic life more accurately, as well as more easily, than do mathematical symbols. [E]xperience seems to show that they give a firmer grasp of many important principles than can be got without their aid; and that there are many problems of pure theory, which no one who has once learned to use diagrams will willingly handle in any other way.*

Then, in the late nineteenth century, diagrams and geometric intuition fell out of favor because of the discovery of non-Euclidean geometries and functions whose properties were difficult to reconcile with the visual metaphor of a *mathematical-function-as-a-curve*; for example, a continuous function that is nowhere differentiable or a function whose one-dimensional curve completely fills a two-dimensional area. Mathematicians realized that their visual metaphors were no longer useful and, in fact, misleading. Terrified that their house of cards was collapsing, they developed a new foundation for mathematics, one that eschewed diagrammatic proofs and was instead based on formal logic. The only acceptable way to prove a mathematical theorem was by manipulating symbolic formulae. No diagrams were allowed.

Nonetheless, despite their rejection of diagrams in proofs, mathematicians continue to use graphics. They are ubiquitous in mathematics education. How could you learn calculus, trigonometry, vector spaces and linear algebra, statistics, or complex analysis without diagrams? They also play an indispensable role in graph, knot and category theory. There is now a belated appreciation by mathematicians and philosophers of the importance of diagrams in day-to-day mathematical practice as tools for insight and discovery. Despite Bertrand Russell's disdain, visual thinking with graphics in the 'mind's eye' or on paper or a computer screen remains widespread across mathematics in the twenty-first century.

Graphics also played another critical role in mathematics. Until computers and the electronic calculator were invented, tables were indispensable tools for calculation. The early seventeenth century saw the invention of the logarithm and the publication of logarithm tables. These tables transformed multiplication and long division into addition and subtraction. Computations that had previously taken hours now took only a few minutes.

Equally important were graphical computing devices such as the slide rule, volvelle (a diagram with rotating parts) and nomogram. Now forgotten, nomograms were once widely used by engineers. Their ingenious design allowed the engineer to quickly calculate the value of an unknown variable in an equation. The engineer laid a straight edge between the known values and observed where the edge intercepted the axis of the unknown variable, as this gave the unknown variable's value.

For instance, the nomogram in Figure 7.9 allows an electrical engineer to swiftly calculate the combined resistance, C, of two resistors, A and B, when connected in parallel. Or suppose the engineer wants a combined resistance of a particular value. In that case, they can use the diagram to find possible values for A and B.

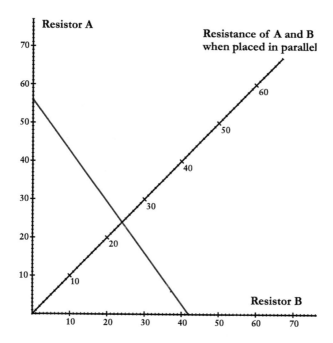

FIGURE 7.9 Nomograms were once widely used to compute the value of an unknown variable from the value of the other variables in an equation. The nomogram above can be used to calculate the resistance of two resistors connected in parallel. It encodes the equation $\frac{1}{C} = \frac{1}{A} + \frac{1}{B}$, which gives the combined resistance, C, of two resistors, A and B, connected in parallel. The red line shows us that if A and B have resistance 56 and 42, respectively, then their combined resistance, C, is 24. Or, if we want a combined resistance of 40, we can draw a line through 40 and vary its slope to find possible values for the resistors to connect in parallel.

Credit: Adaptation of Wikimedia Commons—Nomogram for calculating parallel resistance.

THE IMPORTANCE OF METAPHOR, REVISITED

We have seen how conceptual metaphors underlie visualizations such as family trees, node-link diagrams, timelines, number lines and the Cartesian plane, and how these enable us to visualize kinship, social networks, historical data, numbers and mathematical functions. These graphics ground our understanding and reasoning about these abstract concepts. They make the intangible tangible and form the basis for our mental models of genealogy, social networks, time and mathematics.

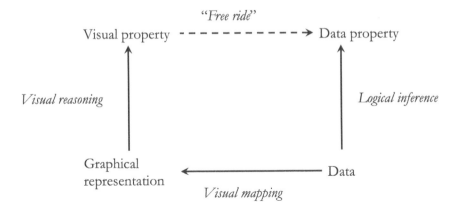

FIGURE 7.10   Data visualizations rely on a precise mapping from the under-lying data to its graphical representation. The viewer can reason visually about the graphic representation and then reverse the mapping to infer properties of the original data.

Graphical representations of abstract data are one of our most surprising and consequential inventions. While they may be built upon conceptual metaphors underlying everyday speech and thought, they take the utility of these metaphors to the next level. The resulting visual metaphors are crisp and precise. The mapping from data values to their graphical representation is exact, enabling the viewer to confidently and precisely reason about the underlying data.

The existence of a precise mapping from the underlying data to its visual representation is central to data visualization (see Figure 7.10). Linear perspective and parallel projections gave an exact method for mapping a three-dimensional object onto a technical drawing. Map projections provided a rigorous way to map the Earth's surface onto a flat map. In this chapter, we saw a new kind of visual mapping, one based on metaphor.

Crucially, in all these mappings, spatial and visual relationships between the symbols in the graphic representation mirror relationships in the under-lying data. The philosopher Atsushi Shimojima has studied how this con-gruence can give rise to cognitive 'free rides'. These occur when the mapping forces relationships hidden in the underlying data to become explicit in the visualization. Scaled plans, for instance, must show the distances between objects, and the Mercator projection must give the bearing between two locations. Euler diagrams are another example. Our sample Euler diagram depicting the relationship between poodles, dogs and cats must show that no poodle is a cat: it is a consequence of the geometric encoding of class containment. In Priestley's timeline of historical figures, the mapping forces us to place people who were born earlier than Descartes to his left, making it immediately clear which philosophers predate him.

Let's look at another example. We can use a position diagram to chart how well our friends play card games. If a player's name appears to the left of another player's name, then they are a better player. If we are told 'Greta is a better player than Sam', we depict this by:

Greta   Sam

If we are also told that 'Phil is a worse player than Sam', our diagram becomes:

Greta   Sam   Phil

Notice how the diagram is forced to show that Greta is a better player than Phil. It is an unavoidable consequence of the underlying mapping. If we add the information that 'Andria is a better player than Greta', then we immediately see from our diagram that Andria is the best player and Phil is the worst:

Andria   Greta   Sam   Phil

The diagram makes explicit information that is implicit in the original statements. Information that we would have had to carefully deduce when reasoning from the sentences describing our friends' card-playing abilities is immediately apparent in the diagram.

The key to designing effective data visualizations is to choose a mapping that allows the viewer to reason visually, reducing demands on working memory and replacing slow conscious processing with fast visual perception. In the next chapter, we will investigate this further. We will see how ingenious visual mappings have allowed us to visualize a wealth of statistical data ranging from population density to profits and losses.

NOTES, REFERENCES AND FURTHER READING

The Importance of Metaphor
Conceptual Metaphors

Lakoff, George. 'The Contemporary Theory of Metaphor.' In *Metaphor and Thought* (2nd ed.). Cambridge University Press, 1993: 202–51.

Lakoff, George, and Mark Johnson. *Metaphors We Live By* (2nd ed.). University of Chicago Press, 2003: Chapters 1–7 and Afterword.

Pinker, Steven. *The Stuff of Thought*. Penguin, 2007: Chapters 4 and 5.

Spatial Metaphors for Time

Boroditsky, Lera. 'Metaphoric Structuring: Understanding Time through Spatial Metaphors.' *Cognition* 75, no. 1 (2000): 1–28.

Boroditsky, Lera. 'How Languages Construct Time.' In *Space, Time and Number in the Brain*. Academic Press, 2011: 333–41.

Casasanto, Daniel, and Lera Boroditsky. 'Time in the Mind: Using Space to Think about Time.' *Cognition* 106, no. 2 (2008): 579–93.

Visual Timelines

Priestley, Joseph. *A Description of a Chart of Bibliography*, 1764. Quote p. 5.

Rosenberg, Daniel, and Anthony Grafton. *Cartographies of Time: A History of the Timeline*. Princeton Architectural Press, 2013: Chapters 1, 2 and 4.

Visual Metaphors

While hundreds of articles have been written about conceptual metaphors, almost all focus on their use in language. Understanding data visualization in terms of conceptual metaphor is uncommon. See, however:

Cox, Donna. 'Metaphoric Mappings: The Art of Visualization.' In *Aesthetic Computing*. MIT Press, 2006: 89–114.

Cybulski, Jacob, Susan Keller, and Dilal Saundage. 'Metaphors in Interactive Visual Analytics.' In *Proceedings of the 7th International Symposium on Visual Information Communication and Interaction* (2014): 212–15.

Risch, John S. 'On the role of metaphor in information visualization.' *arXiv preprint arXiv:0809.0884* (2008).

Woodin, Greg, Bodo Winter, and Lace Padilla. 'Conceptual Metaphor and Graphical Convention Influence the Interpretation of Line Graphs.' *IEEE Transactions on Visualization and Computer Graphics* 28, no. 2 (2021): 1209–21.

Ziemkiewicz, Caroline, and Robert Kosara. 'The Shaping of information by Visual Metaphors.' *IEEE Transactions on Visualization and Computer Graphics* 14, no. 6 (2008): 1269–76.

Visualizing Relationships

Family Trees

Bouquet, Mary. 'Family Trees and Their Affinities: The Visual Imperative of the Genealogical Diagram.' *Journal of the Royal Anthropological Institute* 2, no. 1 (1996): 43–66.

Klapisch-Zuber, Christiane. 'The Genesis of the Family Tree.' *I Tatti Studies in the Italian Renaissance* 4 (1991): 105–29.

Lima, Manuel. *The Book of Trees: Visualizing Branches of Knowledge.* Princeton Architectural Press, 2014: Chapters 1–3.

Structuring and Classifying Knowledge with Trees

Lima, Manuel. *Visual Complexity: Mapping Patterns of Information.* Princeton Architectural Press, 2011: Chapter 1.

Lima, Manuel. *The Book of Trees: Visualizing Branches of Knowledge.* Princeton Architectural Press, 2014: Chapters 1–3.

Evolutionary Trees

Darwin, Charles. *On the Origin of Species.* 1859. Reprinted by Routledge, 2004.

Lima, Manuel. *Visual Complexity: Mapping Patterns of Information.* Princeton Architectural Press, 2011: Chapter 2.

Priest, Greg. 'Diagramming Evolution: The Case of Darwin's Trees.' *Endeavour* 42 (2018): 151–71.

Sociograms

Freeman, Linton. *The Development of Social Network Analysis: A Study in the Sociology of Science.* Empirical Press, 2004: Chapter 3.

Lima, Manuel. *Visual Complexity: Mapping Patterns of Information.* Princeton Architectural Press, 2011: Chapter 3.

Node-Link Diagrams

Kruja, Eriola, Joe Marks, Ann Blair, and Richard Waters. 'A Short Note on the History of Graph Drawing.' In *International Symposium on Graph Drawing.* Springer, 2001: 272–86.

Lima, Manuel. *Visual Complexity: Mapping Patterns of Information.* Princeton Architectural Press, 2011: Chapter 3.

Parsons, Terence, 'The Traditional Square of Opposition.' In *The Stanford Encyclopedia of Philosophy.* Stanford University, Fall 2021.

Euler Diagrams

Lakoff, George, and Rafael Núñez. *Where Mathematics Comes From.* Basic Books, 2000: Chapter 6.

Lemanski, Jens. 'Logic Diagrams in the Weigel and Weise Circles.' *History and Philosophy of Logic* 39, no. 1 (2018): 3–28.

Moktefi, Amirouche, and Sun-Joo Shin. 'A History of Logic Diagrams.' In *Handbook of the History of Logic.* North-Holland, 2012: vol. 11, 611–82.

Visualizing Numbers

Antipathy to Diagrams by Modern Mathematicians

Giaquinto, Marcus. *The Philosophy of Mathematical Practice.* Oxford University Press, 2008: 22–42. The quote from Bertrand Russell is on p. 23.

In the last forty years, several mathematicians have rehabilitated the use of diagrams in mathematical proofs by developing diagrammatic rules of inference that are logically correct and cannot lead to erroneous reasoning. See:

Allwein, Gerard, and Jon Barwise (eds). *Logical Reasoning with Diagrams.* Oxford University Press, 1996.

Mathematics and Conceptual Metaphors

While some parts of Lakoff and Núñez are controversial, the importance of metaphors for conceptualizing number is, I believe, insightful:

Lakoff, George, and Rafael Núñez. *Where Mathematics Comes From.* Basic Books, 2000: Chapters 2–4.

Number Line

Giaquinto, Marcus. *Visual Thinking in Mathematics.* Oxford University Press, 2007: Chapter 6.

Göbel, Silke M, Samuel Shaki, and Martin H Fischer. 'The Cultural Number Line: A Review of Cultural and Linguistic Influences on the Development of Number Processing.' *Journal of Cross-Cultural Psychology* 42, no. 4 (2011): 543–65.

Katz, Victor J. *History of Mathematics* (3rd ed.). Pearson, 2009: 471–2.

Núñez, Rafael E. 'No Innate Number Line in the Human Brain.' *Journal of Cross-Cultural Psychology* 42, no. 4 (2011): 651–68.

Genesis of Cartesian Coordinates

Boyer, Carl B, and Uta C Merzbach. *A History of Mathematics* (3rd ed.). John Wiley & Sons, 2011: Chapters 12 and 15.

Katz, Victor J. *History of Mathematics* (3rd ed.). Pearson, 2009: Chapters 10 and 14.

Invention of Calculus

Boyer, Carl B, and Uta C Merzbach. *A History of Mathematics* (3rd ed.). John Wiley & Sons, 2011: Chapter 16.

Katz, Victor J. *History of Mathematics* (3rd ed.). Pearson, 2009: Chapters 15 and 16.

Nauenberg, Michael. 'Barrow, Leibniz and the Geometrical Proof of the Fundamental Theorem of the Calculus.' *Annals of Science* 71, no. 3 (2014): 335–54.

Complex Plane

Katz, Victor J. *History of Mathematics* (3rd ed.). Pearson, 2009: Chapter 22.

Visualizing the Economy

Blaug, Mark, and Peter John Lloyd. 'Introduction'. In *Famous Figures and Diagrams in Economics*. Edward Elgar, 2010: 1–23.

Larkin, Jill H, and Herbert A Simon. 'Why a Diagram Is (Sometimes) Worth Ten Thousand Words'. *Cognitive Science* 11, no. 1 (1987): 65–100. The quote from Marshall is from p. 94.

Use of Mathematical Diagrams in the Nineteenth and Twentieth Centuries

Carter, Jessica. *Visual Thinking in Mathematics*. Oxford University Press, 2019.

Giaquinto, Marcus. 'Visualizing in Mathematics'. In *The Philosophy of Mathematical Practice*. Oxford University Press, 2008: 22–42.

Mancosu, Paolo. 'Visualization in Logic and Mathematics'. In *Visualization, Explanation and Reasoning Styles in Mathematics*. Springer, 2005: 13–30.

Volvelles

Helfand, Jessica. *Reinventing the Wheel*. Princeton Architectural Press, 2002.

Nomograms

Glasser, Leslie, and Ron Doerfler. 'A Brief Introduction to Nomography: Graphical Representation of Mathematical Relationships'. *International Journal of Mathematical Education in Science and Technology* 50, no. 8 (2019): 1273–84.

Hankins, Thomas L. 'Blood, Dirt, and Nomograms: A Particular History of Graphs'. *Isis* 90, no. 1 (1999): 50–80.

Wikipedia. 'Nomogram'. https://en.wikipedia.org/wiki/Nomogram

The Importance of Metaphor, Revisited

Visual Mappings and 'Free Rides'

Chandrasekaran, B, Janice Glasgow, and N Hari Narayanan. In *Diagrammatic Reasoning: Cognitive and Computational Perspectives*. AAAI Press, 1995: Introduction.

Shimojima, Atsushi. *Semantic Properties of Diagrams and Their Cognitive Potentials*. CSLI Publications, 2015.

Sloman, Aaron. 'Interactions between Philosophy and Artificial Intelligence: The Role of Intuition and Non-Logical Reasoning in Intelligence'. *Artificial Intelligence* 2, no. 3–4 (1971): 209–25.

CHAPTER 8

Visualizing Statistics

IN THIS CHAPTER, WE turn our attention to bar charts, line charts, pie charts, choropleth maps, and the many other graphics used to analyze numerical data gathered by businesses, governments and scientists. Such statistical graphics are central to data visualization. Like sociograms and family trees, they employ visual metaphors to represent abstract quantities. However, unlike these and the other graphics discussed in the preceding chapters, statistical graphics are a modern invention with no precedent in early civilizations. They first appear in the late seventeenth century, at the Scientific Revolution's end and the Enlightenment's beginning, a product of an emerging emphasis on rational analysis.

ARRANGING DATA

Before the invention of statistical graphics, the most common way of dealing with abstract data was to organize it in a table. While a table is not the sexiest of graphics, it is simple to understand and construct—which is why we still rely on them today. Tables allow information to be arranged in two dimensions, each one providing an independent index for the data. Tables make it simple to compare data along each dimension: just run your eye along a row or column. This ability to use spatial location as an index is why tables are so effective.

In general, cues for indexing are one of the great benefits of a graphical representation. Elements related to one another are often close together or linked in a predictable way that allows the reader to quickly move their

DOI: 10.1201/9781003507642-9

focus from one to another. For example, in anatomical diagrams, we have seen how text labels may be placed next to the object they identify, or linked to it by indication lines. Colors can also be used as an index, visually linking related elements or highlighting elements matching search criteria.

Such graphical indexing contrasts with text. We read text sequentially and cannot quickly jump to other logically connected parts of the text. That is why medieval scholars invented the subject index and table of contents, graphical aids for navigating text.

However, while tables are great for understanding small amounts of data, it isn't easy to get an overview of a large dataset with a table. By the late nineteenth century, colors and textures sometimes replaced numeric values in tables, allowing the reader to immediately understand the overall data distribution. Table authors also began to manually rearrange the table to place similar rows and columns together, revealing previously hidden clusters in the data.

Nothing epitomizes the power of tables to organize data and reveal underlying structures more than the periodic table of chemical elements (see Figure 8.1). Eric Scerri writes about how the 'periodic table of the elements is one of the most powerful icons in science: a single document that captures the essence of chemistry in an elegant pattern.'

Like Darwin's evolutionary tree and Copernicus's diagram of the heliocentric system, the periodic table was a scientific watershed. It provided a simple and compelling representation of the discovery by chemists that, if you order the elements by the number of protons in their nucleus, there is an approximate repetition in their properties over regular but varying intervals. The table provided a framework for the whole of chemistry and fueled investigation into the structure of atoms.

The chemist Dmitri Mendeleev is credited with the invention of the periodic table, publishing his first version in 1869. At the time, chemists knew of sixty-one elements, and Mendeleev arranged these carefully in a grid based on their chemical and physical properties. By looking at gaps in his table, Mendeleev predicted the existence of three hitherto unknown elements, inferring their properties from those of their neighbors in the table with uncanny accuracy.

CHARTING DATA

When we think of data analysis, we do not, in fact, usually think of tables. Rather, statistical graphics such as bar or line charts come to mind. The cartographer, mathematician and astronomer Michael Florent van Langren is

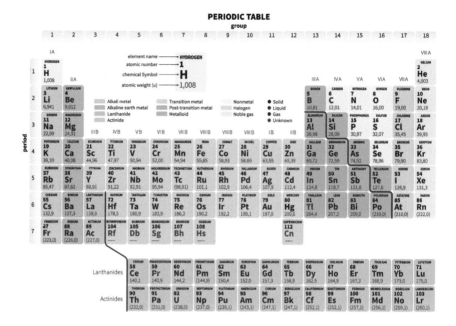

FIGURE 8.1   A modern version of the periodic table, with a cell for each chemical element ordered by the element's atomic number (the number of protons in an atom of that element). The cell gives the element's name, atomic number, chemical symbol and atomic weight. Each row is called a period: at left are the most reactive elements, the alkali metals, which gradually transition to the least reactive elements, the noble gasses, on the right. The color indicates the group the element belongs to, with group members sharing similar chemical and physical properties.

Credit: iStock.com/jack0m.

credited by Michael Friendly and co-authors with creating the first statistical graphic. As discussed in Chapter 5, while latitude was relatively easy to measure, determining longitude proved to be much more difficult as it required comparing the time at the current location with that at a reference location. Around 1630, near the end of the Renaissance, van Langren believed he had discovered an accurate way to determine longitude. While he died before publishing the details, it is thought he wished to use observations of the Moon's rotation to establish the time at the reference location. As part of requests for funding from the Spanish court to pursue his research, he presented variants of a diagram showing the great uncertainty in current estimates of the longitude between the Spanish city of Toledo and Rome (see Figure 8.2). Van Langren's diagrams proved persuasive and he successfully obtained funding.

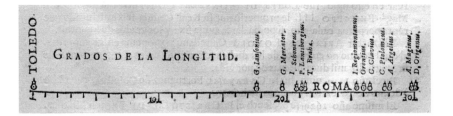

FIGURE 8.2   In 1644, Michael Florent van Langren plotted twelve different estimates of the difference in longitude between Toledo and Rome. These vary from less than 20 degrees to 30 degrees. His diagram clearly shows the wide range in these estimates and, therefore, the difficulty in accurately determining longitude with the techniques then known to Renaissance cartographers. In fact, the correct value, 16.5 degrees, is less than any of the estimates.

Credit: Copyright KBR INC B 635/2 (RP); MIC LP 1308.

However, van Langren's graphic is not a typical statistical graphic. He used a scaled chart to show longitude, an inherently spatial quantity. Therefore, he did not need a visual metaphor to map abstract data onto a graphical representation. It is likely van Langren viewed his graphic as a simplified map. Indeed, another version of his diagram is even more map-like: van Langren drew Toledo and Rome on separate horizontal lines and placed the line with Rome above and to the right of Toledo to indicate their different latitude and longitude.

By the late seventeenth century, however, we see examples of statistical graphics in the physical and social sciences that rely on visual metaphors to show abstract data. These were created by mathematicians and scientists who were likely to have been influenced by the use of Cartesian plane to graph mathematical functions. Their graphs were used to depict new kinds of data that had not been available previously. This included data from new measuring devices such as the pendulum clock, thermometer and barometer. In 1685, Robert Plot produced a stepped line chart showing the barometric pressure in Oxford for each day of the preceding year (see Figure 8.3). By 1771, scientists were using more modern-looking line graphs to record barometric pressure. Data points were now connected with straight line segments rather than steps, and the data was arranged horizontally, not vertically.

Another source of new data was the European states. They began to collect data about population and health after realizing that economic prosperity, tax revenue and military strength relied on the existence of a

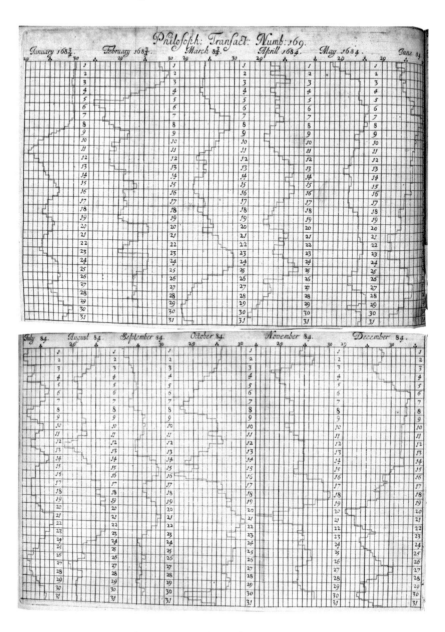

FIGURE 8.3   In 1685, the scientist Robert Plot published one of the first statistical graphics. He recorded the daily weather in Oxford in 1984 and used a stepped line graph to show the barometric pressure.

Credit: Plot, Robert. 'A letter from Dr. Robert Plot of Oxford, …', *Philosophical Transactions of the Royal Society* 15 (1685): 930–43. Courtesy The Royal Society.

large, healthy populace. Starting in 1603, the English Government collected weekly statistics of deaths in London so as to detect the outset of new epidemics and to judge the relative healthiness of different parishes. Six decades later, John Graunt, one of the founders of so-called 'political arithmetic', collated and arranged this data into tables. From this, he estimated London's population and the number of women and men in different age groups, and compared the causes of death. He also created the first life table—a table giving the probability of surviving to a particular age. This was graphed by Christiaan Huygens in 1669.

The aim of political arithmetic—or statistics, as it became known later in the nineteenth century—was to use empirical scientific methods to understand the economy, population, crime and public health. While we now take such an approach for granted, at the time this was a radically new approach to social policy. It was also controversial: collecting evidence and championing public health measures such as vaccination against smallpox was seen as interfering with God's will.

Nonetheless, as we saw from Lisa Best's graph of graphics use in the *Philosophical Transactions* (see Figure 4.13), graphs were rare in the seventeenth and eighteenth centuries. While physical and social scientists had new data sources, this data was not graphed. Instead, it appeared in tables. Even the line graphs of temperature, air pressure, wind speed and direction, or tide height produced by mechanical recording devices were routinely translated into tables for publication.

This began to change in the second half of the eighteenth century. First came Joseph Priestley and his historical time charts. Then came William Playfair, a graphical genius famous for inventing bar and pie charts. Playfair's favorite graphic, however, was the line graph, which he used to chart economic data over time. For instance, line graphs of imports and exports were central to his *Commercial and Political Atlas*, in which Playfair analyzed how England's trade balance had changed over the last century (see Figure 8.4). While he did not invent line graphs—he credits his brother, a scientist, with showing him these—he was the first to use them in economics. Playfair was the original data journalist. His graphs are not the cool, detached graphs of a scientist. They use labels, colors and captions to emphasize Playfair's message, such as the need for economic reform.

Playfair was a colorful character. Trained as an engineer, he worked for a few years as a draftsman for James Watt, the inventor of the first practical

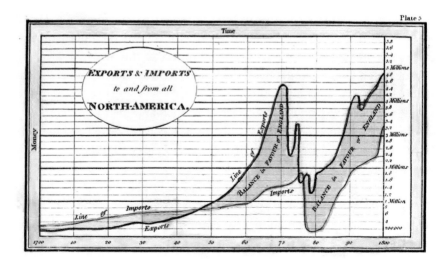

FIGURE 8.4   William Playfair introduced many of the statistical graphics we now take for granted. In his *Commercial and Political Atlas*, he used a series of line graphs to show England's balance of trade with other countries. These show the value of exports and imports since 1700. The area between the two is colored green if the balance of trade is in favor of England and red if not.

Credit: Playfair, William. *Commercial and Political Atlas* (3rd ed.), 1801.

steam engine. However, Playfair was ambitious and left to form a silver-smithing business. This failed, like so many of his ventures, and he decided to get rich by writing about economics. This was when he produced the first of his charts, influenced by the work of Priestley and making use of his technical drawing acumen. Unfortunately, this was also not financially successful. Playfair moved between France and England for the rest of his life, fleeing creditors and prison as one scheme after another proved fruitless. Indeed, at the end of his life, he was so desperate for money he resorted to blackmail—although again, he was unsuccessful. Even more remarkably, it has been suggested that Playfair was a secret agent who, after the French Revolution, helped undermine the French Republic by distributing counterfeit money to destroy confidence in the economy and government.

Playfair had a keen understanding of the benefits of graphics. Nonetheless, like Priestley, he still felt the need to explain and defend the visual metaphor underlying his charts (which he called lineal arithmetic) to a skeptical reader:

This method has struck several persons as being fallacious, because geometrical measurement has not any relation to money or to time; yet here it is made to represent both. The most familiar and simple answer to this objection is given by an example. Suppose the money received by a man in trade were all in guineas, and that every evening he made a single pile of all the guineas received during that day, each pile would represent a day, and its height would be proportional to the receipts of that day; so that by this plain operation, time, proportion, and amount, would all be physically combined.

Lineal arithmetic then, it may be averred, is nothing more than those piles of guineas represented on paper, and on a small scale, in which an inch (suppose) represents the thickness of five millions of guineas, as in geography it does the breadth of a river, or any other extent of country.

To the modern reader, it seems surprising that such an explanation is necessary. After all, the conceptual metaphor *more-is-up* is commonplace: we talk of interest rates *rising* or a *drop* in house prices. Nonetheless, it was a big step in Playfair's time to base a graphical display on this metaphor, and it took time for readers to appreciate the value of his charts. They carried the *more-is-up* metaphor to a new level of usefulness, enabling it to become more precise than is possible with words.

One graph that Playfair did not use is the scatterplot. Exactly who was the first to create a scatterplot is a matter of debate, as this was developed incrementally rather than in a moment of profound insight. In 1760, the mathematician, scientist and cartographer Johann Heinrich Lambert plotted data on the Cartesian plane and then fitted curves to the data to determine the mathematical function that best matched it. Later, in a paper presented to the Royal Astronomical Society in 1832, John Frederick W. Herschel describes how he drew a grid of lines and plotted his two-dimensional data as points on the grid to compute the orbit of a double star. In a wonderful example of visual thinking, he explains:

Our next step, then, must be to draw, by the mere judgement of the eye, and with a free but careful hand, not through, but among them, a curve presenting as few and slight departure from them as possible, consistently with this character of large and graceful sinuosity, which must be preserved at all costs ...

Scatterplots, even more than line charts, bar charts or pie charts, provided scientists with a powerful tool for discovering unexpected patterns and correlations in their data. There are examples in many branches of science. One is the scatterplot published in 1958 by the economist Alban William Phillips. By graphing wage inflation against unemployment, he showed a trade-off between the two. For the first time, economists saw that low unemployment went hand in hand with high wages, and high unemployment led to lower wages.

Another example is the Hertzsprung–Russell (HR) scatterplot (see Figure 8.5). Named after the two astronomers who created it in the early

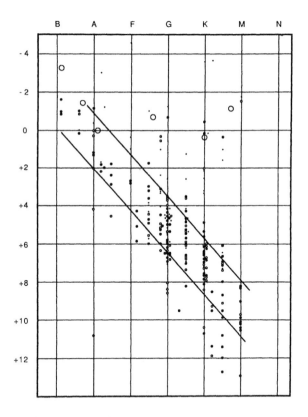

FIGURE 8.5   Redrawn copy of Henry Norris Russell's 1914 scatterplot of star brightness against spectral color.

Credit: Ian Spence and Robert F Garrison 'A Remarkable Scatterplot.' *The American Statistician* 47, no. 1 (1993). © 1993 American Statistical Association and the American Society for Quality, reprinted by permission of Informa UK Limited, trading as Taylor & Francis Group, www.tandfonline.com on behalf of 1993 American Statistical Association and the American Society for Quality.

twentieth century, this had a profound impact on modern astronomy, especially our understanding of star structure and evolution. Astronomers had long observed that stars differed in brightness and color, ranging from blue-white to orange, yellow and red. A scatterplot of brightness (corrected for distance from the observer) against spectral color (which reflects the star's temperature) showed that most stars fell on a diagonal band stretching from high brightness and low spectral color to low brightness and high spectral color. This is now called the main sequence of stars. The plot also revealed another cluster of stars away from this diagonal: the blue- and red-(super)giants, which followed a horizontal line at the top of the scatterplot.

We now know that, for most of their lifetimes, stars lie along the main sequence, with the position depending upon their mass: heavier stars are hotter and brighter, lying in the upper left corner, while lighter stars are cooler and less bright, lying in the lower right corner. As stars age and burn up their hydrogen, they become cooler and less dense, increasing in size and transforming into a (super)giant. Finally, they collapse into a dwarf star, found at the bottom of the scatterplot. Unlike Herschel or Phillips's scatterplots, data in the HR diagram does not lie along a simple curve: without a scatterplot, it would be very difficult to identify these clusters and hence the different stages in stellar evolution.

DATA MAPS

At about the same time that Robert Plot created his stepped line chart of barometric pressure, other scientists began to overlay data on top of maps. Edmond Halley was responsible for two of the first data maps. Halley was one of those larger-than-life European adventurer-scientists who traveled to distant parts of the world, meticulously measuring and recording whatever they saw. He is best known for predicting that a spectacular comet seen in 1682 would return every seventy-five years. The comet was christened Halley's Comet after his prediction proved correct and it returned in 1758. Halley invented the diving bell and was partial to opium. He also argued that the world was much older than the Bible suggested and that the Great Flood might have a natural explanation. (He hypothesized it might have been caused by a comet.)

The oldest of Halley's maps is from 1686 (see Figure 8.6). This shows prevailing wind directions worldwide and is based on data gleaned from navigators and Halley's observations made during an expedition to St Helena. His second data map was one of the first maps to use contours. At the time, understanding how compass readings varied from true north was

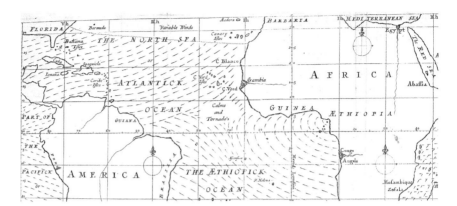

FIGURE 8.6   The scientist Edmond Halley created two of the first data maps. The figure above is part of a map showing prevailing wind directions. Note how he used tapered lines to show direction, except in a tiny region near Cape Verde where he used arrows. After Halley, most maps of wind directions used arrows.

Credit: Halley, Edmond. 'An Historical Account of the Trade Winds,...', *Philosophical Transactions of the Royal Society* 16 (1686): 153–68. Courtesy The Royal Society.

a matter of great practical importance to mariners. Halley used contours to chart this deviation, first in the Atlantic Ocean and then extended to other seas.

Using contours to connect adjacent locations with the same value has proven extremely useful. Apart from showing height or depth, contours are now best known for showing pressure in weather maps. But they have also been used to chart water salinity, rainfall, hours of sunshine, temperature, radiation exposure and many other phenomena. All that is required is that the data being charted varies smoothly across the area of interest.

Early data maps did not only show physical data. A data map from 1741 showed the distribution of languages in Europe, and another map of Europe from 1782 showed where different commodities were produced.

However, despite these examples, the use of data maps in the seventeenth and eighteenth centuries was rare. This changed in the early nineteenth century when the German geographer and scientist Alexander von Humboldt championed a new kind of science. Until then, controlled experiments had been the primary tool for scientists to address questions in physics, chemistry and biology. Humboldt, the foremost natural scientist of the time, advocated the holistic study of physical and biological phenomena. He spent five years traveling through the Americas, carefully observing the plants, animals, climate and geology. No longer were scientists to study nature inside a laboratory. Instead, they should be out in the real world observing and theorizing about more complex objects whose behavior depends on their spatial distribution. In 1817, Humboldt wrote how:

> *The use of graphic means will shed light on phenomena of the greatest interest for agriculture and for the social state of the inhabitants. If instead of geographical maps, we only possessed tables ... a large number of curious connections that continents manifest in their forms and their surface inequalities would have remained unknown.*

While Humboldt more often constructed diagrams than maps, he inspired others to create a multitude of maps, showing ocean currents, the location of underwater volcanoes and trenches, prevailing winds and temperature, geology, vegetation and animal distribution, and meteorology.

The early nineteenth century also saw an increased use of data maps in the social sciences. A map from 1826 by Charles Dupin, an engineer turned social statistician, showed the level of primary school education in different parts of France. He wrote, 'To render the most important of these differences visible, I hit upon the idea of giving those departments that sent fewer pupils to schools the darker shades.' The map quickly became famous for highlighting the sharp divide between France's 'enlightened' northern region and the 'obscure' southern region. This was the first example of what is now called a choropleth map: a map that uses color or shading to show the value associated with sub-regions.

Social scientists were also interested in population and population density. They invented several data maps to visualize these (see Figure 8.7). The first and simplest was to write the total in each map region, just like spot elevations were reported on early military maps. A second approach was to draw a symbol, such as a circle, in the region's center whose size was proportional to the population. Another way was to use a dot or other mark to represent 'x' number of people, and to draw the appropriate number of dots in each region and spread these uniformly across it. This also showed population density, as dot density was proportional to population density. The most common method was the choropleth map. This used discrete colors or patterns to show population density. A cartogram provided yet another approach. In this data

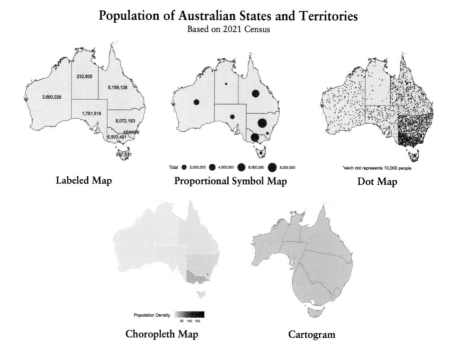

Population of Australian States and Territories
Based on 2021 Census

Labeled Map Proportional Symbol Map Dot Map

Choropleth Map Cartogram

FIGURE 8.7   Cartographers and statisticians invented a variety of data maps to show population and population density.

Credit: Kadek Satriadi.

map, the area of each region in the map is rescaled to become proportional to the region's population while preserving the region's general shape and orientation.

The early nineteenth century saw the invention of another important data map: the weather map. The first weather maps were retrospective records of meteorological data collected by scientists interested in understanding weather and climate. This changed in the 1830s and 1840s when the electric telegraph allowed meteorological data to be collected in real time over large areas. This was data that could, in theory, be used to predict tomorrow's weather. The desire of farmers and the military to predict damaging weather events such as frost or storms fueled the development of modern weather charts called synoptic charts.

By the late nineteenth century, the simultaneous observation of weather conditions—wind direction and force, cloudiness, precipitation, air temperature and pressure—at widely distributed weather stations were routinely transmitted to a central weather bureau. Here, meteorologists plotted these observations onto synoptic charts, identifying weather patterns such as low-pressure systems. Then, using years of experience, they predicted the following day's weather by envisaging how these patterns would progress across the region of interest. Finally, their forecasts were disseminated to newspapers and local weather stations using the electric telegraph.

From the very start, the public embraced weather maps (see Figure 8.8). The first daily weather maps were displayed as a novelty for two months

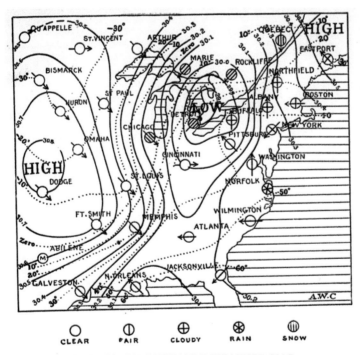

THE BOSTON "HERALD" WEATHER MAP.

FIGURE 8.8   By the end of the nineteenth century, weather maps had become an essential part of the newspaper (above). Their popularity has not declined, and colored animated weather maps are a regular feature in modern news broadcasting (below).   (Continued)

Credit: Top: Weather map from the afternoon issue of the *Boston Herald*, January 24, 1894. From R De C Ward. 'The Newspaper Weather Maps of the United States.' *The American Meteorological Journal*, Vol 11 Issue 3, 1894: 96–100. Bottom: BBC www.bbc.com/weather/map (November 15, 2023). With permission.

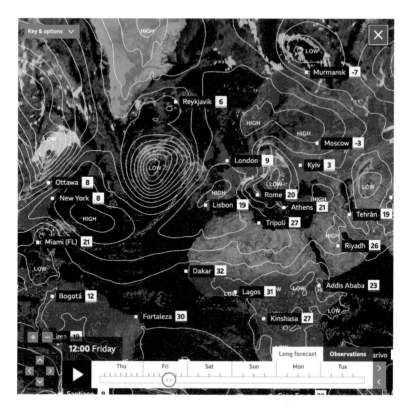

FIGURE 8.8 (Continued)

in 1851 at London's Great Exhibition, held in the Crystal Palace. Then, in 1875, the *Times* of London published the first daily weather map. Other countries followed, and the weather map established itself as a requisite element of the daily newspaper. It remains a regular part of both print and online news services.

SEEING PATTERNS

Before proceeding, it is worth investigating why statistical graphics such as line charts, scatterplots and data maps are so valuable. Why were Playfair and Humboldt so enthusiastic about their charts? Why do we continue to use them?

In the last chapter, we introduced cognitive free rides and how a well-designed graphic enables the viewer to replace slow, conscious processing with fast visual perception. Playfair intuitively understood this. He identified that the advantage of his charts over a table was that they allowed the viewer to more easily see patterns and trends:

The advantage provided, by those charts is not that of giving a more accurate statement than by figures, but it is to give a more simple and permanent idea of the gradual progress and comparative amounts, at different periods, by presenting to the eye a figure, the proportions of which correspond with the amount of the sums intended to be expressed.

We see patterns and trends because our visual system groups visual features into larger regions that are likely to belong to the same object. This occurs without conscious awareness and is essentially instantaneous. Suppose you glance at an animal obscured by trees in a forest (see Figure 8.9). As a

FIGURE 8.9   Our visual system uses rules of thumb to group visual elements together as a precursor to object recognition. Here, regions with similar texture and color are grouped together, and we see the boundaries of these regions as continuous even when obscured by foliage or other elements of the scene, allowing us to recognize the elephant hidden behind the trees.

Credit: João Mateus via Pixabay.

precursor to recognition, the visual system groups regions of similar texture and color to reveal the animal hidden behind the trees.

The rules that the visual system uses to group visual features together were first studied by German psychologists in the early twentieth century. They called them Gestalt laws. Based on their research, we now know that our visual system automatically groups elements for several reasons. The principal rules (see Figure 8.10) are:

Proximity: Elements that are near one another are grouped together. This is why adjacent data points are seen as a cluster on a scatterplot, and a group of buildings on a map is recognized as an entity such as a village.

Similarity: Visually similar elements, such as those having the same color, orientation, shape or texture, are grouped together. That's why coloring cells in a table based on their value allows us to see hitherto unknown patterns in the data.

Connectedness: Connection by lines is another reason for grouping elements. Together with proximity, this is why we see clusters in node-link diagrams.

Continuity: We tend to group region boundaries and lines whose combination forms a smooth, continuous shape. Continuity allows us to see correlations and trends, or to follow individual lines when they cross in a multi-line time series or node-link diagram.

Closure and common region: We like to see closed contours, and our visual system automatically extends lines to close them. We tend to see these contours as 'objects', and being 'inside' the same closed contour is a powerful grouping principle. That's why Euler diagrams and contour lines on maps make so much visual sense.

Parallelism: Elements that mirror each other's shape or direction, such as parallel lines, are also grouped together. This is why adjacent parallel lines in a floor plan are perceptually grouped together and seen as a single object: a wall.

Shared fate: Elements that move together are grouped together. This potent clue permits us to detect a rapidly advancing predator even when it is obscured by thick undergrowth. While not useful for traditional paper-based visualizations, shared fate helps us see patterns in animations.

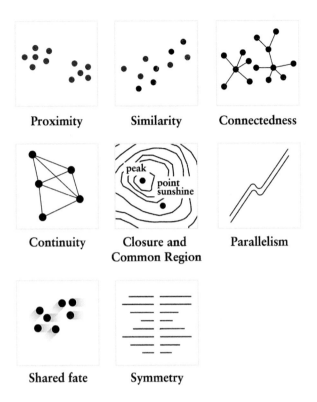

FIGURE 8.10   Our visual system uses a variety of inbuilt rules of thumb to group visual features together. These are automatic and underpin our ability to see patterns in data visualizations.

Credit: Kadek Satriadi.

Symmetry: We readily recognize symmetry, especially around a horizontal or vertical axis, and symmetric elements are grouped together. While I cannot think of a data graphic that utilizes symmetry for grouping, symmetry detection is still valuable. For instance, it lets us immediately notice that a distribution is skewed from its frequency plot, or if two distributions are similar in a paired bar chart.

Part of the reason Gestalt laws are so powerful is that our brain processes visual input in parallel. This allows us to subconsciously obtain an overview of a graphic the moment we see it. However, while it feels like we see all aspects of the scene in front of our eyes at the same level of detail, this is not true. To experience this, shut one eye and look directly at the X in the middle of the line below and see how many characters you can identify to its left and right.

$$U\,H\,H\,G\,C\,K\,G\,V\,G\,P\,O\,P\,\underline{X}\,W\,Q\,P\,L\,C\,H\,R\,S\,J\,I\,O\,P\,N\,R$$

You will have found that you can only read the characters immediately around the X. In fact, the region of acutest vision is only about the size of your thumbnail held at arm's length.

We are usually unaware of this because our eyes are continually moving to whatever region of the visual field we are interested in, focusing for about a third of a second before moving on. Our brain stitches these disparate images together to create the illusion of a single unified view. Furthermore, regardless of where we are focusing, our visual system is subconsciously summarizing visual properties, such as color, texture and line orientation, across our entire field of view. This allows us to extract the gist of a scene from a single glance. In less than one-tenth of a second, we know we are looking at a network diagram, not a bar chart, and that the nodes in the network form two large clusters.

This overview guides subsequent exploration, allowing the eye to focus on those parts of the graphic most relevant to the task at hand. It is in stark contrast to how we read text, where we must laboriously read each word, one at a time, and slowly piece together the overall meaning.

THE GOLDEN AGE OF STATISTICAL GRAPHICS

Despite the cognitive benefits of statistical graphics and the examples set by graphic pioneers like Halley and Playfair, it was not until 1830 that graphical representations of data began to regularly appear in scientific journals. Figure 4.13 illustrates this change, with the percentage of articles containing graphs in *Philosophical Transactions* increasing steadily through the nineteenth century. In particular, between 1850 and 1900, there was an explosion in the use of statistical graphics.

Characterized by an 'unrestrained enthusiasm' for graphics by statisticians and government authorities, this period was regarded as a Golden Age by H. Gray Funkhouser and christened the Golden Age of Statistical Graphics by Michael Friendly. This fervor was enabled by several factors. First, by 1850, the most common statistical charts and data maps had been invented. Second, nineteenth-century improvements in printing reduced the cost and skill required to produce graphics and enabled them to be printed in color.

A third reason was data availability. While the use of graphics in the physical sciences had steadily increased from the start of the nineteenth century, their use in the social sciences had been limited because of a lack of publicly available data. This changed in the early nineteenth century as various countries, including the United States, Britain and France, introduced official censuses, and government bureaucrats began systematically collecting data on health, crime and trade. By the 1830s, Western Europe and the United States were inundated by an 'avalanche of printed numbers'.

The final factor was the changing social context. One of the primary motivations for developing statistics and statistical graphics was the desire to have an empirically grounded method for answering social questions. While the second half of the nineteenth century was a Golden Age for statistical graphics, it was not a Golden Age for the average person. The Industrial Revolution had led to crowding, pollution and deteriorating living conditions as workers and their families were forced to move from the country to the rapidly growing cities to find work. The result was widespread unrest.

Governments wanted a 'social science' that could identify and moderate the causes of poor health, crime and poverty. Like Humboldtian science, this required techniques for identifying trends, correlations and patterns in larger, more complex and often spatially distributed data. By the Golden Age of Statistical Graphics, it had become clear that, while tables were suited to showing individual numbers, graphics were needed to see the trends and patterns. Consequently, there was strong interest in charting 'moral statistics' during the Golden Age: data about poverty, alcoholism, marriages, suicides, crime and prostitution. Data maps and other graphics were used to investigate regional differences and the relationships between these and possible explanatory factors such as living conditions, disease and education.

Charles Booth's maps of London poverty illustrate this (see Figure 8.11). A rich shipping magnate, Booth, like many wealthy Londoners, was concerned by the squalor and poverty of London and wanted to know whether the situation was hopeless. To do so, he and his team visited every street in the city, classifying households into eight classes based on income. Booth found that nearly one-third of London's inhabitants lived under the poverty line (a term he introduced and a good example of a visual metaphor). His reports and accompanying maps were a significant impetus for social reform. They provided a bird's-eye view of the problem, revealing that while poor households were spread throughout London, the extent was not as great as many had feared, and so was manageable. Booth's survey

FIGURE 8.11   Charles Booth mapped household wealth in the late nineteenth century to understand the extent of poverty in London. He found that about one-third of Londoners lived in poverty.

Credit: London School of Economics and Political Science. 'Charles Booth's London.' 2016.

and maps fueled his arguments for an old-age pension, which was subsequently introduced in 1908.

This Golden Age of Statistical Graphics was also when Florence Nightingale produced her famous 'rose' charts. Nightingale was an influential advocate of the power of statistics to inform health policy and was the first woman to be elected to the Royal Statistical Society. In 1854, she volunteered to lead a team of nurses to care for British soldiers fighting in the Crimean War. She soon discovered that the leading cause of death was poor sanitation in the hospitals treating the soldiers, not direct injury on the battlefield. Appalled, she started a campaign for the British Government to improve standards for treating soldiers in field hospitals. Rose charts were not part of her initial report to the queen and the British Parliament. She provided these later when she realized that the tables and recommendations in her first report were being ignored and that she needed a more compelling way to bring home the horrific and unnecessary loss of life (see Figure 8.12).

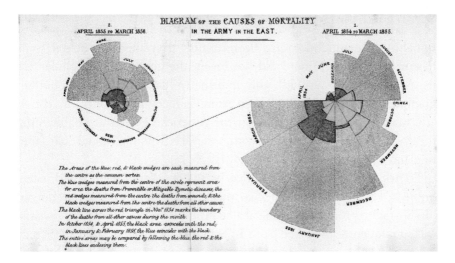

FIGURE 8.12 Nightingale used rose charts, also known as polar-area charts, to convince the British Army of the need to improve hospital hygiene. We immediately see that the number of preventable deaths due to poor sanitation (shown in blue) greatly exceeds the number of deaths from wounds (red) or other causes (black). Nightingale's charts also reveal the impact of basic improvements in sanitation, with the rose on the left showing the death rate after the sewers were cleaned and ventilation improved.

Credit: David Rumsey Map Collection, David Rumsey Map Center, Stanford Libraries.

It is, however, Charles Joseph Minard who perhaps best captures the graphical exuberance and skill of this Golden Age. Minard trained as an engineer, taking responsibility for the construction and maintenance of canals, ports and harbors, as well as France's first railroads. Highly respected, he was forced to retire as a practicing engineer in 1851 when he reached the mandatory retirement age of seventy. This was the beginning of his new career in statistical graphics. Reflecting his background in transport infrastructure, his prime interest was in showing the flow of goods and people.

Figure 8.13 shows two of Minard's graphics. The top chart is one of Minard's first data graphics. It graphs freight transportation along the Canal du Centre between Chalon and Dijon. The horizontal axis lists the intermediate stops along the canal. Stacked 'tiles' between adjacent stops show the goods traveling between them, with an arrow indicating in which direction. The tile's height is proportional to the number of barrels shipped, and its width is proportional to the distance traveled. This gives rise to a clever free ride: the area of each tile reflects the transport cost for that good on that leg.

Minard frequently showed flows using lines whose width was proportional to the magnitude of the flow, running from the flow's source to its destination. While Minard did not invent the flow map, he popularized its use, creating beautiful, highly informative data graphics. The bottom graphic in Figure 8.13 is a splendid example. It compares European cotton and wool imports before and after the American Civil War, highlighting the drastic impact of the war on cotton imports from the United States into England and continental Europe.

French officials from the Office of Public Works were inordinately impressed by Minard's graphics, so much so that they created a new bureau of statistics to produce a graphical atlas. The *Album de statistique graphique* was subsequently published from 1879 to 1897. This series used an incredible variety of charts and data maps and is regarded by Friendly as the 'pinnacle of the Golden Age'.

France was not alone in creating a national graphical atlas. The *U.S. Census Atlas* was produced for the three censuses held between 1870 and 1890. Like the French atlases, these were sumptuously illustrated and highly inventive. They introduced, for instance, the paired histogram to compare distributions for males and females.

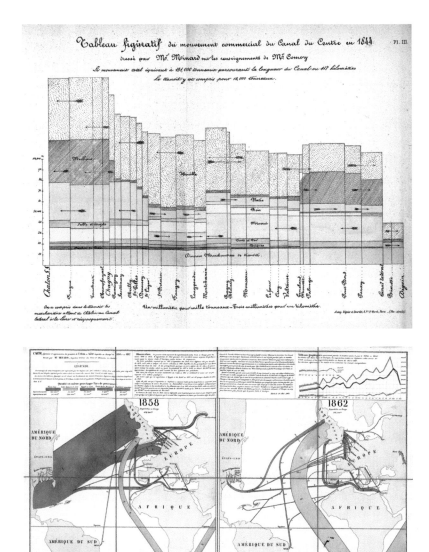

FIGURE 8.13   Two graphics by Charles Joseph Minard. The top graphic shows freight transportation along the Canal du Centre between Chalon and Dijon. The bottom graphic exemplifies Minard's mastery of the flow map.

Credit: Top: *Tableau figuratif du mouvement commercial du Canal du Centre en 1844*; 1845; cote: 4°5299/C307. Bottom: 'Carte figurative et approximative des quantités de coton en laine importées en Europe en 1858 et en 1862' in 'Tableaux graphiques et cartes figuratives par Charles-Joseph Minard', FOL.10975. Collections de l'École nationale des ponts et chaussées.

By the late nineteenth century, statistical charts and data maps were no longer confined to scientific journals. They now played an essential role in informing government policy and communicating national statistics to the public. This was also when the first textbooks on designing and producing statistical graphics were released. And at the International Statistical Congress, delegates showed off new types of charts and data maps and engaged in heated debates on standardization. But then, at the turn of the century, this unbridled enthusiasm by statisticians for graphics collapsed. This was because of the invention of mathematical techniques for statistical analysis. Before this development, visual inspection was the best way of fitting curves to data or determining if two variables were correlated.

During the nineteenth century, mathematicians invented least squares methods for curve fitting and tests for correlation and regression. Then, in the early twentieth century, came statistical tests for significance. In essence, these tested whether the data supported a particular scientific hypothesis by calculating the likelihood that the data would have been observed if the hypothesis was false. If the probability was less than 0.05 (or some other low threshold), the results were said to be statistically significant and the hypothesis was accepted.

The development of a mathematical theory of statistics led to an 'inference revolution' in the social sciences. These developments were the product of insights provided by graphical methods. But, once invented, statistical tests replaced charts and plots, and statisticians began viewing graphics as unnecessary and possibly misleading. Undoubtedly, this rejection was also influenced by the dismissal of diagrams by mathematicians such as Bertrand Russell.

THE SPREAD OF STATISTICAL GRAPHICS

Nonetheless, while statisticians and social scientists turned away from charts and graphs, businesses, schools and newspapers increasingly embraced them. During the second half of the nineteenth century, there was a revolution in the way businesses were organized and operated. Before the 1850s, virtually all businesses were family owned and operated, and most people worked in a family-run farm, shop or trade. It's hard to believe, but business management was not a profession. Businesses were small enough that there was no need for a hierarchy of salaried managers to supervise employees.

Alfred Chandler has charted the rise of the modern business enterprise in the United States. Before 1840, there were no large enterprises with a multilevel management hierarchy. However, by World War I, this had become the dominant business institution in many parts of the American economy.

The reasons for this are rooted in how the Industrial Revolution changed manufacturing, distribution and communication. The railway and electric telegraph allowed the formation of large distributed enterprises; indeed, the first modern businesses were formed to run the railways and telegraph networks. The railways in particular required a large amount of capital to build and then carefully coordinated management to ensure safety, as nearly all railways utilized a single line of track. Control and ownership of railways were separated as the operational tasks were too varied, too burdensome and too complex for company owners to undertake. They employed railway managers with specialized skills organized into an administrative hierarchy. For the first time, professional managers had a career path.

Before the rise of the modern business enterprise, the only type of graphics regularly used in business were tables for recording financial transactions. Bookkeeping was inextricably intertwined with the rise of early capitalism in the late Middle Ages and Renaissance. It encouraged a capitalist view of business as a game of profit and loss, with nothing else mattering but the 'bottom line'. Transparent bookkeeping became even more necessary with the arrival of the joint stock company during the nineteenth century. Dodgy business deals and bankruptcies revealed the need for independent financial auditors and a way of distinguishing income from profit. Accountancy joined business management as a new profession.

The tool in trade of accountants was double-entry bookkeeping. This was first used by merchants in Venice in 1300, soon after the arrival of Hindu-Arabic numerals, and may well be based on Arabic or Indian practices. As its name suggests, in double-entry bookkeeping, every transaction is recorded in a ledger (a table of descriptions and amounts) twice since every credit has a corresponding debit of equal value. For instance, if a merchant buys some cloth, the cost of the fabric will be recorded as a debit entry under cloth assets and a credit entry under cash. This means that, at all times, the running total of all credit entries should equal that of the debit entries: a handy way for the merchant to check that they have not made a mistake.

By arranging the entries under different categories, such as cash and various types of assets, it was possible to understand which products were profitable and which were making a loss. Double-entry bookkeeping was therefore ideally suited to business analysis. Furthermore, the value of the company's assets or capital was clearly separated from the company's income. This distinction between capital and income is at the core of modern capitalism, allowing the calculation of profit and company dividends. It has also shaped economic theories of capitalism. Indeed, Karl Marx's definition of capital is believed to be based on his knowledge of double-entry bookkeeping.

But business managers wanted more than just double-entry bookkeeping. As organizations became more complex, they began to collect data to run the business more efficiently and predict and plan for future demand. At first, managers organized this into tables and forms. Then, in the early twentieth century, as the amount of data grew, they began to use statistical graphics. In a business text by Willard Brinton from 1914, for instance, we find instructions for creating a variety of statistical charts: pie charts; simple, compound and stacked bar charts; line graphs; area charts; scatterplots; and choropleth and proportional symbol data maps.

These were not the only graphics that managers used. The late nineteenth and early twentieth centuries saw the rise of 'scientific management'. Spearheaded by engineers, this viewed an organization as a giant machine, workers as interchangeable cogs, and the manager's job as designing efficient workflows and streamlining processes. Unsurprisingly, given engineers' penchant for graphics, scientific management utilized charts and diagrams. Organization charts detailed administrative hierarchies and responsibilities, flow diagrams depicted business processes, and Gantt charts were used for scheduling. With these, the savvy manager could streamline production and root out inefficiency.

It was not only managers who turned to statistical graphics. Murray Dick writes:

The popularization of abstract graphical forms spread slowly through the first quarter of the twentieth century; in textbooks and gazetteers ... in the illustrated weeklies and popular national press, the serious and financial press and in the 'respectable' provincial press.

The first printed news-sheets date from the seventeenth century. Before this time, only a privileged minority could read, and they relied upon handwritten letters for information. The steam press, cheaper paper and increased literacy led to the modern newspaper in the nineteenth century. However, early newspapers consisted of text with few illustrations. Graphs such as line charts rarely appeared, and if they did, readers had to be instructed on how to interpret these strange diagrams.

The caption for a line graph of deaths due to a cholera outbreak shown in Figure 8.14, which was published in 1849, reveals this unfamiliarity. The editor felt compelled to provide detailed instructions on how to understand it:

> *Each half-inch along the bottom line represents a week. The dates are placed under each. At the end of each half-inch, or week, are upright dotted lines, whose various lengths indicate the number of deaths by Cholera, and other causes, during that week; each inch on these upright lines corresponds to 500 deaths. The numbers are placed at the top of each. The zig-zag lines, which join the ends of these lines, show by their upward or downward slope, whether the deaths during those weeks have increased or decreased, rapidly or slowly.*

This is in striking contrast to the assumption by news media during the recent COVID-19 pandemic that line charts showing deaths from the virus were readily understood.

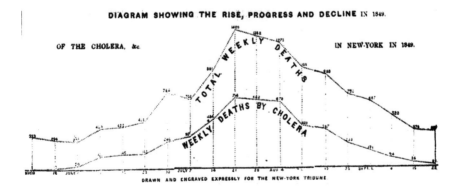

FIGURE 8.14   Line graphs were unfamiliar to most people during the nineteenth century, rarely appearing in newspapers. This line graph from the front page of the *New York Daily Tribune* from September 29, 1849, showing deaths due to a cholera outbreak, is a notable exception.

Credit: Chronicling America, Library of Congress.

In the late nineteenth century, transformations in printing enabled newspapers to use more graphics. By 1901, *The Times* was regularly publishing weather maps and, on occasion, other maps and line graphs of commodity prices. Financial newspapers also began to use line graphs, reflecting their increasing use in the business community. Nonetheless, 'serious' newspapers remained largely graphics-free until the early 1970s.

Populist newspapers and magazines, on the other hand, included line drawings and photographs from the end of the nineteenth century. They also contained maps and some infographics. These were not the sober, unadorned 'scientific' graphics of *The Times* or the *Financial Times*. They were designed to add visual appeal and attract the reader's attention. Pictorial charts showing relative magnitude using different-sized drawings were typical (see Figure 8.15). Such graphics also frequently appeared in school textbooks and atlases.

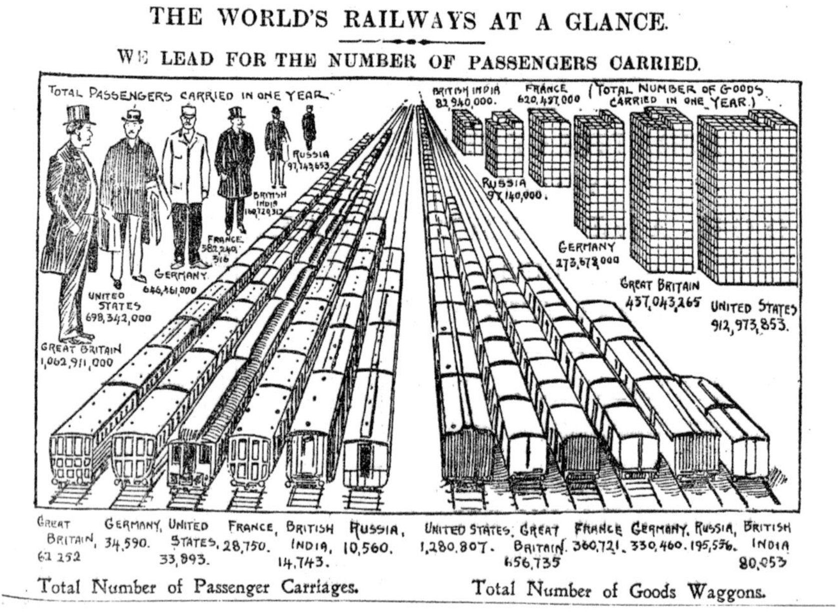

FIGURE 8.15 Pictorial charts like that shown above were common in popular newspapers and educational publications in the early twentieth century. This example from the *Dundee Courier & Argus* of January 12, 1900 compares the size of different countries' railways. These pictures were intended to lend a bit of visual interest to an otherwise dull article.

However, these pictorial charts were difficult to interpret. Brinton railed against their use in his graphics text from 1914, instead advocating using multiple copies of the same-sized icon arranged in a sequence to show magnitude. This approach was taken to the next level of graphical sophistication in the late 1920s by Otto Neurath, Maria Reidemeister and Gerd Arntz. They developed the Vienna pictographs method for presenting economic and social statistics in a way intended to be engaging, emotive and readily understood by the public. This utilized a consistent vocabulary of simple, stylized symbols arranged in horizontal lines in groups of five or ten. For instance, they used a man with his hands in his pocket to represent the unemployed and a coffin to depict annual deaths.

Thus, while statistical graphics fell out of favor with statisticians and social scientists in the early twentieth century, they became increasingly common in business and began to be seen at school and in newspapers. This increased exposure to graphics by the public helped to set the scene for the Golden Age of Data Visualization in the late twentieth century.

NOTES, REFERENCES AND FURTHER READING

The history of statistical graphics has not received the same attention as that of maps and few books are devoted to the topic. A noteworthy exception is:

Friendly, Michael, and Howard Wainer. *A History of Data Visualization and Graphic Communication*. Harvard University Press, 2021.

Michael Friendly has written extensively about the history of statistical graphics, and he and Daniel Denis's Milestones Project provides a comprehensive interactive visualization of the main historical events in statistical data visualization (http://datavis.ca/milestones/). Also see:

Friendly, Michael, Matthew Sigal, and Derek Harnanansingh. 'The Milestones Project: A Database for the History of Data Visualization.' In *Visible Numbers: The History of Data Visualization*. Ashgate Press, 2012: 219–34.

The books by Edward Tufte also provide many examples of early statistical graphics:

Tufte, Edward R. *Envisioning Information*. Graphics Press, 1990.
Tufte, Edward R. *The Visual Display of Quantitative Information* (2nd ed.). Graphics Press, 2001.

Arranging Data
Use of Shading and Permutation
Wilkinson, Leland, and Michael Friendly. 'The History of the Cluster Heat Map.' *The American Statistician* 63, no. 2 (2009): 179–84.

History of the Periodic Table

While a table remains the standard way of visualizing the periodic structure of the chemical elements, other visualizations have been suggested, including spirals, concentric circles, and helixes on cones or cylinders.

Mazurs, Edward G. *Graphic Representations of the Periodic System during One Hundred Years.* University of Alabama Press, 1974: Chapters 2 and 3.

Scerri, Eric R. *The Periodic Table: Its Story and Its Significance.* Oxford University Press, 2007. The quote is from p. xv.

Visual Indexing

Larkin, Jill H, and Herbert A Simon. 'Why a Diagram Is (Sometimes) Worth Ten Thousand Words.' *Cognitive Science* 11, no. 1 (1987): 65–100.

Charting Data

Van Langren's Graphic

Friendly, Michael, Pedro Valero-Mora, and Joaquín Ibáñez Ulargui. 'The First (Known) Statistical Graph: Michael Florent van Langren and the "Secret" of Longitude.' *The American Statistician* 64, no. 2 (2010): 174–84.

Friendly, Michael, and Howard Wainer. *A History of Data Visualization and Graphic Communication.* Harvard University Press, 2021: Chapter 2.

Evolution of the Line Chart

Kostelnick, Charles, and Michael Hassett. *Shaping Information: The Rhetoric of Visual Conventions.* Southern Illinois University Press, 2003: Chapter 4.

Seventeenth-Century Statistical Graphics and Political Arithmetic

Friendly, Michael, and Howard Wainer. *A History of Data Visualization and Graphic Communication.* Harvard University Press, 2021: Chapters 1 and 3.

Funkhouser, H Gray. 'Historical Development of the Graphical Representation of Statistical Data.' *Osiris* 3 (1937): 269–404.

Headrick, Daniel R. *When Information Came of Age: Technologies of Knowledge in the Age of Reason and Revolution, 1700–1850.* Oxford University Press, 2000: Chapter 3.

William Playfair

Berkowitz, Bruce D. *Playfair: The True Story of the British Secret Agent Who Changed How We See the World.* George Mason University Press, 2018: Chapter 7.

Friendly, Michael, and Howard Wainer. *A History of Data Visualization and Graphic Communication.* Harvard University Press, 2021: Chapter 5.

Funkhouser, H Gray. 'Historical Development of the Graphical Representation of Statistical Data.' *Osiris* 3 (1937): 269–404.

Playfair, William. *The Commercial and Political Atlas* (3rd ed.). 1801. Quote from p. xi.

Wainer, Howard. *Graphic Discovery*. Princeton University Press, 2005: Chapters 1–3.

More-Is-Up Conceptual Metaphor

Lakoff, George, and Mark Johnson. *Metaphors We Live By* (2nd ed.). University of Chicago Press, 2003: Chapter 4.

Scatterplots

Friendly, Michael, and Howard Wainer. *A History of Data Visualization and Graphic Communication*. Harvard University Press, 2021: Chapter 6.

Spence, Ian, and Robert F Garrison. 'A Remarkable Scatterplot.' *The American Statistician* 47, no. 1 (1993): 12–19.

Tilling, Laura. 'Early Experimental Graphs.' *The British Journal for the History of Science* 8, no. 3 (1975): 193–213.

Data Maps

Cartographers call maps showing statistical data 'thematic maps'. These are maps that show the spatial distribution of a particular phenomenon or 'theme' rather than general reference maps. Thematic maps, however, are broader than data maps and include, for instance, geological maps. I prefer to use Edward Tufte's term 'data maps' for thematic maps of abstract data.

Edmond Halley

Cook, Alan H. *Edmond Halley: Charting the Heavens and the Seas*. Oxford University Press, 1998.

Dmitri, Levitin. 'Halley and the Eternity of the World Revisited.' *Notes & Records Royal Society* 67 (2013): 315–29.

Jardine, Lisa. *Ingenious Pursuits: Building the Scientific Revolution*. Anchor, 2000: Chapters 1 and 7.

Halley's and Other Early Data Maps

Delaney, John. *First X, Then Y, Now Z: An Introduction to Landmark Thematic Maps*. Princeton University Library, 2012.

Robinson, Arthur H. *Early Thematic Mapping in the History of Cartography*. University of Chicago Press, 1982: Chapters 3 and 4.

Humboldt

Friendly, Michael, and Gilles Palsky. 'Visualizing Nature and Society.' In *Maps: Finding Our Place in the World*. University of Chicago Press, 2007: 207–53. The quote from Humboldt is from p. 105.

Robinson, Arthur H. *Early Thematic Mapping in the History of Cartography*. University of Chicago Press, 1982: Chapters 2 and 3.

Data Maps in the Social Sciences

Delaney, John. *First X, Then Y, Now Z: An Introduction to Landmark Thematic Maps*. Princeton University Library, 2012.

Friendly, Michael, and Gilles Palsky. 'Visualizing Nature and Society.' In *Maps: Finding Our Place in the World*. University of Chicago Press, 2007: 207–53. The quote from Dupin is from p. 240.

Robinson, Arthur H. *Early Thematic Mapping in the History of Cartography*. University of Chicago Press,1982: Chapter 6.

Mapping Population

Nusrat, Sabrina, and Stephen Kobourov. 'The State of the Art in Cartograms.' *Computer Graphics Forum* 35, no. 3 (2016): 619–42.

Robinson, Arthur H. *Early Thematic Mapping in the History of Cartography*. University of Chicago Press, 1982: Chapter 5.

Slocum, Terry A, Robert B McMaster, Fritz C Kessler, and Hugh H Howard. *Thematic Cartography and Geovisualization* (4th ed.). CRC Press, 2022: Chapters 15–20.

Weather Maps

Monmonier, Mark. *Air Apparent: How Meteorologists Learned to Map, Predict, and Dramatize Weather*. University of Chicago Press, 1999: Chapters 2, 3 and 9.

Seeing Patterns

Grouping and Gestalt Laws

Peterson, Mary A, and Ruth Kimchi. 'Perceptual Organization in Vision.' In *The Oxford Handbook of Cognitive Psychology*. Oxford University Press, 2013: 9–31.

Playfair, William. *Lineal Arithmetic; Applied to Shew the Progress of the Commerce and Revenue of England During the Present Century*. 1798. Quote from pp. 6–7.

Visual Attention

Cave, Kyle, and Ruth Kimchi. 'Spatial Attention.' In *The Oxford Handbook of Cognitive Psychology*. Oxford University Press, 2013: 117–30.

Schwartz, Bennett L, and John H Krantz. *Sensation and Perception* (2nd ed.). Sage Publications, 2019: Chapter 9.

Extracting the 'Gist' of a Graphic

Alvarez, George A. 'Representing Multiple Objects as an Ensemble Enhances Visual Cognition.' *Trends in Cognitive Sciences* 15, no. 3 (2011): 122–31.

Cohen, Michael A, Daniel C Dennett, and Nancy Kanwisher. 'What Is the Bandwidth of Perceptual Experience?' *Trends in Cognitive Sciences* 20, no. 5 (2016): 324–35.

Sapra, Akshay. *What Do We See in the First Few Milliseconds?* MSc Thesis. Monash University, 2020.

The Golden Age of Statistical Graphics

The Emergence of the Golden Age

Friendly, Michael. 'The Golden Age of Statistical Graphics.' *Statistical Science* 23, no. 4 (2008): 502–35.

Funkhouser, H Gray. 'Historical Development of the Graphical Representation of Statistical Data.' *Osiris* 3 (1937): 269–404. Quote 'unrestrained enthusiasm' from p. 330.

Tilling, Laura. 'Early Experimental Graphs.' *The British Journal for the History of Science* 8, no. 3 (1975): 193–213.

Reasons for the Golden Age

Friendly, Michael, and Howard Wainer. *A History of Data Visualization and Graphic Communication*. Harvard University Press, 2021: Chapter 7.

Hacking, Ian. 'Biopower and the Avalanche of Printed Numbers.' *Humanities in Society* 5 (1982): 279–95.

Headrick, Daniel R. *When Information Came of Age: Technologies of Knowledge in the Age of Reason and Revolution, 1700–1850*. Oxford University Press, 2000: Chapter 3.

Porter, Theodore M. *The Rise of Statistical Thinking, 1820–1900*. Princeton University Press, 1986: Chapter 1.

Charles Booth

Kimball, Miles A. 'London through Rose-Colored Graphics: Visual Rhetoric and Information Graphic Design in Charles Booth's Maps of London Poverty.' *Journal of Technical Writing and Communication* 36, no. 4 (2006): 353–81.

Florence Nightingale

Brasseur, Lee. 'Florence Nightingale's Visual Rhetoric in the Rose Diagrams.' *Technical Communication Quarterly* 14, no. 2 (2005): 161–82.

Friendly, Michael, and Howard Wainer. *A History of Data Visualization and Graphic Communication*. Harvard University Press, 2021: Chapter 4.

Magnello, M Eileen. 'Victorian Statistical Graphics and the Iconography of Florence Nightingale's Polar Area Graph.' *BSHM Bulletin: Journal of the British Society for the History of Mathematics* 27, no. 1 (2012): 13–37.

Charles Joseph Minard

Friendly, Michael. 'Visions and Re-Visions of Charles Joseph Minard.' *Journal of Educational and Behavioral Statistics* 27, no. 1 (2002): 31–51.

Rendgen, Sandra. *The Minard System: The Complete Statistical Graphics of Charles-Joseph Minard*. Princeton Architectural Press, 2018.

Robinson, Arthur H. 'The Thematic Maps of Charles Joseph Minard.' *Imago Mundi* 21 (1967): 95–108.

Statistical Atlases

Friendly, Michael. 'The Golden Age of Statistical Graphics.' *Statistical Science* 23, no. 4 (2008): 502–35.

International Statistical Congress

Funkhouser, H Gray. 'Historical Development of the Graphical Representation of Statistical Data.' *Osiris* 3 (1937): 269–404.

The 'Inference Revolution' and End of the Golden Age

Friendly, Michael. 'The Golden Age of Statistical Graphics.' *Statistical Science* 23, no. 4 (2008): 502–35.

Gigerenzer, Gerd, and David J Murray. *Cognition as Intuitive Statistics*. Lawrence Erlbaum Associates, 1987: Chapter 1.

The Spread of Statistical Graphics

Rise of the Modern Business Enterprise

Chandler, Alfred Dupont. *The Visible Hand: The Managerial Revolution in American Business*. Belknap Press, 1977.

Gleeson-White, Jane. *Double Entry*. Allen & Unwin, 2011: Chapter 6.

Double-Entry Bookkeeping

Gleeson-White, Jane. *Double Entry*. Allen & Unwin, 2011: Chapters 1, 4, 6 and 7.

Use of Statistical Graphics in Business

Brinton, Willard Cope. *Graphic Methods for Presenting Facts*. The Engineering Magazine Company, 1914: Chapters 1–11.

Smith, William Henry. *Graphic Statistics in Management.* McGraw-Hill, 1924: Chapters 4–10.

Wilson, James M. 'Gantt Charts: A Centenary Appreciation.' *European Journal of Operational Research* 149, no. 2 (2003): 430–7.

Yates, JoAnne. *Control through Communication: The Rise of System in American Management.* John Hopkins University Press, 1989: vol. 3, Chapter 6.

Evolution of Newspapers

Baldwin, Tamara Kay. 'Newspapers in Europe after 1500.' In *The Function of Newspapers in Society: A Global Perspective.* Praeger Publishing, 2003: 89–102.

Frasca, Ralph. 'Newspapers in Europe before 1500.' In *The Function of Newspapers in Society: A Global Perspective.* Praeger Publishing, 2003: 79–87.

Monmonier, Mark. *Maps with the News: The Development of American Journalistic Cartography.* University of Chicago Press, 1989: Chapter 2.

Graphics in Newspapers and School Textbooks

Dick, Murray. *The Infographic: A History of Data Graphics in News and Communications.* MIT Press, 2020: Chapters 3 and 4. The quote is from p. 132.

Drucker, Steven, Samuel Huron, Robert Kosara, Jonathan Schwabish, and Nicholas Diakopoulos. 'Communicating Data to an Audience.' In *Data-Driven Storytelling.* CRC Press, 2018: 211–31.

Monmonier, Mark. *Maps with the News: The Development of American Journalistic Cartography.* University of Chicago Press, 1989: Chapter 2.

Vienna Pictographs

Jansen, Wim. 'Neurath, Arntz and ISOTYPE: The Legacy in Art, Design and Statistics.' *Journal of Design History* 22, no. 3 (2009): 227–42.

CHAPTER 9

Modern Visualization

W E INTRODUCED THE GOLDEN Age of Statistical Graphics in the previous chapter and the Golden Age of Dutch Cartography in Chapter 5. We are now in a new Golden Age. In the last fifty years, data visualization and information graphics have become pervasive. We use them at work and home and view them on popular media. Unlike previous Golden Ages, this time, *everyone* is using data visualization. We will investigate the reasons for this dramatic increase in this and the next chapter.

VIRTUAL BUILDINGS AND MACHINES

The obvious explanation for this upsurge is the computer, undoubtedly the greatest invention of the twentieth century and one of the greatest inventions of all time. Its genesis lies in World War II. Before the electronic computer, mathematical calculations were performed by hand. Indeed, the original meaning of 'computer' was a person who computes or calculates. But while graphics such as logarithmic tables, nomograms and mechanical calculators helped, manual calculation was time-consuming and error-prone.

Matters came to a head when, as part of the war effort, the US military employed hundreds of mainly female 'computers' to produce firing tables for new types of artillery. If the target's position was known, the firing table gave the gunner the elevation and direction in which they had to aim the gun. However, it took a month to produce a new firing table, a significant bottleneck in the deployment of new weapons. The US military realized it

DOI: 10.1201/9781003507642-10

needed a way to do this more quickly. As a result, it funded the development of the electronic computer. While not finished in time to help the US war effort, the Electronic Numerical Integrator and Computer, or ENIAC, completed in 1946, is regarded as the world's first general-purpose electronic computer.

Improvements to the ENIAC came quickly. Soon, universities, governments and large businesses were using large and hugely expensive mainframe computers for scientific calculation and data processing. It also became apparent that computers could be used to create engineering and architectural drawings.

In 1963, Ivan Sutherland submitted his PhD thesis to MIT. Sutherland had built Sketchpad, the world's first interactive computer graphics editor (see Figure 9.1). Sketchpad allowed a designer to fashion graphics from

FIGURE 9.1   Sketchpad was the first interactive graphics editor. Created by Ivan Sutherland in the early 1960s, it established computer graphics and CAD as new research fields. The photograph above shows Sutherland using Sketchpad to create an engineering drawing.

Credit: Courtesy of MIT Lincoln Laboratory and courtesy of the Computer History Museum.

straight lines and circular arcs. These could be resized and repositioned using a light pen, a forerunner of today's computer stylus. Sutherland demonstrated the creation of scientific, mathematical and engineering drawings using his program. His work helped establish computer-aided design (CAD) and gave rise to a new field of computer science known as computer graphics, which underpins modern data visualization. In 1988, Sutherland was awarded the ACM A.M. Turing Award, the computer science equivalent of a Nobel Prize, for 'his pioneering and visionary contributions to computer graphics, starting with Sketchpad'.

The first commercial CAD systems ran on mainframes and then on personal computers (PCs) when these came onto the market in the late 1970s. These early tools were drafting aids, facilitating the manual creation of engineering and architectural drawings. The main advantage of these tools over manual drafting was that they made it quicker and easier to modify an existing design. They could also perform simple housekeeping functions like keeping a tally of each off-the-shelf component, such as screws or bolts, used in the design. Nonetheless, their chief purpose was to produce technical drawings identical to those previously drafted by hand.

This changed with Pro/ENGINEER. Released in 1987, Pro/ENGINEER required the designer to construct a 3D computer model rather than a technical drawing, a shift from relying on the indirect representation afforded by the lines and points in a technical drawing. While Pro/ENGINEER was not the first CAD tool to utilize 3D computer models, it was groundbreaking because it forced the designer to view the 3D model as the primary goal of the design process (see Figure 9.2). While Pro/ENGINEER could automatically generate orthogonal, perspective, isometric or whatever kind of view the designer wanted from the 3D model, these were optional by-products.

Access to a complete 3D model allowed CAD tools to provide significantly more assistance to the designer. They could analyze how the design would respond to pressure or stress, and check that moving components had sufficient clearance. Furthermore, as the tool automatically generated technical drawings from the 3D model, inconsistencies between drawings were eliminated. In fact, in some engineering applications, technical drawings were no longer needed as the CAD system could directly generate instructions from the 3D model for software-controlled machining tools to manufacture the object, reducing production time and errors.

FIGURE 9.2   Modern CAD tools allow the designer to construct a digital 3D model. If technical drawings are required, they can be generated automatically from the model.

Credit: iStock.com/Evgeniy Shkolenko.

Early computer graphics systems like Sketchpad required a large mainframe computer system, tools that only large corporations could afford. It was not until the 1980s that computers powerful enough to generate realistic images of the type of 3D models used in Pro/ENGINEER in real time came onto the mass market. Known as workstations, they were more expensive than a PC but much less costly than a mainframe. Like PCs, they were designed for a single user, usually a designer or scientist. But, unlike early PCs, they were perfect for 3D graphics because they came with lots of computing power and a large, high-resolution screen.

Workstation screens were the result of a breakthrough in display technology. The first computer displays, such as that used in Sketchpad, had a cathode-ray tube and could only show lines drawn in monochrome. The new computer display technology worked quite differently. The display was composed of a grid of tiny dots called pixels. An electron beam repeatedly scanned the screen, 'painting' each pixel in turn. The high resolution of these displays enabled photorealistic images. And, on the more expensive models, three layers of pixels, each in a different hue, provided color.

By the 1980s, computer graphics researchers had developed software for generating photorealistic images from virtual 3D objects. Called rendering, this requires simulating the behavior of light, which is computationally tricky because light sources emit trillions of photons, each of which can interact with the objects they reach in complex ways. This means that computer programs for rendering use shortcuts and approximations, and even then, photorealistic rendering requires powerful computers.

Rendering algorithms are based on the geometry of vision invented in the Renaissance. One technique, called ray casting (see Figure 9.3), conceptually resembles Albrecht Dürer's apparatus for constructing perspective drawings (see Figure 3.6). The critical insight is you don't need to consider the paths of all photons, only those that reach the viewer's eye. Ray casting constructs these paths backward from the viewer. Lines or 'rays' are projected from the viewer's point of view, one ray for each pixel in the display. The rendering algorithm calculates the point of contact with the first object that the ray encounters. It then computes the intensity and color of light reflected in the ray's direction from the contact point.

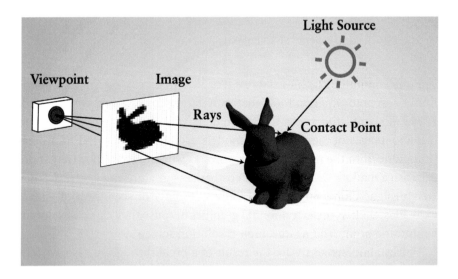

FIGURE 9.3 Applications like Pro/ENGINEER rely on computer-generated renderings of 3D models. Ray casting is one popular approach. In essence, this works by tracing lines of sight backward from the viewer until they hit an object in the scene. The color and its intensity at that point is then calculated by summing the illumination from all light sources.

Credit: Kadek Satriadi.

CAD tools like Pro/ENGINEER have fundamentally changed engineering and architecture practice. Manual drafting is a skill of the past. Nonetheless, information graphics and visual thinking remain central. The designer still sketches and explores different ideas using pencil and paper before finalizing the design with their favorite CAD tool. Almost certainly, the interface to the tool is inherently graphical. In the case of Pro/DESIGNER, the designer fashions their 3D model from 3D shapes created by using a drawing tool to sketch a 2D cross-section and then extruding the section in the third dimension, rotating it around an axis or moving it along a path in 3D space. They then interact with their model through realistic illustrations of the model on the 2D computer display. Furthermore, in many cases, technical drawings continue to be used to communicate the final design to the builder or manufacturer; it's just that these are produced automatically, not manually.

VIRTUAL SCIENCE

Science has also been profoundly changed by the computer. The change most noticeable to non-scientists is that digital images and animations have become integral to teaching science and communicating science to the public.

In the late 1970s, NASA pioneered computer-generated animations in its short films of the *Voyager 1* and *Voyager 2* missions to Jupiter, Saturn and Neptune. Impressed by these, astronomer and science writer Carl Sagan used computer animation in his documentary *Cosmos: A Personal Journey* (1980) to show, among other things, two colliding galaxies. Awarded an Emmy and watched by 600 million people in sixty different countries, *Cosmos* is one of the most popular documentaries of all time.

Driven by Hollywood's desire of to create ever more spectacular sci-fi blockbusters, computer-generated imagery (CGI) has grown increasingly lifelike. It is now a staple of popular science documentaries and presentations, illustrating the evolution of the universe, cell replication, extinct animals and archaeological sites. If something no longer exists or is too small or too large to photograph or film, CGI can bring it to life.

Computer-generated images are not only used by scientists to communicate with the public but also to communicate with one another. *Nature* is one of the world's most prestigious scientific journals. Since its inception in the late nineteenth century, *Nature* has encouraged graphics. Every scientist dreams of having an illustration from one of their papers on its front cover. At first, images in *Nature* were uncolored printed engravings. But nowadays, as likely as not, the cover image will be computer-generated, and the online edition will include computer animations.

Long before the arrival of CGI, however, photography had already revolutionized the creation of scientific illustrations. The first practical method for creating photographs was invented in 1839 by Louis Daguerre. By the end of the nineteenth century, photographs of scientific phenomena (in black and white) appeared in *Nature*. Photographs were a distinctively new kind of information graphic. While scientists had been using graphic recording devices to monitor changes in air pressure and wind direction since the seventeenth century, photography took automatic graphics creation to the next level.

From photography's inception, scientists have been fascinated by its promise of an impartial and objective record of reality. In 1880, French astronomer Pierre Janssen spoke about how 'The sensitive photographic film is the retina of the scientist', declaring it 'faithfully preserves the images which depict themselves upon it'. Of course, photographs are also shaped by the scientist, who chooses what to photograph and which features to emphasize—and who may touch up the image to clarify details, or color a monochrome image to differentiate elements or show other aspects of the data.

Traditional photography, just like human vision, relies on visible light. In the twentieth century, scientists discovered new ways of seeing that did not depend on visible light. The accidental discovery of X-rays in 1895 by the physicist Conrad Röntgen initiated this revolution. Experimenting with a Crookes tube, a type of vacuum tube through which an electric current is passed, Röntgen noticed that a nearby piece of cardboard coated with a fluorescent material was glowing. He realized the Crookes tube was emitting a hitherto unknown type of ray. Röntgen placed various materials between the tube and the cardboard, discovering that the rays could go through a thin sheet of aluminum but not a sheet of lead. While holding the lead, he saw the unimaginable: the outline of his thumb and finger threw a pale shadow, and within this, there were darker shadows that he suspected were cast by the bones inside his hand!

Röntgen's discovery took the scientific world by surprise. It also enthralled the public. Soon, coin-operated X-ray machines allowed the curious to see the bones in their hand, and fashionable shoe stores provided X-ray booths so that customers could see how snugly their feet fitted inside the shoes they were about to purchase. The main application of X-rays, of course, was in medicine—to begin with, allowing doctors to check for bone fractures or embedded shrapnel in soldiers injured during World War I.

However, X-rays did not show soft tissue and were dangerous to pregnant women. Medical researchers and practitioners wanted other ways of seeing inside a patient's body. They learned that if radioactive markers were ingested by, or injected into, the patient, they could track them as they traveled through the patient's body. They discovered that if pulses of high-frequency sound waves called ultrasounds were directed into a patient's body, these were reflected by boundaries between tissues of different densities, revealing the shape and position of the patient's internal organs. And they found that if they placed the patient in a high-intensity magnetic field, the hydrogen atoms in water and fat molecules in the patient's body were excited. The level of excitement could be measured, allowing the location and concentration of water and fats to be mapped. Called magnetic resonance imaging (MRI), this process does not expose the body to harmful radiation and can reveal injuries and tumors in soft tissue.

It is difficult to overstate the impact of medical imaging on medical prac-tice and the number of lives it has saved. Doctors can check for breaks and fractures in bones, and identify heart disease; dentists can check for tooth cavities; and expectant parents can see their unborn baby in utero. Before medical imaging, the chief use of information graphics in medicine was to educate medical practitioners; now, graphics play an essential role in diagnosis.

Imaging has also impacted the life and physical sciences, including astronomy (see Figure 9.4). Photographic film revealed that radioactive elements such as radium emanated mysterious rays. Uncovering the origin of these rays led to our modern understanding of the atom. Photographs of the trails left by elementary particles racing through cloud and bubble chambers were key in this endeavor. For instance, one groundbreaking image from 1931 shows the trail of a new particle with the same mass as an electron but with a positive charge rather than a negative charge. This was totally unexpected and revealed the existence of anti-matter.

Soon after X-rays were discovered, physicists determined they were another kind of electromagnetic radiation, just like visible light, but with a much shorter wavelength. They realized that this smaller wavelength meant that X-rays could be used to 'see' objects too small to see with visible light.

FIGURE 9.4 Photography and other imaging techniques have revolutionized astronomy. This iconic image of the Crab Nebula was assembled from twenty-four exposures taken by the Hubble Space Telescope. Once restricted to observing only the visible light portion of the electromagnetic spectrum, astronomers now study the cosmos using radio waves, microwaves, infrared, ultraviolet, X-rays and gamma rays.

Credit: NASA, ESA and Allison Loll/Jeff Hester (Arizona State University). Acknowledgment: Davide De Martin (ESA/Hubble).

This insight led to X-ray crystallography. This reveals the arrangement of atoms in a crystal, enabling scientists to see the structure of molecules for the first time. Famously, images created by the chemist and talented X-ray crystallographer Rosalind Franklin allowed James Watson and Francis Crick to establish the helical structure of DNA, one of the most significant biological discoveries of the twentieth century. The diagram drawn by Odile Crick, Francis Crick's wife, of DNA's structure resembled a spiral staircase. It formed the centerpiece of Watson and Crick's 1953 *Nature* article and has become an icon for molecular biology.

The sociologist Michael Lynch has studied this reliance of modern scientists on what he calls an 'externalized retina' to see objects and processes that are too big, too inaccessible, or too small to be seen with the naked eye. In the early 1980s, he joined a biological laboratory, observing the scientists for several months. He was struck by the centrality of graphics to the lab's day-to-day practice, and how the primary function of the technicians and scientists was to create representations that could be viewed and analyzed.

The production of scientific and medical images is a significant application of what is now known as scientific visualization. At first, scientific visualization focused on creating 2D images from sensors and imaging devices. The goal was to automate the production of information graphics that scientists had previously drawn by hand, such as bar charts, line graphs and contour plots. While scientists from the late nineteenth century might have been astonished that these graphics had been created by a computer, they would have immediately recognized and understood the visual conventions they employed.

This changed in the 1980s. Just as for CAD, graphics workstations allowed scientists to create and visualize 3D models (see Figure 9.5). Now they could generate a 3D model of the sea floor from sonar imaging or a 3D model of a patient from a computerized tomography (CT) scan (CT combines information from a sequence of 2D X-ray 'slices' to create a 3D model). Scientists studied their models on large graphics workstation displays, rotating them to see them from a better angle or zooming in to see fine details. If required, they could quickly generate new visualizations to display other aspects of the data. This ability to use a series of visualizations to interactively explore data was unprecedented. Scientists could even create animations, a marvelous new way of viewing time-varying data and escaping the 'deadland' of paper graphics.

Interactive 3D visualization was a breakthrough, and in 1987 the US National Science Foundation (NSF) funded a workshop highlighting the effectiveness of visualization as a technique for understanding the 'fire hose' of data that was now becoming available to scientists. Attendees spoke of the wealth of data from radio telescopes, space probes and satellites, medical scanners and sonar imaging. This was data scientists were currently warehousing because they did not have a way of understanding it—data they could use visualization to understand.

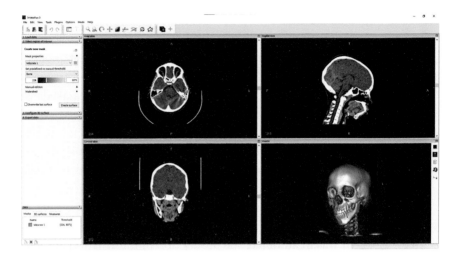

FIGURE 9.5   As computers became more powerful, they allowed something unprecedented: interactive visualization. Above is an interactive visualization of a CT scan of a human head created with the medical imaging tool InVesalius. The visualization combines transverse (horizontal plane), sagittal (vertical plane from front to back) and coronal (vertical plane from left to right) slices through the scan with a volume-rendered 3D image of the scan. The viewer can interactively rotate the 3D image and scroll through the slices. As they do so, the visualization software immediately updates the graphics. Note how, in the volume-rendered image, the soft tissue has been made semitransparent to reveal the underlying skeleton.

Credit: CTI Renato Archer, Campinas-SP, Brazil.

A key challenge facing scientific visualization was that, while imaging techniques such as CT scans captured the internal structure of solid objects, it was difficult to show this. In a traditional view of an object, occlusion hid the internal components. The alternative was to present the scan as a series of 2D slices through the object. However, it was cognitively demanding to build a mental model of the 3D structure from these.

Shortly after the NSF workshop, computer graphics researchers devised two ingenious solutions. Both relied on thinking of the three-dimensional space as a 'volume' composed of tiny little cubes, each with its own data value. For instance, with a CT scan, the value of each cube is the amount of X-ray absorbed by the tissue or bone at the associated location. One solution, called volume rendering, uses color to show a cube's value. The trick is to make the cubes semitransparent so that the viewer can see into the volume and discern the color of the internal cubes (see Figure 9.5). The second solution uses a generalization of contour lines known as contour 'surfaces'. Like a contour line, these connect adjacent points with the same value. But because the points lie in a three-dimensional space, this results in a surface.

Scientists were not only interested in visualizing data from sensors and imaging devices. They also wanted to visualize data generated by computer programs—programs that were revolutionizing scientific practice by simulating natural processes.

Before the computer, there were two ways of doing science. Experimental scientists observed the world and conducted experiments. The other way of doing science was to devise new theories. This was the responsibility of theoretical scientists who invented simplified models of some aspect of the world, often expressed as mathematical formulae. The two were intertwined: theories were based on the data collected by experimental scientists, and theoretical scientists made predictions or hypotheses that could then be tested experimentally.

Then came the computer. One of the main motivations for developing the computer was to solve mathematical equations, such as those used to predict an artillery shell's trajectory. As computers became more powerful, scientists began to use them to test and explore more complex models. Rather than running an experiment in the real world, they could simulate a scientific model on their computer and use this to test their theories. Called computational science, this new technique enabled scientists to run experiments that weren't possible in real life, and to study phenomena too small, large, quick, slow or dangerous to observe directly.

Computation now plays a central role in all kinds of science, from astronomy, quantum physics, chemistry and biology to the social sciences. Astronomers, for instance, use the computer to go back in time and simulate the universe's birth in the Big Bang, or the collapse of a galaxy into a massive black hole. During the COVID-19 pandemic, epidemiologists used computer simulations to determine how best to control the spread of the virus.

Computational science has also played a pivotal role in our understanding of the impact of carbon dioxide and other gasses on the Earth's climate. The climate is affected by many interconnected factors, such as the quantity and types of greenhouse gasses in the air, the amount and kind of land vegetation, and the ocean currents. It is clearly impossible to run experiments to test the impact of different levels of CO_2 and other greenhouse gasses on the climate. Instead, climate scientists have created complex computer models of the climate and use these to simulate possible scenarios and their likely impact. Visualizations of these predictions form core arguments in the debate on climate change.

Figure 9.6 (including the caption) is from an IPCC report. It shows the predicted impact of two hypothetical scenarios on the climate, based on the expected change in average temperature and precipitation for 2081–2100 compared to 1986–2005. The first scenario, RCP2.6, assumes a stringent

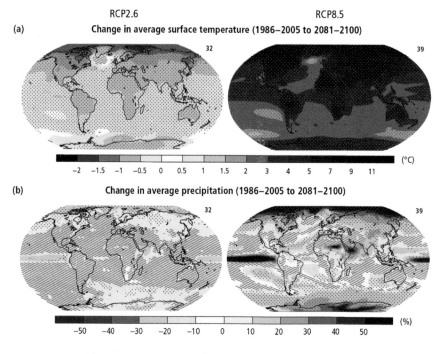

FIGURE 9.6   Change in average surface temperature (a) and change in average precipitation (b) based on multi-model mean projections for 2081–2100 relative to 1986–2005 under the RCP2.6 (left) and RCP8.5 (right) scenarios. The number of models used to calculate the multi-model mean is indicated in the upper right corner of each panel. Stippling (i.e., dots) shows regions where the projected change is large compared to natural internal variability and where at least 90 per cent of models agree on the sign of change. Hatching (i.e., diagonal lines) shows regions where the projected change is less than one standard deviation of the natural internal variability.

Credit: Figure SPM.7 from IPCC, 2014: *Climate Change 2014: Synthesis Report.* Contribution of Working Groups I, II and III to the Fifth Assessment Report of the Intergovernmental Panel on Climate Change [Core Writing Team, RK Pachauri and LA Meyer (eds)]. IPCC, Geneva, Switzerland.

reduction in greenhouse gas emissions, while the second, RCP8.5, assumes very high emissions.

The 1987 NSF workshop highlighted visualization's critical role in computational science. Computer programs like those used to predict the weather are large and complex. The first implementations are often wrong, but it's difficult to detect errors if you are only looking at tables of numbers. Visualizations let scientists see if their computer models work. Even better, they allow them to see how their models might be improved and can provide unexpected insights into the underlying natural phenomenon. In science, like CAD, visualizations have become the interface to sophisticated computer models.

We can see that computer-generated graphics, photography, and medical and scientific imaging fundamentally changed the practice of science, medicine, engineering and architecture during the late twentieth century. However, in most cases, this directly impacted only those people employed in these disciplines. In the next chapter, we investigate how these new technologies have affected the wider population and their use of data visualization.

NOTES, REFERENCES AND FURTHER READING

While there are many books about how to design and create data visualizations for the computer, the history of data visualization after the introduction of the computer has received much less attention.

Virtual Buildings and Machines

Early Computers

Campbell-Kelly, Martin, William Aspray, Nathan Ensmenger and Jeffrey R Yoost. *Computer: A History of the Information Machine* (3rd ed.). Routledge, 2013: Chapters 4, 10 and 11.

The Birth of Computer Graphics

ACM. *A.M. Turing Award Citation for Ivan Sutherland.* https://amturing.acm.org/award_winners/sutherland_3467412.cfm

Peddie, Jon. *The History of Visual Magic in Computers: How Beautiful Images Are Made in CAD, 3D, VR and AR.* Springer-Verlag, 2013: Chapters 4 and 5.

Sutherland, Ivan E. *Sketchpad: A Man-Machine Graphical Communication System.* PhD thesis. MIT, 1963. Reprint available as Technical Report 574 from University of Cambridge Computer Laboratory, 2003.

Pro/ENGINEER

Pro/ENGINEER was also groundbreaking because its models were parametric. As the designer constructed the model, Pro/ENGINEER recorded the steps and the geometric relationships between the surfaces and parts. If the designer changed something in the model, this allowed Pro/DESIGNER to automatically update the rest of the model.

Shih, Randy. *Parametric Modeling with Pro/ENGINEER Wildfire 3.0.* SDC Publications, 2006.

Weisberg, David E. *The Engineering Design Revolution: The People, Companies and Computer Systems That Changed Forever the Practice of Engineering.* Shapr3D Blog, 2008: Chapter 16. www.shapr3d.com/history-of-cad/

Rendering

Hughes, John F, et al. *Computer Graphics: Principles and Practice* (3rd ed.). Pearson Education, 2014: Chapters 1, 3 and 15.

Impact of CAD on Engineering and Architectural Professions

Meyers, Frederick. 'Engineering Design Graphics: Into the 21st Century.' *The Engineering Design Graphics Journal* 71, no. 3 (2007).

Pierce Meyer, Katie. 'Technology in Architectural Practice: Transforming Work with Information, 1960s–1990s.' *Information & Culture* 51, no. 2 (2016): 249–66.

Virtual Science

Computer-Generated Imagery (CGI)

Sito, Tom. *Moving Innovation: A History of Computer Animation.* MIT Press, 2013: Chapters 3 and 8–14.

Imagery in Nature

Belknap, Geoffrey. 'The Evolution of Scientific Illustration.' *Nature* 575, no. 7781 (2019): 25–8.

Graphic Recording Devices

Hoff, Hebbel E, and Leslie A Geddes. 'The Beginnings of Graphic Recording.' *Isis* 53, no. 3 (1962): 287–324.

Scientific Photography

Daston, Lorraine, and Peter Galison. *Objectivity.* Princeton University Press, 2007: Chapter 3.

Goldberg, Vicki. *The Power of Photography: How Photographs Changed Our Lives.* Abbeville, 1991: Chapter 1.
Turner, Peter. *History of Photography.* Hamlyn Publishing. 1987: Chapter 10. Quote from Pierre Janssen on p. 190.
Wilder, Kelley. *Photography and Science.* Reaktion Books, 2009: Chapter 1.

X-Rays: Discovery and Use
Crowther, JA. 'Röntgen Centenary and Fifty Years of X-Rays.' *Nature* 3934 (1945): 351.
Goldberg, Vicki. *The Power of Photography: How Photographs Changed Our Lives.* Abbeville, 1991: Chapter 2.
LeVine III, Harry. *Medical Imaging.* ABC-CLIO, 2010: Chapter 3.
Watson, James D, and Francis HC Crick. 'Molecular Structure of Nucleic Acids: A Structure for Deoxyribose Nucleic Acid.' *Nature* 171, no. 4356 (1953): 737–8.

Medical Imaging
LeVine III, Harry. *Medical Imaging.* ABC-CLIO, 2010: Chapters 6–9.
Umar, AA, and SM Atabo. 'A Review of Imaging Techniques in Scientific Research/ Clinical Diagnosis.' *MOJ Anatomy & Physiology* 6, no. 5 (2019): 175–83.

Scientific Imaging
Goldberg, Vicki. *The Power of Photography: How Photographs Changed Our Lives.* Abbeville 1991: Chapter 2.
Kherlopian, Armen R, et al. 'A Review of Imaging Techniques for Systems Biology.' *BMC Systems Biology* 2, no. 1 (2008): 74.
Turner, Peter. *History of Photography.* Hamlyn Publishing. 1987: Chapter 10.
Umar, AA, and SM Atabo. 'A Review of Imaging Techniques in Scientific Research/ Clinical Diagnosis.' *MOJ Anatomy & Physiology* 6, no. 5 (2019): 175–83.
Wikipedia. 'X-Ray Crystallography.' 2023. https://en.wikipedia.org/wiki/X-ray_crystallography
Wilder, Kelley. *Photography and Science.* Reaktion Books, 2009: Chapters 1 and 2.

Externalized Retina
Lynch, Michael. 'The Externalized Retina: Selection and Mathematization in the Visual Documentation of Objects in the Life Sciences.' *Human Studies* 11, no. 2 (1988): 201–34.

History of Scientific Visualization
Brodlie, Ken. 'Scientific Visualization: Past, Present and Future.' *Nuclear Instruments and Methods in Physics Research Section A: Accelerators, Spectrometers, Detectors and Associated Equipment* 354 (1995): 104–11.

Collins, Brian. M. 'Data Visualization: Has It All Been Seen Before?' In *Animation and Scientific Visualization: Tools & Applications.* Academic Press, 1993: 3–28.

The outcomes of the 1987 NSF Workshop on scientific visualization are presented in: McCormick, Bruce H, Thomas A DeFanti and Maxine D Brown (eds). *Visualization in Scientific Computing. Computer Graphics* 21, no. 6 (1987).

Scientific Visualization Techniques

Kaufman, Arie E, and Klaus Mueller. 'Overview of Volume Rendering.' In *The Visualization Handbook.* Elsevier, 2005: 127–74.

Schroeder, William J, and Kenneth M Martin. 'Overview of Visualization.' In *The Visualization Handbook.* Elsevier, 2005: 3–35.

Yoo, Terry S. 'Taking Stock of Visualization in Scientific Computing.' *ACM SIGGRAPH Computer Graphics* 38, no. 3 (2004): 4–6.

Computational Science

DeFanti, Thomas A, and Maxine D Brown. 'Visualization in Scientific Computing.' In *Advances in Computers.* Elsevier, 1991: vol. 33, 247–307.

Denning, Peter J. 'Computational Thinking in Science.' *American Scientist* 105, no. 1 (2017): 13–17.

National Science Foundation. 'Visualization: A Way to See the Unseen.' www.nsf. gov/about/history/nsf0050/pdf/visualization.pdf

Robertson, Douglas S. *Phase Change: The Computer Revolution in Science and Mathematics.* Oxford University Press, 2003: Chapter 7.

Wilson, Kenneth G. 'Grand Challenges to Computational Science.' *Future Generation Computer Systems* 5, no. 2–3 (1989): 171–89.

Climate Change Modeling and Visualization

O'Neill, Saffron J, and Nicholas Smith. 'Climate Change and Visual Imagery.' *Wiley Interdisciplinary Reviews: Climate Change* 5, no. 1 (2014): 73–87.

Pasini, Antonello. *From Observations to Simulations: A Conceptual Introduction to Weather and Climate Modeling.* World Scientific, 2005: Chapter 7.

CHAPTER 10

The Democratization of Visualization

A DEFINING FEATURE OF OUR current Golden Age of Data Visualization is the democratization of data visualization. Now data visualizations are understood and used by most people daily, not just by people working in a few professions.

THE ASCENT OF VISUAL CULTURE

The 1970s and 1980s were a watershed moment in the use of graphics in print media. An article from 1971 in the *Bulletin of the American Society of Newspaper Editors* tells of the 'explosion in graphics' and the rise of the art department. As a case in point, the bestselling newspaper *USA Today* was launched in 1982. It featured a large, full-color daily weather map, a daily 'USA Snapshot' graphic with a colorful illustration enhancing a table of data, and a locator map accompanying the 'USA Journal' feature about an obscure American town. In the case of Australian newspapers, the number of tables and graphs increased by 900 per cent between 1976 and 1996, and the number of maps, diagrams and illustrations by more than 400 per cent.

One of the reasons for this was the computer. In 1985, Apple released the first inexpensive laser printer and, in collaboration with Aldus and its PageMaker software, announced the arrival of 'desktop publishing'. Now, anyone could create a newsletter or brochure. Desktop publishing heralded a fundamental change in the production of printed information graphics.

DOI: 10.1201/9781003507642-11

No longer were they drawn by hand. Computer programs such as Adobe Illustrator, Microsoft Chart, MacDraw and Mac Atlas made the creation of technical illustrations, maps and charts quick and straightforward (see Figure 10.1).

However, desktop publishing is only part of the reason newspapers and magazines increased their use of graphics. They were already beginning to provide more illustrations before the advent of desktop publishing because this was what their readers demanded. This demand was because of television and the rise of popular visual culture. At the start of the twentieth century, the average person saw relatively few graphical images; by its end, they were bombarded with them. Historian and journalism and mass communication expert Mitchell Stephens writes of how 'in the second half of the

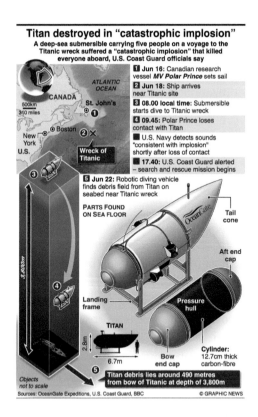

FIGURE 10.1   Desktop publishing made creating infographics like the one shown above straightforward. Infographics have now become a staple of print and online news media.

Credit: © GRAPHIC NEWS.

twentieth century—for perhaps the first time in human history—it began to seem as if images would gain the upper hand over words'.

Modern visual culture started with photography. At first, taking a photograph was messy and cumbersome. Most photographers were professionals, catering to the burgeoning middle class and its desire for family portraits. By the beginning of the twentieth century, however, photography was no longer just for experts. The release of the Kodak Brownie camera in 1901, with the promise that 'You press the button, we do the rest', led to an avalanche of photographic images. Photography had reached the mass market.

The beginning of the twentieth century also saw the arrival of the motion picture. By 1920, movie theatres were popular entertainment venues, with newsreels providing an update on current affairs before the main feature. But the technology most responsible for creating modern visual culture is television. Full-scale commercial television broadcasting started in the United States in 1947. Eight years later, half of all American homes had a TV. By the 1990s, the average American was spending more than three hours a day viewing television. And Americans were not unusual in this: all around the world, anyone who could afford a TV bought one and started to watch it.

By the 1970s, television had replaced newspapers as the primary news source for the American public. The competition with television and its inherently visual message drove the increasing use of graphics in newspapers. As television news matured, it integrated more sophisticated graphics: animations, cartoons, illustrations, maps, graphs and diagrams. Perhaps the first display of an information graphic on television occurred in December 1941, when CBS's experimental TV station WCBW used a map to explain the Japanese attack on Pearl Harbor.

While maps of war continue to feature on TV news, the most common TV map is undoubtedly the weather map. During the 1950s and 1960s, the weather presenter would stand in front of an outline map showing state boundaries and major cities. Then, while explaining the forecast, the presenter would use a marker pen to draw warm and cold fronts, airflow and temperature on the map. The ability to draw a snowman or umbrella was a definite asset. Then, in the 1980s, hand-drawn maps were replaced by satellite imagery and increasingly sophisticated computer-generated animations that showed the predicted movement of weather patterns across the forecast region. Regardless, the weather forecast remained a core part of the daily newscast.

Photography, cinema and television are the most evident reasons for the image's ascendance over text. Less obviously, as the twentieth century progressed, people became increasingly accustomed to monitoring and controlling their household devices through graphical interfaces. At the start of the twentieth century, cars came with little instrumentation. In 1908, for example, the only instrument provided on the standard Ford Model T dashboard was a meter allowing the driver to check that the battery was charging. By the middle of the century, however, the typical dashboard had gauges showing the car's speed, level of fuel, engine rotation speed, engine temperature, oil pressure, battery charge, and controls for the car radio.

The PC provides another example. The first PCs were released in the late 1970s. However, many users found the command-line interface intimidating. This changed in 1984 with the release of the Apple Macintosh. It was the first commercially successful PC to provide a graphical interface. Based on ideas pioneered at Xerox PARC, the Macintosh featured windows and icons controlled with a mouse and keyboard. It introduced the visual metaphor of a 'desktop': computer files were physical objects you could move around on the desktop or place in a folder or waste bin using the mouse. Now, even our phones have a graphical user interface.

The increasing use of graphics in popular culture led to far-reaching educational changes. Teaching materials became more visual, and new kinds of visual materials, such as educational videos, were introduced. Educators recognized the need to teach 'graphic literacy'—that is, the use of maps and charts alongside numeracy and literacy—and 'visual literacy', or the ability to communicate visually and critically evaluate images in the mainstream media. This created a virtuous cycle. Popular media could use more complex information graphics as the public became more graphically literate, which in turn reinforced the need to teach graphic literacy at school.

FROM SPREADSHEETS TO VISUAL ANALYTICS

In our current Golden Age, not only are people encountering data visualizations at school and on popular media, but they are also using them at work. One reason for this is the kind of jobs that most of us have. During the twentieth century, mechanization dramatically decreased the number of people working as laborers, farmers and household servants. Offsetting this was a rise in teachers, accountants, engineers, mechanics and repairers, health workers, and managers and office workers, all of which are professions utilizing graphics. Particularly noteworthy was the increase in the number of managers and office workers. In the United States in 1910, about 12 per cent of the workforce managed a business or worked in an office. By 2000, this had risen to almost 30 per cent.

The computer has also driven the use of graphics at work. The arrival of desktop publishing in 1985 was closely followed by the first desktop presentation software, PowerPoint. Released by Forethought, Inc. in 1987, this ran on the Apple Macintosh. Designed for business, it led to a new presentation genre, one that made heavy use of charts and other graphics.

Spreadsheets also date from this time. The world's first spreadsheet application, VisiCalc, was released in 1979. It is credited with legitimizing the use of PCs in business. Undoubtedly, the spreadsheet is one of the most successful computer applications ever created. We now take spreadsheets for granted, but they were a revelation when they first appeared, allowing non-programmers to perform complex calculations using an intuitive graphical interface: a grid of cells whose value was automatically updated if other cells changed value.

While VisiCalc could not generate charts from the data in a spreadsheet, subsequent spreadsheet applications could. This became one of the most valued features of newer products such as Microsoft Excel. Analysts used these charts to understand their data and for presentations and reports designed to impress their bosses. By the mid-1990s, Excel had become the default business analytics tool.

The use of graphics in analysis has been taken one step further in visual analytics. Visual analytic tools combine visualizations with automated data analysis techniques. In these tools, charts are not just a helpful add-on; they have become a defining characteristic (see Figure 10.2).

Tableau was one of the first commercially available visual analytics tools. Released in May 2003, Tableau allowed business and government analysts to create an almost endless variety of visualizations by dragging and dropping data fields onto the tool's main panel. They could effortlessly create standard visualizations like choropleth maps and bar charts or craft their own custom chart. The resulting visualizations were interactive. When the analyst moved their mouse over a graphic element, they saw details of the underlying data. They could zoom, pan and scroll across larger visualizations. And they could sort and reorder their data or use checkboxes and slider bars to filter it. Tableau made it easy for anyone to explore data and see trends, patterns and anomalies. And once you found something, Tableau made it simple to publish visualizations on the web.

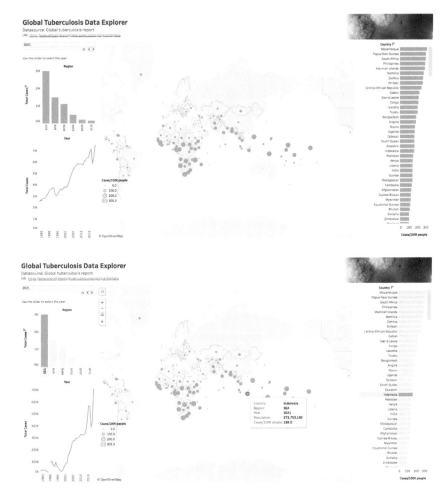

FIGURE 10.2   Visual analytics applications allow analysts to create compound visualizations that support the interactive exploration of data. The screenshots above show a dashboard for exploring the prevalence of tuberculosis. Initially, the dashboard shows information for all countries (top). When the mouse moves over a country (bottom), additional information about the number of cases in that country is shown, the country and region are highlighted in the bar charts on the right and upper left, and the time series on the bottom left is updated to display total cases for that country rather than for the entire world.

Credit: Kadek Satriadi.

The genesis of tools like Tableau lies in the work of two great data visualization pioneers: Jacques Bertin and John Tukey. Tableau's drag-and-drop interface for constructing visualizations stems from the research of cartographer Bertin, who recognized that the mapping from the underlying information or data to its visual representation is central to data visualization. He formalized this, regarding an information graphic as a mapping from data elements and attributes to graphical marks and their associated visual variables.

That's quite a mouthful, so let's step through this. A data element corresponds to an object or observation, and attributes are the characteristics or measurements associated with the element. These are the things being visualized. Marks are the core graphical elements in the visualization and their position and appearance are controlled by visual variables.

For example, consider the bubble chart (see Figure 10.3), popularized by Hans Rosling. An outstanding communicator, he used these to show the relationship between a country's wealth and the health of its inhabitants. Underlying each chart is a data element for each country. This has four attributes: measure of income (GDP per capita), average life expectancy, population and geographic region (Africa, Americas, Asia-Pacific or Europe). Each data element (a country) has a corresponding mark (a circle)

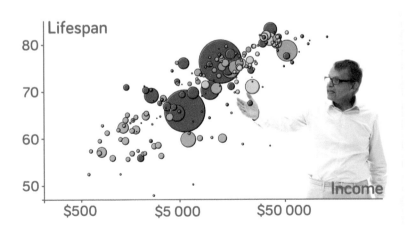

FIGURE 10.3 The physician and health statistician Hans Rosling was a consummate data storyteller. Here, he uses a bubble chart showing the relationship between income and the health of its inhabitants to argue that health is dictated by wealth.

on the bubble chart. The mark's visual variables—its horizontal and vertical position, size and color—are determined by the element's data attributes.

Before Bertin, an analyst had a fixed collection of information graphics. After Bertin, they had a framework that allowed them to imagine new ways of mapping data to marks and visual variables to create their own bespoke graphics. Supporting this flexibility was a critical difference between Tableau and the visual data exploration tools that preceded it. While Tableau provided standard built-in chart types, it also allowed the analyst to arbitrarily map data elements and attributes to marks and visual variables.

The research of the great statistician John Tukey in the early 1970s was equally critical to Tableau's design. Originally trained as a chemist and with a PhD in mathematics, Tukey's passion was data analysis. We have seen that, while graphics were used by statisticians in the nineteenth century, they had lost favor by the early twentieth century. Instead, statisticians concentrated on developing mathematical techniques to determine the probability of a particular set of observations given a hypothesis about the population the sample was drawn from. Tukey argued this was only half the story. He contended these techniques did not support the vital first step in data analysis in which the analyst explores the data, endeavoring to make sense of it and discover its underlying patterns and trends. Only then could these mathematical techniques come into play, allowing the analyst to calculate the likelihood that a particular pattern or trend was simply the result of chance. Tukey championed the use of graphics as an essential component of data exploration, writing: 'The greatest value of a picture is when it *forces* us to notice what we never expected to see.' (Emphasis in the original.)

In his book on exploratory data analysis, Tukey spelled out that the analyst's role was to explain the general behavior of the data. Like the astronomer John Frederick W. Herschel, Tukey did this by fitting a line to it. Statisticians call this a model for the data as the line captures a hypothesized relationship between the variables in the data. To ascertain how well the line explained the data, Tukey advocated graphing the difference between each data point and the value predicted by the line. By looking at this plot, the analyst could immediately see the model's accuracy and, if necessary, use the errors it revealed to guide their search for a more exact model.

The techniques Tukey described in his book were designed to be used manually. However, Tukey was well aware of the computer. In 1972, he

and Mary Anne Fisherkeller developed one of the first interactive graphical applications for exploratory data analysis. By the late 1980s, Tukey,
Fisherkeller and their fellow pioneers had invented many interactions that
were later employed in Tableau. The 1980s was also when interactive statistical graphics moved from the laboratory into commercial data analysis
products, because of the availability of graphic workstations and more
powerful PCs.

The computer allowed statisticians to explore larger, more complex
datasets, automating the generation of plots and charts that would have
taken too long to draw by hand. They started with the visualizations
invented in the previous two centuries, such as bar charts, choropleth
maps, scatterplots and pie charts. These, however, were designed to show
the relationship between two variables, or the distribution of a single variable. Unfortunately, real-world problems are usually more complex and
involve multiple variables. So a critical question facing statisticians was
how to visualize such multivariate data.

They invented two main ways of doing so (see Figure 10.4). One approach
shows the high-level structure of the multivariate data, exposing its clusters
and outliers. It does this by projecting the entire multidimensional space
of the variables onto the two-dimensional space of the display. It's a bit
like placing each data element on a map. Data elements with similar variable values are positioned close to one another, while those with disparate
values are separated.

The second approach combines multiple charts, each showing a different
aspect of the data, into a compound visualization. A widely used example is
the scatterplot matrix. Invented in 1975, this is a square grid of scatterplots.
Scatterplots in the same row have the same variable on their vertical axis,
while scatterplots in the same column have the same variable on their
horizontal axis. Thus, there is a scatterplot for each pair of variables. The
scatterplot matrix is also known as the 'generalized draftsman's display',
reflecting how it extends the three-view arrangement used in engineering
drawings to multiple variables.

A limitation of the scatterplot matrix is that it does not reveal which
points in its constituent scatterplots correspond to the same underlying
data element. Statisticians invented a clever technique to address this: they
used interaction to link the scatterplots. When the viewer selects points in
one scatterplot, the points corresponding to the same underlying objects or
observations are highlighted in the other scatterplots.

PCA of USA Cereal Dataset

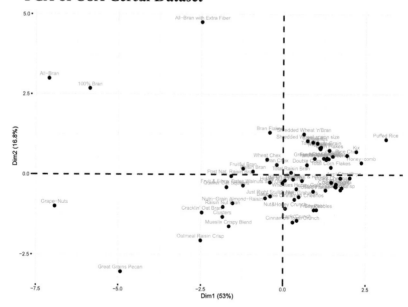

SPLOM of USA Cereal Dataset

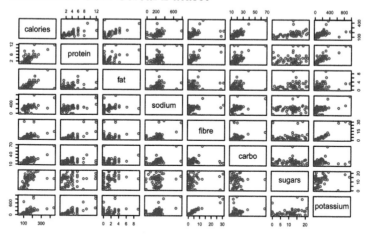

FIGURE 10.4 Visualizing multivariant data is a significant challenge. Two techniques are shown above, visualizing the same dataset comparing the nutritional value of US breakfast cereals. One method is to project the multidimensional variable space onto the two-dimensional space of the display (top). This suggests that, for instance, All-Bran and 100% Bran are outliers. Another method is to arrange scatterplots in a square grid to form a scatterplot matrix (bottom). This suggests that high fiber levels correlate with high potassium.

Credit: Kadek Satriadi.

Combining several graphics to show different aspects of the data and then using interaction to link these has proven to be a highly effective way of understanding multivariate data. That is why visual analytics tools allow the analyst to create compound visualizations, like that in Figure 10.2. Behind the scenes, these tools link the different graphics in the visualization allowing the visualization to immediately respond to user interaction such as mouse hovering above a country. It is this kind of feedback that makes interactive data visualization so powerful. As one of the pioneers of statistical graphics, Peter Huber, declared, 'We see more when we interact with the picture—especially if it reacts instantaneously—than when we merely watch.'

Interaction also plays a crucial role in handling large datasets. Revealing more information on a mouse hover, search, filtering, sorting and reordering, zooming, scrolling, and panning allows the viewer to focus on the information that is relevant to them. Tamara Munzner writes about how:

Interactivity is crucial for building vis[ualization] tools that handle complexity … For example, an interactive vis tool can support investigation at multiple levels of detail, ranging from a very high-level overview … to a fully detailed view of a small part of it. It can also present different ways of representing and summarizing the data in a way that supports understanding the connections between these alternatives.

THE INTERNET AND BIG DATA

The World Wide Web has also contributed to the escalating use of data visualization in business and government. One reason is that there is more data to analyze. While the internet has existed in a limited form since the late 1960s, it was not until the early 1990s that the World Wide Web was created. At first, the web was primarily seen as a communication tool and a source of free information. Then came online shopping and social media. This led to an avalanche of digital data: census data, financial data, YouTube videos, tweets on Twitter (now X), Google searches and orders from Amazon.

Furthermore, as work practices have moved online, organizations have been able to collect data in real time, allowing them to continuously monitor performance. Tools such as Splunk or Tableau have made it simple for analysts to create online dashboards that managers can use to track how they and their teams are going. Inspired by the automobile dashboard, these have a clean, uncluttered design aesthetic, and they use graphics such as gauges and dials that can be understood at a glance.

The volume of digital data that is available is so large that analysts have christened it 'Big Data'—it is estimated we now produce 330 million terabytes of data daily, and this amount is increasing exponentially. Big Data has led to new professions, one of which is data science. Everyone wants to hire data scientists to make sense of their data. They help banks identify unusual patterns of transactions suggesting fraud, and companies like Google to better target their ads. They also played a vital role in the pandemic, assisting epidemiologists in modeling the behavior of COVID-19.

Like Tukey, data scientists fit mathematical models to the data to identify patterns, clusters or trends. Models that predict that, if a customer has bought 'X' and 'Y', they are likely to buy 'Z'. But, while Tukey constructed his models by hand, data scientists use the latest data mining and machine learning techniques (now simply known as 'AI'). Nonetheless, data scientists continue to visualize the data to 'get a feel for it', find outliers, and ascertain how well a model fits the data. And they use data visualization to communicate what they have found to the health scientists, government officials or business executives who hired them. Few people understand deep learning or spectral clustering. They can, however, see trends in a time series and clusters in a scatterplot.

Big Data isn't only characterized by the volume of data but also the variety. Much online data isn't the sort of data that analysts were used to. It's messy, and it's not numbers. A prime example of this is text. Before the twenty-first century, text analysis was the preserve of the humanities. Analysis was restricted to an in-depth examination of a single text or a few related texts. Information graphics played little part. With the web and digitization of print, analysts suddenly had email, tweets, tags, blogs, webpages, online magazines, newspapers and digitized document collections to analyze.

New analysis and visualization techniques were required. One of the most common is the word cloud. As best I can tell, they first appeared in 1991. Then, in the early 2000s, word clouds took off after appearing on the photo-sharing site Flickr. For a while, they were everywhere, prompting a backlash against their use. Used in moderation, however, I feel word clouds can be an engaging way of summarizing text.

Other visualizations of text and documents rely on more sophisticated analyses that convert the textual data into data that can be visualized using standard techniques. For instance, sentiment analysis uses natural language processing to determine whether a tweet or some other text is positive or negative about its subject. Another kind of analysis measures the similarity of two documents by analyzing the number of words they have in common. Once you know how similar each pair of documents in a collection is, you can draw a 'map' of a document collection in which similar documents are placed near one another.

Another change associated with Big Data and the web has been the emergence of networks as a way to organize and understand interconnected systems. In the twentieth century, data was arranged in tables. But in the twenty-first century, networks are favored. Analysts see networks everywhere. The internet is a network of interconnected computers. Webpages comprise another mammoth network, as do social media users, who are connected by their posts, likes and tweets. Biologists have also realized the importance of networks. Interactions between proteins and those between proteins and genes form complex networks. The biochemical reactions in living organisms create metabolic networks (see Figure 10.5), and the neurons in the brain form yet another network. Economists study trade networks, intelligence analysts piece together terrorist networks, and journalists draw networks showing media influence.

Data science isn't the only new profession created by Big Data. The internet has provided journalists with unprecedented access to government and corporate data, prompting the emergence of data journalism. *The New York Times*, *BBC News Online*, *The Guardian* and *The Washington Post* now employ dedicated data journalists. As the name suggests, data journalism merges journalism with data science. Its practitioners explore data to find thought-provoking patterns or anomalies and then craft a story around these.

Data visualization plays an integral role in data journalism. There has been a steady rise in the use of graphics by newspapers and magazines since the late nineteenth century, and data journalism has further accelerated this. In data journalism, the graphics are no longer add-ons to the text. Graphics and text are equal partners, and sometimes the graphic *is* the story.

This has been facilitated by newspapers moving online. Graphics no longer take up valuable space on the printed page. Now, journalists have unlimited white space in which to tell their stories. Furthermore, a younger audience is demanding more visually appealing and engaging news. Monitoring click-through rates has made it amply clear that readers stay longer on pages with data visualizations.

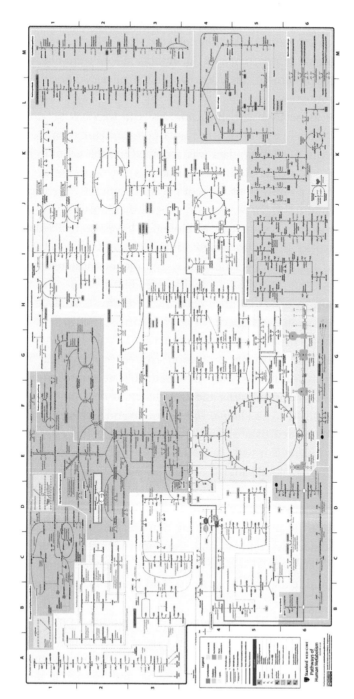

FIGURE 10.5   Networks and network visualizations are now commonplace, particularly in the life sciences. Most networks are drawn using variants of the node-link diagrams that Jacob Moreno used to show social networks. The network above was manually created by Stanford University medical researchers and summarizes the pathways in human metabolism.

Credit: Pathways of Human Metabolism Map. Copyright 2013-2023 Stanford Medicine. All rights reserved. Freely available at https://metabolicpathways.stanford.edu/.

Data journalism is part of a general trend to use data visualizations in public discourse, with 1999 being a turning point. That year, three climatologists published a graph detailing a reconstruction of the Northern Hemisphere's average temperature from the year 1000 to 1998. It showed the temperature falling slightly before a dramatic increase starting around 1900, and culminating in the 1990s as the hottest decade on record. Christened the 'hockey stick graph' because of its shape, it featured in the Intergovernmental Panel on Climate Change's (IPCC) *Third Assessment Report, Climate Change 2001* as evidence of climate change. The graph and original caption are shown in Figure 10.6. I think it's fair to say that no

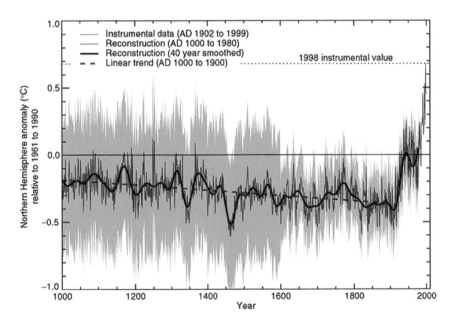

FIGURE 10.6   Millennial Northern Hemisphere (NH) temperature reconstruction (blue) and instrumental data (red) from AD 1000 to 1999, adapted from Mann et al. (1999). Smoother version of NH series (black), linear trend from AD 1000 to 1850 (purple-dashed) and two standard error limits (grey-shaded) are shown.

Credit: Figure 2.20 from Folland, CK, TR Karl, JR Christy, RA Clarke, GV Gruza, J Jouzel, ME Mann, J Oerlemans, MJ Salinger, and S-W Wang, 2001. 'Observed Climate Variability and Change.' In *Climate Change 2001: The Scientific Basis. Contribution of Working Group I to the Third Assessment Report of the Intergovernmental Panel on Climate Change* [Houghton, JT, Y Ding, DJ Griggs, M Noguer, PJ van der Linden, X Dai, K Maskell, and CA Johnson (eds)]. Cambridge University Press, Cambridge, United Kingdom and New York, NY, USA.

other graphic has created so much controversy. The graph, the underlying science and the lead researcher, Michael Mann, were fiercely attacked by climate change skeptics. The dispute led to an independent review by the US National Academy of Sciences in 2006 which found that, while there were some statistical failings, these had little effect on the overall findings.

What was different about this debate was that it centered around data and data visualizations, with both sides using graphs. The other novelty was that it was one of the first public discussions to go online. Before 2000, it was rare for homes to have an internet connection. Public discourse consisted of debates by politicians, TV interviews and panels, newspaper articles and editorials, and the occasional demonstration. Since 2000, digital media has played an increasingly important role in public discussion. In the case of the hockey stick graph, online blogs, which were a novelty then, have been credited with engaging the public and fueling the controversy.

Campaigns to raise public awareness about environmental and social issues are now built around digital media and marketing. Visualizations figure prominently. Hans Rosling's Gapminder project is one example (see Figure 10.3). Another is the Global Forest Watch Fires map. Released in 2014 by the World Resources Institute, a research NGO, this online map tracks the health-threatening haze produced by the illegal burning of forests and peatlands in Indonesia. It is based on satellite images, air quality data, government data and crowdsourcing. The map has fueled debate in Indonesia about the problem. It has mobilized collaboration between environmental groups and local communities to combat haze, and was used as evidence in a trial leading to the Indonesian Government being found guilty of negligence.

More recently, we saw that data visualizations were prominent in public debate during the COVID-19 pandemic. They were on government websites and in the news media. They also appeared on social media (see Figure I.2), with a study finding that COVID-19–related tweets containing visualizations led to significantly more reader engagement (as measured by likes, replies, retweets and quotes). And it is this ability to engage that ensures we will continue to see data visualization in public discourse.

VIRTUAL MAPS: YOU ARE HERE

While our smartphones now enable us to access a wealth of online data visualizations, maps are the graphics we view most frequently. It's hard to

FIGURE 10.7 Smartphone mapping applications like Google Maps have revolutionized how we navigate and how we think about maps.

Credit: By deepanker70 via Pixabay.

overstate the change smartphone mapping applications such as Google Maps have made to our lives (see Figure 10.7). They have replaced street directories and maps in travel guides and enabled new types of businesses like Uber. By combining computerized cartography, satellite imagery, Global Positioning System (GPS), the internet and smartphones, these mapping applications provide a radically new, context-aware way of visualizing and experiencing geography, one that has transformed how we think about maps.

In 2006, Steve Jobs recognized that Google Maps was the killer application he needed for Apple's soon-to-be-released iPhone. Sure enough, at the iPhone's carefully choreographed launch on January 9, 2007, Google

Maps stole the show. Jobs tapped on the Google Maps icon and a map appeared on the iPhone's (for the time) large screen—a map that (using the magic of the inbuilt GPS) was centered on Jobs's current location, shown as a pulsing blue dot. He typed 'Starbucks', and fourteen pins dropped onto the map indicating nearby stores. He clicked on one of the pins and called the Starbucks store directly from the map interface, ordering 4000 lattes before apologizing and hanging up. The audience erupted, laughing and applauding. But Jobs wasn't finished. He switched Google Maps to satellite mode and explored the world, from the Giza pyramids in Egypt to the Statue of Liberty. Effortlessly panning, zooming in and out with swipes and two-finger pinches, he showcased the power and immediacy of the iPhone's groundbreaking multi-touch interface. There was no doubt this was a phone like nobody had ever seen before, and this was a map like nobody had ever seen before.

The origin of Google Maps lies with geographer Roger Tomlinson. In 1962, he was working with an aerial survey company in Canada on a government-funded project to assess current land use and the land's future capacity for agriculture, forestry or wildlife conservation. The government soon discovered it had a problem. While it could collect and map the required data, it estimated it would need to employ another 500 skilled technicians for three years to analyze the information. There were simply not enough trained staff for this, so Tomlinson suggested a different approach, explaining that:

maps could be put into numerical form and linked together to form a complete picture of the natural resources of a region or of a nation or a continent. The computer could then be used to analyse the characteristic of those resources and provide information that was useful and timely for land planning decisions.

Tomlinson pitched his idea to the Canada Land Inventory. It accepted, and work began on what he called a geographic information system (GIS). Tomlinson wasn't the first to think about how computers could automate cartography. Previously, however, the focus had been on storing maps digitally so that it was faster to update them. Just as in early CAD and desktop publishing, the computer was viewed as a tool to reduce the cost of producing a printed visual artefact—in this case, a traditional map. Tomlinson's insight was that computers could do much more than this. They could be programmed to analyze spatial data.

By the end of the 1960s, Tomlinson's system had been built, and his idea had inspired the creation of dozens of other GIS tools. The desire to better manage land resources and environment protection laws were the main drivers for their development. Rachel Carson's book *Silent Spring*, published in 1962, had awoken a generation to the dangers of pesticides. It fueled a rising concern for the environment as the community became more aware of industrial and agricultural pollution and their risks. For instance, in the United States, the *National Environment Policy Act* of 1970 funded the development of GIS systems to improve land management and help with environmental impact assessment.

At its core, a GIS is a spatial database. It knows the location of natural and artificial geographic features such as lakes and rivers, political and county boundaries, roads and buildings. It also contains non-spatial data associated with these geographic features, such as a city's population and a building's address and owner. This means the user can search for geographic elements that satisfy a mix of spatial and non-spatial requirements. GIS tools also support more specialized geographic operations and analyses. For example, they can convert postal addresses to a geographic position, compute distances and areas, or find the shortest route between two locations.

The first GIS tools worked in batch mode, and the resulting maps and charts were printed using line printers, yielding makeshift, low-resolution graphics. Then, with the arrival of graphics workstations in the 1980s, an analyst could view the results on a high-resolution computer display. GIS became interactive, with an interface built around maps, allowing the analyst to zoom and pan to explore a map or select a region on the map as part of a new query or operation.

By the end of the twentieth century, GIS tools were indispensable and a new profession had emerged: experts in GIS known as spatial analysts. GIS continued to be used for natural resource planning and management but were now also used for many other applications, including disaster management, land records management, public health, crime analysis and town planning. Businesses, for instance, used them to plan where to place warehouses to minimize transport costs, and governments used them to determine the position and height of new levee banks to protect a region from flooding.

One reason for the increasing use of GIS was that geographic data became quicker and cheaper to collect. As we saw in Chapter 6, the military recognized the value of aerial photography for reconnaissance during World War I. By the middle of the twentieth century, aerial surveying was commonplace. Then came aerial radar. Based on microwaves, this allowed mapmakers to see through clouds and mist. They could now map tropical rainforests such as the Amazon. Sonar provided even more data. It allowed ships to systematically survey the ocean beds for the first time, revealing unexpected mountain ranges and chasms, and providing evidence for the sea-floor spreading version of continental drift.

It was satellite imaging, however, that had the most significant impact on cartography. At first, mapmakers thought the primary cartographic use of artificial satellites would be to reveal the Earth's shape. Minuscule changes in the orbit exposed that the Earth was pear-shaped, bulging slightly in the Southern Hemisphere. Then, in 1963, Gordon Cooper, an American astronaut, took photographs of the Earth with his handheld camera. To the surprise of those on the ground, his images were clear of atmospheric distortion. They revealed an inaccessible region of Tibet in detail, allowing it to be mapped for the first time.

A decade later, NASA launched Landsat 1, the first non-military reconnaissance satellite. Circling the Earth fourteen times a day, its orbit was designed to pass above the entire planet. Landsat took three photographs of the region beneath it every twenty-five seconds: one in red, one in green and one in infrared. In combination, these gave a detailed picture of the area's terrain and vegetation. Landsat 1 and its successors produced an incredible amount of data—data that required a computer and GIS to make sense of.

Computers store graphics in two distinct ways. Images such as those taken by satellites are represented as a grid of points, each with a color or value. This is called a raster graphic. Schematic graphics like charts and maps, however, are usually encoded as geometric shapes, such as points, lines or polygons. This is called a vector graphic.

The first GIS systems used vector graphics, storing geographic data as geometric shapes whose coordinates were specified using latitude and longitude. By the 1990s, as satellite images became more common, most GIS tools handled both vector and raster data. Nonetheless, reflecting their cartographic origins, these systems remained firmly based on vector representations of geographical features and their presentation using traditional maps.

This changed in 2001. A US start-up called Keyhole launched EarthViewer. Based on satellite images, this computer application showed the world as a 3D globe, not a 2D map. Given an address, it would fly into the location, zooming in as it drew closer and closer until you could see streets and individual buildings. It was intuitive and visually exhilarating, making traditional GIS look tired and old-fashioned. EarthViewer was the brainchild of 3D computer graphics programmers, not cartographers, and its ancestry was in computer games and flight simulators. While it didn't provide all the functionality of a traditional GIS, it certainly had the gee whiz factor in spades.

Google recognized the potential of EarthViewer and bought the company in 2004, along with Where 2 Technologies, a small mapping software company based in Australia. Google's original mission had been 'to organize the world's information'. By 2004, it had realized that much of this information was spatial, and it now wanted to link information about objects in the real world with the objects' physical location. The goal was to extend Google Search from 'indexing web pages' to 'indexing the world around us'. In 2005, Google launched Google Earth, a slicker version of EarthViewer, and Google Maps, an entirely new product.

Google Maps was viewable in a web browser. While it wasn't the first browser-based mapping tool, it was light years ahead of the competition. It had a simple interface, was fast, and integrated satellite imagery. Even better, its maps were up to date, as Google regularly scraped webpages for geographic information. This allowed Google to check, for instance, that a company's address on its webpage was consistent with its location on Google Maps. However, a critical difference to today's Google Maps was that it did not use GPS, forcing the user to type in their location.

GPS (Global Positioning System) was invented by the US military in the 1970s. It relies on twenty-four satellites that circle the Earth twice each day. Their orbits are designed so that any point on the Earth will always be in radio contact with at least four satellites. Each satellite has a highly accurate clock and continuously broadcasts the time, correct to a billionth of a second, along with its position. When a GPS receiver on the Earth receives a broadcast, it uses the time taken for the signal to arrive to compute its distance to the satellite. Using the distances from each of the four satellites within radio contact and their positions when they sent the signal, the receiver can precisely calculate its latitude, longitude and elevation.

At first, only the US military was allowed to use GPS. This changed in 1983 when a Korean Air civilian airliner was shot down by Soviet jets when it mistakenly entered Soviet airspace, killing everyone on board. President

Ronald Reagan then mandated free civilian access to GPS to avoid such disasters in the future. Undoubtedly, GPS is the handiest device for navigation that the world has ever seen. It is a massive advance for map-making and navigation, on par with the invention of the compass and the chronometer.

The first GPS receivers were bulky and expensive. But as prices and size fell, manufacturers such as TomTom introduced GPS-equipped car navigation systems. Then, from 2000, all mobile phones sold in the United States were required to have a GPS chip so that it was possible to know the caller's location in case of an emergency call to 911.

Google Maps on GPS-equipped smartphones has brought about a revolution in map use. In 2020, Google Maps was used by over one billion people every month, mostly on smartphones. It relies on data from satellite imagery, aerial footage, real-time traffic information, street view scenes filmed from cars, official city and regional maps, and crowdsourced corrections and updates from users. This data is merged into a master map, 'Ground Truth', which underpins both Google Maps and Google Earth. Ground Truth is now the world's most extensive and detailed GIS.

It costs Google billions of dollars to collect the data for Ground Truth. Just consider the amount of footage required for Google Street View and the cost of obtaining this. Yet both Google Maps and Google Earth are free. This is because of Google's business model: businesses pay to appear on Google Maps. If you use Google to search for a bookstore, you get back a list of nearby stores and a map showing their locations with pins. Whenever you click on a pin or follow a link to the store's website, Google makes money. Is this good? I am not sure. Advertising revenue means that Google Maps is more reliable and up to date than any map ever seen before. But it does mean that what we see on it is mediated by the business interests of Google.

That said, Google Maps is more than a new advertising model. It has become a platform for new businesses and applications. From the beginning, Google encouraged its users to create 'mash-ups' in which their data was overlaid on top of a Google map. Google Maps is now a regular feature of applications like Airbnb, providing information about the location of products and services. More profoundly, Google Maps and similar platforms have enabled new types of urban transport. Companies such as Uber, Lyft and Lime that provide ride-sharing, car-sharing, bike, e-bike and e-scooter sharing could not exist if we didn't have smartphones and locationally aware maps.

THE NEW GOLDEN AGE

In this and the previous chapter, we have seen that the 1980s was a watershed moment in data visualization. We saw how engineers, architects, medical practitioners, scientists, managers and cartographers embraced computer-mediated data visualization. We also saw the emergence of new professions—spatial analyst, data scientist and data journalist—that rely on data visualization. Most of us now make regular use of graphics at work, be it calendars, spreadsheets or PowerPoint presentations.

However, a hallmark of this Golden Age is that data visualization is not restricted to the workplace. We are taught how to use tables, maps and statistical charts at school. Graphics pervade our private life. We use digital maps on our smartphones for navigation. And, because of Google, maps have become integral to finding out where to shop or dine, and specifying where we would like to be picked up by an Uber. We use spreadsheets to manage our personal finances. The interface to our smartphone, tablet, PC or TV is an information graphic. Our built environment is replete with information graphics: from dials and gauges on the car dashboard to maps and directories in shopping centers to markings on the road.

Data visualization has become part of popular culture. We know Tony Stark from *Iron Man* is a technical genius because of the diagrams and graphs he conjures up on his futuristic computer display. Animated weather maps (see Figure 8.8), financial charts and sports graphics enliven the mainstream press. People share entertaining and informative visualizations on social media. Visual artists turn data into artwork. Never before have so many people routinely used data visualization and information graphics.

One reason is that we have more data to visualize. The computer has led to a tsunami of what is known as Big Data. This includes medical and scientific images, data from satellites and wearables, social media data, and government and corporate data on the internet and private networks.

The second reason is that the computer has revolutionized the production and presentation of information graphics. The first computer applications supported traditional workflows in which graphics were manually designed and printed on paper. Computer graphics software and hardware advances soon allowed graphics to be automatically generated from digital data and viewed on a computer display. While the computer

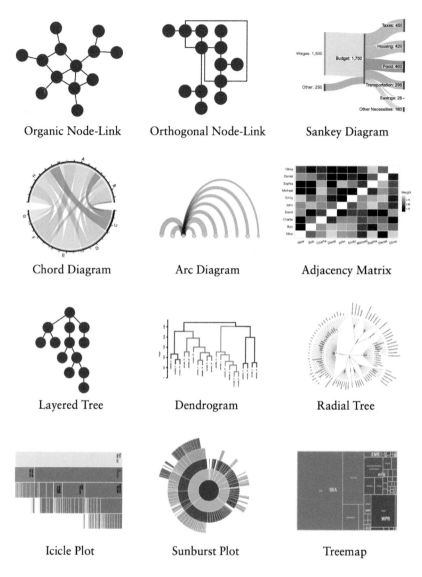

FIGURE 10.8   The Golden Age of Data Visualization employs a rich visual language of graphics. For example, data analysts can choose from a variety of network and hierarchy representations or, if necessary, invent their own representation.

Credit: Kadek Satriadi.

was not the first device to automatically create an information graphic, it was the first to provide a generic capability.

Automatic generation allowed visualizations to scale up to large datasets with hundreds of thousands of data elements, which is simply impossible if done by hand. Without the computer, it would not be possible to visualize data generated from a CT scan or the network of computers forming the internet.

The automatic generation of graphics has fundamentally changed the economics of graphics use, reducing the cost of production to essentially zero. If Google or Tableau had to pay someone to manually draw a map or chart every time you used their products and then print it on paper, they would be losing money hand over fist. Applications like these are only viable because of computer-generated graphics and computer displays. Furthermore, the web has fundamentally changed the cost of distributing graphics. It costs almost nothing to publish a data visualization online or post it on social media.

The computer has also brought about another significant change: graphics are no longer static but can change their appearance. Animation allows us to escape the 'deadland' of printed graphics. We can step through animated weather maps or 'scrollytell' through an online visualization. Even more usefully, user interaction enables us to visualize larger, more complex datasets. The invention of interactions, such as showing details on demand, sorting, searching, filtering, zooming, scrolling and panning, and techniques linking graphics in compound visualizations, is a notable contribution of our current Golden Age.

Even more profoundly, the computer has transformed the function of information graphics. Graphics are no longer used as calculating devices: slide rules and nomograms are now curiosities of the past. Instead, they have become the interface to sophisticated computer analysis and modeling tools in CAD, computational science, GIS and business analytics. Indeed, the computer interface itself is a kind of interactive information graphic.

As a case in point, think of how Google Maps has transformed mapping. Its interactive maps allow the viewer to search, filter, zoom in or out, and pan to tailor the view to their needs. The map is the interface to a computer application with unprecedented amounts of geospatial data. It is an application that can perform sophisticated analyses, such as finding an optimal navigation route considering current traffic densities. Perhaps even more astonishingly, the application is aware of where it is being viewed, allowing it to center the map on the viewer's position and align its orientation with the external geography.

One reason for these tremendous changes and innovations is that data visualization has emerged as a profession and area of study in its own right. Each year, tens of thousands of university students study data visualization, and dozens of books and online courses can teach you how to design and create your own visualizations. The 1987 NSF workshop proved pivotal in creating this new field, leading to regular conferences on computer visualization.

Building on Jacques Bertin's taxonomy of visual variables, visualization researchers have explored new data visualization designs (see Figure 10.8). They have systematically compared the effectiveness of different visualizations for a wide variety of tasks using experimental methods from perceptual psychology; for example, we now know that values can be more accurately compared on a bar chart than a pie chart. They have developed new algorithms for generating graphics from data and new visualization software. Tableau, for instance, was the brainchild of data visualization researchers from Stanford University.

But for all of the changes engendered by the computer, the Golden Age of Data Visualization has its roots in the past. Computer rendering of 3D models is based upon the 'geometry of vision' developed in the Renaissance, and many other algorithms are based on pre-existing manual processes such as those used to calculate contour lines from the heights of multiple locations.

Modern data visualizations utilize visual notations developed over thousands of years. For instance, maps in the twenty-first century look remarkably like those from the pre-computer age. They use lines to show roads and boundaries, contours to depict relief, and color and symbols to show spatially embedded data. Satellite and aerial imagery, while more detailed, resembles bird's-eye views of cities from the Renaissance. Even the projections remain unchanged—Google Maps uses a standard Mercator projection, and Google Earth is a virtual globe.

Furthermore, this Golden Age builds upon the visual cultures of scientists, engineers, architects and business managers. It builds upon the increasing use of graphics in newspapers during the early twentieth century and the rise of our modern visual culture. It builds upon the introduction of compulsory education and the expanding use of graphics in schools. Without these foundations, our current Golden Age could not exist.

NOTES, REFERENCES AND FURTHER READING

The Ascent of Visual Culture

Desktop Publishing

Crocker, Suzanne. 'Paul Brainerd, Aldus Corporation, and the Desktop Publishing Revolution.' *IEEE Annals of the History of Computing* 41, no. 3 (2019): 35–41.

Monmonier, Mark. *Maps with the News: The Development of American Journalistic Cartography*. University of Chicago Press, 1989: Chapter 4.

Romano, Frank and Miranda Mitrano. *History of Desktop Publishing*. Oak Knoll Press, 2019.

Increased Use of Graphics in Newspapers and Magazines

Dick, Murray. *The Infographic: A History of Data Graphics in News and Communications*. MIT Press, 2020: Chapter 4.

Gottlieb, Agnes Hooper. 'Newspapers in the Twentieth Century.' In *The Function of Newspapers in Society: A Global Perspective*. Praeger Publishing. 2003: 127–37.

Monmonier, Mark. *Maps with the News: The Development of American Journalistic Cartography*. University of Chicago Press, 1989: Chapter 4.

Sexton, William C. 'The Explosion in Graphics.' *Bulletin of the American Society of Newspaper Editors*, no. 547 (January 1971): 16–22.

Tiffen, Rodney. 'Changes in Australian Newspapers 1956–2006.' *Journalism Practice* 4, no. 3 (2010): 345–59.

The Rise of Visual Culture

Stephens, Mitchell. *The Rise of the Image, the Fall of the Word*. Oxford University Press, 1998. Quote from p. 5.

However, the twentieth century also saw a rising distrust of vision by philosophers and humanity scholars. *USA Today* was accused of 'dumbing down' its audience because of its heavy use of graphics, and this sentiment may have fueled Betty Boothroyd's disdain for graphics discussed in the introduction.

Jay, Martin. *Downcast Eyes: The Denigration of Vision in Twentieth-Century French Thought*. University of California Press, 1993.

Photography

Goldberg, Vicki. *The Power of Photography: How Photographs Changed Our Lives*. Abbeville, 1991: Introduction.

Turner, Peter. *History of Photography*. Hamlyn Publishing, 1987: Chapters 1 and 4.

Wajda, Shirley Teresa. *'Social Currency': A Domestic History of the Portrait Photograph in the United States, 1839-1889.* PhD thesis. University of Pennsylvania, 1992.

Television

Blank, Ben, and Mario R Garcia. *Professional Video Graphic Design.* Focal Press, 1986: Chapters 5 and 6.

Foote, Joe S, and Ann C Saunders. 'Graphic Forms in Network Television News.' *Journalism Quarterly* 67, no. 3 (1990): 501–7.

Heflin, Kristen. 'The Future Will Be Televised: Newspaper Industry Voices and the Rise of Television News.' *American Journalism* 27, no. 2 (2010): 87–110.

Monmonier, Mark. *Maps with the News: The Development of American Journalistic Cartography.* University of Chicago Press, 1989: Chapter 5.

Stephens, Mitchell. *The Rise of the Image, the Fall of the Word.* Oxford University Press, 1998.

Xiaoming, Hao. 'Trend: Television Viewing among American Adults in the 1990s.' *Journal of Broadcasting & Electronic Media* 38, no. 3 (1994): 353–60.

Graphical Interfaces

Campbell-Kelly, Martin, William Aspray, Nathan Ensmenger, and Jeffrey R Yoost. *Computer: A History of the Information Machine* (3rd ed.). Routledge, 2013: Chapters 4, 10 and 11.

Mattern, Shannon. 'Mission Control: A History of the Urban Dashboard.' *Places Journal* (March 2015). https://doi.org/10.22269/150309

Terkourafi, Marina, and Stefanos Petrakis. 'A Critical Look at the Desktop Metaphor 30 Years on.' In *Researching and Applying Metaphor in the Real World.* John Benjamins, 2010: 145–64.

Graphic Literacy

Avgerinou, Maria, and John Ericson. 'A Review of the Concept of Visual Literacy.' *British Journal of Educational Technology* 28, no. 4 (1997): 280–91.

Balchin, William GV, and Alice M Coleman. 'Graphicacy Should Be the Fourth Ace in the Pack.' *Cartographica: The International Journal for Geographic Information and Geovisualization* 3, no. 1 (1966): 23–8.

Danos, Xenia. *Graphicacy and Culture: Refocusing on Visual Learning.* Loughborough Design Press Limited, 2014.

From Spreadsheets to Visual Analytics
Changes in Work

Wyatt, Ian D. 'Occupational Changes During the 20th Century.' *Monthly Labor Review* 129 (2006): 35–57.

Presentation Software

Mace, Scott. 'Presentation Package Lets Users Control Look.' *Info World News.* March 2, 1987: 5.

Yates, Joann, and Wanda Orlikowski. 'The PowerPoint Presentation and Its Corollaries: How Genres Shape Communicative Action in Organizations.' In *Communicative Practices in Workplaces and the Professions: Cultural Perspectives on the Regulation of Discourse and Organizations.* Baywood Publishing, 2007: 67–92.

Spreadsheets

Campbell-Kelly, Martin. 'Number Crunching without Programming: The Evolution of Spreadsheet Usability.' *IEEE Annals of the History of Computing* 29, no. 3 (2007): 6–19.

Visual Analytics and Tableau

Wikipedia. 'Tableau Software.' 2023. https://en.wikipedia.org/wiki/Tableau_Software

Zhang, Leishi, Andreas Stoffel, Michael Behrisch, Sebastian Mittelstadt, Tobias Schreck, René Pompl, Stefan Weber, Holger Last, and Daniel Keim. 'Visual Analytics for the Big Data Era—A Comparative Review of State-of-the-Art Commercial Systems.' In 2012 *IEEE Conference on Visual Analytics Science and Technology* (VAST). IEEE, 2012: 173–82.

Formalization of Information Graphics

Bertin, Jacques. *Semiology of Graphics: Diagrams Networks Maps.* (Translation of *Sémiologie graphique*, 1967). University of Wisconsin Press, 1983: Part II.

Tukey and Exploratory Data Analysis

Brillinger, David R. 'John W Tukey: His Life and Professional Contributions.' *The Annals of Statistics* 30, no. 6 (2002): 1535–75.

Tukey, John W. *Exploratory Data Analysis.* Addison-Wesley, 1977: Preface, and Chapters 2 and 4. The quote is from p. vi.

Early Interactive Computer Graphics for Data Analysis

Becker, Richard A, William S Cleveland, and Allan R Wilks. 'Dynamic Graphics for Data Analysis.' *Statistical Science* 2 (1987): 355–83.

Cook, Dianne. 'The Twentieth-Century Computer Graphics Revolution in Statistics.' In *Visible Numbers: Essays on the History of Statistical Graphics.* Routledge, 2016: 207–18.

Friedman, Jerome H, and Werner Stuetzle. 'John W Tukey's Work on Interactive Graphics.' *Annals of Statistics* 30, no. 6 (2002): 1629–39.

Tukey, John W, and Paul A Tukey. 'Computer Graphics and Exploratory Data Analysis: An Introduction.' *Proceedings of the Sixth Annual Conference and Exposition of the National Computer Graphics Association.* National Computer Graphics Association, 1985: 773–85.

Visualizing Multivariate Data

Data with multiple variables is often called multidimensional, but I have chosen to use the term 'multivariate' so as not to confuse it with data that has inherent spatial dimensions, such as scientific images.

Few, Stephen. 'Dashboard Confusion Revisited.' *Visual Business Intelligence Newsletter* (March 2007): 1–6, Perceptual Edge.

Munzner, Tamara. *Visualization Analysis and Design.* CRC Press, 2014: Chapters 12 and 13.

Ward, Matthew O, Georges Grinstein, and Daniel Keim. *Interactive Data Visualization: Foundations, Techniques, and Applications* (2nd ed.). CRC Press, 2015: Chapter 8.

Interaction

Becker, Richard A, and William S Cleveland. 'Brushing Scatterplots.' *Technometrics* 29, no. 2 (1987): 127–42.

Card, Stuart K, Jock Mackinlay, and Ben Shneiderman. Interaction. In *Readings in Information Visualization: Using Vision to Think.* Morgan Kaufmann, 1999: 231–4.

Few, Stephen. 'Dashboard Confusion Revisited.' *Visual Business Intelligence Newsletter* (March 2007): 1–6, Perceptual Edge.

Huber, Peter J. 'Statistical Graphics: History and Overview.' In *Proceedings of the Fourth Annual Conference and Exposition of the National Computer Graphics Association.* National Computer Graphics Association, 1983: 667–76. The quote is from p. 675.

Munzner, Tamara. *Visualization Analysis and Design.* CRC Press, 2014: Chapters 1 and 12. The quote is from p. 9.

The Internet and Big Data

Big Data

Diebold, Francis X. 'On the Origin(s) and Development of the Term "Big Data".' PIER working paper 12-037. Penn Institute for Economic Research, University of Pennsylvania, 2012.

Statista. 'Volume of Data/Information Created, Captured, Copied, and Consumed Worldwide from 2010 to 2020, with Forecasts from 2021 to 2025.' 2021. www. statista.com/statistics/871513/worldwide-data-created/

Digital Dashboards

Few, Stephen. *Information Dashboard Design: The Effective Visual Communication of Data.* O'Reilly, 2006.

Mattern, Shannon. 'Mission Control: A History of the Urban Dashboard.' *Places Journal* (March 2015). https://doi.org/10.22269/150309

Data Science

Kelleher, John D, and Brendan Tierney. *Data Science.* MIT Press, 2018: Chapter 1.

Miller, Steven, and Debbie Hughes. 'The Quant Crunch: How the Demand for Data Science Skills Is Disrupting the Job Market.' *Burning Glass Technologies,* 2017. www.bhef.com/sites/default/files/bhef_2017_quant_crunch.pdf

Visualizing Text

Ward, Matthew O, Georges Grinstein, and Daniel Keim. *Interactive Data Visualization: Foundations, Techniques, and Applications* (2nd ed.). CRC Press, 2015: Chapter 10.

Wikipedia. 'Tag Cloud.' 2023. https://en.wikipedia.org/wiki/Tag_cloud#History

Networks

Barabási, Albert-László. *Network Science.* Cambridge University Press, 2016: Introduction.

Lima, Manuel. *Visual Complexity: Mapping Patterns of Information.* Princeton Architectural Press, 2011: Chapters 3 and 4.

Munzner, Tamara. *Visualization Analysis and Design.* CRC Press, 2014: Chapter 9.

Newman, Mark. *Networks: An Introduction.* Oxford University Press, 2018: Chapters 2–5.

Ward, Matthew O, Georges Grinstein, and Daniel Keim. *Interactive Data Visualization: Foundations, Techniques, and Applications* (2nd ed.). CRC Press, 2015: Chapter 9.

Data Journalism

Dick, Murray. *The Infographic: A History of Data Graphics in News and Communications.* MIT Press, 2020: Chapter 5.

Weber, Wibke, Martin Engebretsen, and Helen Kennedy. 'Data Stories: Rethinking Journalistic Storytelling in the Context of Data Journalism.' *Studies in Communication Sciences* 2018, no. 1 (2018): 191–206.

Yau, Nathan. *Visualize This: The FlowingData Guide to Design, Visualization, and Statistics*. John Wiley & Sons, 2011: Introduction.

The 'Hockey Stick' Graph

Mann, Michael E. *The Hockey Stick and the Climate Wars: Dispatches from the Front Lines*. Columbia University Press, 2012: 141–5.

Newburger, Eric C. *Home Computers and Internet Use in the United States: August 2000*. No. 207. US Department of Commerce, Bureau of the Census, 2001.

Pearce, Fred. 'Climate Change Debate Overheated after Sceptic Grasped "Hockey Stick".' *The Guardian*, February 10, 2010. www.theguardian.com/environm ent/2010/feb/09/hockey-stick-michael-mann-steve-mcintyre

Zorita, Eduardo. 'The Climate of the Past Millennium and Online Public Engagement in a Scientific Debate.' *Wiley Interdisciplinary Reviews: Climate Change* 10, no. 5 (2019): e590.

The original hockey stick graph appeared in:

Mann, Michael E, Raymond Bradley, and Malcolm K Hughes. 'Northern Hemisphere Temperatures During the Past Millennium: Inferences, Uncertainties, and Limitations.' *Geophysical Research Letters* 26, no. 6 (1999): 759–62.

Use of Visualizations in Public Discourse

Berti Suman, Anna. 'The Role of Information in Multilateral Governance of Environmental Health Risk: Lessons from the Equatorial Asian Haze Case.' *Journal of Risk Research* 25, no. 8 (2022): 959–75.

Kasumba, Robert, Saugat Pandey, Vishesh Patel, Micah Wolfson, and Alvitta Ottley. 'User Engagement with COVID-19 Visualizations on Twitter.' https://doi.org/10.31219/osf.io/es6ua

Nærland, Torgeir Uberg, and Martin Engebretsen. 'Towards a Critical Understanding of Data Visualisation in Democracy: A Deliberative Systems Approach.' *Information, Communication & Society* 26, no. 3 (2023): 637–55.

Virtual Maps: You Are Here

Google Maps on the iPhone Release

Kilday, Bill. *Never Lost Again*. Harper Business, 2018: Chapter 18.

History of GIS

Brotton, Jerry. *A History of the World in Twelve Maps*. Viking, 2012: Chapter 12.

Coppock, JT, and DW Rhind. 'The History of GIS.' In *Geographical Information Systems: Principles and Applications*. Longman, 1991: vol. 2, 21–43.

Foresman, Timothy W. 'GIS Early Years and the Threads of Evolution.' In *The History of Geographic Information Systems: Perspectives from the Pioneers.* Prentice Hall, 1998: 3–17.

Tomlinson, Roger F. 'Geographic Information Systems: A New Frontier.' In *Introductory Readings in Geographic Information Systems.* Taylor & Francis, 1990: 15–27. The Tomlinson quote comes from p. 17.

Wilford, John Noble. *The Mapmakers* (2nd ed.). Vintage, 2001: Chapter 23.

Modern GIS Systems and Their Use

Chang, Kang-Tsung. *Introduction to Geographic Information Systems* (7th ed.). McGraw-Hill Higher Education, 2014: Chapters 1, 9, 10, 13, 14, 16 and 17.

DeMers, Michael N. *Fundamentals of Geographic Information Systems* (4th ed.). John Wiley & Sons, 2008: Chapters 8–14 and 16.

Peuquet, Donna J, and Menno-Jan Kraak. 'Geobrowsing: Creative Thinking and Knowledge Discovery Using Geographic Visualization.' *Information Visualization* 1, no. 1 (2002): 80–91.

From Aerial Photography to Satellite Imaging

Wilford, John Noble. *The Mapmakers* (2nd ed.). Vintage, 2001: Chapters 15, 16, 19 and 22.

EarthViewer

Kilday, Bill. *Never Lost Again.* Harper Business, 2018: Chapters 2–4.

History of Google Maps

Kilday, Bill. *Never Lost Again.* Harper Business, 2018: Chapters 8–13.

GPS

Kilday, Bill. *Never Lost Again.* Harper Business, 2018: Chapter 15.

Wikipedia. 'Global Positioning System.' 2023. https://en.wikipedia.org/wiki/Global_Positioning_System

Wilford, John Noble. *The Mapmakers* (2nd ed.). Vintage, 2001: Chapter 21.

Google Maps Today

Some GIS experts do not consider Google Maps a true GIS system as it does not have general-purpose spatial analysis capabilities. However, its origins lie in GIS and it has a wide range of spatial analysis capabilities.

The business model for Google Maps is not unprecedented. Before Google, it was common for printed tourist maps to be available for free, the cost of map production being paid for by local businesses who used the map to advertise their products and show their location. However, Google has taken this business model to an entirely new level.

Kilday, Bill. *Never Lost Again*. Harper Business, 2018: Chapter 19.

Rijo, Daniel. 'Google Maps Now Used by over 1 Billion People Every Month.' *PPC Land*, February 2020. https://ppc.land/google-maps-now-used-by-over-1-billion-people-every-month/

The New Golden Age

Built Environment Is a Graphic

Tversky, Barbara. *Mind in Motion: How Action Shapes Thought*. Hachette UK, 2019: Chapter 10.

Modern Plethora of Information Graphics

Harris, Robert L. *Information Graphics: A Comprehensive Illustrated Reference*. Oxford University Press, 1999.

Munzner, Tamara. *Visualization Analysis and Design*. CRC Press, 2014: Chapters 7–9.

Ward, Matthew O, Georges Grinstein, and Daniel Keim. *Interactive Data Visualization: Foundations, Techniques, and Applications* (2nd ed.). CRC Press, 2015: Chapters 5–10.

Data Visualization Research

Munzner, Tamara. *Visualization Analysis and Design*. CRC Press, 2014.

Ward, Matthew O, Georges Grinstein, and Daniel Keim. *Interactive Data Visualization: Foundations, Techniques, and Applications* (2nd ed.). CRC Press, 2015.

Ware, Colin. *Information Visualization: Perception for Design* (4th ed.). Elsevier, 2021.

CHAPTER 11

Visualization
without Vision

I N THE LAST CHAPTER, we saw that data visualization and information graphics have become pervasive in our modern world. However, what if you are blind? Worldwide, it is estimated that thirty-six million people are blind. Lack of access to graphical information is one of the most disabling consequences of blindness. It can restrict educational opportunities and employment, especially in science and technology, reduce the enjoyment of cultural institutions, such as art galleries and museums, and limit access to information in popular media and websites. More recently, the lack of access to graphical information about COVID-19 was recognized as a significant equity and public health issue.

I became aware of the need for accessible graphics fifteen years ago when I taught a university course on computer algorithms and data structures to a student who was blind. He struggled, as the lecture slides were full of diagrams. His difficulty made me realize the significant disadvantage faced by university students who are blind and the need for more equitable access to graphical information.

Staff from Disability Support Services helped my student understand the diagrams in two ways. Usually, they described them to him. This remains the most common way for people who are blind to access graphical information. However, a description has severe limitations. For more complex graphics, it necessarily misses out on details and can only provide an

DOI: 10.1201/9781003507642-12

overview. Nor can the listener independently explore the data or check the description is accurate. Furthermore, the listener must expend considerable cognitive effort to create a mental image from the description, and they miss out on the cognitive benefits associated with visual graphics identified in the previous chapters.

Because of these limitations, my student was also given raised-line drawings of the most important diagrams. Such drawings are called tactile graphics. They are a graphical analog to braille and use elements with different textures and heights to represent the graphic. Like braille, they are read with the hands (see Figure 11.1). Guidelines for providing accessible information to people who are blind recommend using tactile graphics rather than a description whenever understanding the graphic's geometry is required.

In this chapter, we will explore the little-known story of tactile graphics: their history, and how they provide an accessible alternative to visual representations. Not only are they fascinating in their own right, but understanding the cognitive benefits of tactile graphics provides an insight into the cognitive benefits of visual graphics.

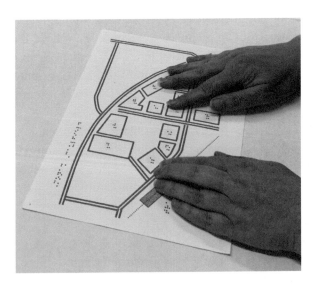

FIGURE 11.1   Raised-line drawings known as tactile graphics allow people who are blind to access graphics. Here, a person is touch reading a tactile map of a university campus printed on swell paper.

Credit: Sam Reinders (photography) and Leona Holloway (tactile graphic).

THE RISE OF TACTILE GRAPHICS

Tactile graphics have been in use for hundreds of years. In 1760, the philosopher and writer Denis Diderot (co-editor of the *Encyclopédie* discussed in Chapter 4) met Mélanie de Salignac, a young woman from a well-off family who was blind. He writes:

> *I have seen the maps with which she studied geography. The parallels and meridians were made of wire; the boundaries of kingdoms and provinces of embroidery in linen, silk or wool of various thickness; the rivers and streams and mountains of pins' heads of various sizes; and cities and towns of drops of wax of various sizes.*

However, in 1760, it is fair to say, only a few lucky children would have encountered tactile graphics.

It was at the first school for blind students that tactile graphics came into more frequent use. This was founded in Paris by Valentine Haüy in 1784 and revolutionized the education of children who are blind. As part of his instruction, Haüy made maps for his students. He would take a print map and painstakingly lay wire along the country and regional borders, pasting a copy of the print map over the top. He would then use nails with different heads to mark towns and, finally, shellac the result.

The history of tactile graphics is inextricably linked to our evolving attitudes to disability. Before the Industrial Revolution, the education and care of people who were blind was the responsibility of their families and the local community. But social disruption and the movement of people from rural areas to cities because of industrialization meant that families and communities no longer had the resources to provide for people with disabilities.

As a result, charitable organizations and governments created institutions to care for people who were blind during the nineteenth century. Specialized schools for blind students were built throughout Europe and the United States. Loosely modeled on Haüy's school, most offered a basic education—reading, writing, arithmetic, geography and religion—and vocational training in music and other crafts deemed suitable for people who were blind, such as basket weaving or massage.

Tactile graphics and three-dimensional models were a regular part of this teaching. At first, tactile graphics were made by gluing materials with distinctive textures, such as velvet, sandpaper or thread, onto paper or cardboard. Soon, rising demand led to mass production. By the end of the nineteenth century, tactile maps and diagrams for physics, botany and zoology were being manufactured by pressing damp paper between two molds.

During the twentieth century, self-advocacy and activism by disability groups led to a revolution in attitudes towards people who are blind. Previously, most people had viewed disability as a medical problem: individuals were disabled by their impairments or differences, and the focus was on fixing these. In the second half of the twentieth century, this view was replaced by a more nuanced understanding of disability. It was recognized that most of the difficulties facing people with disabilities were, in fact, the result of other people's attitudes and architectural, economic or educational barriers. Many countries introduced anti-discrimination laws, and people with disabilities were integrated into the broader community. Many children who were blind no longer attended specialist schools; instead, they studied at their local schools and had the same educational opportunities as their sighted peers. Nonetheless, regardless of which school they attend, tactile drawings, diagrams and maps have continued to play an essential role in the education of students who are blind.

The twentieth century saw another significant change: the introduction of orientation and mobility training. Originally developed to support veterans injured during World War II, this was quickly recognized as critical for all people who are blind. It equips people who are blind to travel independently by teaching them to use travel aids such as guide dogs and canes. Tactile maps are frequently used in orientation and mobility training. They are used to teach children about traffic flow and different kinds of street crossings, and to help travelers build a mental model of a new location before they travel to it.

In the last fifty years, new technologies have reduced the cost of tactile graphic production. In one approach, a braille embosser punches raised dots into thick paper. Another technique is to print the graphics onto swell paper which contains microcapsules of alcohol that rise when heat is applied.

Regardless of the production technology, most tactile graphics are designed by professional translators called transcribers using computer graphics-editing software. Transcription is not straightforward. Text labels must be replaced by braille, and colors and patterns by different textures. The transcriber may have to introduce braille keys and a legend if the labels do not fit or there are too many colors and patterns. As fingers are much less sensitive to detail than eyes, the transcriber must carefully simplify the graphic while preserving its essential message. If the graphic is particularly complicated, they may need to create a series of less complex drawings, with an overview drawing showing the main components and the following graphics presenting the details.

READING TACTILE GRAPHICS

Tactile graphics are read using the fingers of both hands. An experienced touch reader uses faster, more fluid movements to identify different textures and the approximate position of the components, then slower, more careful exploration with one or two fingers to follow lines or boundaries.

Touch reading a tactile graphic is slower and less immediate than seeing a visual graphic. As the reader can only touch a small part of the graphic at one time, the field of view of the touch reader is considerably more limited than that of the sighted reader. Extracting the gist of a graphic and finding perceptually salient features such as rougher textures or regions of raised height takes conscious effort and exploration with the fingers. This means that reading a tactile graphic is a bottom-up process requiring the reader to construct a mental image as they sequentially explore it. Doing so places a high load on working memory, and it is common for a touch reader to be provided with a spoken or written overview of the graphic to facilitate their exploration.

Learning to touch read a tactile graphic is challenging, and blind children must be taught how to interpret tactile pictures. In part, I believe this is because of a perceptual disconnect between haptic perception and the conventions used in tactile drawings. Drawings, whether visual or tactile, use lines to show an object's outline and its surface features. We saw in Chapter 3 that this reflects how the visual system works, as identifying region boundaries and surface edges is the first step in object recognition. But this is not true for haptic perception. Here, texture is more salient. For instance, when you feel a spoon, you immediately notice its smoothness, hardness and coldness. Determining its shape comes later and requires conscious exploration.

Furthermore, the pictorial convention of showing a scene from a single viewpoint is intimately tied to visual perception. Touch, unlike vision, allows different sides of an object to be felt simultaneously, effectively showing it from multiple viewpoints. Moreover, pictorial depth cues, such as linear perspective, shadows, or a horizontal line to show the horizon, make little sense to someone who has been blind from birth.

These perceptual mismatches explain why people, regardless of whether they are sighted or blind, can readily identify familiar objects such as a spoon or comb by touch, but identification from a tactile drawing is slow and error-prone. They also explain why the recognition rate is even lower for those who have been blind from an early age.

Nonetheless, despite these challenges, many people who are blind strongly desire tactile graphics. Some, including my former student, say that they think visually. As discussed in Chapter 4, visual thinking by sighted people frequently involves reasoning with schematic mental models of spatial layout. It is this kind of spatial reasoning that I believe people who are blind are referring to when they say they think visually.

For centuries, philosophers have been fascinated by the relationship between blindness and spatial reasoning, and whether spatial awareness can exist independently of visual perception. In 1932, the German scientist Marius von Senden published the results of one of the first empirical investigations into these issues. He examined several case histories in which, mainly because of the removal of cataracts, people who had been blind obtained the use of sight. He concluded that:

> not one [case history] has provided evidence to support the hypothesis of a space of touch; they may be said, indeed, to have shown beyond doubt that the congenitally blind patient lacks everything that would entitle one to speak of a tactile awareness of space.

Subsequent research, however, has shown that von Senden was completely wrong. Multiple studies demonstrate that people who have been blind from birth generate, manipulate and store mental images that are functionally similar to those used by sighted people. For instance, when shown a shape on a tactile graphic, a person who is blind can mentally rotate it. And, just as when a person who is sighted mentally rotates a visual image, the greater the angle of rotation, the longer it takes. This does not mean that the mental images of someone who has been blind from birth are identical to those of someone who is sighted. But they do contain broadly equivalent information about shape and location.

Because of this, spatial cognition is now believed to rely on an abstract representation independent of any particular sense. Our brain combines information from sight, touch, sound, smell, taste and natural language descriptions into a single, unified spatial image. This spatial image is linked to information in long-term memory and sensory-specific representations containing additional details such as color, texture or temperature.

Likewise, cognitive maps of our environment are abstract representations of space independent of any particular sense. In contrast to the views of von Senden, we now know that people who are blind, regardless of when they became blind, create cognitive maps of their surroundings that are functionally similar to those produced by sighted people. However, for people who are blind, the primary way of building this model is from touch and sound rather than vision.

One difference is that people who are blind tend to understand their environment in terms of sequential routes rather than in a more connected, map-like representation: without sight, it is difficult to know how the routes fit together. Tactile maps help overcome this difficulty and enable people who are blind to build an allocentric, map-like model of their environment.

The usefulness of tactile maps has been demonstrated in several studies. One tested how well thirty adults who were blind could construct a cognitive map of an unfamiliar area in Madrid. They were divided into three groups, all learning the same highly convoluted route of two kilometers. The first group learned it only through direct experience. One of the researchers guided them along the path and told them the names of eight landmarks as they passed them, but they received no other information. The second group was given more information. As they were directed along the route, they were told the names of streets, landmarks and the direction in which to turn. The third group was given a tactile map detailing the route and landmarks. People in this group were guided along the path and could refer to the map whenever they liked.

Two kinds of knowledge were measured. The first was how well the participants could retrace the route. The second was the accuracy of the cognitive map they had built of the route. This was evaluated by asking each participant to plan a shortcut that connected three landmarks on the route and, when they were at a particular landmark, to point in the direction of each of the other landmarks. The group with the tactile map was significantly better at all tasks. They could retrace the route with fewer wrong turns and were better at estimating the direction to other landmarks and planning the shortcut.

Other studies have found that children who are blind can learn new environments from a tactile map as well as they can from direct experience.

Simon Ungar, a leading researcher in this field, argues that tactile maps are crucial tools for teaching students who are blind about their environment. They not only enhance the child's understanding of their geography, but also help train the child to conceptualize their environment using an allocentric reference frame in which the position of objects is understood relative to one another rather than in terms of their distance along a route.

Thus, we find that, while maps are undoubtedly helpful to sighted people, they are at least as beneficial to people who are blind, which is why they are an essential part of orientation and mobility training.

But what about graphics showing more abstract kinds of data? Do the spatial metaphors underlying scatterplots or timelines continue to make sense to someone who is blind? Studies with people who are blind from Western countries have found that they conceptualize both numbers and time in terms of space. Just like sighted people, they tend to think about numbers and time as locations on a horizontal line, with smaller numbers and earlier times on the left and larger numbers and later times on the right. This suggests that tactile graphs and charts will be understandable to people who are blind. However, do they offer cognitive benefits?

Two recent studies shed some light on this. One compared a tactile scatterplot to a tactile table of data values. This study indicated that people who are blind could more quickly and accurately identify the relationship between two variables using a scatterplot than a tactile table.

Another study was conducted in our lab. We compared a tactile node-link diagram of a social network with a braille list detailing each person and their friends on separate lines (see Figure 11.2). Our participants, who were blind, identified clusters of friends in the node-link diagram more quickly and accurately than with the list. They were also quicker at finding a path of friends between two people with the node-link diagram, using the position of the nodes to guide their search—just like a sighted person does with a visual node-link diagram. We also found that, while none of the participants had previously seen a tactile node-link diagram, all thought this was a more intuitive way of showing the social network.

BEYOND TRADITIONAL TACTILE GRAPHICS

We have discussed how most tactile graphics are now designed digitally and then printed on swell or embossed paper. In the case of visual graphics, we saw that the computer revolutionized data visualization by enabling animation and interactive exploration of automatically generated

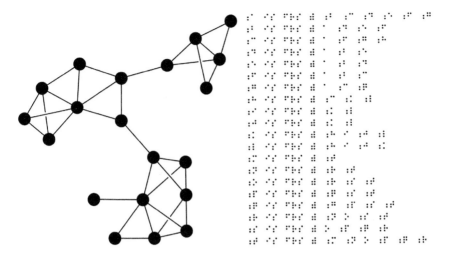

FIGURE 11.2 We conducted a study comparing a tactile node-link diagram of a social network (left) with a braille list detailing each person and their friends (right). People who are blind, just like people who are sighted, found it easier to follow paths and to identify clusters using the node-link diagram.

Credit: Yang, Yalong, Kim Marriott, Matthew Butler, Cagatay Goncu, and Leona Holloway. 'Tactile Presentation of Network Data: Text, Matrix or Diagram?' In *Proceedings of the 2020 CHI Conference on Human Factors in Computing Systems*. (2020): 1–12.

graphics. Digital technology has not yet brought a similar transformation to tactile graphics use. Modern tactile maps are fundamentally no different from those used by Mélanie de Salignac. I believe, however, that emerging computer technologies are about to radically alter how tactile graphics are produced and viewed.

The first change is the arrival of low-cost, refreshable tactile displays (see Figure 11.3). These consist of a grid of round-tipped pins that can be raised and lowered to form a tactile graphic. Their great advantage over a traditional raised-line drawing is that it takes only a few seconds to display a new graphic, and the cost of doing so is virtually nothing. In other words, a refreshable tactile display is the tactile equivalent of a standard computer display. And, as with a standard display, the viewer can interactively explore their data. For the first time, people who are blind can zoom into a tactile map or interactively filter the data shown in a tactile line chart.

Previously, an A4-size, refreshable tactile display would set you back tens of thousands of dollars, putting it out of reach of most people who are blind.

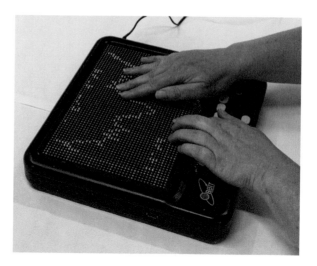

FIGURE 11.3   A touch reader exploring a line graph on a refreshable tactile display.

Credit: Samuel Reinders.

Fortunately, displays suitable for presenting tactile graphics and costing less than ten thousand dollars are expected to be on the market in 2024.

Another technology transforming tactile graphic production is 3D printing. 3D printers, which were invented in 1986, repeatedly print thin layers of plastic or some other material on top of one another, stopping when the desired shape has been reached. The great thing about 3D printing is that you can buy a printer for US$300. As a result, 3D printers are now commonplace: home hobbyists own them, and many schools are buying them.

While 3D models have been used to educate blind children since the first school for the blind, up until now, they were either expensive because they had to be made by hand, or cheaper but mass-produced and designed for sighted students rather than blind children. 3D printing has changed this. It is now inexpensive and straightforward to create 3D models. Around the world, teachers are excited by the potential of 3D printing to provide blind students with 3D models of cells, the solar system or the Sydney Opera House (see Figure 11.4).

As you might expect, children who are blind find it much easier to understand a 3D model than a tactile drawing. They are also more engaging. Often, when a blind child or adult is given a 3D model, they will smile as

⠠⠎⠽⠙⠝⠑⠽⠀⠠⠕⠏⠻⠁⠀⠠⠓⠕⠥⠎⠑

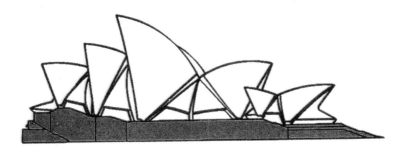

FIGURE 11.4 If you are blind, it's a lot easier to understand the shape of the Sydney Opera House from a 3D printed model (top) than from a tactile drawing (bottom).

Credit: Jacquie Johnstone (photograph) and Leona Holloway (model and tactile graphic).

they explore it. They love that the models are three-dimensional. As one of my collaborators who is blind said: 'It is more like a sighted person looks at things. You get it all at once.'

Another wonderful thing about 3D-printed models is that you can use electronics to make them interactive. Adding touchpoints that read out a pre-recorded label when you tap them is straightforward. More ambitiously, Samuel Reinders, who is a PhD student in our lab, has integrated a 3D model of the solar system with an intelligent conversational agent similar to Siri or Alexa. If you pick up a planet, the model can tell you its name and answer questions about it. If you mistakenly return the planet to the wrong position on the platform, the model will alert you. And if the model doesn't know something, it will look up the information online. That's a lot more fun than a tactile graphic!

Stepping back, I believe the take-home message of this chapter will be surprising to many sighted people: you do not need to be able to see a graphic for it to be helpful. There is considerable evidence that tactile maps and charts are valuable to people who are blind and offer some of the same advantages as visual graphics. As a broad generalization, if the cognitive benefits of a visual graphic are due to its spatial layout, then the corresponding tactile graphic is likely to provide similar advantages.

On the other hand, if the advantages rely on the properties of visual perception, then tactile graphics are unlikely to provide analogous benefits. For instance, people who have been blind from birth find pictorial depth cues showing three-dimensional objects in tactile graphics confusing rather than helpful. In this case, a 3D model will be easier to understand than a tactile graphic because it is tactually perceptually similar to the original object.

However, the usefulness of tactile graphics highlights a severe equity issue. It is not yet a Golden Age of Tactile Graphics. Around the world, people who are blind are clamoring for equitable access to graphical information and more tactile graphics. And this lack of access is not confined to people who are blind. People who are neurodiverse can find data visualizations challenging to understand or unpleasant to look at. People with motor impairments can find interaction difficult or impossible. Given the prevalence of data visualization, we need to ensure that, to the greatest extent possible, visualizations are designed to be accessible by people who are blind or have low vision, lack the motor skills to interact using a mouse, or are neurodiverse.

NOTES, REFERENCES AND FURTHER READING

Chapter Introduction

Demographics of Blindness

Bourne, Rupert R, et al., 'Magnitude, Temporal Trends, and Projections of the Global Prevalence of Blindness and Distance and Near Vision Impairment: A Systematic Review and Meta-Analysis. *The Lancet Global Health* 5, no. 9 (2017): e888–e897.

Impact of Inaccessible Graphics

Butler, Matthew, Leona Holloway, Kim Marriott, and Cagatay Goncu. 'Understanding the Graphical Challenges Faced by Vision-Impaired Students in Australian Universities.' *Higher Education Research & Development* 36, no. 1 (2017): 59–72.

Holloway, Leona, Matthew Butler, Samuel Reinders, and Kim Marriott. 'Non-Visual Access to Graphical Information on COVID-19.' In *Proceedings of the 22nd International ACM SIGACCESS Conference on Computers and Accessibility*. 2020: 1–3.

Siu, Alexa F, Danyang Fan, Gene SH Kim, Hrishikesh V Rao, Xavier Vazquez, Sile O'Modhrain, and Sean Follmer. 'COVID-19 Highlights the Issues Facing Blind and Visually Impaired People in Accessing Data on the Web.' In *Proceedings of the 18th International Web for All Conference*. 2021: 1–15.

Tactile Graphic Guidelines

The Braille Authority of North America. *Guidelines and Standards for Tactile Graphics*. 2010. www.brailleauthority.org/tg/index.html

The Rise of Tactile Graphics

Changing Attitudes to Blindness

Bledsoe, Warren C. 'The Originators of Orientation and Mobility Training.' In *Foundations of Orientation and Mobility* (3rd ed.). AFB Press, 2010: vol. 1 (*History and Theory*): 434–85.

Braddock, David L, and Susan L Parish. 'An Institutional History of Disability.' In *Handbook of Disability Studies*. Sage Publishing, 2001: 11–68.

Farrell, Gabriel. *The Story of Blindness*. Harvard University Press, 1956: Chapter 2.

Roberts, Ferne K. 'Education for the Visually Handicapped: A Social and Educational History.' In *Foundations of Education for Blind and Visually Handicapped Children and Youth: Theory and Practice*. American Foundation for the Blind, 1986: 1–18.

Roy, Archie WN, and Gisela Dimigen. 'The History of Access to Education of People with Visual Impairments in Great Britain from 1656 to 1999.' In *The Routledge History of Disability*. Routledge, 2017: 258–72.

Scotch, Richard K. 'American Disability Policy in the Twentieth Century.' In *The New Disability History: American Perspectives*. New York University Press, 2001: 375–92.

History of Tactile Graphics

Eriksson, Yvonne. *Tactile Pictures: Pictorial Representations for the Blind, 1784–1940*. University of Gothenburg, 1998.

Eriksson, Yvonne, Gunnar Jansson, and Monica Strucel. *Tactile Maps: Guidelines for the Production of Maps for the Visually Impaired.* Swedish Braille Authority, Swedish Library of Talking Books and Braille, 2003: Introduction.

Farrell, Gabriel. *The Story of Blindness.* Harvard University Press, 1956. Quote from Diderot on p. 16.

Designing Tactile Graphics

Edman, Polly. *Tactile Graphics.* American Foundation for the Blind, 1992: Chapters 4 and 7.

Eriksson, Yvonne, Gunnar Jansson, and Monica Strucel. *Tactile Maps: Guidelines for the Production of Maps for the Visually Impaired.* Swedish Braille Authority, Swedish Library of Talking Books and Braille, 2003.

The Braille Authority of North America. *Guidelines and Standards for Tactile Graphics.* 2010. www.brailleauthority.org/tg/index.html

Reading Tactile Graphics

Recognition of Tactile Drawings

Cattaneo, Zaira, and Tomaso Vecchi. *Blind Vision: The Neuroscience of Visual Impairment.* MIT Press, 2011: Chapter 4.

Heller, Morton A, and Edouard Gentaz. *Psychology of Touch and Blindness.* Psychology Press, 2013: Chapter 8.

Picard, Delphine, and Samuel Lebaz. 'Identifying Raised-Line Drawings By Touch: A Hard But Not Impossible Task.' *Journal of Visual Impairment & Blindness* 106, no. 7 (2012): 427–31.

Spatial Reasoning

Von Senden, Marius. *Space and Sight: The Perception of Space and Shape in the Congenitally Blind before & after Operation.* Methuen, 1960. Quote is from p. 279.

Mental Imagery

Cattaneo, Zaira, and Tomaso Vecchi. *Blind Vision: The Neuroscience of Visual Impairment.* MIT Press, 2011: Chapter 4.

Cattaneo, Zaira, Tomaso Vecchi, Cesare Cornoldi, Irene Mammarella, Daniela Bonino, Emiliano Ricciardi, and Pietro Pietrini. 'Imagery and Spatial Processes in Blindness and Visual Impairment.' *Neuroscience & Biobehavioral Reviews* 32, no. 8 (2008): 1346–60.

Heller, Morton A, and Edouard Gentaz. *Psychology of Touch and Blindness.* Psychology Press, 2013: Chapter 7.

Sensory Mode Independent Understanding of Space

Cattaneo, Zaira, Tomaso Vecchi, Cesare Cornoldi, Irene Mammarella, Daniela Bonino, Emiliano Ricciardi, and Pietro Pietrini. 'Imagery and Spatial Processes in Blindness and Visual Impairment.' *Neuroscience & Biobehavioral Reviews* 32, no. 8 (2008): 1346–60.

Cecchetti, Luca, Ron Kupers, Maurice Ptito, Pietro Pietrini, and Emiliano Ricciardi. 'Are Supramodality and Cross-Modal Plasticity the Yin and Yang of Brain Development? From Blindness to Rehabilitation.' *Frontiers in Systems Neuroscience* 10 (2016): Article 89.

Loomis, Jack M, Roberta L Klatzky, and Nicholas A Giudice. 'Representing 3D Space in Working Memory: Spatial Images from Vision, Hearing, Touch, and Language.' In *Multisensory Imagery*. Springer, 2013: 131–55.

Schinazi, Victor R, Tyler Thrash, and Daniel-Robert Chebat. 'Spatial Navigation by Congenitally Blind Individuals.' *WIREs Cognitive Science* 7 (2016): 37–58.

Cognitive Maps of People Who Are Blind and Benefits of Tactile Maps

Cattaneo, Zaira, and Tomaso Vecchi. *Blind Vision: The Neuroscience of Visual Impairment*. MIT Press, 2011: Chapter 5.

Espinosa, M Angeles, Simon Ungar, Esperanza Ocháita, Mark Blades, and Christopher Spencer. 'Comparing Methods for Introducing Blind and Visually Impaired People to Unfamiliar Urban Environments.' *Journal of Environmental Psychology* 18, no. 3 (1998): 277–87.

Golledge, Reginald G, Daniel R Jacobson, Robert Kitchin, and Mark Blades. 'Cognitive Maps, Spatial Abilities, and Human Wayfinding.' *Geographical Review of Japan, Series B*. 73, no. 2 (2000): 93–104.

Noordzij, Matthijs L, Sander Zuidhoek, and Albert Postma. 'The Influence of Visual Experience on the Ability to form Spatial Mental Models Based on Route and Survey Descriptions.' *Cognition* 100, no. 2 (2006): 321–42.

Schinazi, Victor R, Tyler Thrash, and Daniel-Robert Chebat. 'Spatial Navigation by Congenitally Blind Individuals.' *WIREs Cognitive Science* 7 (2016): 37–58.

Thinus-Blanc, Catherine, and Florence Gaunet. 'Representation of Space in Blind Persons: Vision as a Spatial Sense?' *Psychological Bulletin* 121, no. 1 (1997): 20–42.

Ungar, Simon, Mark Blades, and Christopher Spencer. 'The Role of Tactile Maps in Mobility Training.' *British Journal of Visual Impairment* 11, no. 2 (1993): 59–61.

Ungar, Simon. 'Cognitive Mapping without Visual Experience.' In *Cognitive Mapping: Past, Present, and Future*. Routledge, 2000: 221–48.

Spatial Metaphors for Numbers and Time

Rinaldi, Luca, Lotfi B Merabet, Tomaso Vecchi, and Zaira Cattaneo. 'The Spatial Representation of Number, Time, and Serial Order Following Sensory Deprivation: A Systematic Review.' *Neuroscience & Biobehavioral Reviews* 90 (2018): 371–80.

Effectiveness of Tactile Diagrams

Watanabe, Tetsuya, and Hikaru Mizukami. 'Effectiveness of Tactile Scatterplots: Comparison of Non-Visual Data Representations.' In *International Conference on Computers Helping People with Special Needs.* Springer, 2018: 628–35.

Yang, Yalong, Kim Marriott, Matthew Butler, Cagatay Goncu, and Leona Holloway. 'Tactile Presentation of Network Data: Text, Matrix or Diagram?' In *Proceedings of the 2020 CHI Conference on Human Factors in Computing Systems.* 2020: 1–12.

Beyond Traditional Tactile Graphics

Refreshable Braille Displays

Holloway, Leona, Swamy Ananthanarayan, Matthew Butler, Madhuka Thisuri De Silva, Kirsten Ellis, Cagatay Goncu, Kate Stephens, and Kim Marriott. 'Animations at Your Fingertips: Using a Refreshable Tactile Display to Convey Motion Graphics for People Who Are Blind or Have Low Vision.' In *Proceedings of the 24th International ACM SIGACCESS Conference on Computers and Accessibility.* 2022: 1–16.

3D Printed Models

Jafri, Rabia, and Syed Abid Ali. 'Utilizing 3D Printing to Assist the Blind.' In *2015 International Conference on Health Informatics and Medical Systems (HIMS '15) (Las Vegas, Nevada, 2015).* 2015: 55–61.

Ngo, Tuan D, Alireza Kashani, Gabriele Imbalzano, Kate TQ Nguyen, and David Hui. 'Additive Manufacturing (3D Printing): A Review of Materials, Methods, Applications and Challenges.' *Composites Part B: Engineering* 143 (2018): 172–96.

Reinders, Samuel, Matthew Butler, and Kim Marriott. 'Hey Model!': Natural User Interactions and Agency in Accessible Interactive 3D Models.' In *Proceedings of the 2020 CHI Conference on Human Factors in Computing Systems.* 2020: 1–13.

Accessible Data Visualization

Marriott, Kim, Bongshin Lee, Matthew Butler, Ed Cutrell, Kirsten Ellis, Cagatay Goncu, Marti Hearst, Kathleen McCoy, and Danielle Albers Szafir. 'Inclusive Data Visualization for People with Disabilities: A Call to Action.' *Interactions* 28, no. 3 (2021): 47–51.

CHAPTER 12

What's Next?

O UR HISTORY OF DATA visualization has now reached the present day. But what will happen in, say, the next decade? Will our current Golden Age continue, or will data visualization lose its shine?

BROADENING USE OF VISUALIZATION

One reason for our Golden Age has been the increasing availability of data. I only see this trend continuing. The era of Big Data is not going to end anytime soon. Low-cost sensors, including cameras, mean that our world is increasingly instrumented. These can remotely monitor patient health, temperature and energy usage in buildings, traffic flow, public transport and air pollution in cities, soil moisture on farms, and biodiversity in national parks. And these sensors are networked, meaning that as their use ramps up, they will create an unbelievable amount of digital data.

The growing availability of data allows decision-making to become more data-driven in virtually all professions. There is increasing pressure on employees to be data-literate. A 2022 report from Forrester Consulting suggests that, by 2025, 70 per cent of employees will work extensively with data, compared to only 40 per cent in 2018. This doesn't mean that all employees will need to have the analytic skills of a data scientist. However, they will be expected to use tools like Excel or Tableau to identify patterns and trends, and then use these as the basis for their decisions. Inevitably, graphs, charts and data maps will play a significant role. Educators have

DOI: 10.1201/9781003507642-13

recognized the need for data literacy—including the ability to create and critically interpret data visualizations—to become part of the school curriculum.

Data-driven decision-making will not just occur at work. We now have a wealth of personal data available to us. Banks provide us with financial data. Wearables such as Fitbits allow us to track physical activity and monitor health data such as heart rate, calories burnt, and time spent in different stages of sleep. Social media provides data about our social networks. Sensors and smart devices in our homes increasingly allow us to scrutinize, for instance, electricity usage.

We are seeing the emergence of a new kind of analyst: the personal analyst. Typically, these are not professional data analysts but ordinary people interested in monitoring their health, mood, time management or spending behavior. As more personal data becomes available and data literacy skills increase, I believe personal data analytics will become commonplace.

That's one example of a cultural shift: the general public will increase their use of personal data visualization. But who do I mean when I refer to the 'general public'? I am talking about people from the economically developed world. People who are rich enough to buy the latest computer technology. People with a high degree of graphic literacy because of their schooling and exposure to graphics in popular media. People who can see a graphic on a computer screen. However, this is, of course, only a fraction of the world's population. In Chapter 11, I suggested that refreshable tactile displays and conversational agents will improve access to data visualizations for people who are blind. I believe another historic social change is also underway. During the next ten years, the consumption of computer-mediated data visualizations will become widespread in developing countries. Soon, for the first time, most data visualization viewers will no longer be living in the economically developed world.

The driver of this massive change is the smartphone. Over the last decade, the smartphone has democratized the internet. In India, for example, there are nearly 700 million smartphone users, and, as a consequence, half of India's population is now connected to the internet. The majority are new internet users who are poor and have only a basic education and limited graphic literacy. As these people start to use apps such as Google Maps, it is inevitable they will be exposed to a broader range of information graphics and that their understanding and use of data visualization will increase.

EVOLVING TECHNOLOGIES

Data visualization use will also be impacted by emerging technologies such as virtual and mixed reality and, of course, artificial intelligence (AI). The relationship between data visualization and AI is fascinating. I used to teach a class in data visualization, and I always asked my students what they thought the future of data visualization would be. There was always a handful of students who believed that AI would mean we would no longer need data visualization. In the future, we would simply ask our AI application to analyze data and it would provide the necessary answer.

Indeed, recent progress in AI has been spectacular. Voice assistants like Amazon's Alexa and Apple's Siri are now part of everyday life. Generative AI tools such as DALL·E 2 and ChatGPT are creating new artworks and writing our reports. And, if Elon Musk is to be believed, it will only be a few years until we have driverless cars.

Most AI applications are based on what's known as deep learning. They work a little like our brains and contain an artificial neural network trained on millions of examples. Training strengthens and weakens the connections between the neurons, leading to behavior that can surprise even their creators. But this is also a problem. Deep learning applications are black boxes that make recommendations without justification or explanation. Sometimes they get things wrong, decisions that may have life-or-death consequences. For instance, the Correctional Offender Management Profiling for Alternate Sanctions (COMPAS) is a commercial AI tool used in the United States to predict whether a prisoner seeking parole will reoffend. Unfortunately, it turns out that it is biased against African Americans. ChatGPT, meanwhile, is infamous for its 'hallucinations' whereby it makes things up, things that sound plausible.

As we become more aware of the bias and unreliability of AI systems, governments, businesses and society in general are demanding that AI-based decision-making becomes more transparent and accountable. I suspect visualization will play a role in the solution. I believe that, in the future, AI systems will be required to generate a mix of text and graphics to explain and justify their recommendations, just as human decision-makers do now.

Many people see the future as human-in-the-loop AI in which decision-making is a collaboration between a human and an AI assistant. Alex Singla, a senior partner at McKinsey, has said, 'For most generative AI insights, a human must interpret them to have impact. The notion of a human in the loop is critical.'

For this reason, I believe that new products combining visual analytics tools with AI assistants are compelling. Tableau has just released Tableau GPT, which extends Tableau with an AI assistant. The assistant understands natural language and can recommend appropriate visualizations. It can summarize findings and suggest new questions that the user might ask. Microsoft's new Copilot application provides similar capabilities. It works with Office 365 products, including Excel, and Microsoft's visual analytics tool Power BI.

This is the future of data analysis. Visualization remains important, but rather than a human carefully crafting the visualization, the choice of representation and even the decision to create a graphic will increasingly be left to an AI assistant.

AI is not the only technology that is set to transform data visualization. In 2016, Facebook (now Meta) released the Oculus Rift, the world's first consumer-friendly virtual reality (VR) headset. VR aims to create a digital experience indistinguishable from reality, and Facebook's intended market was computer gamers. At US$599, it took the gaming world by storm. In Chapter 2, we saw how Renaissance painters took advantage of pictorial depth cues such as occlusion, foreshortening, shading and shadows to give the illusion of depth. The Oculus took this illusion to the next level by adding stereoscopic and motion depth cues.

Stereoscopic depth perception infers the distance to an object from the minor differences between the images falling on each eye. The Oculus encased the gamer's eyes in a pair of goggles which, by showing a slightly different image to each eye, allowed the gamer to see the virtual world in stereo. You might remember the enthusiasm for 3D movies and TVs in the 1990s. These also provided stereo vision. However, while stereoscopic depth cues help give a more immersive 3D experience, they are not that important in practice. In fact, more than one in five people have limited stereoscopic vision, and many never notice its absence. This is perhaps why 3D TVs and movies never really took off. That and the annoying glasses.

The game-changer (sorry, couldn't resist) was that the Oculus also provided motion depth cues. These occur when an object moves with respect to the viewer, allowing the viewer to see it from multiple viewpoints. Standard computer displays already support some motion cues because a 3D object shown on the screen can be animated or rotated to show it from different viewpoints. The Oculus took this to the next level by continuously tracking the position and orientation of the viewer's head, allowing it to update the image shown to the viewer whenever their viewpoint changed. Combined with pictorial and stereoscopic cues, this provided a compelling viewing experience that felt genuinely 3D. This feeling of immersion was further enhanced by the viewer's ability to interact with the virtual environment, as they were free to walk about and could even manipulate virtual objects using handheld controllers.

The Oculus resulted from decades of work by computer graphics researchers in VR. This was initially driven by training applications such as flight simulators. Architecture, engineering and scientific applications also played a role. VR allowed the architect and client to walk through a new building before it was built, and an engineer to check for headroom in the latest design of a new aircraft. It also permitted scientists to travel to Mars and to visualize and manipulate virtual molecules. But the main driver for the development of modern VR has been the computer games industry and its desire to make the gaming experience as immersive and lifelike as possible.

While the Oculus Rift was not designed for data visualization, it and its successors are now used by architects and engineers to showcase new designs and by educators to simulate real-world scenarios, or when it is critical to understand the three-dimensional structure of the object of study. Like several other research labs worldwide, my lab recognized that VR also offered the potential for new ways to visualize abstract data. These approaches utilized realistic 3D graphics and provided more direct and natural interactions than were possible with a mouse and keyboard to provide a data visualization experience that was far more immersive and engaging than traditional computer visualizations of graphs and charts.

To demonstrate this potential, Maxime Cordeil and other researchers at my lab and the University of South Australia created a data visualization tool, ImAxes, explicitly designed for VR. Data variables are represented by embodied axes: 3D rods with an arrow at one end. These are placed on a shelf. You can walk over to the shelf and pick up an axis with the handheld controller. If you position two axes together at right angles, a scatterplot magically appears. Adding another axis at right angles creates a 3D scatterplot. Or, if the two axes are held parallel to one another, thin lines materialize, connecting the corresponding data points to form parallel coordinates. Once you have created a plot, you can leave it resting in mid-air and walk around it, moving your head closer to see the details. This sounds clunky and a bit gimmicky, but the actual experience is compelling. The data and visualizations are tangible and concrete, providing a very different experience from viewing data on a desktop display and using a mouse and keyboard for interaction.

We have also used VR to show the residents of Elwood, a bayside suburb in Melbourne, where I live, the potential impact of rising sea levels due to climate change, and the effectiveness of different flood mitigation strategies. Comparing flood overlays on your computer screen is one thing. Putting on a pair of VR glasses and flying over your virtual neighborhood or walking down your virtual street and watching the water rise is entirely different. Visualization doesn't get much more visceral than this!

However, despite these two examples, I don't believe pure VR will ever play more than a niche role in data visualization. In VR, the viewer is trapped inside a virtual world, unaware of their physical environment, whereas much of the time, we also need to be aware of what is happening around us. Because of this, I think way of the future is mixed reality (MR). So do Meta and Apple: Meta Quest Pro, the successor to the Oculus, and Apple's new Vision Pro are both MR displays.

In MR, the viewer inhabits a magical new world in which the virtual and physical are seamlessly blended (see Figure 12.1). MR, for instance, can equip a surgeon with X-ray vision, allowing them to see into their patient during a complicated operation. It can enable a farmer to see data from sensors monitoring moisture content overlaid on top of their fields. In the future, MR will direct you when assembling furniture from IKEA—at each step, virtual arrows will point to the relevant components, and a virtual wireframe will guide the assembly. MR is a radically new kind of data visualization, one that allows data to be embedded in the real world.

I believe that, as new head-mounted MR displays improve, they will replace smartphones, tablets, PCs and laptops as the primary interface to computers. While this will probably not happen as quickly as Meta and Apple hope, in the not-too-distant future, we will inhabit a world in which the virtual and physical are merged in an unprecedented way.

Data visualization researchers are exploring how data visualization should look in MR. MR offers similar benefits to VR: natural interactions and 3D visualizations. But it also provides physically embedded visualizations in which the placement and orientation of graphics reflect the viewer's physical environment and position. We have already seen that Google Maps can rotate a map on a smartphone to align with the phone's orientation. MR takes this kind of contextual awareness to the next level. For instance, imagine you are shopping for breakfast cereal in your local supermarket. Your MR headset might highlight ingredients you are allergic to or overlay

FIGURE 12.1 Mixed reality enables a radically new type of in-situ construction drawing. The image above shows bricklayers building a complex curved bench as part of a new hospital. They are wearing a Microsoft HoloLens, the world's first commercially available head-mounted MR display. The display overlays the current layer of bricks with a diagram of where the next bricks should be placed. This diagram is directly generated from a CAD model and reduces the need for the bricklayers to consult architectural plans. Using this technology, novice bricklayers can quickly and accurately construct complex organic shapes that were previously beyond the skill of all but the most expert artisan.

Credit: Fologram.

nutritional information on a cereal packet when you pick it up. Or, if you pick up two products, it might show a paired bar chart that allows you to quickly compare their nutritional value and cost.

If MR does take off, I believe it will create another revolution in data visualization, potentially as far-reaching as those resulting from the invention of the printing press and the computer.

NOTES, REFERENCES AND FURTHER READING

Broadening Use of Visualization

Sensors and the Internet of Things

Khanna, Abhishek, and Sanmeet Kaur. 'Internet of Things (IoT), Applications and Challenges: A Comprehensive Review.' *Wireless Personal Communications* 114 (2020): 1687–762.

Data Literacy

Forrester Research. *Building Data Literacy*. February 2022. www.tableau.com/sites/default/files/2022-03/Forrester_Building_Data_Literacy_Tableau_Mar2022.pdf

Wolff, Annika, Daniel Gooch, Jose J Cavero Montaner, Umar Rashid, and Gerd Kortuem. 'Creating an Understanding of Data Literacy for a Data-Driven Society.' *The Journal of Community Informatics* 12, no. 3 (2016).

Personal Data Analytics

Choe, Eun Kyoung, Nicole B Lee, Bongshin Lee, Wanda Pratt, and Julie A Kientz. 'Understanding Quantified-Selfers' Practices in Collecting and Exploring Personal Data.' In *Proceedings of the SIGCHI Conference on Human Factors in Computing Systems*. 2014: 1143–52.

Huang, Dandan, Melanie Tory, Bon Adriel Aseniero, Lyn Bartram, Scott Bateman, Sheelagh Carpendale, Anthony Tang, and Robert Woodbury. 'Personal Visualization and Personal Visual Analytics.' *IEEE Transactions on Visualization and Computer Graphics* 21, no. 3 (2014): 420–33.

Lee, Bongshin, Eun Kyoung Choe, Petra Isenberg, Kim Marriott, and John Stasko. 'Reaching Broader Audiences with Data Visualization.' *IEEE Computer Graphics and Applications* 40, no. 2 (2020): 82–90.

Increasing Use of Data Visualization in the Developing World

Jena, Amit, Matthew Butler, Tim Dwyer, Kirsten Ellis, Ulrich Engelke, Reuben Kirkham, Kim Marriott, Cecile Paris, and Venkatesh Rajamanickam. 'The Next Billion Users of Visualization.' *IEEE Computer Graphics and Applications* 41, no. 2 (2021): 8–16.

Statista Research. 'Smartphone Users in India 2015–2025.' 2021. www.statista.com/statistics/467163/forecast-of-smartphone-users-in-india/

Evolving Technologies

Limitations of AI

Mehrabi, Ninareh, Fred Morstatter, Nripsuta Saxena, Kristina Lerman, and Aram Galstyan. 'A Survey on Bias and Fairness in Machine Learning.' *ACM Computing Surveys* 54, no. 6 (2021): 1–35.

Schardt, David. 'ChatGPT Is Amazing. But Beware Its Hallucinations!' Center for Science in the Public Interest. March 20, 2023. www.cspinet.org/blog/chatgpt-amazing-beware-its-hallucinations

Explainable and Human-in-the-Loop AI

Alicioglu, Gulsum, and Bo Sun. 'A Survey of Visual Analytics for Explainable Artificial Intelligence Methods.' *Computers & Graphics* 102 (2022): 502–20.

McKinsey & Company. 'A Human in the Loop Is Critical: McKinsey Leaders on Generative AI at US Media Day.' July 23, 2023. www.mckinsey.com/about-us/new-at-mckinsey-blog/keep-the-human-in-the-loop. Source of quote from Singla.

AI and Data Visualization

Tableau. 'How Tableau GPT and Tableau Pulse Are Reimagining the Data Experience.' 2023. www.tableau.com/blog/tableau-pulse-and-tableau-gpt

Virtual Reality (VR)

Cordeil, Maxime, Andrew Cunningham, Tim Dwyer, Bruce H Thomas, and Kim Marriott. 'ImAxes: Immersive Axes as Embodied Affordances for Interactive Multivariate Data Visualization.' In *Proceedings of the 30th Annual ACM Symposium on User Interface Software and Technology*. 2017: 71–83.

Dwyer, Tim, Kim Marriott, Tobias Isenberg, Karsten Klein, Nathalie Riche, Falk Schreiber, Wolfgang Stuerzlinger, and Bruce H Thomas. 'Immersive Analytics: An Introduction.' In *Immersive Analytics*. Springer, 2018: 1–23.

Mazuryk, Tomasz, and Michael Gervautz. 'Virtual Reality: History, Applications, Technology and Future.' Research paper. TU Wein, 1996.

Sito, Tom. *Moving Innovation: A History of Computer Animation*. MIT Press, 2013: Chapter 8.

Depth Perception

Hess, Robert F, Long To, Jiawei Zhou, Guangyu Wang, and Jeremy R Cooperstock. 'Stereo Vision: The Haves and Have-Nots.' *i-Perception* 6, no. 3 (2015). https://doi.org/10.1177/2041669515593028

Schwartz, Bennett L, and John H Krantz. *Sensation and Perception* (2nd ed.). Sage Publications, 2019: Chapter 7.

Ware, Colin. *Information Visualization: Perception for Design* (4th ed.). Elsevier, 2021: Chapter 7.

Mixed Reality (MR)

Mixed reality is also known as augmented reality.

Bensley-Nettheim, Tilli. 'Bricklayers Meet Augmented Reality.' *Australian Design Review*, April 14, 2020. www.australiandesignreview.com/architecture/bricklayers-meet-augmented-reality

Dwyer, Tim, Kim Marriott, Tobias Isenberg, Karsten Klein, Nathalie Riche, Falk Schreiber, Wolfgang Stuerzlinger, and Bruce H Thomas. 'Immersive Analytics: An Introduction.' In *Immersive Analytics*. Springer, 2018: 1–23.

ElSayed, Neven AM, Bruce H Thomas, Kim Marriott, Julia Piantadosi, and Ross T Smith. 'Situated Analytics: Demonstrating Immersive Analytical Tools with Augmented Reality." *Journal of Visual Languages & Computing* 36 (2016): 13–23.

Schmalstieg, Dieter, and Tobias Hollerer. *Augmented Reality: Principles and Practice*. Addison-Wesley Professional, 2016: Chapter 1.

Thomas, Bruce H, et al. 'Situated Analytics.' In *Immersive Analytics*. Springer, 2018: 185–220.

Conclusion

A S I EXPRESSED IN the introduction, my aims for writing this book were twofold: to understand how the current Golden Age of Data Visualization came about, and to highlight information graphics and data visualization's pivotal role in shaping the modern world. To investigate these issues, we have examined the history of data visualization from 30,000 years ago to the present day. What have we learned?

REASONS FOR THE GOLDEN AGE

We have seen that four factors explain the increasing use of data visualization that has culminated in our present-day Golden Age.

One factor is *changes in production and presentation technologies.* Broadly speaking, as these technologies have evolved, the cost of creating and viewing a graphic has reduced, encouraging greater use.

The invention of woodblock printing and then copperplate engraving revolutionized graphics production. It allowed graphics to be faithfully reproduced and dramatically reduced the cost of reproduction. The nineteenth century saw more transformation: photography introduced a radically new type of graphic; lithography provided affordable colored illustrations; photomechanical processes automated the production of the printing plate; and mechanized printing presses reduced the cost of printing.

Then came another revolution: the computer. The first computer applications were tools for manually creating graphics, but soon they generated graphics automatically. Computer displays increased their

DOI: 10.1201/9781003507642-14

resolution and became cheaper, replacing paper as the primary presentation device. By the end of the twentieth century, most graphics were produced in a few seconds or less and cost next to nothing to make and display, and could be distributed anywhere in the world using the internet.

The second factor driving data visualization use is *the increasing amount of data to visualize*. As governments became larger and more bureaucratic, they collected more data for administration and planning. This included commissioning surveys for topographic map series and introducing national censuses in the nineteenth century. The invention of new instruments allowed scientists to collect more and more data, ranging from air pressure and wind speed to observations of the night sky and organisms in a water droplet.

The twentieth century, in particular, saw an explosion of data. New types of sensors and scans, such as radio telescopes, CT scanners and electron microscopes, provided a wealth of medical and scientific data. Aerial photography and satellite imaging drove the development of GIS. Data was increasingly digital, and we entered the age of Big Data. No wonder that businesses, governments, scientists and the public turned to data visualization to make sense of this deluge.

The third factor explaining the increasing use of data visualization use is *the availability of visual representations that are effective cognitive aids*. In the Renaissance, artists, architects, engineers and cartographers invented visual conventions built around a geometry of space and vision in which three-dimensional objects, such as a building or the surface of the Earth, could be projected onto a two-dimensional canvas. They developed a comprehensive visual language for representing three-dimensional objects on paper—a language that allowed them to escape 'flatland' and 'deadland'.

Then, in the eighteenth and nineteenth centuries, we saw the development of a new kind of graphic. This used mathematically exact visual metaphors to provide abstract data with a graphical representation, and it gave rise to a rich visual language of statistical charts and data maps.

The final breakthrough occurred in the late twentieth century. While information graphics with moving parts, such as the slide ruler and volvelles, had existed before the computer, they were uncommon. The computer changed this. Now it was straightforward to create animations and interactive graphics. User interaction fundamentally changed data visualization practice, allowing the analyst to explore larger and more complex datasets than had been possible with paper graphics.

These inventions fed into the current Golden Age, providing analysts, scientists, data journalists, indeed, anyone who wanted to visualize something, with a rich visual vocabulary of information graphics and ways of interacting with them.

We need a variety of representations because different graphics provide different cognitive benefits, and the best way to visualize data depends on the purpose. Beck's map of the London Underground, for instance, makes planning travel easier but can mislead travelers about the quickest or shortest route.

In a well-designed visualization, the spatial and visual relationships between the symbols in the graphic representation mirror relationships in the underlying data. They provide cognitive free rides by making relationships hidden in the data perceivable by our visual system, allowing the viewer to reduce demands on working memory and replace slow, conscious reasoning with fast visual perception. This is possible because visualizations take advantage of the human visual system. For instance, drawings perceptually resemble the objects they represent, diagrams support visual and spatial indexing, and the Gestalt laws mean patterns and trends jump out in charts and graphs.

But this is not the whole story. Visualizations also leverage the way we think. They build upon our innate understanding of space, geometry, magnitude and numerosity. Maps, for example, provide a concrete realization of our internal cognitive maps. We can internalize visual representations and use these to reason about the world because our brains support mental imagery. We have also seen that many graphics leverage our propensity to use conceptual metaphors grounded in our experiences of the external world to reason about abstract concepts. Family trees, Euler diagrams and Playfair's line graphs make kinship, categories and the balance of trade tangible. They allow us to use spatial reasoning to think about these abstruse concepts. Indeed, the cognitive benefits of graphical representations are frequently independent of visual perception, which is why tactile graphics provide many of the benefits of visual graphics to people who are blind.

The final factor impacting data visualization use is the *societal and cultural context*. This has several aspects. One is the prevailing attitude to graphics. During the Renaissance, visual experience was increasingly given precedence over the written word. This encouraged early scientists to carefully observe and draw their specimens. In the twentieth century, photography, film and television created a popular culture that was image-based rather than word-based, establishing an environment primed for the Golden Age. Another aspect is the degree of graphic literacy: mandatory schooling and exposure to graphics at school also primed the general population for the Golden Age.

Cultural attitudes can be specific to a particular profession and its visual culture. The ability to read and construct technical drawings was long regarded by engineers as central to the engineering profession. For thousands of years, geometric diagrams were central to mathematics. But graphics can also drop out of favor. We saw this at the beginning of the twentieth century when mathematicians and statisticians abandoned graphs and charts.

Another aspect is societal needs. These determine the uses for data visualization. New demands have driven the invention of new kinds of visualization. For instance, the desire to separate construction from design spurred the development of technical drawings. Larger cities and new modes of transport led to street directories and urban transit maps.

These needs are linked to the invention of new tools and technologies. For example, the discovery of writing reduced the need for graphics to be used as mnemonic aids. On the one hand, the computer removed the need for graphical calculating devices, but on the other hand, it introduced a new role for graphics as the interface to computer applications.

In combination, these four factors—new technologies for graphics production and presentation, access to more data, the cultural and societal context, and the invention of visual languages that take advantage of our visual system and the way we reason, and the cultural and societal context — have led to our ubiquitous use of visualization and the current Golden Age. They explain the increasing use and diversification of data visualization in Western culture during the Modern Era, ever since the Renaissance. They also underpin how the use of information graphics has gradually spread from mathematicians, scientists and technicians to administrators, social scientists and business managers, and then to the public.

HOW VISUALIZATION HAS SHAPED OUR MODERN WORLD

My second reason for writing this book was to draw attention to data visualization's crucial role in shaping the modern world. For me, this has been the most surprising learning. I knew that data visualization was essential in the twenty-first century. What I hadn't realized is that, without it, our modern world would not have come into existence.

The invention of writing and mathematics in the first civilizations was underpinned by information graphics. Proto-writing relied on graphical representation, and counting aids such as tallies and pebbles made numbers concrete and tangible. Geometric diagrams were central to the Greek invention of deductive mathematics. In the seventeenth century, mathematical diagrams took on a significant new role with the discovery of Cartesian coordinates and analytic geometry, which underpinned the invention of differential and integral calculus. It is fair to say that modern mathematics would not exist if it were not for diagrams.

I was surprised to discover the pivotal role that information graphics played in the European Renaissance and the birth of the Modern Era. We learnt how maps played a crucial role in the emergence of the modern state by providing a tangible representation of the state and enabling the transition from a feudal state to one in which a sovereign ruled a geographic region with clear boundaries.

We saw that maps underpinned European colonization. As Europeans sailed further and further during the Renaissance, they mapped the new lands and seas they encountered. Maps encouraged them to see these new lands as empty, helping legitimize the enslavement and displacement of their indigenous inhabitants. Maps allowed European ships to safely travel to their new colonies. They facilitated the control and exploitation of natural resources, resources that later fueled the Industrial Revolution.

We also saw that the emergence of architecture and engineering as new professions during the Renaissance was inextricably linked to the invention of a new type of information graphic: the technical drawing. This enabled design to be separated from construction, allowing the creation and production of more complex buildings and machines and the Industrial Revolution.

Modern science is yet another product of the Renaissance, and again, information graphics were vital. Without illustrations, it would have been impossible for early scientists to share their observations of human anatomy, the new animals and plants encountered by early European explorers, and the new worlds visible through the telescope and microscope. Geometric diagrams were key in early reasoning about the physical world. Illustrations depicted novel experimental apparatus, while drawings of experiments built confidence by allowing other scientists to virtually witness the events described.

It is impossible to overstate the importance of graphics to science. Copernicus's diagram of the heliocentric system, Darwin's evolutionary tree, Mendeleev's periodic table of the elements, Odile Crick's drawing of DNA's helical structure, and Wegener's drawings of continental drift are just a few of the graphics that have revolutionized scientific thinking. And now, more than ever, science relies on an 'externalized retina' to study the macroscopic and the microscopic, the future and the past.

We even saw that the emergence of capitalism in the Renaissance was linked to the invention of double-entry bookkeeping and its tabular arrangement of credits and debits. It is fair to say that, if not for information graphics, many of the most significant developments of the European Renaissance would not have occurred. While most histories dwell on the beauty and impact of Renaissance sculptures and paintings, I hope to have convinced you that Renaissance information graphics are at least as important.

Visualization was also at the heart of the immense changes during what has been called the 'long nineteenth century', the period of rapid industrialization and technical invention between the French Revolution and World War I. Trains, bicycles and then the car revolutionized transport. Low-cost steel allowed the construction of elegant bridges and soaring skyscrapers. The telegraph, telephone and radio transformed communication. Gas lights, then electric lights, lit cities at night. Steamships created a global trading network. Mass production led to cheap consumer goods and unheralded wealth before the unheralded carnage of World War I. These advances in engineering and science were the product of technical and scientific drawings and charts. Maps also played a role: topographic maps for planning the transport networks—roads, canals and railroads—required to transport goods, and geological maps for finding the coal, oil and minerals that fueled industrialization.

It was in the long nineteenth century that, for the first time, medical treatment was more likely to extend a patient's life than curtail it. Epidemiologists plotted cases on maps to determine the origin of cholera and yellow fever outbreaks. Pathological atlases allowed doctors to diagnose disease. X-rays allowed doctors to check for fractures. Nightingale's rose charts led to improved hospital hygiene. Photographs and drawings of bacteria convinced medical researchers of the bacterial origin of anthrax, tuberculosis and cholera, leading to better controls and new treatments.

The Humboldtian revolution in the physical and life sciences and the invention of statistics are inextricably linked to the rising use of statistical charts and data maps in the long nineteenth century. These facilitated the emergence of the modern business enterprise, and graphics such as Booth's poverty map provided a way of understanding and quantifying the social problems that industrialization had created, spurring the introduction of the old-age pension in Britain and the establishment of the welfare state.

This reliance on data visualization only increased as we moved forward to our present Golden Age of Data Visualization. We have seen how visualization now underpins almost every aspect of life, and how our contemporary world could not function without it.

Undeniably, our modern world has been shaped by data visualization. Information graphics are one of our most significant and valuable cognitive artefacts. They rank alongside writing, mathematics and the computer. Indeed, I would argue that information graphics provide the foundation for these other cognitive aids because they underpinned the invention of writing and mathematics, and enabled the technical culture that allowed us to design and manufacture the computer.

Furthermore, we have seen that our use of data visualization is unlikely to slow down. I'm confident that new audiences in the developing world, new data sources, and new technologies like mixed-reality displays, AI-generated visualizations and refreshable tactile graphic displays, mean the current Golden Age of Data Visualization will not end anytime soon.

Index

For Product Safety Concerns and Information please contact our
EU representative GPSR@taylorandfrancis.com Taylor & Francis
Verlag GmbH, Kaufingerstraße 24, 80331 München, Germany